THE YALE EDITIONS OF

The Private Papers of James Boswell

(Research Edition)

Boswell's Correspondence, Volume 1
General Editor: Frederick W. Hilles

THE CORRESPONDENCE OF
JAMES BOSWELL AND
JOHN JOHNSTON OF GRANGE

THE CORRESPONDENCE

OF

James Boswell

AND

John Johnston

OF GRANGE

EDITED BY

RALPH S. WALKER

MOLSON PROFESSOR OF ENGLISH
MCGILL UNIVERSITY

McGRAW-HILL BOOK COMPANY

NEW YORK   TORONTO

Library of Congress Catalog Card Number: 66–11589

06610

PRINTED IN GREAT BRITAIN

GENERAL EDITORIAL NOTE

THE research edition of the Private Papers of James Boswell will consist of at least three co-ordinated series: Boswell's journal in all its varieties, his correspondence, and the *Life of Johnson* in an arrangement which will show the method and progress of its composition. The undertaking is a co-operative one involving many scholars, and publication will proceed in the order in which the volumes are completed for the press. It is expected that the whole edition will consist of not fewer than thirty volumes.

In the parallel "reading" or "trade" edition, which began publication in 1950 and has now reached its ninth volume, those portions of the papers have been selected which appeared likely to interest the general reading public, and the object of the annotation has been to illuminate the documents themselves as compositions. The annotation in that series may be said to be turned in towards the text.

The annotation of the research edition, on the contrary, is turned out from the text, and is intended to relate the documents to the various areas of scholarship which they are capable of illuminating: history in many of its varieties (literary, linguistic, legal, medical, political, social, local), biography, bibliography, and genealogy. The comprehensiveness and coherence of the papers that Boswell chose to preserve make them almost uniquely useful for such exploitation.

The journal and its related notes and memoranda will be presented in one chronological sequence, but the correspondence will appear in three different kinds of volumes: *subject* volumes, which will select letters relatable to a topic or theme (for example, Boswell's correspondence concerning the *Life of Johnson*); *single-correspondence* volumes, of which the present volume is a good illustration; and *miscellaneous-correspondence* volumes, which will collect the remaining letters in chronological sequence. Since, with all its gaps, the journal provides a more continuous and detailed record of Boswell's life than the correspondence does, it has been taken as the primary document for the annotation of his daily activities and the identification of the persons he met or mentioned. In particular, the volumes of the journal will contain, in alphabetized Biographical Supplements, condensed biographical accounts of all the contemporaries of Boswell whom he mentions in those volumes in more than an allusive way. The correspondence volumes will deal in a more summary fashion with matters that are to receive systematic "depth" annotation in the journal volumes, but will themselves provide "depth" annotation on their own special topics and on persons and events not mentioned in the journal.

FREDERICK W. HILLES
FRANK E. TAYLOR
HERMAN W. LIEBERT

FREDERICK A. POTTLE
Chairman

CONTENTS

"You have drawn a more naive and truer family picture of yourself than Raphael could have done if you had sat to him, and fitter to be deposited in your family library at Auchinleck in memory of you to the latest future times, for the instruction of your posterity and the true friends of your ancient house (and particularly the honest Johnstons) of hundreds of years yet to come. You have immortalized with yourself the worthy Johnston of the present age, and indeed as it were embalmed yourselves both in one catacomb. . . ."

Letter to Boswell from Sir Alexander Dick, 10 Aug. 1782 (spelling and punctuation modernized)

INTRODUCTION

THE chief interest of this correspondence does not, I think, lie in the narrative of events unfolded in it. The story behind it can be pieced together only with the help of other sources, for the correspondence is discontinuous, not only through the loss of many of the letters, but because there were considerable gaps of time during which no letters were exchanged. Nor is there very much profundity or variety of thought in it to engage the reader's mind, for most of the letters were obviously written hurriedly and without much serious reflection. What is of continuous interest and should prove its main attraction for most readers is the record it contains of a remarkable friendship between two men of opposite temperaments who so grew together in a relationship of "reciprocity and mutual convenience" that they became almost indispensable to each other. The correspondence adds little, except in details, to the knowledge of Boswell and his circle which can be gathered from his Journal and Memoranda, but it does show his many-faceted character in a new and favourable light and it brings the retiring figure of Johnston, about whom so little has been known, out of its obscurity into the foreground.

If they often seem lacking in factual interest, it has to be remembered that many of the letters were intended merely to accompany the full account of his daily doings which Boswell was writing for Johnston in his Journal: "I must not rob my Journal to tell you what I have seen",[1] he says at one point. And the later letters are no more than occasional exchanges between close neighbours accustomed to meeting each other continually and separated only for short periods. But their informality of style and lack of studied content make the letters in this volume all the more revealing as expressions of personal affection. Boswell's letters to Johnston are usually unreserved and unaffected, free of the uneasy desire to impress which so often betrays itself in his attitude to other correspondents. His Journal often depicts him as volatile and inconstant, and we come to think of him as alternating between shame at his own lack of steadfastness and delight at seeing himself in the character of a bright, attractive butterfly; but in the correspondence

[1] To JJ, 30 Dec. 1765.

with Johnston he shows himself capable of unwavering loyalty. Even Johnston's apparent neglect, when it led Boswell to protest against such unresponsiveness, left his affection unchanged: "I must . . . forgive you; for what can I do? I love you, and I fear you never will be better; so I must bear with you as you are."[1] However foolish, insensitive, or weak Boswell may have been from time to time in his conduct towards others, he was admirable in the consistency of his friendship for Johnston.

The correspondence stretches from the time of Johnston's law-apprenticeship to the year of his death, and from Boswell's student-days to the time of his ill-advised abandonment of the Scottish for the English bar, when, though the *Life of Johnson* had still to be compiled, his best days were past. At its start, in September 1759, Boswell was not yet nineteen, though it was already six years since he had entered as a student at Edinburgh University,[2] for in those days the Arts course at a Scottish university, which was taken regularly before the more specialized professional courses, was roughly equivalent, as a stage in the educational process, to the secondary schooling of today. He and Johnston had been intimate friends for several years before the first letter was written. They had probably first met as members of Professor Robert Hunter's Greek class of 1755–56.[3] Sitting on the same hard benches in the

[1] To JJ, 25 Apr. 1768.

[2] JB's signature appears in the Edinburgh University Matriculation List of George Stuart's class of 1753–54, and again in Robert Hunter's class-list dated 10 Mar. 1756, where the number 3 occurs after it, indicating that he was then, though only in his sixteenth year, completing his third year at the University (MS. Edin. Univ. Matric. Office).

[3] Hunter's Matriculation Roll, 10 Mar. 1756 (see the note preceding this), contains a signature "John Johnston" which appears to be JJ's. JB, in summarizing his University days for Rousseau, implies that his intimacy with JJ began at about the same time as that with W. J. Temple ("Á la fin, Je me suis lié avec un Anglois nommé Temple . . . et avec un Ecossois nommé Johnston"; Yale MS. L 1111, discarded leaf). In strict chronology, however, JJ's name should have come first, for at the time of his death JB

referred to him as "my oldest friend" (To Alexander Boswell, 4 Aug. 1786; quoted *post*, p. xxxvii). In a letter in the printed Erskine correspondence dated 8 May 1762 (*Letters between the Hon. Andrew Erskine and James Boswell, Esq.*, 1763, p. 107) JB says he has lived in intimacy with JJ "more years than the Egyptian famine lasted", which, if taken literally, would push the beginning of the intimacy back to some time before May 1755. Perhaps we should take it literally. But the sentence was added to the original letter as a compliment to JJ when the copy was being prepared for the printer (Mem. 10 Feb. 1763; To Andrew Erskine, 9 May 1762) and may assume Feb. or Mar. 1763 as its point of reference rather than May 1762. JB and Temple both placed the beginning of their intimacy at Christmas 1755 (Journ. 25 Dec. 1776; From W. J. Temple, 4 Jan. 1786).

same bare room, they had been daily in each other's company. But the class was a large one, of forty-six members, whose ages probably ranged from thirteen to well over thirty, and they might never have come to know each other if Johnston's maturity (for he was the older by fully ten years),[1] combined with something distinctive about his clothes, had not attracted Boswell, always readily drawn to men who seemed more experienced in the ways of the world than himself: "You had a straw-coloured lining to your coat and I thought you quite the genteel gentleman."[2] On better acquaintance, Johnston had appealed to him still more, perhaps, because of the glamour of his status. Though he was only about twenty-six, he was already a laird and styled "of Grange", his father having died when he was about twenty and left him heir to a small estate, with his own independent income. No doubt his way of life fascinated Boswell, for he was entirely free from the sort of family restriction Boswell found so irksome.

Johnston was the owner of three farms in Dumfriesshire. The largest, Grange, situated in the lovely upland valley of the Milk, a tributary of the Annan, had been in the possession of his kinsmen from an early time. The family of Johnston, Johnstone, or Johnstoun (spelt also, but less frequently, Johnson or Jonson), at one time because of its size and strong kin-loyalty the most formidable of the border clans, with a black history of violence and lawlessness, had many branches in Dumfriesshire. In the seventeenth century numerous Johnstons, all claiming kinship in some degree with the main line which produced the Earls of Hartfell and Marquesses of Annandale, were to be found as owners or tenants in manors and farms throughout the county. The many small estates in Johnston hands passed from generation to generation, coalescing or dividing into smaller holdings according as the branches of the race diminished or increased in the number of offspring to be provided for, and though the lands were sometimes let or sold outside the immediate families of their owners, it was an almost unfailing rule that they should remain in the hands of Johnstons, or of members of the allied families of Graham, Irving, Armstrong, Scott, Carlyle, Eliot, Carruthers, and Bell.

As early as 1611, Grange had been the property of a namesake of Johnston. In that year John Johnston of Castlemilk, advocate in Edinburgh and commendator of Holywood in Dumfriesshire, was

---

[1] See Appendix 2. [2] To JJ, 19 July 1763.

accidentally drowned while crossing the swollen river Milk on horseback.[1] It is recorded that he left Grange to his cousin, Thomas Johnston, younger of Fingland,[2] who was a red-handed member of the notorious Wamphray Johnston gang and had played his part in the outrages that led in 1592 to the battle of Dryfe Sands, at which the Johnstons, under their outlawed chief, had defeated a party of Maxwells, Crichtons, and others who were attempting to enforce the will of the government against them.[3] Thomas Johnston died about 1629, but even after death he was a cause of strife and slaughter, for in a family *stramash* over the burial of his body, three of the Lockerbie Johnstons and two of the Johnstons of Tundergarth lost their lives.[4]

From him Grange passed to Christopher Johnston, husband of the Blanche Armstrong, who, when a widow of nearly eighty, was condemned to transportation for harbouring escaping Covenanters —a sentence which it is comforting to know was remitted on account of her age.[5] In 1653, Christopher Johnston of Grange acquired by feu from James Johnstone, Earl of Hartfell, the neighbouring farms of Persbiehall and Priestbutts.[6] His son, John Johnston of Persbiehall, who was a member of the last Scottish parliament, died in 1720 without inheriting Grange, which passed to his own son, another John, also called "of Persbiehall".[7] This younger John of Persbiehall disponed Priestbutts to David Bell of Newhall, and Grange, in 1730, to John Johnston of Heithat, son of John Johnston, tenant-farmer in Upperbanks.[8] John Johnston of Heithat, who thus became "of Grange", and was subsequently also "of Upperbanks", when he bought the farm in which his father and grandfather had been tenants,[9] was the father of Boswell's friend.

Heithat (a good-sized farm in Hutton parish which incorporated the smaller farm of Bandrigg or Banriggs) had come to him from a Walter Johnston, perhaps an uncle, who had been disbarred from his own inheritance because of his father's active support of the Covenanters' cause, but who had made a small fortune abroad

[1] C. L. Johnstone, *History of the Johnstones*, 1909, p. 113.
[2] Grange MSS.
[3] Sir William Fraser, *Annandale Family Book*, 1894, i. xcvii, 32 f.; ii. 26.
[4] Grange MSS.
[5] C. L. Johnstone, *op. cit.*, p. 147.
[6] James Steuart, *The Bell Family in Dumfriesshire*, 1932, p. 82.
[7] Services of Heirs, 26 Jan. 1721; 28 June 1739, S.R.O.
[8] Register of Deeds, Mack. 3 Aug. 1730; Dur. 16 July 1739, S.R.O.
[9] Tombstone in Tundergarth parish churchyard.

and returned to his native district, drawn there by the strong homing instinct of the Johnstons.[1] John Johnston had died in 1749,[2] and his eldest son John coming of age shortly after, had succeeded to the lands of Grange, Upperbanks, and Heithat.[3]

Boswell's friend had behind him an immediate ancestry of hard-working farmers, strong in clan-loyalty but stern in their revulsion against the centuries of anarchy experienced by the border-lands. They had been staunch in their adherence to the Covenant, and prepared to suffer for their principles, even in the "Killing Time", when many Dumfriesshire lairds recanted and became (to curry favour with the government) particularly ferocious with recalci-trants. But though Johnston loved the district in which his fore-bears had lived for so long, and was full of the lore of his clan, he seems to have rebelled against the tameness of the farmer's life led by his father and grandfather, and against their puritan aus-terities and narrow moral standards. He belonged, like Boswell, to the first generation of romantic revolt, and was out of sympathy with his Covenanting predecessors; nostalgic for the freer, wilder, gayer times associated with an earlier age; converting in his fancy, no doubt, all the gruesome Johnston history of robbery and blood-shed into an epic of heroism and romance.

There seems to have been little love between him and his mother,[4] Agnes Laggart, originally from Kirtlehead in the same county, who may have represented in his mind the cramping author-ity of the previous generation, as Lord Auchinleck did in Boswell's. At any rate he seems to have decided to leave home as soon as he could possibly be spared, though it meant leaving Grange, his mother, his four sisters, and his youngest brother Andrew in the not very competent hands of his brother Thomas; and so he set out to enlarge his experience, to live a life of independence in lodgings in Edinburgh, and by studying law to prepare for a career which might provide some scope for ambition. He was older than many of his colleagues in making a start, because he had been unable to leave home until his younger brother should be of an age to assume responsibility, but this meant that he had had plenty of time to make up his mind. Since he did not feel cut out to be a farmer, the legal profession was an obvious one to adopt: it offered

[1] W. R. Rogerson, *Hutton under the Muir*, 1908, p. 3.
[2] Services of Heirs, 28 Apr. 1786,
S.R.O.
[3] *Ibid.*, 3 May 1759.
[4] Journ. 13 Mar. 1780.

the likeliest means to a good livelihood, and if it did not lead to the enlargement of his estate should at least enable him to look after what he already possessed. And so it seems he found himself taking a class at the University (as all hopeful young lawyers did) in which there were boys ten years younger than himself. Among them he may well have cut something of a dash—though not deliberately, for he was modest by nature, and, knowing his own property to be small in comparison with the expectations of many of them, would have deprecated or treated as good-natured banter the nicknames of "laird" and "your honour" which they accorded him.[1]

Boswell gives us a glimpse of their friendship in its first stage when he recalls in a letter to Johnston[2] their Saturday walks to the shore at Leith, accompanied sometimes by John Dun, the parish minister from Auchinleck, who at a still earlier period had been tutor in the Boswell household. Their way home would lead them to the Canongate by way of the Abbey Close, where the tarts in Mrs. Bird's shop-window proved irresistible to appetites whetted by exercise and sea-air. Trudging up the long slope of the High Street and climbing the Customhouse steps, they would arrive at last, pleasantly tired, at Lord Auchinleck's fourth-floor flat in Parliament Close. There (after dining no doubt with the family) Boswell and Johnston, we may suppose, would retire to a room by themselves, where Johnston would stretch out contentedly in an easy chair to talk, and would fascinate the young, impressionable Boswell with his tales of Scotland's past, Edinburgh's regal days, and the stirring events in Johnston's own home-county when his ancestors, the Annandale Johnstons, won renown for their prowess in Border warfare. They would while away the evening by the high fourth-story window, gazing over the cluster of tiled and crow-stepped gables towards the moon-lit slopes of Arthur's Seat, while Johnston idealized and romanticized those harsh old times (as so many sentimental historians and poets were to do later), and filled the boy's mind, already attuned by the influence of his home and circumstances, with seductive fancies, and a taste for all that seemed heroic, ceremonious, and picturesque in the Scots tradition. Boswell's love of ritual, symbol, and romance, of Jacobitism, Episcopalianism, and Catholicism, though not entirely derived from the infection of Johnston's enthusiasm, must have been fanned and

[1] To JJ, 16 Apr. 1763.   [2] To JJ, 19 July 1763.

fostered by it. Ever afterwards he associated such things with Johnston's name, and years afterwards, in Rome, at what he thought the very fountain-head of all such sentiment, his mind was fixed on Johnston: "Get near Cardinal", he adjured himself before attending a service to be conducted at Frascati by Cardinal York, the Pretender's younger son, in one of those memoranda by which he tried to regulate his conduct, "and think of Grange and old Scots kings and Chapel of Holyrood".[1] There can be little doubt that Johnston's talk at this impressionable age, during those "many tea-drinking afternoons which we have past both in your room and mine",[2] helped to give form and direction to the vague, rebellious energies which were rising in Boswell and were to drive him for a time, even in spite of Johnston's restraining counsel, into revolt against his upbringing, his parents, and the future prescribed for him by his birth and circumstances, while at the same time they enriched his imagination and his personality.

The companionship of Boswell and Johnston was probably of four years' standing when the first of the letters in this volume was written. There are many indications from the very beginning of the correspondence of the shared experiences and mutual tastes which had brought them into closer and closer association. In Johnston's company Boswell had sampled pleasures more daring than the Saturday walks with Mr. Dun, Mrs. Bird's jam-tarts, or lavish indulgence in the milk biscuits and currant jelly which Johnston's landlady kept in a cupboard in his room.[3] Johnston was at home in the sociable club-life of legal Edinburgh: in time he seems to have gathered some small renown among his legal cronies as an organizer of convivial parties.[4] We may assume that it was he who introduced Boswell to the social life of the many small, dark taverns, reached by basement steps from the High Street and the closes off it, and that together they fixed on Thom's as their favourite haunt or "howf". In such company Boswell had been captivated by the gaiety of tavern-life and had rapidly acquired the taste for sociable drinking without which his preparation for a legal career in eighteenth-century Edinburgh would have been seriously defective. More daring (at any rate for Boswell) were the visits

---

[1] Mem. 26 May 1765.
[2] To JJ, 21 July 1763.
[3] To JJ, 11 Jan. 1763.
[4] Grange MSS.: William Hay to William Loch, 19 Jan. 1768; round robin signed by W. Loch, W. Hay, J. Loch, J. Baillie, and R. Hamilton [undated, but written on same sheet].

we must suppose they frequently paid to the theatre in the Canongate.[1] In the eyes of old-fashioned Presbyterians like his mother a theatre was a far more questionable resort than a tavern—little better than a brothel—and even the recent success of *Douglas*, a tragedy of the highest moral tone by a Presbyterian minister, did not remove the long-established prejudice of churchmen against players and play-houses. Boswell had been intoxicated by his taste of the forbidden joys of the theatre. He had sought out the company of actors and made friends with West Digges and James Love. He had been fired with ambition to become a patron of playwrights, to be a dramatic critic, and to write plays himself: he had even had thoughts of running away with an actress and marrying her. Johnston, though he was no doubt Boswell's companion and confidant throughout, was older, more stable, of less inflammable material, and he was probably not himself affected by any such yearnings.

It was probably Temple who introduced Boswell to the Episcopalian form of worship, but it appealed also to Johnston and their common liking for it was a bond through life. The pastors and members of the Scottish Episcopalian congregations, though no longer persecuted, were still officially proscribed and their activities were conducted under the disabilities imposed by the penal statutes of 1746 and 1748. But there were also congregations ministered to by "qualified" clergy in Church of England orders, and to one of these they attached themselves. On a Sunday afternoon, after spending the morning with his family in the Presbyterian New Kirk, Boswell would escape with Johnston into a different atmosphere. Turning off the High Street into the old-world aristocratic purlieus of Carrubber's Close, they would attend a second service there held by a "qualified" Episcopalian clergyman; then, with a lighter step, relieved from the depression produced by the sternly minatory sermon of the morning, they would walk out, past Holyrood and the fields beyond, to Restalrig, talking of religion and morality in a way which neither John Dun nor Lord Auchinleck would have approved.[2] And investigations along the same lines may have carried them farther than Carrubber's Close. They may have had, perhaps, more dealings than we can ever know about

[1] To JJ, 27 Oct. 1762. In JB's absence in Glasgow, JJ was his confidential informant about theatrical affairs in Edinburgh (To JJ, 26 Sept. 1759; 11 Jan. 1760).

[2] To JJ, 27 Oct. 1762.

with the still unemancipated Roman Catholics. What had they to do with that mysterious "little Mr. Duchat, the popish priest" whom Boswell remembered so vividly as calling sometimes in the evenings at Johnston's lodgings and entertaining them with stories of foreign parts, while he sat with his chair pulled close in to the fire, taking snuff and drinking green tea?[1] Characteristically Boswell reacted sharply to the stimulus of such contacts. He was seized with a determination to become a Roman Catholic himself, to renounce the world and enter a monastery, and in London in 1760 he went so far as to enter for a short time into the communion of the Church of Rome.[2] Johnston, though he shared his tastes and inclinations up to a point, probably never seriously contemplated taking such positive steps.

Boswell, the adolescent, may well have caught his first glimpse of a world beyond the rather grim and narrow circle of his upbringing in the company of Johnston, the countryman who had escaped to the town and was still savouring the delights of his independence. Both were in revolt against the restrictive code which survived among their elders as a legacy of the social strains and stresses of the seventeenth century: but they responded differently, according to their opposite temperaments. To Johnston, it is clear, such glimpses were merely food for the fancy. He was essentially a dreamer, content as he grew older to compensate for outward conformity to a conventional way of life by living largely in his imagination. To Boswell they were incentives to action, experiment, and adventure, for his nature constantly impelled him to try, with all his might, to make his dreams come true.

With Temple, his other intimate friend, Boswell's relationship during their student-days was different. His description of himself as Temple's "grave, sedate, philosophic friend"[3] was a playful exaggeration, but for all the warmth of their subsequent intimacy it seems not unlikely that he was first drawn to Temple by curiosity of an intellectual sort rather than by instinctive sympathy. In Temple he saw something of the refinement of mind and manners which he associated with an English rather than a Scottish background, and a wider, more critical interest than Johnston's in things literary and intellectual. For all their cordiality, he was never *en rapport*, in the same homely, comfortable way with

[1] To JJ, 26 July 1763.
[2] Journ. 5 Dec. 1764.
[3] To Temple, 29 July 1758.

Temple, with his different upbringing and uncongenial whiggish outlook, though Temple's gentle, unassuming nature made him easy to confide in. As he developed his Scottish sympathies and home-bred tastes through contact with Johnston, who whetted his enthusiasm for Scotland's colourful Stuart and Catholic past, so he cultivated the anti-Scot in him through contact with Temple, acquiring, along with a taste for contemporary writers and philosophers, some comprehension of the attitude of the Whig and Democrat. The "antisyzygy" of the post-Union Scot, as familiar today as in Boswell's day, is nowhere more vividly exemplified than by Boswell's conflicting selves—the one so deeply attached to the past, to Johnston, and to home; the other reaching out to Temple and aspiring to some higher and larger self-realization. Boswell seems to have thought of his friends as like the two sides of his nature, antipathetic to each other—at any rate he appears to have done nothing during his university days to bring them together, class-fellows as they were, for in 1767, when he had known them both for ten years, he wrote to Temple of Johnston as of a stranger whom Temple had never met.[1]

As we read through the correspondence, and still more clearly if we supplement it by reference to the Journal, we realize how much Johnston meant to Boswell, and how firmly Boswell's affection for him came to be founded on certain needs in Boswell which only Johnston could supply. If Johnston had a special function to perform in the earliest stages of their friendship, when he helped to people Boswell's thoughts with "stately men and lovely women with lines of black hair down their backs like Lady Mary Douglas",[2] stimulating his fancy, introducing into the ferment of his vague longings a catalyst which gave them imaginable shapes, he had, as time went on, to undertake certain other functions of a very different sort. Yet the two complementary personalities grew together and became so closely interlocked that their relationship could modify itself with no disharmony when altered circumstances called for adaptations. Thus Johnston, from being the stimulator and instigator, quite readily assumed the receptive part and accepted the office of appreciative listener when Boswell went out into the world to court adventure and try to be a hero of romance. Like any actor, Boswell could not bear to be without his audience, and the knowledge that the letters and the Journal enabled Johnsto

---

[1] To Temple, 30 Mar. 1767.   [2] To JJ, 19 July 1763.

to lead the sort of vicarious life he loved gave part of its zest to all that Boswell did.[1] At the same time Johnston, by a natural transition, from being a source of restless thoughts inciting to daring enterprises, became a restraining, steadying influence on the more volatile Boswell. As he matured into staid, respectable bachelorhood, with his amiable, mild, contemplative nature, he became to Boswell the embodiment of moderation and practical good sense— almost the very opposite of what he once had seemed.

Early in the correspondence we find Boswell intent on strengthening the bond between himself and Johnston, as if he fully realized the needs in himself which the older man could supply. The first seven letters are merely occasional communications between friends who have parted recently and expect to meet again before long, but after that Boswell's grow more frequent, and, in a sense, more purposeful. In the autumn of 1762 he went to London, with the grudging consent of his parents, to try to get for himself the commission in the Guards which his father refused to buy for him. He was by no means certain of success, but he had made influential acquaintances on his previous visit in 1760, and he had a high opinion of his own very considerable personal charm, which he counted on to gain him the backing he needed. He no sooner arrived in London than he wrote to Johnston (he had already written to him briefly from Durham on the way south) and proposed a regular interchange of letters: "You must write to me a great deal . . . I shall keep a journal of every day; and send it to you weekly . . . I shall send you franks."[2] To keep the correspondence going was a matter of urgent concern to him. His letters are full of assurances of his own friendship for Johnston and appeals to him, sometimes reproachful, sometimes indignant, to respond more often. But Johnston had formed his own circle of cronies in Edinburgh, among lawyers nearer to his own age, and it is doubtful if he realized how vital his friendship was to Boswell at this time. He did not really approve of Boswell's excursion to London, and had argued against it[3]—for in spite of his rhetorical praise of enterprise and vigorous action, when it came to the point he was nowadays, lawyer-like, in favour of caution. He wrote gratefully now and then, in his hurried way, excusing his own neglect. Boswell's fervour was plainly a little bewildering to him: "What do I owe

[1] To JJ, 21 Dec. 1762; 23 July 1763.   [3] From JJ, 27 June 1763.
[2] To JJ, 20 Nov. 1762.

you for this goodness?" he exclaims on receipt of the first packet of journal.[1] He himself has little pleasure in writing, and takes little trouble to express himself effectively: he does not seem at first to understand that Boswell's reiterated appeals and commands to him to acknowledge regularly the arrival of the weekly packets are requests as much for some return gesture of affection and appreciation as for assurance of the safety of the Journal; and he becomes impatient at Boswell's importunity, irritated by his reproaches.

He certainly did not understand the importance which Boswell attached to his presence at the moment of his setting out from Edinburgh to strike a blow for freedom and romance against the ways of tame conformity, and he had failed to turn up, merely, or so he would have Boswell believe, because he was suffering from one of his recurrent fits of lethargy.[2] Boswell, though he had planned the occasion months before and given Johnston long notice of his intentions,[3] had been obliged to make his ceremonious farewell to Holyrood Palace and Arthur's Seat alone;[4] but the symbolism had been incomplete for him without the living symbol always associated with the others in his mind, and he had felt a superstitious pang lest his romantic venture, lacking the ritual sanction of Johnston's blessing, was foredoomed to failure. That fear lay working in his mind, in spite of all the high spirits engendered by the journey. Ten days later it produced a vivid nightmare, which he described to Johnston in his Journal: "I had been in a bad situation during the night for I dreamt that Johnston did not care for me. That he came to see me set off on a long journey, and that he seemed dissipated and tired, and left me before I got away. I lay abed very gloomy. I thought London did me no good. I rather disliked it; and I thought of going back to Edinburgh immediately. In short, I was most miserable."[5] Boswell needed Johnston at this time as a substitute for the parents who were out of sympathy with him. He believed that, if nobody else did, Johnston understood and loved him: he thought of him as something stable and lasting, unaffected by the flux of his London experience, to which he could always return, however far he might drift. Even though he did not respond sufficiently to satisfy Boswell, the knowledge that he was there to be written to was important: "I value myself much on

[1] From JJ, 13 Dec. 1762.
[2] To JJ, 6 Dec. 1762.
[3] To JJ, 17 Aug. 1762.

[4] To JJ, 20 Nov. 1762.
[5] Journ. 25 Nov. 1762.

feeling that my friendship is firm and permanent and not confounded by the infinite variety of this metropolis."[1]

Johnston had his faults. He was lazy—and a trifle selfish, like all men who make a protestation of busyness to excuse their own indolence; and he was given to excessive drinking and occasional drabbing. But his shortcomings made part of his appeal for Boswell, for they were the source of his sympathy with Boswell's own weaknesses, and it was sympathy above all that Boswell needed from him. Whether his much-valued advice had any considerable influence on Boswell's actions may well be doubted. It is commonsensical and platitudinous, and Boswell is always delighted to have it, for it shows Johnston's interest in him. Sometimes, in small matters he may have acted on it, as when he changed his mind about refusing to lend some money to Andrew Erskine because Johnston convinced him that it would be unfriendly to deny the loan if he could possibly afford it.[2] But Johnston's advice is usually attuned to Boswell's inclinations, and when it is not, as in the case of Boswell's intrigue with Mrs. Dodds (of whom Johnston strongly disapproved),[3] or in momentous matters like the attempt to get a commission in the Guards and the decision to transfer to the English bar, it does not weigh against the strong impulses of Boswell's passion or ambition. In choosing Johnston at this time as his confidant in all private and personal matters, Boswell was not looking for a moral censor, but rather, without realizing it, for someone who could be relied on to find a sane and moderate formula of words in which to sanction his actions and condone his lapses. Johnston's steadying influence on Boswell in this early phase was not exerted through precept or example: his service to Boswell in his roving days was to provide him with an object for his homing affections, an assurance that somewhere he would be welcome in the future whatever happened, the fixed point in a relationship of two "twin compasses".

When, after eight months in London, Boswell abandoned hope of a commission in the Guards and obtained his father's willing permission to go abroad to the University of Utrecht to resume his study of law, he began rapidly to strengthen the lifeline between himself and Johnston. He dreaded the voluntary exile he was going into, and shrank from the prospect of a lonely, monotonous

---

[1] To JJ, second letter of 14 Dec. 1762. [3] Journ. 14 Mar. 1767; 16 Mar. 1767.
[2] To JJ, 21 Sept. 1768.

existence in Holland.[1] Hitherto he had been sending Johnston a letter a week along with the packets of Journal, but now, in the five weeks left him before going where mails would be less frequent and postage more expensive, he sent a letter by every post, whether he had anything to say or not. In those thirty-six days, from 30 June to 4 August 1763, "with a successive velocity equal to the rattling hail, or the words of a talkative woman",[2] he sent off seventeen letters to Johnston—without receiving more than two in return. His apprehensions, occasionally voiced, are in the main repressed, and these letters are mostly optimistic and high-spirited. The end of hesitation, the reconciliation with his father, and the prospect of a journey unite to exhilarate him for the time being: but his last words before setting out point forward to his return and envisage a time when he and Johnston will meet again to read over the Journal and letters, which he is so insistent to have Johnston lay by and preserve with meticulous care.[3]

As Boswell foresaw, correspondence became more difficult after his arrival in Utrecht. He went on writing his Journal, but instead of entrusting instalments periodically to the post, as he had done in London, he laid it up to be sent back later for Johnston to read entire—though as it happened, Johnston never saw the Dutch portion, which was lost in transit between Holland and Scotland. But this, with the letters he wrote occasionally to London acquaintances within easier reach, was not enough to provide the sense of intimate contact with home the correspondence with Johnston had given him, and six weeks after his arrival he made an attempt to resume the exchange of confidences. He wrote to Johnston, as he had just written to Temple, describing vividly the state of dejection he had been living in, and asking his advice on a highly impracticable design to carry on a courtship with Archibald Stewart's sister in Scotland by means of postscripts added to her brother's letters from Rotterdam.[4] This was, as he knew, a mere whim, and when at last, many weeks later, the reply (which had at first miscarried) reached him, he was well pleased to find in it the advice he had invited and expected. In his next letter, written in January,[5] he asked Johnston to write to him often, but there is no indication that Johnston replied before the death of Boswell's natural son

[1] To JJ, 5 July 1763.
[2] To JJ, 9 July 1763.
[3] To JJ, 6 Dec. 1762; 21 Dec. 1762;

1 Mar. 1763; 20 Jan. 1764.
[4] To JJ, 23 Sept. 1763.
[5] To JJ, 20 Jan. 1764.

Charles (whose guardian he had been since his birth in the previous winter) produced from him a letter which Boswell received on 8 March.[1] Johnston wrote once more, and Boswell acknowledged his letter on 9 April, asking for more news of him; but two months later there had been no response, and Boswell wrote reproachfully as he set out on his travels into Germany: "More than two months ago, I sent you a long letter to the care of Provost Graham. If it has been lost or miscarried, I am very sorry. Yet I think at any rate you might have written to me again, before this time." The letter ends affectionately, holding out the prospect of future meetings: "Go my friend by yourself to Arthur-Seat; think of me in distant regions. Love me ever and let us hope for many happy days together. God bless and preserve you my worthy Sir."[2]

Boswell left Utrecht in June to make the continental tour which Lord Auchinleck had conceded him as a reward for his compliance in adopting a legal instead of a military career. No letter had come from Johnston by 10 September, when Boswell wrote to him from Berlin protesting that there could be no excuse for such protracted silence, since he could have found out his address at any time from David (Boswell's younger brother), then an apprentice in the Edinburgh bank of John Coutts & Co. He still kept his Journal up to date, with Johnston in mind as its reader, but as he drew farther away from home, the image of Johnston in his mind, linking the past with the future and signifying security and continuity amidst all the shifting scenes of the present, seems to have grown in significance, and he devised a new and more intimate method of communing with the symbolic wraith to supplement his journal-keeping. During the nineteen months of his absence in Germany, Switzerland, Italy, Corsica, and France, he seems to have sent Johnston only three letters; but he *wrote* him no fewer than fifty-four!

He began the series on 1 October 1764 at Anhalt-Dessau and before he received, in the following March, his first letter from Johnston since leaving Utrecht, had already written twenty-two unposted letters to him. He continued to add to these, without hearing more than twice again from Johnston, until he reached Auxerre on 9 January 1766 on his way home from Corsica. No doubt his aim was partly to catch and preserve for his own future

[1] To JJ, 9 Apr. 1764.   [2] To JJ, 11 June 1764.

amusement the various moods of these exciting times, but his avowed intention was to keep alive friendship: "I would not wish to make my friend Johnston pay postage for frequent letters while I am abroad, yet to write to him often is agreeable, and keeps alive friendship. I shall therefore, at every court and city where I reside any time, write him a letter. These letters I shall direct and seal so that I shall have as little to do with them as if they were really sent off."[1] To keep the memory of Johnston fresh in mind as a talisman against nostalgia and the sense of aimless drifting was obviously of importance to him. The letters permitted him to express frank personal feelings of a sort precluded by the narrative form of the Journal, and so brought Johnston nearer. When low-spirited, in alien, uncongenial surroundings, a vision of Johnston was apt to flash into his thoughts to comfort him: at a firework show in Berlin, when "hyp'd" and dissatisfied with his company, suddenly he thought "of Canongate—Johnston— Mrs. Bird's tarts".[2] Even to pretend to commune with Johnston at each new stopping-place on his journey quieted his restless apprehensions and eased the strangeness of his surroundings.

After the long period of separation, when Boswell had come home again to Scotland, the correspondence naturally grew more intermittent, though the friendship grew still closer. For a few months, while Boswell was at Auchinleck, preparing under his father's guidance for the trials which, in the summer of 1766, admitted him to the Scottish bar as a member of the Faculty of Advocates, it continued to be the main link between them; but after that they were both in Edinburgh during the law-court sessions, living within a very short distance of each other, and there was no need for letter-writing, except during the vacations, which Boswell spent sometimes at Auchinleck, sometimes in London, and Johnston usually at Grange.

Boswell's letters in the spring of 1766 are partly concerned with his arrangements for a meeting with Johnston at Moffat to celebrate their reunion. There they appear to have spent some hilarious days together, perhaps going over in the evenings, in the candle-lit parlour of their lodgings, the journal of Boswell's adventures abroad and the series of unposted letters. The conviviality of their meeting has its echo in an astonished letter, which tells more about Johnston than most of his own, sent by their crony Andrew Erskine,

---

[1] Journ. 1 Oct. 1764.   [2] *Ibid.*, 9 Sept. 1764.

the gifted, scatter-brained younger brother of the Earl of Kellie, in reply to an ebullient invitation from Johnston to join them: "Instead of that warm love of your country—that blaze of patriotism, that tender sensibility and strong affection for Mary King's Close—instead of these William Wallace and Fletcher of Saltoun-like qualities that I used so much to admire you for, how am I astonished to get a letter from you full of pert wit, and coxcombical vivacity!" To Erskine, as to Boswell, Johnston appears a combination of sentimental romancer, staid citizen, and sympathetic companion, whose outstanding qualities are modesty and warmth of heart: "I can say to you Johnston with safety", he says, "that you have an honest good heart, because you don't pride yourself on these qualities. . . . The only way to get praise is to seem not to expect it; I don't know whether this is a secret to you but I'm sure it's one to Boswell";[1] and elsewhere he says, "I hope dear Johnston your head is better. I have no hopes of bettering your heart."[2] The picture of Johnston which emerges at this time from the Journal, and from the letters of Boswell and Erskine, corrects the impression of him which a reader of the correspondence may have been forming up to this point as a result of his unresponsiveness during Boswell's long absence from Scotland. We see him as "worthy", "mild", and "comfortable" (in the old sense of "comforting"); and we can appreciate the special flavour given to his company by the idiosyncrasies so familiar to his friends—his habit of advocating lost causes, of championing Mary Queen of Scots, of ceremoniously "becking on", or saluting, Arthur's Seat[3] as a ritual tribute to Scotland's past, of glorying in the wild doings of his ancestors without the least desire to emulate them, of hymning the superiority of Spartan brose (of which we may be sure he never partook from choice) over all the culinary delicacies of a decadent age. Whatever his defects as a correspondent, he was the best of companions, with his easy-going fondness for tippling and his undemonstrative good nature—so undemonstrative that he forgot to thank Boswell for the fifty-one unposted letters till several months after he had read them.[4]

The contrast with Boswell is very striking: even the vices they had in common seem to have sprung from opposite poles of charac-

[1] From Andrew Erskine to JJ, 2 June 1766.
[2] From Erskine to JJ, 9 Feb. 1769.
[3] From Erskine to JJ, 4 Aug. 1767
[4] To JB, 25 July 1766.

ter. During the early stages of their reunion, Johnston admitted on one occasion to a moral lapse of a kind familiar to Boswell, which had been a consequence of drunkenness and which had affected his health. Boswell assumed the role of comforter and adviser: "Be very careful against drinking. It is a vice to which both of us are inclined but which you are in most danger from because you want my obstinacy and cannot refuse an honest fellow who asks you."[1] There is some unconscious irony in this, and it appears at first sight to conflict with Boswell's later confession: "My inclination towards drinking is twice as strong as your honour's; and that is saying not a little",[2] but the distinction he was drawing was, at bottom, probably sound. Boswell's vices sprang from superabundance of vital energy, whereas Johnston's were the weaknesses of a too-pliable good nature. Even the "antiquity" or hypochondria they both so readily succumbed to seems to have been induced in them by opposite causes: in Boswell as a product of frustrated energies or the violent reaction from high spirits; in Johnston as the intensification, through dullness or misfortune, of a natural tendency to languor.

However differently induced, their common susceptibility to this disease, like their common vices, bound them together. Their letters contain so many plaintive references to it that the subject grows tedious to any reader not prepared to sympathize to some extent with their condition. Only a fellow sufferer could hope to establish a lasting intimacy with Boswell, and to admit susceptibility to it was at once to provoke his interest: "I was recommended to one of the first nobles of this republic", he wrote to Johnston from Lucca, "a knowing, sensible, polite man, a man truly of the world for he has the prejudices of no particular country. You and I my dear friend must like him for another reason. He is often as hypochondriac as we are. His name is Signor Romano Garzoni."[3] Temple and Dr. Johnson were both periodically afflicted, and so indeed were very many of their contemporaries. The incidence of a tendency to "spleen" among the intelligent and cultivated in the middle of the eighteenth century seems to have been so high that it is fair to conclude that something in the mental climate of that age of uneasy social transition and metaphysical deadlock was peculiarly conducive to it. The hypochondria of Boswell and his

[1] To JJ, 18 May 1767.
[2] To JJ, 21 Sept. 1768.

[3] To JJ, 5 Oct. 1765.

friends was frequently accompanied by religious doubts and a horror of death, as if the sudden confrontation of the reasoning mind with something beyond its scope produced a baffling mental struggle and a species of nervous breakdown. Certainly this malaise was not in Boswell's case (like the *fin-de-siècle* boredom fashionable in the 1890's) mere affectation or a form of self-indulgence: it was an alarming neurotic condition which he felt to be continually threatening him, and for which he never ceased to search for the cause and cure: "The spleen is a most unaccountable thing. It comes and goes like the wind."[1]

The topic recurs so frequently in his letters partly because of a serious concern to probe to the roots of the condition by collecting evidence of its symptoms from every source ("I study hypochondria as a science"),[2] and partly owing to a conviction, obviously shared by Johnston, that the very acts of examining and expounding were themselves curative. They were both dismayed at Dr. Johnson's reception of Boswell's doleful complaints[3] as weak and undignified: "Do not treat me . . . as your learned and eminent friend used to treat you when in the like state", says Johnston, after describing a fit of melancholy, "I alwise thought it unkind, nay unpardonable in him, who had suffered so much himself in that way."[4] The clash of creeds and standards between an older and a younger generation, between the age of reason and the new age of romance, so fascinatingly exemplified at every point of the Boswell story, both in Boswell's personal relations with others and in his own internal strife, is reflected in this misunderstanding between him and Dr. Johnson. Boswell and Johnston were clear that to disburden the mind by communicating its symptoms to a sympathetic listener was not weakness but wisdom, however unwelcome such Rousseauistic extravagances might appear to Dr. Johnson. The confessions in their letters were part of a policy pursued deliberately—and even at times with a certain disinterestedness, for Boswell in assembling his thoughts and experiences as a hypochondriac for publication in *The London Magazine*, believed himself to be performing a public service.[5] To control the mysterious disease, which he regarded half-scientifically, half-superstitiously, was a matter of so much moment to him that he made it his life-

[1] To JJ, 29 Mar. 1763.
[2] To JJ, 10 Sept. 1764
[3] *Life* iv. 379.
[4] From JJ, 21 Apr. 1785.
[5] *Hypochondriack* 63, Dec. 1782.

study. If one of the principal motivating forces in Boswell's life was ambition, another was to keep the spleen at bay, and it is often hard to tell, at a particular juncture, which of these impulses was the stronger.

In the twenty years of their life together in Edinburgh, Boswell made Johnston his *alter ego*. Though he never went with Boswell on any of the many excursions to London and elsewhere, and showed no inclination to accompany him into the society of the eminent, the aristocratic, or the notorious, preferring to hear of them at second hand through Boswell's eager *reportage*, he was otherwise closely involved in almost all Boswell's affairs. No continuous narrative emerges from the intermittent correspondence of the Edinburgh years, but there are hints and echoes in it of nearly all the matters which most occupied Boswell. Little is to be gathered from it of Johnston's own private concerns, for he was not, like Boswell, driven by an inner urge to dramatize himself, to put everything he felt and did and saw into words, to capture every moment of precious life and store it up for future contemplation. Boswell's social life was lived partly among men of place and prominence (cultivated sometimes because he "collected" notabilities as another might collect rare coins, sometimes because by their influence he hoped to further his ambitions); partly among lawyers and professional men, into whose circles his calling inevitably drew him; and partly among old friends like Erskine and his sisters. From these three sources, in the main, the gossip of his letters to Johnston is drawn: in addition, their correspondence touches on the legal matters in which both were interested, the literary activities which represented Boswell's most persistent line of ambitious endeavour, and the love-affairs and family problems in which he made Johnston his confidant. Johnston acted in these years as a comforter, a prop to self-respect, a moderating counsellor, an appreciative critic, a sympathetic fellow sufferer—the mirror in which Boswell viewed himself, sometimes anxiously, sometimes complacently; the shelter to which he had recourse in times of storm.

The correspondence of these years is a mere bridging of occasional gaps in an otherwise continuous association, for while Johnston lived in Roxburgh's Close, very near Boswell's home, there was no need for written communication between them, other than a note, now and then, appointing a meeting—and even this was seldom necessary, since both men's business took them almost daily to the Parliament House. For more than a year after his marriage, in November 1769, to his cousin Margaret Montgomerie, Boswell lived farther off, first in the Cowgate and then at Chessel's Court in the Canongate,[1] but in May 1771 he removed to a flat in the large block of buildings off the Lawnmarket known as James's Court.[2] Johnston's lodgings were only a few hundred yards away, off the north side of the High Street opposite the Luckenbooths, but even this small intervening distance was reduced to the extent of a staircase, when, sometime in the seventies, abandoning his lodgings for an establishment of his own, he also moved into James's Court and set up house there in a lower flat.[3]

But though Boswell's letters to Johnston in this period have no coherent narrative running through them to hold the reader's interest to the events referred to, they continue, at their best, to exert the intrinsic appeal of things written vividly and imaginatively out of sheer zest for life. And even the great variability in merit of his letters contributes to their interest, for though they are sometimes consummate in their unaffected literary ease, sometimes strained in their virtuoso-like exploitation of a self-conscious literary gift, sometimes alight with unforced vivacity and sheer gaiety of spirit, sometimes heavily sententious, and occasionally frothy with laboured triviality, they reflect in every mood the richly varied personality of their writer, and are aglow with his singular, unfailing affection for the one man towards whom he felt "cordially and steadily *semper idem*",[4] and to whom he could say with confidence: "I know everything that I write must please you."[5]

The Journal shows in more detail than the letters how closely Johnston was drawn into the very texture of Boswell's daily life in Edinburgh. He had been Boswell's confidant in the intimate matter of Peggy Doig's pregnancy, and had acted in Boswell's absence as guardian to the child during the whole of its short life: and he

[1] To JJ, 31 May 1770.
[2] To JJ, 22 May 1771.
[3] There is no record of the date of his removal, but it may be deduced from the Journal that it was between Sept. 1774 and Oct. 1775. On 20 Sept. 1774 JB mentions meeting JJ in the Grassmarket, which would scarcely have seemed worth recording if he had been living then in James's Court. On 10 Oct. 1775 the entry reads: "I drank tea in my wife's room and then went down to worthy Grange's."
[4] To JJ, 27 Mar. 1772.
[5] To JJ, 20 Nov. 1762.

continued to receive Boswell's confidences about all his real or imaginary loves, whether these were connected with his plans to get married or were merely what he called "amorous adventures". Even the engagement to Margaret Montgomerie was made and carried through to the accompaniment of sage advice from Johnston, who "argued me quite out of my mercenary views for marriage, and was clear for *My Lady* if I thought myself sure of happiness".[1] So, too, it was Johnston who listened to all Boswell's complaints against his father and strove for reconciliation: in the matter of a career; at the time of the publication of the correspondence with Erskine (which Boswell knew would exasperate his father);[2] in the difficult period when Lord Auchinleck was contemplating a second marriage, the very thought of which filled Boswell with so violent a revulsion against his father that Johnston was reduced to tears and to threatening a severance of their friendship;[3] later, when the quarrel blew up between father and son over the entailing of the estate;[4] and at a time when relations were severely strained because of Lord Auchinleck's coldness towards Margaret Boswell.[5]

Because of his peculiar healing, sedative effect on Boswell's restless passions and disordered nerves, he became Boswell's constant resort in moments of distress. On the morning after that day in August 1770 when Margaret Boswell bore her first child, only to lose him almost immediately, Boswell wrote with a petulance possible only where there is perfect understanding between friends: "It was not kind in you to leave me alone yesterday. I had a terrible day. . . . Pray come to me directly."[6] Johnston could always be counted on to speak for moderation, the reasonable course, the abandonment of fear and suspicion. When Boswell began his Journal, Johnston advocated the cautious policy of using fictitious names where the use of real ones might chance to give offence[7]— a policy which would have saved Boswell from a number of awkward scrapes if he had followed it when compiling his *Life of Johnson* and *Tour to the Hebrides*, though it would have greatly reduced the savour of his writing for posterity. Johnston was always for avoiding enmities: for tolerating the slights of Lord

---

[1] Journ. 16 June 1769.
[2] From JJ, 28 Apr. 1763.
[3] Journ. 16 July 1769.
[4] *Ibid.*, 6 Feb. 1776.
[5] *Ibid.*, 6 Jan. 1778.
[6] To JJ, 29 Aug. 1770.
[7] From JJ, 13 Dec. 1762.

Eglinton;[1] for admitting culpability and apologizing when an unwise letter to Margaret Montgomerie brought a sharp rejoinder which turned Boswell's head "giddy";[2] for "laughing off with indifference" the offensive comments of the Lord Advocate on Lord Auchinleck's conduct on the bench during the Fife election case,[3] though Boswell proposed to challenge him for them; and he was for speaking well of an old friend like Lord Kames—and not, if possible, even *thinking* ill of him—however strong the temptation to criticize him might be.[4] He could be relied on to oppose headstrong or dangerous courses, such as the proposal to flout the sentence of the court by reviving John Reid, Boswell's sheepstealing client, after his execution on the gallows;[5] and though he could talk sharply to Boswell on occasion, about his indiscretions and his lack of morals, he could also soothe him by his advocacy of contentment and a settled way of life, and through his habit of meeting Boswell's complaints about the frustration of his ambitions by recalling his blessings: "Betake yourself now to business and the management of your estate."[6] "Remember you have reputation to support, and I hope much to acquire; think not my good friend of floating any longer in uncertainty, but of casting anchor on a good bottom."[7]

Margaret Boswell, far from resenting her husband's intimacy with Johnston, found him a useful ally, and like Boswell considered him "a real comfortable friend".[8] She obviously valued his steadying influence on Boswell's wild moods and recognized the unvarying sanity of his counsels. She even favoured his admission to confidences of the most private kind, and on one occasion encouraged Boswell to consult Johnston after a breach of marital faithfulness which he had just (as his practice was) confessed to her.[9] At moments of domestic strain, it was to Johnston that she, too, had recourse: on the day following a memorable public exhibition of indiscretion by Boswell, who had been acting under the influence of drink and, now sober, was in great distress of mind, he records that she "[was] sensible [and] called Grange. He consoled me, [though he] gave me an acc[oun]t of myself yesterday, [and scolded me on] three points: [on behaving so at a] funeral; [on annoying a]

---

[1] From JJ, 13 Dec. 1762.
[2] Journ. 13 July 1769.
[3] *Ibid.*, 9 Mar. 1776.
[4] *Ibid.*, 25 Jan. 1780.
[5] *Ibid.*, 20 Sept. 1774.
[6] From JJ, 17 June 1783.
[7] From JJ, 21 Apr. 1785.
[8] Journ. 7 Oct. 1774.
[9] *Ibid.*, 3 Sept. 1776.

young gilr; [on doing it before] Methodists";[1] and at her wits'
end on the dreadful morning which was expected to bring a challenge from William Miller, offended by Boswell's references in an
article in *The London Chronicle* to his father, the Lord Justice-Clerk,
she rose at six o'clock, after a sleepless night, to summon Johnston
to come immediately and join them.[2] If Johnston lost his temper
with her once, because of a too pointed comment on his fondness for
the bottle, and flung out of the room in a rage to go and sulk alone
in his flat,[3] it was the merest family tiff—sorely repented by him,
laughingly treated by Boswell[4] and no doubt readily forgotten by
Mrs. Boswell.

Johnston's solemn, fatherly admonitions may seldom have
really swung Boswell from a course of action to which his temperament impelled him, yet they plainly came to be of the greatest
value to him psychologically, giving him a sense of being morally
buttressed from without, assisted in his perpetual struggle to
solidify his fluid personality round a core of principle. "You know
my sad changeable humour. Help me to get the better of it",[5]
he begged with his usual disarming frankness. His fascinated
interest in the people he conceived of as possessing integrity—
Sir Alexander Dick, Lord Kames, Paoli, Dr. Johnson, his father,
and a host of others—was partly due to his longing to emulate their
consistency of character. He was exceptionally aware of his own
diversity and many-sidedness, and constantly in search of wholeness,
by a process of introspection and comparison with others, whom he
studied and analysed as if he hoped to discover at last some
secret character-making formula common to all. When he listened
gratefully to Johnston's platitudes, and voiced in his turn moral and
religious sentiments hardly in keeping with many of his actions, he
was not hypocritical (though he sometimes betrays doubts about
this himself); he was profoundly sincere in his desire to accept, as
the necessary basis of sound character, standards which were, after
all, open and obvious, not hidden secretly away beneath the com-
plexities of human nature. The commonsensical code preached by
Johnston did not really satisfy him, for instinctively he felt its
limitations, but in times of peculiar stress it offered a temporary
reassurance at which his restlessly questing mind was eager to grasp.

[1] Journ. 25 Aug. 1777; expanded by
F. A. Pottle (BP xii. 219).
[2] Journ. 17 Oct. 1774.
[3] From JJ, 21 Apr. 1785.
[4] Reg. Let. 4 Apr. 1785.
[5] To JJ, 10 Sept. 1764.

As time passed Johnston, for all his common sense and quiet competence, had been getting steadily into deeper waters. His last years were to be clouded with anxiety. Grange had not been entirely free of embarrassments when it came into his hands, for there had been legacies and annuities to pay under his father's will,[1] and it may have been partly doubt about the capacity of the estate to support all its dependants that had sent him out in search of a career and, if possible, a fortune. His brother Thomas had never been able to pay his way, and as early as 1763 had been in such difficulties that John had felt obliged to make a legal contract with him defining their respective responsibilities. He let Grange to Thomas on an eleven-year lease at a rent of £50 a year, and undertook to pay him £6 a year for the maintenance of their mother (who survived till 1780),[2] reserving for himself the right to occupy a "sufficient lodgeable house" on the estate, with a garden of half an acre. Thomas agreed to build on to the older house, before Whitsunday 1765, the present house of Grange; to keep a cow for John among his own cattle; and to leave to his elder brother's care "the little parks or enclosures which are planted with firs and other forest trees, with full power and liberty to enclose such pieces of ground on the said lands as he shall think proper for planting".[3] John made a grant of £10 towards the cost of building the new house, and in addition lent Thomas £148 to clear him of his debts to others.[4]

But things had gone from bad to worse. Although three of his sisters, Janet, Sarah, and Jean had married and left Grange, and Thomas had married a wife with good expectations (James, or Jemina, one of the three daughters of John Paxton of New Orchard, a man of considerable property), Thomas, with a constantly increasing family, had plunged always more deeply in debt. From 1768 no rent was being paid,[5] and by 1775 John had been obliged to undertake the stocking of the farm himself.[6] In 1779 Thomas had declared himself bankrupt and had summoned a meeting of his creditors to ask them to discharge him in exchange for all his

[1] Grange MSS.: Discharge and Assignation, Jean and Agnes Brown to William Johnston, 11 Apr. 1798.

[2] Journ. 13 Mar. 1780.

[3] Grange MSS.: Contract between JJ and Thomas Johnston, 10 Nov. 1763.

[4] Ibid.: Account of Charge and Discharge between JJ and Thomas Johnston, 6 Nov. 1767.

[5] Ibid.: Decree against Thomas Johnston by the Trustees of JJ, 1789.

[6] Ibid.: Book of accounts for livestock at Grange, 1775 to 1786.

goods. Fifty creditors had appeared; but finding, perhaps, that Thomas had few possessions, since the livestock on the farm belonged to John, only seventeen had accepted his terms,[1] so that he had had to make a new start under the appalling handicap of "notour", or undischarged, bankruptcy.

Such a state of affairs was crippling to John, who remained loyal to his brother and anxious to do what he could for the growing family. Not only could he draw nothing from his best property, but all he made in other ways was insufficient to stop the drain caused by Grange on his resources. Though he borrowed money right and left from his friends, he knew that, at latest, the day of reckoning must come when he died, and that he could no longer hope to pass on intact to his kin the lands of which he was so patriarchally proud. Nothing could be left to Thomas, for it would be immediately claimed by creditors, and as time went on it grew increasingly doubtful whether much could be saved even for the children.

Johnston had had one early stroke of fortune, when in 1760, while the future still looked reasonably bright, his relative Francis Scott, an Edinburgh solicitor, who was unlikely to live long and wished to straighten his involved affairs, had sold him the farm of Johnston in Eskdalemuir, in return for his bond for £600, and an annual sum of £120, to be paid to him during his lifetime and after his death to his daughter Isabella.[2] Francis Scott had died in 1762, leaving the affairs of his widow and daughter in Johnston's charge, and in the same year Isabella had disponed to him, "for the friendship and respect I have to John Johnston of Grange, writer in Edinburgh, my cousin", the five-room house in James's Court in which the Scotts had previously lived (and in which, later on, he himself lived while in Edinburgh), reserving to herself only the life-rent.[3] For the time being this had meant an added burden, which in 1768 he had had to ease by borrowing £400 from Isabella; but at her death in 1773 both properties became his own outright, and his liability towards her other heirs was no more than the annual interest on the two heritable bonds of £600 and £400.[4]

In 1771, as we learn from certain hints in Boswell's letters,

---

[1] Grange MSS.: Petition to Lords of Council and Session by William Armstrong, 16 Feb. 1804.

[2] *Ibid.*: Bond of Corroboration, JJ to Isabella Scott, 10 July 1762; Register of Deeds, Mack. 215, p. 180; 245, p. 494;

240, p. 117, S.R.O.

[3] *Ibid.*: Deed of Assignation, Isabella Scott to JJ, 11 May 1762.

[4] *Ibid.*: Discharge and Assignation, Margaret Eliot to William Johnston, 15 Sept. 1800.

Johnston had contemplated marriage with Grace, eldest daughter of William Johnstone of Lockerbie[1]—a match which might have solved his financial difficulties, for she was co-heiress with her two sisters to their father's large estate—but after showing him some kindness, which he must have interpreted as encouragement, she rejected him in favour of Boswell's cousin William Douglas of Kelhead, whom she married in 1772. The disappointment seems to have affected him deeply and to have necessitated a period of rest and change about Eastertime during which he made a tour of Stirlingshire, Perthshire, and Fife.[2] With Thomas and his family (which increased at the rate of a child every second year) as a constant liability, there was nothing for John to do, since his legal practice was much too small to produce the fortune he had hoped for, but to go on borrowing, and to trust that he would get some pension or sinecure to provide for his old age.

In 1778 he had borrowed £700 from Thomas's father-in-law John Paxton, presumably for Thomas's use, and given the farm of Heithat as security,[3] but that had not saved Thomas from being shut up in 1780 in Lochmaben jail by the most insistent of his remaining creditors.[4] He had borrowed £150 from Boswell, £300 from a Miss Helen Bertram,[5] and various sums at different times, his friends and colleagues, Abercrombie, Gordon, and Baillie, acting as his sureties.[6] In the last years of his life his troubles and the blighting of his prospects weighed heavily on his mind, making his fits of melancholia more frequent, more pronounced, and more prolonged: he seems to have been kept going largely by Boswell's optimism and reiterated promises of help, and to have come to look upon Boswell's sympathy as a necessity of life.

It was an admirable characteristic of Boswell that where his affections were aroused he was unwearying in his efforts on behalf of others. Gradually a new change had taken place in their relationship, and whereas at first Boswell had been dependent on Johnston's friendship to supply the parental affection he supposed wanting in his father, it was Johnston, latterly, who needed Boswell. No doubt the Boswell household provided a substitute for the family life

[1] To JJ, 20 Oct. 1771; 3 June 1772.
[2] From JJ, 18 Apr. 1772.
[3] Register of Sasines, Dumfries, 28 Feb. 1781: MS. Heritable Bond, 7 Sept. 1778, S.R.O.
[4] Grange MSS.: Petition to Lords of Council and Session by William Armstrong, 16 Feb. 1804.
[5] *Ibid.*: Extract Bond, 29 May 1794.
[6] Register of Deeds, Mack. 240, p. 117, S.R.O.

he lacked, and in sharing Boswell's hopes and fears he experienced something of the self-fulfilling responsibility usually denied to those who have no families of their own. In these last years of his life Boswell was his constant support and comforter, rallying him, consoling him, holding out prospects of better times, lending him money in spite of his own difficulties (and in such a way that it would seem to be doing a favour to accept it),[1] exerting himself in every possible way to get some office or pension for Johnston. In 1782 he tried to get the Lord Advocate to give him some office about the Edinburgh courts, and extracted a promise from Burke that he would see what could be done about a pension as soon as the Duke of Portland's government got "well settled".[2] For nearly a year he buoyed up Johnston's spirits with the assurance that Burke would succeed, and when nothing came of it, managed to get him nominated for a half-share in the Clerkship to the Justices of Ayr—though this prospect also came to nothing when it was found that a prior claim to the vacancy existed.[3] In 1784 he was writing to Dundas urging him to find some office for Johnston;[4] and in 1785 he wrote to Sir James Erskine, Director of the Chancery in Scotland, disavowing any claim on him in return for having promised to vote for him in the Fife election, but taking the liberty of soliciting him as a cousin to appoint Johnston his deputy in case of a vacancy.[5] As Johnston sank under the weight of his low spirits, Boswell grew more clamant on his behalf, and risking a rebuff, approached Pitt himself.[6] When the inevitable rebuff followed, he was undaunted, and in September 1785 wrote to assure Johnston that "the *Premier* shall not be allowed to have peace until he grants me something *for you*, which is all I ask of him".[7] He was still writing to Pitt in the early summer of 1786, little knowing that it was then too late, and that Johnston had barely two months to live.[8]

It was in January of that year that Boswell supped with Johnston for the last time, on the evening before his departure for London to open a new chapter of his life at the English bar.[9] Johnston had tried to dissuade him from this step to the last, but Boswell, after long hesitation and much consultation with his various friends, had

[1] Reg. Let. 9 May 1782.
[2] To JJ, 22 Apr. 1783.
[3] To JJ, 27 Apr. 1784; Reg. Let. 22 May 1784.
[4] To JJ, 12 Sept. 1784.
[5] Grange MSS.: To Sir James Erskine, 3 Mar. 1785.
[6] Reg. Let. 7 June 1786.
[7] To JJ, 19 Sept. 1785.
[8] Reg. Let. 7 June 1786.
[9] Journ. 26 Jan. 1786.

INTRODUCTION

"resolved to try [his] fortune" there.[1] Johnston's plea had been urged partly on personal grounds, for he dreaded the separation, but Boswell had done all he could to console him, assuring him that they would meet every year, and that he would exert himself to get some office for him in the south. Johnston's health had broken down in the spring of 1785,[2] and though he had recovered, the parting with Boswell and consequent break-up of his customary way of life at James's Court seem to have brought on, early in 1786, a new illness which lingered on and prevented him from leaving Grange when the Edinburgh courts resumed their session after Easter. Boswell plied him with cheerful letters, tried to rouse him to hope and to some delight in life—even pressed him to adopt his own method of conquering spleen and viewing events with objectivity by writing a daily journal;[3] but Johnston had insufficient energy even to reply. He rallied in May and made a trip into England in search of health, accompanied by his friend George Graham of Shaw; but a relapse followed, and early in June, hearing nothing from him, Boswell grew anxious and dreamt that Johnston was very ill.[4] As July came and still no word from Johnston, Boswell grew seriously alarmed and wrote to Graham begging for news, and asking him to tell Johnston how much he longed for an answer to the many letters he had sent.[5] But still no answer came from Johnston, and on 3 August came a letter from John Lawrie (who had been Boswell's clerk, and after he left Edinburgh had become clerk to Johnston) telling him of Johnston's death.[6] The day had come which, fully twenty-three years before, he had begun to anticipate with dread: "Certain it is that one or other of us *must* hear of his friend's death."[7] Next day he wrote to his son Alexander: "The death of my oldest friend, Grange, who was steady to me upon all occasions, is a melancholy event. I was much shocked last night when I came home from the circuit at Maidstone and found a letter from Mr. Lawrie with this sad intelligence. It is a loss that never can be made up to me. My comfort is that he was a benevolent and pious man, so that I trust he is gone to a better place, where it may please God that we may meet, never to undergo the distress of being separated."[8]

1 Reg. Let. 22 May 1784.
2 From JJ, 21 Apr. 1785.
3 To JJ, 13 Feb. 1786.
4 Reg. Let. 7 June 1786.
5 *Ibid.*, July 1786.
6 *Ibid.*, 3 Aug. 1786.
7 To JJ, 4 Jan. 1763.
8 To Alexander Boswell, 4 Aug. 1786.

Johnston had remained through the spring at Grange, not in the house of Grange, which was filled with the family of Thomas (whose wife James Paxton had now borne him five sons and five daughters, of whom nine were alive), but in his own little house near by, Milkside, which subsequently came to be used as a sort of dower-house for Grange.[1] Here he was no doubt cared for by his eldest and favourite sister Janet, the widow of George Brown of Cleughside, who had been staying with him for some time past in James's Court. Her life, like his own, was overshadowed with financial troubles, for her elder son John was proving a ne'er-do-well, and she had become entangled in a network of debt in the effort to save him from the consequences of his own thriftlessness.[2] As Johnston lay in bed, he was visited several times by Joseph Fergusson, who had been his parish minister for twenty-five years and whose friendship with Boswell and Johnston went back to their student-days in Edinburgh. Now in his seventieth year, he found it hard going to travel to and fro on horseback over the four miles between Tundergarth manse and Grange, but his dying parishioner greeted him with pleasure, and he was able to write later to tell Boswell how affectionately his friend had remembered him on his deathbed.[3]

Johnston's will, in which Boswell was named an executor, was drawn up with care in an effort to preserve what could be saved of his property for the lineal descendants of his brother Thomas. The whole was assigned to a board of trustees with a formidable array of lawyers on it: besides Boswell, there were Alexander Abercrombie, W.S., John Gordon, W.S., James Baillie, writer in Edinburgh, James Loch, King's Remembrancer in Exchequer, Alexander Gordon of Campbelton, George Graham of Shaw, John Paxton of New Orchard, and George Kirkpatrick, Depute Clerk of Session. They were appointed "tutors and curators or guardians and managers" to Thomas's children; and Grange, Upperbanks, Heithat, Johnston, and the Edinburgh house were entrusted to them for the ultimate behoof of Thomas's heirs. In addition, by a codicil written within four months of his death, certain separate bequests were made to his sisters and to his house-

[1] It was occupied to 1834 by Thomas Johnston's widow, and subsequently by his unmarried daughter Margaret, who died in 1857.

[2] Grange MSS.: Discharge and Assignation, Jean and Agnes Brown to William Johnston, 11 Apr. 1798.

[3] From Joseph Fergusson, 24 July 1786.

keeper and housemaid at James's Court. To Janet, his "well-beloved sister", he left an annuity of £20 "for her extraordinary trouble and attention to me when I was indisposed"; to her elder son John, the black sheep, fifty guineas; and to her younger son Thomas, a hundred guineas. He also left to Janet his household and personal effects, both at Grange and in Edinburgh; his rings, silver plate, china, linen, furniture, bedding, and blankets. To Sarah, his second sister, the wife of John Graham, formerly owner of Corrie-law, who had fallen on evil times and was now no more than tenant at Linton, he left an annuity of £5, so phrasing the bequest that the money could not be claimed by her husband's creditors; and to Jean, his youngest sister, wife of John Bell of Priestbutts, an annuity of £10. His younger brother Andrew had died in 1785; and because of his insolvency no fixed bequest was made to Thomas, who was appointed a sort of residuary annuitant, the amount to be paid him resting in the discretion of the trustees and depending on what should be available when all other claims were met.[1]

Although it had been conceived for the ultimate benefit of his own family, Thomas was dissatisfied with the terms of the will, and particularly resented the bequests made in the codicil, fore-seeing that little of his own annuity would materialize after the rest had been paid. He even contemplated an action for its reduc-tion, on the ground that Janet exerted an undue influence at the last, miscalled her in private an unworthy sister, and did all he could to obstruct the winding up of Johnston's affairs by the trus-tees.[2] They found him "a very troublesome man" to deal with,[3] raised an action of multiplepoinding to circumvent his obstructions, and to silence his demands even obtained a decree against him in 1789 for the £1,050 he owed the estate in arrears of rent from 1768 to 1788.[4] Debts and bequests were paid only gradually, by instalments, and all the annuities fell into arrears. It was not until more than thirteen years after Johnston's death, when the farms of Heithat and Johnston and the Edinburgh house had all been sold[5] (and of the board of trustees only Abercrombie and Baillie survived), that it was possible to dissolve the trust and

[1] Register of Deeds, Mack. 240, pp. 117–21, S.R.O.
[2] From Thomas Johnston, 3 Oct. 1786.
[3] Reg. Let. John Gordon to JB, Feb. 1788.
[4] Grange MSS.: Decree and Letters of Horning, 1789; Answers for William Johnston to Petition of William Arm-strong, 19 Apr. 1804.
[5] Ibid.: Account of the Intromissions of the Trustees of JJ, 1797.

convey what remained of his property to Thomas's second son William, who was by then established as a partner in the flourishing Glasgow manufacturing firm of Lillie and Johnston, and was in a position to settle all the remaining claims. On 2 April 1800 he became William Johnston of Grange.[1]

Boswell's first concern, when he recovered from the shock of Johnston's death, was to regain the letters which had been in Johnston's keeping. He wrote to John Gordon asking him to make sure of their safety, and congratulating himself that they "are in the hands of gentlemen".[2] He also wrote to John Lawrie, asking him to send the box of papers by a sure conveyance.[3] A later thought was for the debt which Johnston owed him, and he asked his cousin Robert Boswell, who acted as his man of business in Edinburgh, to put forward his claim.[4] There ensued a lengthy correspondence in the course of which the claim was admitted by the other trustees (in spite of some irregularity in the drawing up of one of the bonds), but two years later Boswell was still writing to Robert "wishing to hear of money from . . . Grange's Trustees",[5] and more than seven years later, in 1795, he was still entering the debt, amounting now to £195, on the credit side of his New Year balance sheet.[6] That same January, only four months before Boswell's death, a large instalment was repaid,[7] but it was not until 1798 that Sir William Forbes, Boswell's executor, acknowledged receipt of the final payment from John Johnston's trustees.[8]

When Johnston died, Boswell was already surrounded by new scenes and new company, and perhaps the immediate pain of his loss was rendered less intense by his new problems and preoccupations; but there was no one to fill the gap adequately, and in the autumn of 1786 "the death of worthy Grange came upon me from time to time with a melancholy weight. I shrunk from the practice of the law of England; I read almost nothing and went on very slowly with Dr. Johnson's *Life*."[9] He no longer felt that sense of anchorage in the past, the traditional, the unchanging, which contact with Johnston had given him when he had launched forth into his earlier adventures. Courtenay and Malone, who helped

[1] Register of Deeds, Dur. 285, pp. 676–82, S.R.O.
[2] Reg. Let. 5 Aug. 1786.
[3] *Ibid.*, 20 Nov. 1786.
[4] *Post* c. 26 Sept. 1787.
[5] *Post* 29 Dec. 1789.
[6] Yale MS. A 52.
[7] Grange MSS.: Account of the Intromissions of the Trustees of JJ, 1797.
[8] *Ibid.*: Receipt and Discharge, 5 Dec. 1798.
[9] Journ. Oct. 1786.

him with the compilation of the *Life*, were new intimates and did not share the Scottish background and early memories he had had in common with Johnston. Temple, though as old a friend, had not latterly been wholly sympathetic. Margaret Boswell survived only till 1789, and Boswell's last years, though they brought him the literary success he had coveted for so long, were notably rudderless in their activity, years of premature decline unchecked by his wife's steadying influence or Johnston's affection, with its singular power to restore his self-respect.

Since he had moved to England, he could not take an active part in the work of trusteeship; but in befriending Johnston's nephew, Thomas's eldest son John, he found an opportunity of acting as a "tutor and curator or guardian and manager" to the heir of the estate. John Johnston, junior, though Boswell accorded him the honorific title of "Johnston of Grange",[1] never came into his inheritance. The events of his short career may be traced in a series of letters still extant which he wrote to his father and mother at Grange and to his younger brother William in Glasgow.[2]

From these we learn that after training as a surgeon he had hoped to find an opening as a ship's doctor in the service of the East India Company,[3] but failing in this had dallied for a couple of years at home, in the belief that he might soon inherit the Dumfriesshire property. A visit to the trustees in Edinburgh in 1792 disillusioned him. The demands on the estate, they told him, amounted to £3,000; to settle arrears of salary due to him, Lawrie had appropriated all the furniture in the Edinburgh house; Thomas's annuity could not possibly be fixed for a long time, and his own prospects must remain indefinite. His obvious course, since he was already almost twenty-three, was to find an opening in his profession without more delay; and so, in the following spring, hearing of a vacancy for a surgeon's mate in the 3rd Regiment (the Buffs), then stationed partly at the Tower of London and partly at Windsor Castle, he set off for London. There Boswell took him in charge and introduced him to some influential people. Shortly after his arrival he passed his examination, and having given a handsome bribe to Du Pré, the Surgeon-General's secretary, was

[1] Journ. 11 Oct. 1793; 15 Nov. 1793.
[2] Grange MSS.: 21 letters, written between 1 Feb. 1792 and 16 Mar. 1794.
[3] From Joseph Fergusson, 18 Feb. 1790.

appointed to the staff of the government hospital in Jamaica. It was arranged that he should travel in one of the transports then being prepared to convey an expeditionary force under the command of Sir Charles Grey against the French West Indies: but in November, just before he was due to sail, he was recalled from Portsmouth to London by an urgent message from Boswell, who had meanwhile been moving heaven and earth to get him a better post, and had extracted from Gunning, the Surgeon-General, the promise of a regimental surgeoncy for him, even though this should mean promotion over the heads of forty previous applicants: "I can scarcely give you an idea of the friendship and activity Mr. Boswell has shown in this affair", he wrote to his mother: "my being so very young requires much more interest than it would otherwise do."[1]

Some delay over the appointment was, however, likely, and young Johnston decided, after all, to retain his bird-in-the-hand. He sailed as previously planned in the *Roebuck* on 24 November, under convoy of Sir John Jervis's fleet, saw some gruelling active service as a surgeon's mate with the forces which captured Martinique and Guadeloupe, and reached his destination in Jamaica, only to succumb, within a few weeks, to the tropical fever which had played such havoc among the troops he had just left. He died in the spring of 1794, within six months of leaving England.[2]

His brother William, with his manufacturing business at his back, proved a good laird, and undertook the improvements which converted Grange into the attractive, fertile, pleasantly wooded property it now is. It had been his uncle's ambition to plant trees, as every progressive Scottish landowner was doing at the time; but without stretching his credit,[3] as he told Boswell, he could not afford to do so, and he had had to be content with a gift of young larches raised at Auchinleck by James Bruce, the overseer there, which Boswell sent him.[4] But in 1834 Thomas Little, minister of Tundergarth, writing his account of the parish for inclusion in the *New Statistical Account of Scotland*, was able to praise William, above all the proprietors of the neighbourhood, for the extent of his planting: "The improvements on the estate of

[1] Grange MSS.: From John Johnston, junior, to Mrs. Thomas Johnston, 15 Nov. 1793.

[2] Grange: MSS. Power of Attorney, Thomas Johnston in favour of Eaglesfield Smith, 28 Oct. 1795.

[3] From JJ, 24 Apr. 1767.

[4] To JJ, 31 Mar. 1769.

Grange, the property of William Johnston, Esq., are chiefly re-markable. About eighteen years ago, that gentleman planted extensively; and the plantations, which consist of timber of all sorts, are thriving uncommonly well."[1]

William Johnston of Grange and his wife Mary Newbigging left no children, and when William died in 1835 his brother James, Thomas's third son, who had been tenant-farmer in Cowburn, suc-ceeded.[2] James's wife Isabella Bell died in giving birth to their only child Isabella Margaret, who in 1860 married David Williamson Stewart, factor to the Hope Johnstones of Annandale, having at James's death in 1857 (after some family litigation) inherited Grange. Isabella Margaret (who reverted for the spelling of her maiden name to "Johnstone", in order, no doubt, to mark her family connexion with the more aristocratic branches of the clan, with whom that spelling had long been usual) survived her hus-band by six years and died in 1932, leaving Grange to her elder son James Hope Stewart. At his death in 1944 it passed to his brother, David Williamson Stewart, junior, who sold it in 1947.[3] Its history in the possession of John Johnston's relatives can thus be traced to a recent date for nearly three hundred and fifty years.

Many descendants of the family of Johnston of Grange are scattered about the world, some no farther off from Grange than the neighbouring parishes; and its memory is well preserved in the inscriptions on several stones in Tundergarth parish church-yard. No stone in the family burial enclosure records the name of Boswell's friend, but there is one small rectangular block, about two feet long by nine inches broad, much overgrown by lichen, moss, and grass, on which is carved the one word GRANGE, and some sentimental satisfaction may be derived from associating this modest inscription with the man who loved the place so much and was familiarly known by its name to all his dearest asso-ciates.

But if his trustees did not see fit to put his burdened estate to the expense of a memorial, no doubt a vivid memory of him remained in the minds of all who had known him—black-bearded,[4] broad-

---

[1] *New Statistical Account of Scotland*, 1845, iv. 202.
[2] Tombstone in Tundergarth church-yard.
[3] Information furnished by Messrs. J. C. & A. Steuart, W.S., Edinburgh.
[4] To JJ, 19 Dec. 1764.

shouldered, thick-legged,[1] wanting in the exterior graces,[2] and indifferent to the fashions;[3] modest, loyal, and sensible—though much given to gloominess; indolent and inclined to betake himself to bed, with a book of Scottish history, a cup of tea, and some biscuits spread with currant jelly,[4] rather than rouse himself to more active pleasures: but when drawn out and exhilarated by good company and good drink, eloquent in his defence of Scotland's past, of Catholic Mary, the Jacobite cause, and the doughty *"auld lairds* of Johnston",[5] in the days of "brose and border incursions";[6] in whom all his friends discovered a tolerant good-nature making for restful companionship, the outcome of what Boswell called his "ancient *stark love and kindness"*.[7]

[1] From Andrew Erskine to JJ, 2 June 1766.

[2] To JJ, 28 May 1763.

[3] To JJ, 19 Dec. 1764.

[4] To JJ, 26 July 1763.

[5] To JJ, 19 July 1763.

[6] From Andrew Erskine to JJ, 2 June 1766.

[7] To JJ, 22 May 1771.

ACKNOWLEDGEMENTS

ACKNOWLEDGEMENTS for generous help and advice in the preparation of this volume are due to the members of the Editorial Committee of the Boswell Papers, and to Dr. Robert Metzdorf, Mrs. Marion Pottle, Dr. Robert Warnock, Mr. Benjamin F. Houston, and other research workers and secretarial helpers who have been from time to time in the Boswell Room at Yale. I want to thank also certain friends and correspondents applied to for information, some of whom were able to supply it, some to suggest where I could find it for myself, and others, after searching, to assure me it was unobtainable: C. C. Bayley, Professor of History, McGill University; Mons. Carlo Castiglioni, Prefetto, Biblioteca Ambrosiana, Milan; Rev. W. D. Cooper, Theological College, Edinburgh; J. C. Corson, Deputy Librarian, University of Edinburgh; Antonio D'Andrea, Professor of Italian, McGill University; Robert Donaldson, Reference Librarian, University of Edinburgh; Sir James Fergusson, Keeper of the Records of Scotland; R. A. Houston, Grange, Lockerbie; Rev. J. W. Ingram, Tundergarth Manse, Lockerbie; Mrs. Molly Johnston, Carlisle; Rev. Douglas Lockhart, Old St. Paul's Church, Edinburgh; C. T. McInnes, Curator of Historical Records, Edinburgh; J. B. McKeeman, Assistant Keeper of Printed Books, National Library of Scotland; Mrs. M. D. McLean, County Librarian, Dumfries; C. A. Malcolm, Librarian, Signet Library, Edinburgh; David Murison, Editor, *Scottish National Dictionary*; B. C. Skinner, Assistant Keeper, Scottish National Portrait Gallery; D. S. Walker of Messrs. J. C. & A. Steuart, W.S., Edinburgh; and R. A. Wilson, Keeper of Printed Books, British Museum.

I should like to make particular mention of the work of Mr. N. S. Curnow, Johannesburg, who most generously gave to the enrichment of certain of the notes and to the correction of the proofs the benefit of his researches among the Boswell papers and material related to them.

Thanks are due to Mr. and Mrs. Donald F. Hyde for permission to include material from the Hyde Collection, and to the Misses

ACKNOWLEDGEMENTS

Carlyle, Waterbeck, Dumfriesshire, for permission to print certain letters in their possession, as also for their kindness in making family papers available for research.

To the University of Aberdeen and the Carnegie Trust for the Universities of Scotland I want to express my gratitude for enabling me, while Lecturer in English Literature at Aberdeen, to accept the invitation of the Editorial Committee to spend a period at Yale and undertake the editing of this volume.

R. S. W.

TEXTUAL NOTE

THE text of the original manuscripts has been reproduced exactly, as to spelling and word order, except where footnotes indicate editorial emendations, or where editorial additions are enclosed in square or angular brackets. Passages in square brackets are additions made to clarify the sense or supply something inadvertently omitted by the writer. Angular brackets indicate defects in the manuscript and passages printed between them are conjectural.

The original punctuation and capitalization have been retained except in a very few instances where a writer, through haste or carelessness, has obscured his meaning by omitting a comma or failing to mark the end of a sentence. Conventional epistolary contractions, such as *wt* for *with* and *agt* for *against*, have been expanded, superior letters lowered, and interlinear or marginal additions incorporated in the running text without editorial comment.

Datelines are printed at the head of the letter regardless of their position in the original; salutations are not printed on a separate line, but are marked off by a colon from the opening sentence; and abbreviations used in salutations and complimentary conclusions are expanded.

Where, in a few instances, a writer has omitted to underline titles of books or plays, these have been italicized; and in a few cases, where direct speech is quoted without the use of inverted commas, these have been supplied.

The heading to each letter records anything of significance, apart from the text, which appears on the manuscript or its wrapper, such as the address, the postmark, or an endorsement. It records also any mention made of the letter in Boswell's own register of letters sent and received by him, and the location of the original manuscript. Unless otherwise specified all endorsements are the recipient's.

The existence at one time of certain letters now missing from the series can be inferred from references made to them in the correspondence as we have it, or in Boswell's journal or register of letters. These are noted in their chronological order, so far as this can be determined, with a summary of as much information as can be gathered about their contents.

Notes have frequently been amplified beyond what may be thought strictly necessary for the explanation of the text. This has been done partly because the temptation to pursue by-paths of such interest to the student of eighteenth-century Scotland is hard to resist, and partly because the Editorial Committee, looking ahead to future volumes, has been concerned to make sure that a record is kept at suitable points in the series of all that can be discovered from the study of the Boswell Papers about Boswell and his associates. If some of the footnotes in this volume appear unduly long and detailed in comparison with others, it is because they deal with matters not likely to be so fully handled elsewhere in the series.

Though not covered by the title of this book, the letters to Johnston from Andrew Erskine, and those concerning Johnston's affairs written after his death, could not well have been excluded from a volume which aims at presenting as complete a view as possible of Johnston's life, character, and relationship with Boswell.

LIST OF ABBREVIATIONS USED
IN THE NOTES

BP: *The Private Papers of James Boswell from Malahide Castle, in the Collection of Lt.-Col. Ralph Heyward Isham*, edited by Geoffrey Scott and Frederick A. Pottle, 1928–36.

Burke, *Peerage and Baronetage*: Sir Bernard Burke, *A Genealogical and Heraldic Dictionary of the Peerage and Baronetage*: edited by Sir Desmond Burke.

College of Justice: George Brunton and David Haig, *An Historical Account of the Senators of the College of Justice*, 1832.

Comp. Bar.: George Edward Cokayne, *Complete Baronetage*, 1900–09.

Comp. Peer.: George Edward Cokayne and Jeffrey H. White, *Complete Peerage*, 1910–55.

Consultation Book: Boswell's MS. Consultation Book, 1766–72, National Library of Scotland.

Donaldson's *Collection*: *A Collection of Original Poems by Scotch Gentlemen*, vol. 1. 1760; vol. 2. 1762.

Faculty of Advocates: *The Faculty of Advocates in Scotland, 1532–1943*, edited by Sir Francis J. Grant, 1944.

Fasti Scot.: *Fasti Ecclesiae Scoticanae*, edited by Hew Scott, 1915–28.

Forbes: Sir William Forbes, *Memoirs of a Banking House*, 1860.

Gent. Mag.: *The Gentleman's Magazine*.

Grange MSS.: Family papers in the possession of the Misses Catherine and Margaret Carlyle, Waterbeck, Dumfriesshire.

Hist. MSS. Comm.: *Reports of the Royal Commission on Historical Manuscripts*.

Hyde Collection: The collection of Mr. and Mrs. Donald F. Hyde, Somerville, New Jersey.

JB: James Boswell.

JJ: John Johnston of Grange.

Journ.: Boswell's MS. Journal, Yale.

Life: Boswell's *Life of Johnson*, edited by G. B. Hill, revised by L. F. Powell, 1934–50.

Lit. Car.: Frederick A. Pottle, *The Literary Career of James Boswell*, 1929.

Lond. Journ.: *Boswell's London Journal, 1762–1763*, edited by Frederick A. Pottle, 1950.

Lond. Mag.: *The London Magazine*.

Mem.: Boswell's MS. Memoranda, Yale.

MS.; MSS.: Manuscript; manuscripts.

Notes: Boswell's MS. Journal Notes, Yale.

OED: The Oxford English Dictionary.

Old and New Edinburgh: James Grant, *Cassell's Old and New Edinburgh*, 3 vols., ?1881–83.

LIST OF ABBREVIATIONS USED IN THE NOTES

Original Portraits: John Kay, *A Series of Original Portraits and Caricature Etchings*, 1877 (paginated as two vols., often bound as four).

Reg. Let.: Boswell's MS. Register of Letters, Yale.

Scotland and Scotsmen: John Ramsay, *Scotland and Scotsmen in the Eighteenth Century*, edited by A. Allardyce, 1888.

Scots Mag.: *The Scots Magazine.*

Scots Peer.: *The Scots Peerage*, edited by Sir James Balfour Paul, 1904–14.

SJ: Samuel Johnson.

S.R.O.: Scottish Record Office, H.M. General Register House, Edinburgh.

Tour: Boswell's *Journal of a Tour to the Hebrides with Samuel Johnson, LL.D.*, edited by Frederick A. Pottle and Charles H. Bennett, 1936, 1961 (1963).

Writers to the Signet: *The Society of Writers to His Majesty's Signet*, 1936.

I

September 1759–October 1762

During this period, from his twentieth to his twenty-second year, Boswell was a student of law. The law studies he had begun earlier in Edinburgh, he now continued, first at the University of Glasgow, and then (after a few months' interval spent in London in the spring of 1760) at home under his father's direction.

I

September 1759–October 1762

From Johnston, September 1759

Missing. A letter sent to Auchinleck. JJ wrote to say that he could not, as he had intended, pay a visit at that time to Auchinleck, and gave JB some news of theatrical affairs in Edinburgh. It appears from the reply below that he may also have asked JB to request Lord Auchinleck to use his influence on behalf of Joseph Fergusson, a candidate for presentation to the vacant charge of Tundergarth parish in Dumfriesshire.

To Johnston, Wednesday 26 September 1759

MS. Yale (L 675).

Auchinleck, 26 Septr 1759

DEAR SIR: Although it may appear an odd introduction to an Epistle, yet I must begin with saying that I don't know whether your letter gave me more satisfaction or uneasiness; satisfaction at hearing of your wellfare, uneasiness at being informed that you had lay'd aside the thoughts of your intended visit. I am pretty sure, had it been convenient for you to favour us with your Company, you would have found the jaunt very agreable.

Auchinleck is a most sweet, romantic Place. There is a vast deal of Wood and Water, fine retired shady walks, and every thing that can render the Countrey agreable to contemplative Minds. I can here indulge those pleasing dispositions which must have inspired the breast of my favourite Poet Horace, when in his Ode to Mæcænas he breaks out into this elegant and beautifull Exclamation

> Me doctarum ederæ præmia frontium
> Dis miscent superis; me gelidum nemus
> Nympharumque leves cum Satyris choræ
> Secernent Populo, si neque tibias
> Euterpe cohibet, nec Polyphymnia
> Lesboum refugit tendere Barbiton.[1]

---

[1] Horace, *Odes* I. i. 29-34. "The ivy-wreath, the poet's reward, associates me with the gods: inspired by the light dance of nymphs and choral satyrs in the cool

3

I beg you may not think me pedantic for inserting this quotation, for it is realy so delicate, so picturesque, that I could not resist the pleasure of transcribing it at full length.

I dare say you will be saying by this time to what purpose is all this Rhapsody about his place? What can he mean by it? Have patience Sir—what I intended by it was to say that your presence would have been no small addition to my happiness, and likewise to encourage you to make out your visit another time.

I am sorry that Tundergirth cannot be procured for Mr. Fergusson,[2] as I hear that Mr. Blacklock has got a promise of the Presentation.[3] Besides, though that were not the case, I am affraid My Lord Auchinleck's interest could be but of very little service as He was on the opposite side to Scotstarvet, at the Elections.[4]

woodlands, I am set free from the vulgar throng, so long as Euterpe does not check her flute, nor Polyhymnia refuse to tune her Lesbian lyre." In this ode the poet contrasts the different ways in which men spend their lives and the different goals they set themselves. It is his desire, he says, to be a lyric poet and to spend his life in the seclusion of the country. For "chorae", "secernent", and "Polyhymnia" JB should have written "chori", "secernunt", and "Polyhymnia". "Polyphymnia" is perhaps a slip of the pen, but "chorae" (for "choreæ") and "secernent" make sense and are more probably unconscious substitutions in a memorized text. Lord Auchinleck had promised JB a shilling for every ode of Horace he got by heart, and at one time he could repeat "upwards of forty of them" (To Alexander Boswell, 7 Feb. 1794).

[2] Joseph Fergusson (1718–91), who had been tutor some years before to JB and his brothers, had just been licensed. He had been hoping for the presentation to the vacant charge of Tundergarth parish, in which Grange lay, and of which JJ was a principal heritor. There was delay over the settlement, but Fergusson was inducted on 17 Sept. 1761 (*Fasti Scot.* ii. 223).

[3] Thomas Blacklock (1721–91), the blind poet, had been advised by Hume (who befriended him after the publication of his first volume of verse) to enter the ministry of the Church of Scotland. When in 1758 he was licensed, there was considerable difficulty about his settlement. He was not, after all, presented to Tundergarth, but to the united parishes of Kirkcudbright, Galtway, and Dunrod, where he was received with protests by the parishioners, unwilling to accept a blind minister (*Fasti Scot.* ii. 417–18). He demitted the charge in 1765 and moved to Edinburgh, where he kept a boardinghouse for students, whose work he supervised.

[4] David Scott of Scotstarvet (d. 1766), advocate, was M.P. for the county of Fife, 1741–47, and for the Aberdeen group of burghs from 1751 until his death. His near relative, David, 7th Viscount Stormont, possessed the right to present to the charge of Tundergarth.

Lord Auchinleck, who had become a Fife voter on 9 Apr. 1734 for the superiority of the lands of Nether Glassmount, Kinghorn parish, was elected praeses at the election meeting at Cupar, 31 July 1747, and voted for James Oswald of Dunnikier, who was elected with 43 votes to Scott's 38. Though Lord Auchinleck did not cast his vote either at the by-election of 2 Jan. 1752 or the general election of 2 May 1754, and Oswald was not personally a candidate for the county of Fife in 1754, it is sufficiently clear that Oswald and Scott continued to be opposed, and that Lord Auchinleck continued to

No doubt but You would have been very well pleased to have had so old and intimate an Acquaintance for your Parish Minister, but as that cannot be you must endeavour to exercise the amiable virtue of contentment.

I am sure it would have made him very happy for he greatly commends the place, says he knows *the People* and (as his usual phrase is) declares they would all be for him.

You obliged me not a little with your Theatrical News. I am highly diverted that a certain Mock Hero has now fixed the dramatic Criticisms[5] on a different Author from what he did formerly. You have raised my curiosity by mentioning a Satyrical piece upon the Players.[6] I should take it kind if you would drop a line to any of your Acquaintances who might, if possible, yet pick up a copy of it.

Would you beleive it? The report of my affection for Sylvia has allready reach'd the ears of my friend Temple.[7] Well might the Mantuan Bard say

give his interest to Oswald (Freeholders' Minutes, Sheriff Court Records, Fife, in the Register House, Edinburgh; *Memorials of . . . James Oswald*, 1825, pp. 330–41, 343–44).

[5] During the summer, a series of critical reviews of the performances at the Canongate theatre had appeared in *The Edinburgh Chronicle*. F. A. Pottle conjectures that JB had some part in their composition (*Lit. Car.*, pp. 263, [284]–291). The exaggerated praise given to his favourite actress Mrs. Cowper, and to his stage hero West Digges (whose name is always printed in capitals), together with something characteristically pert and juvenile in the style, does suggest that JB was the author.

Digges was in Ireland at the time, having failed to obtain a partnership he had hoped for with Callender and Beat, the managers of the Edinburgh theatre (J. C. Dibdin, *The Annals of the Edinburgh Stage*, 1888, p. 104). The articles in the *Chronicle* contrast unfavourably with Digges's the acting of a substitute named Dexter, and indirectly attack the managers for failing to secure the services of Digges when they had the opportunity. The "dramatic criticisms" referred to here are

almost certainly the *Chronicle* reviews, and the "mock hero" may well be Dexter.

[6] Possibly *The Rival Theatres, or a Playhouse to be Let: a Farce. To Which Is Added the Chocolate-makers, or Mimickry Exposed: an Interlude; with a Preface, and Notes Commentary and Explanatory*, by *Mr. George Stayley, comedian, Dublin*, satirizing the Irish players and their quarrels, which had been published in London in May and briefly reviewed in *The Monthly Review* (1759) xx. 463. At this time the Edinburgh company was constantly recruited from Dublin and there was much passing to and fro of the leading actors between the two cities. George Stayley (1727–?79) later himself acted in Edinburgh during the 1765–66 season, and it was the management's failure to re-engage him, against public opinion, which led to the riot that wrecked the Canongate theatre on 24 Jan. 1767 (*Annals of the Edinburgh Stage*, pp. 135–43).

[7] "I heard an odd story here, of you and one Mrs. Cooper. I scarce imagined my grave friend wou'd have turned a gallant so soon. You are continually in the Playhouse, I am told, and I hear you and Mr. Love have differed" (From

Fama malum quo non aliud velocius ullum[8]

Be so good as write me soon and beleive me to be Dear Sir your very sincere Friend

JAMES BOSWELL

From Johnston, January 1760

Missing. Sent from Edinburgh and received by JB in Glasgow, having presumably been forwarded there from Auchinleck. It contained some news of theatrical affairs in Edinburgh, as is shown in JB's reply.

To Johnston, Friday 11 January 1760

MS. Yale (L 676). The paper has perished, in part, from damp.

ADDRESS: ⟨T⟩o ⟨Mr. John Johnston at t⟩he house of Mr. ⟨?James Hay⟩[1] C⟨lerk⟩ to the Signet, Wardro⟨p's Cour⟩t, Edi⟨nbur⟩gh.

ENDORSEMENT: Glasgow 11th January 1760. James Boswell.

University of Glasgow, ⟨11 January, 1760⟩

DEAR SIR: Your very agreable Epistle ⟨came safe to hand,⟩ which, as it informed me of your ⟨welfare, gave me⟩ much Satisfaction.

W. J. Temple, Autumn 1759, MS. Yale C 2656). In the *Chronicle* reviews Mrs. Cowper is invariably praised, Mrs. Love comes in for sharp criticism, and Love is treated without enthusiasm. Little is known of Mrs. Cowper and even her Christian and maiden names have not been ascertained. JB's reference to her as "Sylvia" probably merely reflects the fact that one of her best parts was that of Sylvia in *The Recruiting Officer*. She must have been several years older than he, for she was acting at Richmond in 1749. Theatrical records also show that she played at Bath, Drury Lane, and Dublin during the next ten years, and that she took the leading female roles in the Edinburgh theatre during the summer of 1759. Temple saw her act in Newcastle later in the year but was not greatly impressed: "She is a pretty good actress, but I cannot say I was much taken with her. Both her manner of acting and her voice were far from transporting me. Her person is tolerable. You are the best judge of the charms of her conversation. In my opinion however, by marrying her

musick-master she has given but a bad specimen both of her taste and judgment" (From W. J. Temple, 25 Dec. 1759–14 Jan. 1760). Her later theatrical career, if any, and ultimate fate have not been traced.

[8] Virgil, *Aeneid* iv. 174. "Nothing travels more quickly than scandal." Modern texts have *qua*, but *quo* appears in several important manuscripts and is the reading generally found in 18th-century texts: e.g. Burmann (1746), Warton (1753), and Heyne (1767).

---

[1] Various Edinburgh Window Tax and Stent Rolls for the period 1759–60 (S.R.O.) indicate that one of the three "possessors" (i.e. occupiers) of a property in Wardrop's Court was "Mr. James Hay, Clerk to the Signet". This was James Hay of Cocklaw (d. 1771), W. S. since 1728 (*Writers to the Signet*, p. 187). It seems likely that he was the "Mr. Hay" referred to *post* 21 Dec. 1762, and that JJ received his legal training as a clerk in Hay's chambers.

I dare say you would ⟨be greatly surprised on⟩ hearing that I was ⟨come hither as the result of⟩ an unexpected ⟨Decision of my father in whose⟩ judgment it beca⟨me wise for me to leave Edinburgh.⟩[2]

I must confess that it made me n⟨ot a⟩ little uneasy at first, to think of being de⟨prived⟩ of the happiness I usually enjoyed, and h⟨oped⟩ for this Winter, in my good friends and Ac⟨quai⟩ntances at Edinburgh, but I resolved to br⟨ing m⟩y mind to be contented with the Situat⟨ion which⟩ was thought proper for me.

My greatest inducement for c⟨oming hi⟩ther, was to hear Mr. Smith's lectures ⟨which are tr⟩uly excellent.[3] His Sentiments ⟨are striking, profound⟩ and beautifull, the method in ⟨which they⟩ are aranged clear, accurate and ⟨orderly, his lan⟩guage correct perspicuous and elegan⟨tly phrased⟩. His private character is realy amiable. He ⟨has⟩ nothing of that formal stiffness and Pedantry which is too often found in Professors. So far from that, he is a most polite well-bred man, is extreamly fond of having his Students with him and ⟨treats them⟩ with all the easiness and affa⟨bility imaginab⟩le.

⟨There is likew⟩ise a very able Professor of Ci⟨vil Law,⟩ D⟨oc⟩tor Hercules Lindsay, who is, in⟨deed one of the⟩ best teachers I ever saw.[4]

⟨I lead qu⟩ite an academical life, am boar⟨ded in my lodgings⟩

[2] It was not unknown for men who had passed through the arts course at Edinburgh University to attend law classes afterwards in Glasgow. Lord Auchinleck may have been prejudiced in favour of the teaching at Glasgow University, but the unexpectedness of his decision to send JB there suggests rather that he considered the company JB had been keeping in Edinburgh, and the literary and theatrical proclivities he had recently been indulging, likely to distract him from making satisfactory progress.

[3] Adam Smith (1723–90), after giving private lectures in Edinburgh on Rhetoric and Belles Lettres, had returned to Glasgow in 1751 as Professor of Logic and in 1752 had been appointed to the Chair of Moral Philosophy. His *Wealth of Nations* did not appear until 1776. "I remember Dr. Adam Smith, in his rhetorical lectures at Glasgow, told us he

was glad to know that Milton wore latchets in his shoes instead of buckles" (*Tour*, p. 9, previously recorded in Journ. 18 Oct. 1762; see Journ. 22 Jan. 1763 for another recollection of Smith's lectures). In a letter of this period (not now known to exist) Smith had remarked on JB's "happy facility of manners," and JB long treasured and often repeated the compliment (To Andrew Erskine, 8 Dec. 1761; Journ. 22 Dec. 1765, 12 Sept. 1773, 3 Apr. 1775).

[4] Hercules Lindsay (d. 1761) son of Robert Lindsay, minister of Edzell and Newdosk, had been a member of the Faculty of Advocates since 1745, Professor of Law at Glasgow since 1750, and Dean of Faculties there since 1758 (*The Matriculation Albums of the University of Glasgow from 1728 to 1858*, ed. W. Innes Addison, 1913, entry 1436).

and very seldom go down ⟨to Auchinleck or pay any⟩ visits except to my ⟨teachers and a few stude⟩nts.

⟨I was glad to have⟩ the Story of your ⟨ad⟩ventu⟨re with⟩ the ⟨. . . . .⟩t; I may safely inform y⟨ou tha⟩t I wrote the Elegy, but I beg you may cont⟨radict i⟩t.[5] I am surprised how he suspected me. ⟨His⟩ lines in answer to it (for which I thank y⟨ou⟩ do⟩n't want Spirit. I in reality did not in⟨tend to⟩ affront *him* in the least, so that if I w⟨rote an⟩y thing which he could interpret in⟨vidiousl⟩y, it has been owing to inadvertency. ⟨I shou⟩ld be glad to know if Love saw it,[6] ⟨an⟩d ⟨if it was to⟩l⟨er⟩ably circulated.

⟨I see by the *C*⟩*hronicle*, that Theatrical P⟨assions at p⟩resent run high.[7] Pray be so good ⟨as give me a⟩ number of particulars, which

[5] The only poem known to be JB's which is styled "elegy" in the title is *An Elegy on the Death of an Amiable Young Lady*, published in quarto in Aug. 1761, but it has not hitherto been supposed that this piece was composed so early (see *Lit. Car.*, pp. 5–6), and it is hard to see how even a poet could have found in it matter of affront. The "elegy" in question was probably some unrecovered burlesque or satirical piece, JB's contribution to the controversy then raging over the management of the Canongate theatre. A speculative but highly attractive restoration of the lacuna in the sentence preceding that to which the present note is attached would be "the ⟨great Bea⟩t". Callender having withdrawn from the business, David Beat was left in charge, but though he had a fresh opportunity to strengthen the company by taking into partnership the very popular leading actor West Digges, who returned post-haste from Ireland in November, he quarrelled with him, and their squabble became a public concern. Digges published a statement of his case in *The Edinburgh Courant* on 20 Nov., and Beat replied in the same paper on 1 Dec. (J. C. Dibdin, *The Annals of the Edinburgh Stage*, 1888, pp. 108–10). There is no doubt on which side JB's sympathies lay, for his admiration for West Digges at this time knew no bounds. F. A. Pottle conjectures that JB was the author of a pamphlet dedicated to Digges which appeared in Feb. 1760

(a reprinting of the reviews mentioned *ante* 26 Sept. 1759, n. 5), and which formed part of the ammunition in a feud between the actor Francis Gentleman, with whom JB had formed an acquaintance, and the management of the theatre (*Lit. Car.*, pp. [284]–291). Gentleman had by this time gone, like JB, to Glasgow.

[6] James Dance (1722–74), an Englishman who took the name of Love when he went on the stage, had first acted in Edinburgh during the 1753–54 season, when he was among the new talent imported by John Lee, the manager. After returning in 1756, Love and his wife acted in Edinburgh regularly until 1762 and Love also for some years assisted Beat in the management of the theatre. He was a man of good education and considerable talent, and had long been a confidential friend of the young JB. Indeed, it was at his desire that JB in 1758 wrote his first recorded journal, which is not now known to exist (To W. J. Temple, 16 Dec. 1758). In 1762 he joined Garrick's company at Drury Lane, but for many years after continued to be energetic in his efforts to promote theatrical ventures in Scotland and the provinces, where he and Digges, along with others, were anxious to establish a chain of theatres (DNB; J. C. Dibdin, *Annals of the Edinburgh Stage*, 1888, *passim*; John Jackson, *The History of the Scottish Stage*, 1793).

[7] Dramatic reviews, by unknown hands, were appearing regularly in *The*

⟨will⟩ aff⟨o⟩rd me some entertainment, when de⟨pr⟩ived of the exalted pleasures of the Stage. In compliance with your request, accept a small Poetic Essay which you must not give a Copy of. I am My Dear Sir Your sincere and Affectionate Friend

JAMES BOSWELL

When y⟨ou⟩ see Mr. ⟨. . . ma⟩ke my kind Com⟨pt⟩s to him.

Ode

I.

Ye elves! who stated vigils keep,
When Mortals sunk in balmy sleep,
   Forget the live-long night:
Ye, who soft trip it late and soon,
While the faint-shining, paly Moon
   Affords her gratefull light.

II.

On you I call whom oft I've seen
Upon the flow'r-enamel'd green
   Your sportive meetings hold,
While I distrest with gentle fears
Have to your kindly-listning ears
   My tender story told.

III.

Bear witness, ye: how oft I've sighed,
How oft in fancy'd anguish died,
   Ah! struck by Cupid's dart!

Edinburgh Chronicle. In the issue current when JB wrote this letter (5–7 Jan., pp. 385 ff.) a "critical review" praises Digges extravagantly as an actor. The next article in the same issue thoroughly damns him. Besides the tension over the management of the theatre, and the old prejudice against theatre-going as conducive to immorality (which had produced a letter in the *Chronicle* as recently as 29–31 Dec., complaining that certain spectators were appearing in the company of women of doubtful character), a new cause of unrest was the announcement that Garrick's farce *High Life Below Stairs,* which had had a successful run in London, was to be given on 16 Jan. An organized riot took place on the opening night (five days after the date of JB's letter) in the free gallery reserved for the footmen, who objected to the satirizing of servants. They were at this time peculiarly sensitive about their rights and prerogatives, because of a movement which had been set afoot by several bodies, including the Company of Hunters, the Faculty of Advocates, the Clerks to the Signet, and the Select Society, to abolish the practice of giving "vails", i.e. tipping servants (J. C. Dibdin, *op. cit.*, p. 110; *Scots Mag.*, 1760, xxii. 42).

How oft in nature's artless strains
Have plaintive sung the cruel pains
That pierce my wounded heart.

IV.

Unhappy me, who, in the bloom
Of youth, must bear the heavy gloom
Of a grief-clouded mind;
Unhappy me! who thus must prove
The torments of despairing love,
Which no relief can find.[8]

To Johnston, Monday 22 September 1760

MS. Yale (L 677).

ADDRESS: To John Johnston Esqr.

Auchinleck[1] 22 Sepr. 1760

DEAR SIR: It gave me much pleasure to hear from Mr. Fergusson that You had got so far safe upon the road. I hope the rest of your

[8] Several words and phrases are missing in the copy of these verses sent to JJ, which is in a tattered condition, but they have been supplied from a fair copy in a collection of his own verses made by JB (Bodleian, MS. Douce 193). Though headed "Plan of a Volume of Poems to be published for me by Becket and De-hondt", the collection was never printed.

[1] Since the last letter to JJ, from Glasgow, there had occurred the most momentous event in JB's life up to this date. Early in the morning of 1 Mar. 1760 he had run away from Glasgow University with the intention of becoming a Roman Catholic, despite all the practical penalties and disabilities this act would have cost him when it became known. Riding hard, he reached London on the 5th and plunged into an existence in which dissipation mingled oddly with his fervour for his new faith. But, within a week or two and before Catholicism had claimed him irredeemably, the Earl of Eglinton, an Ayrshire neighbour, alerted by Lord Auchinleck, had located him

and come to the rescue. Eglinton quickly effected a cure by introducing the well-connected young man into the exclusive circles of high and gay society. The experience so inflamed JB's fancy with a predilection for this type of life that he forsook Catholicism and turned his ambition towards obtaining a commission in the Guards. These were based permanently in London, and, as one of their officers, he expected to be able to enjoy constantly the delights of high life. Lord Auchinleck cannot have been greatly pleased by this turn of events, but at least it was better for the family than that his heir should turn Catholic. Accordingly, he allowed his son to remain in Eglinton's care until the end of May, when he journeyed to London himself and carried JB back to Edinburgh for the Summer Session, and thereafter, as this letter shows, to Auchinleck (To Sir David Dalrymple, 22 Mar. 1760; "Memoirs" in *Europ. Mag.*, 1791, p. 324, reprinted *Lit. Car.*, p. xxxi; Journ. 25 Jan. 1763; Loudoun papers, Lord Auchinleck to Lord Loudoun, 6 June 1760).

journey was equaly safe and agreable, and that You found all your friends well.

My being carried away so suddenly, was very unlucky. You may, however, in some measure be blamed; as You did not keep your Appointment of coming out 10 days after the Session, when I lay'd my account to be at home. But I hope the transient sight You have had of this Place, will make You wish to be here some other time, when we can settle matters so as to rove about, like *Youths of Nineteen*,[2] for a good while.

I came home upon Tuesday; But found myself not a little injured by the Exercise, and high living which good Company and a love to Sociality led me into.

I am now taking a regular course of Medecines, and keeping within doors, with spare diet, in order to get effectualy rid of my Indisposition, that troublesom Companion and bar to my innocent Pleasures.[3]

I have been sometimes *Sixty* since You left me. But I must shake it off. For Juvenility is absolutely necessary for carrying on *Give Your Son his Will*.[4]

Write me soon and beleive me Your sincere Affectionate Friend

JAMES BOSWELL

[2] The phrase may have been borrowed from a contemporary play or song. Nineteen was JB's actual age at this time, although JJ was older (*post*, Appendix 2). But terms of age have special significance in the context of this correspondence. As indicated later in the letter, JB and JJ were accustomed to liken the sensations they experienced during their periodic fits of depression to those they supposed to accompany old age.

[3] "Last Summer, indeed, I went to a house of recreation in [Edinburgh], and catch'd a Tartar too, with a vengeance" (To Temple, 1 May 1761). This, presumably, was the "visitation" that lasted four months (Journ. 22 Jan. 1763), for the earlier one of ten weeks had happened during JB's visit to London (Journ. 22, 25 Jan. 1763).

[4] The first Act of this ballad opera, in JB's youthful handwriting, is extant (MS. Yale M 116). It takes the form of a discussion between Sir Solomon Positive and a friend named Sagely who sympathizes with the aspirations of Sir Solomon's son Charles to join the army instead of going into his father's business. Sir Solomon's arguments are plainly on the lines of those used by Lord Auchinleck in his attempts to reason with JB, and the comic mannerisms in his speech may be Lord Auchinleck's too. The opera was never completed nor does the dialogue contain any suggestion of action out of which further developments might arise.

To Johnston, Friday 21 August 1761

MS. Yale (L 678).

ENDORSEMENT: Auchinleck 21st August 1761. James Boswell.

Auchinleck 21 August 1761

MY DEAR SIR: We had a good journey west and have been in good health and spirits. I was so much hurried that I could not have an opportunity to take leave of you, in form, before I left Edinr.[1]

My Father and Mother set out upon the Circuit on the 11 or 12 of next Month.[2] I insist upon your coming to me then—I shall expect you on the 12 or 13. I am reading law hard—You shall just soap your own beard[3] and shall see som⟨e fine pro⟩ductions of your fr⟨iend⟩[4]

JAMES BOSWELL

No excuse will serve
Try if you can Get the Book, and bring it with You.[5]

---

[1] At the close of the session of the Edinburgh law-courts, the Boswells customarily left their Edinburgh house in Blair's Land, Parliament Close, and transferred the whole household to Ayrshire, where they spent the vacation at Auchinleck. "Came to Auch[inleck] middle of Augt." (Notes, undated entry preceding entry for 14 Aug.). In 1761 the Court rose on Wednesday, 12 Aug.

[2] Besides being a Judge in the Court of Session, Lord Auchinleck was a Judge in the Justiciary Court, and, as such, went during the vacation on one or other of the three justiciary court circuits. In Sept. 1761 he went on the western circuit, accompanied by his colleague Lord Strichen, and held courts at Stirling, Glasgow, and Inveraray (*Scots Mag.*, 1761, xxiii. 554).

[3] "Every man soap his own beard" was the motto of the Soaping Club, founded by JB at some festive gathering in Thom's tavern and celebrated by him in the verses called "B——, a Song", which were printed in the second volume of Alexander Donaldson's *Collection of Original Poems by Scotch Gentlemen* (1762). (The

first volume had appeared in October 1760.) A note (ii. 90) explains that "Every man", etc., was "the reigning phrase for Every man in his humour".

[4] A reference, perhaps, to JB's contributions to the second volume of Donaldson's *Collection*, which was to be published early in the following year (*post* 13 Sept. 1762, n. 12). It included thirty pieces of verse by JB, among them epigrams, odes, epistles, and songs.

[5] JJ arrived at Auchinleck on 8 Sept. "Was excessively happy to see him. All our fine ideas rushed into my mind: Holyroodhouse, etc. and Mr. Digges and chapel" (Notes). He left on 21 Sept., the day before JB's father and mother returned. It is not known to what book JB refers. Donaldson had published his *Elegy on the Death of an Amiable Young Lady* on 8 Aug. (*Lit. Car.*, pp. 5–6; *Letters of George Dempster to Sir Adam Fergusson*, ed. Sir James Fergusson, 1934, p. 57), but he should have had no difficulty in getting copies before he left Edinburgh.

To Johnston, Tuesday 17 August 1762

MS. Yale (L 679).

ADDRESS: To Mr. John Johnston, Writer in Edinburgh.

ENDORSEMENT: Auchinleck 17th August 1762. James Boswell.

Auchinleck, 17 August 1762

DEAR SIR: After a very safe and very composed sort of a journey, I arrived here. I am now in the new house, where I have a neat elegant Apartment which contributes to render me chearfull and well.[1] Immediatly on my arrival I gratified the strange whim you heard me mention of shaving my forehead, which indeed was agreable at first by letting the heat of my brain evaporate but as it requires a long time to grow, I am quite confined can see no Company, and am obliged to wear my Nightcap. I shall take care of playing such a trick in time coming.[2]

And now my friend to serious business. I shall be here for about three weeks then I shall go to Galloway, then to Kames, and then jaunt about near Edinburgh.[3] Remember you are to be ready to attend me in the Abbey of Holyroodhouse whenever I write to you. Is not this quite in taste for us? quite romantic and old Scotch? I hope to keep myself in good humour, till you and I set out in our Post-Chaise for Berwick,[4] and after that let Fortune and I have at it.

I have written to Cairnie to meet with you and concert a plan about my little affair,[5] as he will probably be gone before you[6] return. Doctor Mcquhae[7] was with me last night. He is very happy

---

[1] The new house at Auchinleck, in the fashionable Grecian style, had just been completed. It replaced an outdated 16th-century mansion which had superseded a still older fortified keep. Dr. Johnson found himself in 1773 "less delighted with the elegance of the modern mansion, than with the sullen dignity of the old castle" (*A Journey to the Western Islands of Scotland*, ed. R. W. Chapman, 1924, p. 147).

[2] JB's hair was evidently very thick and heavy. In his journal for 17 Mar. 1776 he records having it cropped because he thought his health and spirits hurt by the heat it occasioned.

[3] JB was planning the tour which he

described in his "Journal of my Jaunt, Harvest 1762".

[4] JB hoped that, when he set out for London to try to obtain a commission in the Guards, JJ would accompany him part of the way (*post* 20 Nov. 1762, n. 1).

[5] John Cairnie (d. 1791) the Edinburgh doctor in whose charge JB had put the girl, Peggy Doig, who was to bear him a son in December (*post* second letter of 14 Dec. 1762, n. 2).

[6] MS. "your" ("r" del.).

[7] William McQuhae (1737–1823), nicknamed "the doctor of Divinity", a son of Baillie David McQuhae of Wigtown, had been tutor for a time to the

and regards you as usual. Write to me soon and beleive me your very affectionate friend

JAMES BOSWELL

From Johnston, September 1762

Missing. Sent to Auchinleck and received there on 10 Sept. JJ wrote complaining of low spirits, as appears from JB's reply.

To Johnston, Monday 13 September 1762

MS. Yale (L 680).

To John Johnstone Esq: of Grange
The Epistle of James Boswell Esq:
Wittily Sheweth

That your Corespondent had the pleasure to receive yours on Friday last, and in order to engage your attention to the Answer he has thought proper to prefix this Petition to it.

Auchinleck, 13 Sepr. 1762

MY DEAR SIR: I was very happy at having a Letter from you, but was uneasy to hear of your age. We are both Antiquarians[1] which is not the most agreable sort of feeling. However when we consider what infinite pleasure we feel in our hours of Juvenility, we ought to be content with our fate; as upon the whole we have much more satisfaction than the dull Sons of Equality.[2] I can assure you, that even when I am in the very deepest dungeon of

Boswell boys. He was not much older than JB and was at this time one of his most intimate friends. It was for his perusal that JB wrote the Journal of his Harvest Jaunt in 1762. In Feb. 1763 he still thought of him as one of his three surest friends: "Thank heaven! I have some true friends. Johnston is most strictly so. Temple is also one. Honest McQuhae is also one. To these I can unbosom my anxious mind; from these I am sure of sympathy and kindness" (Journ. 16 Feb. 1763). He wrote a long and very friendly letter to McQuhae on 26 July 1763, shortly before leaving for the Continent, but discontinued the correspondence during the three years that he was abroad, and found on his return that the friendship had evaporated. Some grounds may be discovered in JB's own admiring description of McQuhae's character and aims (Journ. 26 Feb. 1763) for believing that he could not have served for long as a satisfactory confidant. He was too even in temperament, too well-adjusted to circumstances, too surely in command of himself and his fortunes to be permanently interesting to JB or fully in sympathy with him. Cheerful, successful, well-liked, he lived a long, peaceful life in the Ayrshire parish of St. Quivox, marrying twice and bringing up a family of fifteen (*Fasti Scot.* iii. 66–67).

[1] That is, hypochondriacs (*ante* 22 Sept. 1760, n. 2).

[2] That is, equanimity.

Age, I can argue in this manner, which tends to alleviate, tho' not to remove my distress. I think the severest circumstance attending that distemper is the want of hope; for when you are truly bad, you never expect to get rid of it. Since my arrival here I have had days of it, but am now (thank God) extremely chearfull, have good health and a moderate flow of lively spirits. I have read Robertson's *History* for the first time, which has carried me back in Imagination to the ancient days of Scottish Grandeur; has filled my mind with generous ideas of the valour of our Ancestors, and made me feel, a pleasing sympathy for the beautifull accomplished Mary.[3] I had a letter from C[airnie] lately who said he thought it needless to talk to you of the Affair till Novr. At that time we shall meet with him, and you will have a charge committed to you, and your mind will be filled by him with curious ideas of France[4]—churches lighted with wax Candles,—gilded prayer Books—Prince Charles with a white feather in his hat,—Old Jacobite Ladies drinking tea in an old carved room down a north closs,[5] in the month of January[6]—The Duke of Perth's family[7]—

[3] *A History of Scotland during the Reigns of Queen Mary and of King James VI till his Accession to the Crown of England* (1759) was much admired at the time both for its style and for the handling of its contents. Following its success, William Robertson (1721–93) had recently been appointed Principal of Edinburgh University. Walpole, Hume, and Chesterfield thought the book showed undue partiality for Queen Mary, but Jacobite and Royalist sympathizers like Tytler and Whitaker attacked it on quite opposite grounds.

[4] Cairnie had been an active Jacobite and had spent many years abroad (From Sir William Forbes, 28 May 1791).

[5] Probably Carrubber's Close, on the north side of the High Street, the headquarters of Episcopalianism and Jacobite sentiment in Edinburgh. It was much longer than it now is, contained some fine old houses, and was considered an old-world, aristocratic locality (*Old and New Edinburgh* i. 238–39).

[6] In the Episcopal church year the commemoration of the martyrdom of Charles I fell on 30 Jan. and at that season Royalist sentiments may be supposed to have been at their warmest.

[7] The Dukedom of Perth was a creation of the Pretender, and so not officially recognized in Britain. James Drummond (1648–1716), 4th Earl of Perth and 1st titular Duke, had died in exile at St. Germain. His son James (1673–1720) served in the Irish campaign and in the Fifteen, and was one of the ablest Jacobite leaders. He also died in France. He was succeeded by his elder son James, his younger son John, his half-brother John (1679–1757), and his half-brother Edward (1690–1760), who was Gentleman-in-Waiting at the Court of St. Germain, and who died without issue, as his three predecessors had done. There was thus no Duke of Perth at the time when JB was writing, though there were three dowager Duchesses still living (*Scots Peer*. vii. 50–57).

Sir William Forbes (To JB 28 May 1791) says that Dr. Cairnie had been private secretary to "the son" of the 1st Duke. Cairnie's employer was presumably one of the last two Dukes, John and Edward, the latter being the more plausible choice.

A coach and Six—An Apartment with a large fire on—with a yellow damask Bed and Window Curtains—fine carpet—splendid Looking Glasses—soft chairs etc. O Johnstone Johnstone! what a lively fertile Imagination I have. Are you not greatly diverted? The generosity of Captain Blair is great.[8] I rejoyce to find such instances as it gives me a good opinion of human Nature, and I am very happy to find that I have friends in case of need. I set out for Galloway tomorrow. I shall write to you from Kirroughtree.[9] Direct there to me by Minnigaff. I expect to be very happy in Galloway. I am to be at Lord Kenmore's on Wednesday.[10] I intend to keep a journal in order to acquire a method, for doing it, when I launch into the Ocean of high life. Dr. Mcquhae is well. I have been often with him, and he has often relieved me from age, and inspired me with notions of activity and spirit. My Brother John[11] has been with us for ten days and is now gone. I have heard nothing of Captain Andrew[12] since I saw you. But I have wrote to

[8] "Captain" Blair was at this time in Scotland, recruiting (*post* 10 Mar. 1763). After he returned to London with his "Little Army" in Apr. 1763, he is several times mentioned in JB's journal. The fact that one of their meetings took place, on 26 May, at Lord Eglinton's suggests that he was John Blair of Dunskey, whose mother, Anne Kennedy, was a first cousin of the Earl. JB was at this time accustomed to give all junior army officers the courtesy rank of "Captain", but Blair was actually an ensign (commission dated 11 Aug. 1759) in the Third Foot ("Scots") Guards. As this was one of the three regiments of Guards which JB wished very much to join, it is likely that the generosity mentioned here refers to some offer by Blair to assist him if possible.

John Blair remained in the Third Foot Guards, purchasing a lieutenancy in 1767 (*Scots Mag.*, 1767, xxix. 224), until his death in 1772 (*ibid.*, 1772, xxxiv. 582).

[9] Kirroughtrie, near Newton Stewart, in the parish of Minnigaff, was the home of Patrick Heron of Heron, whom JB visited during his tour of the south of Scotland (Journ. 18 Sept. 1762).

[10] JB was entertained at Kenmure Castle in Kirkcudbrightshire during his

Harvest Jaunt by John Gordon (1713–69), who would have been 8th Viscount Kenmure, but for the part played by his father in the Fifteen, for which he had been attainted and executed (Journ. 16–18 Sept. 1762).

[11] John Boswell (1743–c. 1798), Lord Auchinleck's second son, had attended the University of Glasgow (*The Matriculation Albums of the University of Glasgow from 1728 to 1858*, ed. W. Innes Addison, 1913, entry 1869, dated 14 Nov. 1758) and on 21 Apr. 1760 had joined the Earl of Loudoun's 30th Regt. of Foot as an ensign. For further notes on his troubled life see *post* 8 Feb. 1763, n. 3; 31 March 1769, n. 1.

[12] Andrew Erskine (1740–93), third son of the Jacobite 5th Earl of Kellie, was at this time a lieutenant in the 71st Regt. of Foot. He and JB were drinking companions and fellow members of the Soaping Club, and they had similar literary aspirations. It was Erskine who induced the publisher Alexander Donaldson to accept a number of JB's pieces of verse for the second volume of his *Collection*, to both volumes of which Erskine was a contributor. His name occurs often in the Boswell–Johnston letters, particularly in connexion with the correspondence with

him and hope to hear soon. You see I have complied with your request for a long letter. Farewell my worthy friend. Be happy and well.

JAMES BOSWELL

I am pleased to think that this Letter may put you into good humour—may make you thankfull to your bountifull Creator, affectionate to your fellow-creatures, and satisfied with yourself.

To Johnston, Wednesday 27 October 1762

MS. Yale (L 681).

Edinburgh, 27 October 1762

MY DEAR FRIEND: I know it will revive your spirits to see from whence this Epistle is dated, even from a Place in which the happiest moments of your life have passed. While the multitude consider it just as *the town of Edinburgh* and no more; How much more valuable is it to you, who look upon it as an ancient City—the Capital of Scotland—in which you have attended the Theatre, and there had your soul refined by gentle Music, by the noble feelings of Tragedy, by the lively flashes of comedy and by the exalted pleasure resulting from the view of a crowd assembled to be pleased, and full of happiness. To the generous contemplative mind nothing can afford a more sublime satisfaction than to see happiness diffused thro' a number of our fellow creatures mutualy participating of the same entertainment. You also think of the Royal Palace of Holyroodhouse, the venerable church, the lofty Mountain Arthurseat, the romantic Salisbury craigs and the extensive King's Park, where You and I have had so many walks of pleasing Meditation. You also think of the Church of England Chapels,[1] the decent form of prayer, a well-drest Clergyman and the grand sound of the Organ which lifts the soul to the

---

JB which was shortly to be published (*post* 16 Apr. 1763), and later in connexion with his gambling debts (*post* 2 Aug. 1768).

[1] "Qualified" Episcopal chapels, chapels served by clergymen in English or Irish orders, who read the liturgy of the Church of England and conducted

their congregations as peculiars or independents, without obedience to the Scots bishops. It was only in "Church of England" chapels that one could have heard an organ in Scotland in 1762, for the Establishment did not admit organs and the Episcopal Church in Scotland, being under severely repressive statutes because of the persistent Jacobitism of its clergy, met obscurely and quietly.

17

celestial Regions. O what elevated what delightfull Notions of a future state have I sometimes had! Have not you and I of a sunday's afternoon in Grants,[2] been full of chearing views of the immortality of the Soul and the state of bliss in the world above? Have we not had our hearts warm'd with devotion to the supreme Lord of the Universe? have we not been posest of the sincerest gratitude to our allmighty Benefactor and did we not take a sweet walk to Restalrig[3] and cherish and preserve that heavnly frame? My worthy friend does not this raise a glow of delight in your honest Bosom, to have such a golden train of ideas called up to view. If you are in high Spirits you will relish it highly; if in low it will contribute to sooth and relieve the anxiety of your Mind. After leaving Galloway, I was six nights in Annandale and should have been with you, had not I heard that you was from home. I then went thro' the skirts of England to Kames and came here by myself last night.[4] I am to be about this and the Neighbour-

[2] Grant was clearly incumbent or assistant at the qualified Episcopal chapel which JB and JJ attended. Perhaps he is the same as the James Grant who had been assistant to the minister of Inveresk, but in 1746 had taken orders in the Church of England and in Jan. 1747 had opened a chapel in Edinburgh in Skinner's Close (*Scots Mag.*, 1747, ix. 47). At that time such chapels were springing up rapidly in Edinburgh, three (of which Grant's was the most recent) having been opened in 1746 and the first month of 1747. Among the 18th-century documents preserved in the Theological College of the Scottish Episcopal Church in Edinburgh is a pamphlet, dated 21 Dec. 1748, which expresses the resentment then felt against the new breed of "qualified" clergy by the proscribed Scottish Episcopalians. *A Letter to the Reverend James Grant at his Chapel in Skinner's Close* by Philalethes (probably Robert Forbes of Leith, later a bishop of the Scottish Episcopal Church) purports to be written by a student of languages and mathematics who has recently arrived in Edinburgh and hopes to attach himself to an Episcopalian congregation: he finds two obstacles in the way of associating himself with Mr.

Grant's; first, he understands the nonjurors in England to be the true Church of England, and the Establishment (with which Grant is in communion by virtue of his ordination by the Bishop of London) to be in schism; second, he feels that the English Establishment has no business to obtrude its clergy into Scotland, where there are already bishops— those of the proscribed Scottish Episcopal Church.

[3] The village of Restalrig, a mile and a half east of Edinburgh, had its sacred and historical associations. The ruined church of St. Triduana, near which was the old pilgrimage well of St. Margaret, would have been of great interest to two such enthusiasts for ecclesiastical antiquities as JB and JJ. Restalrig kirk-yard was the favourite cemetery of the nonjuring Scottish Episcopalians of the time, the use of the burial-service being proscribed in the city burial-grounds (Hugo Arnot, *The History of Edinburgh*, 1788, pp. 256–57; Daniel Wilson, *Reminiscences of Old Edinburgh*, 1878, ii. 282–90).

[4] JB had just completed his six-week Harvest Jaunt in the south of Scotland. Early in his tour he had visited, at Kirroughtrie, the home of Mrs. Patrick Heron, Lord Kames's daughter, with

hood visiting till Saturday when I go to Kelly to our worthy friend Captain Erskine. I shall be back here, before the Session sits down. I beg you may be in town by the 10th of Novr. I ever remain yours affectionately

JAMES BOSWELL

whom he seems to have carried on an adulterous affair ("Ébauche de ma vie", 5 Dec. 1765: MS. Yale L 1107). There he had found Lord and Lady Kames staying with her. They had invited him to visit them later at Kames in Berwickshire (Journ. 18 Sept.). Lord Kames was already well known as a writer on legal, philosophical, and historical subjects, and had recently published his *Elements of Criticism*. He took a kindly, half-humorous interest in JB, who, sensing in the judge's character a richness inviting to a biographer, conceived the plan of writing his biography, and collected materials for it which are still extant (MS. Yale M 135).

II

November 1762–August 1763

This period, during his twenty-third year, Boswell spent in London attempting through the influence of patrons to obtain the commission in the Foot Guards which his father refused to purchase for him.

II

November 1762–August 1763

To Johnston, Tuesday 16 November 1762

Missing. Written from Durham. See next letter.

To Johnston, Saturday 20 November 1762

MS. Yale (L 682).

ADDRESS: To Mr. John Johnstone at Mrs. Fergusson's, Don's Close, Edinburgh.

ENDORSEMENT: London 20th Novr. 1762.

London, 20 Novr. 1762

MY DEAR FRIEND: At last I am got to this great Metropolis the object of my wishes for so long; The Place where I consider felicity to dwell and age to be a stranger to. I am all in a flutter of joy. I am full of fine wild romantic feeling to find myself realy in LONDON. O Johnstone my worthy friend! I wish you was with me to partake of my happiness. I wrote a line to you from Durham reproving you for neglecting to come to town Indeed my friend it hurt me; that we did not meet and bid a cordial adieu. I am sure it would hurt you more when you came to Edinburgh and found that I was gone.[1] However let this be forgot and let us consider how to be most happy in time to come. You must write to me a

[1] JB had planned this leave-taking well in advance, and had hoped at one time that JJ might travel with him to Berwick, on the first stage of his journey, and so escort him off the soil of Scotland (*ante* 17 Aug. 1762). He had asked him to come to town by the 10th (*ante* 27 Oct. 1762), and had not set out for London till the 15th. The romantic salute to the spirit of Scotland described in the Journal (15 Nov. 1762), which involved bowing from the piazzas at Holyrood to the palace, to the crown over the gate, and to the chapel, and standing in the forecourt to make three bows to Arthur's Seat, was a ceremony of the kind JJ understood and practised himself; but he was not entirely in sympathy with JB's decision to go to London in face of his father's disapproval, and this, rather than the indisposition he pleaded (*post* 6 Dec. 1762), may have caused him not to comply with JB's invitation: "I called upon my friend Johnstone, but found he was not come from the country which vexed me a little, as I wished to bid him cordially adieu" (Journ. 15 Nov. 1762). That it vexed him more than "a little" may be gathered from his account of a nightmare it induced ten days later (Journ. 25 Nov. 1762).

great deal write freely and easily and if you are old it will releive you to open your heart. I shall burn all your letters that have any thing of that kind in them. I shall keep a journal of every day; and send it to you weekly so as to come on Saturday night and comfort you on Sunday. I know every thing that I write must please you. I must first hear from you, and get your exact address that my packets may go safe. I shall send you franks.[2] Address for me at Mr. Douglasse's Surgeon Pallmall London.[3] This Gentleman has kindly insisted that I shall stay in his house till I get a lodging to my mind.

Expect a longer letter soon. I ever am your very affectionate friend

JAMES BOSWELL

To Johnston, Wednesday 24 November 1762

MS. Yale (L 683).

ADDRESS: To John Johnstone Esq: of Grainge.

London, 24 Novr. 1762

MY DEAR FRIEND: I left 4 parcels with my mother sealed up[1] which I left for you to get the charge of. I beg you may go up and make Davie[2] get them for you, and cause a Cadie[3] carry them down

[2] JB in London was in a better position than JJ for obtaining franks, for there were, among his own and his father's friends, several Scottish M.P.s of whom he might ask so small a favour. His friend George Dempster, member for Perth, was probably his chief source of supply. The loss of revenue to the Post Office through the abuse of the franking privileges of the members of both Houses of Parliament was causing concern at this period, and in Mar. 1764 a parliamentary committee was appointed to inquire into the question. As a result of its recommendations an Act of Parliament was passed in 1764 requiring each peer or M.P. to write in his own hand the whole superscription on any cover franked by him (*Scots Mag.*, 1765, xxvii. 299–301). The favour thus became a little more difficult for friends to ask, and the traffic in unaddressed franked covers was largely eliminated. No further change in the system took place until 1784, when additional limitations were imposed (*Gent. Mag.*, 1784, liv. 648).

[3] Andrew Douglas, JB's host during his first few days in London, is described as "a kind-hearted, plain sensible man" (Journ. 19 Nov. 1762). His practical advice was useful, and before the visit to London was over, JB had occasion to consult him professionally (Journ. 20 Jan. 1763).

[1] The parcels contained letters, among them copies of those written by JB to Andrew Erskine, which he was perhaps already planning to publish, though he did not send for them till nearly three months later (*post* 10 Feb. 1763).

[2] David Boswell (1748–1826), the youngest of Lord Auchinleck's sons, was JB's favourite brother.

[3] Public messenger and odd-job man. See *post* 15 Feb. 1763, n. 6.

before you to your lodging, then lock them up till I send for them. Also leave a line at Stewart & Lindesay's shop for Cairnie, and tell him where to meet with you immediatly. Go and meet him and talk to him about my girl.[4] I left £10 in his hands for her behoof. Enquire every thing about the affair. Go and see her. Let me hear all you can. When she is delivered go and see the Child. Observe it's marks. And do every thing you see proper. Let Grant[5] baptize it; and be you Godfather. Consult with C[airnie] in all respects about the affair. This will be delivered to you by Davie. I have desired him to be much with you. He regards you. Be kind to him; and write to me about him. Encourage him in his scheme of being a Banker. It pleases his parents, and will be best for himself. I have been hurried; yet I have written twice to you. You will be happy with my Journal by and by. I shall not forget you; but remain your cordial friend

JAMES BOSWELL

To Johnston, Wednesday 1 December 1762

Missing. Sent from London to Edinburgh and received by JJ on 10 Dec. "A few lines concerning the boy" referred to in JJ's letter of 13 Dec., the note was probably a request to be told of the birth as soon as it took place, and to be given full particulars. JJ replies in his letter of 13 Dec. that he has already written "fully on that subject".

From Johnston, December 1762

Missing. Sent to London from Edinburgh and received on 5 Dec. JJ wrote to apologize for his failure to come to Edinburgh, as he had promised, to see JB off on his journey to London. "I found a letter from my friend Johnston which gave me much satisfaction, brought many comfortable ideas into my mind and put me on a regular plan of sending him my Journal" (Journ. 5 Dec.).

To Johnston, Monday 6 December 1762

MS. Yale (L 684).

London, 6 December 1762

MY DEAR SIR: Your kind letter gave me very great satisfaction. I am glad to find you giving a circumstantial excuse as it shows

[4] Peggy Doig (*ante* 17 Aug. 1762, n. 5).
JB and JJ attended (*ante* 27 Oct. 1762, n. 2).

[5] Priest at the Episcopal chapel which

your being in earnest to clear yourself from the imputation of Neglect. Indeed my good friend I am sure that you had all the inclination in the world to have seen me before I left Scotland and indeed I regretted much my being obliged to go before you came as I knew the uneasiness you would be in. Your description of what you felt is very strong. Well can I imagine your situation. I dare say your Age was excessive at that time   I realy sympathize heartily with you and I dare say you are somewhat uneasy even now with impatience to hear particular and fresh accounts of me. I am quite elated at the thoughts of your happiness at receiving these two Packets, and of reading the first Sheets of my Journal. You must stay at home on Sunday forenoon never open the Packet till then so as that you may read it when warm and comfortable in bed, which will make you enjoy it more fully and with a more cordial satisfaction. I have now sent you 28 Pages of Journal.[1] You must write regularly by the Monday's Post or by the Saturday's when you can acquainting me of the safe arrival of the Packet; and to preserve exactness mention in each letter to what page the parcel received comes down. You will see that I have written my Journal hitherto very plain and with a large margin. I shall continue to do so. You must lay it by carefully in the full Quarto size. I may perhaps send for some of the papers numbered 1 2 3 4 sometime hence. My Journal will give you so full an account of me that I need say little in my letter. I cannot as yet give you any certain accounts of my Commission;[2] but depend on hearing every thing at very great length. Beleive me you have my sincere regard and if I can make you happy I shall never neglect it. Lady Betty Mcfarlane Lady Ann and Captain Erskines[3] came here last week. Would you beleive it. It vexed me. It confounded my ideas of London to find there just my auld fife hameliness.[4]

[1] The entry for 27 Nov. ends on p. 29.

[2] The commission in the Foot Guards which it was the purpose of JB's visit to London to obtain, through the influence of the Duke of Queensberry, Privy Councillor and Keeper of the Great Seal of Scotland, or any other influential patron whom he could contrive to interest in his affairs.

[3] The plural surname is according to Scots usage.

[4] Since coming to London, JB had adopted a pose of metropolitan refinement which could not be maintained without ridicule in the company of familiar Scottish friends. "I was vexed at their coming. for to see just the plain *hamely* fife family hurt my grand ideas of London. Besides I was now upon a plan of studying polite reserved behaviour which is the only way to keep up dignity of character" (Journ. 1 Dec.). JB's vexation must have been clearly visible to the Erskines (*post*, Andrew Erskine to JJ, 2 June 1766).

The Erskines had become intimate

However I cannot be much with them which is lucky. Altho' I like them as I used to do. Address to me at Mr. Terrie's Downing Street Westminster London.[5] I remain your friend

JAMES BOSWELL

> Johnston to whom each tuesday goes
> A heavy packet of plain prose
> Sheets of that Journal which contains
> All your friend's pleasures and his pains
> The real good and real ill
> He meets in clamb'ring up life's hill
> And all the fancies which posess
> His whirling brain which moves by guess
>   Tell me good Johnston when you view
> This portrait most exactly true
> What think you of poor Boswell's mind
> Can you ought there of reason find
> Or don't you with himself agree
> That from it's influence he is free.
> Whim and extravagance indeed
> You may in his existence read
> But small acquaintance can he claim
> With the reflecting sober Dame.[6]

From Johnston, Thursday 9 December 1762

Missing. Sent from Edinburgh to London and received by JB on 14 Dec. This letter gave JB an account of his son's baptism. It is referred to in JJ's letter of 13 Dec. as "my letter on Thursday last". In it JJ complained of low spirits, as appears from JB's reply of 14 Dec.

friends and were entirely unreserved with JB. Elizabeth had been, since 1760, the wife of Walter Macfarlane of Macfarlane, the antiquary, but was fond of associating with those nearer her own age than her elderly husband. She and Anne, her unmarried sister, were lively, quick-tempered, and by JB's newly acquired standards, unpolished in manner. Their eldest brother Thomas had succeeded in 1756 to the impoverished earldom of Kellie in Fife.

[5] Thomas Terrie (or Terry), a Moray-shire man, was chamber-keeper at the Office for Trade and Plantations. JB spent the winter with him and his wife in their Downing Street house, making himself so acceptable to them, in spite of the hauteur which he thought it desirable at first to adopt towards them, that to accommodate his limited means they twice lowered their charges (Journ. 30 Nov. 1762; 9 Feb. 1763). Terrie proved, however, to be passionate and rude, and JB left his house after a violent quarrel (*post* 7 July 1763).

[6] It is not certain with which letter these verses (MS. Yale M 271) were enclosed. JB's first cast for line 8 was: "His whirling mind which goes by guess."

From Johnston, Monday 13 December 1762

MS. Yale (C 1615).

[Edinburgh] Monday 13th Decr. 1762

DEAR SIR: Yesterday about one o'Clock I received the 2 packets, (it being So late on Saturday's night when the post arrived, That the letters were not given out till Sunday). I put them up Snug in my pocket, went to Dinner, and returned with Joy to my room, and spent the afternoon in feasting upon the sheets of your Journal, no less then 28. pages. What do I owe you for this Goodness? it's next to your presence, and Contributes much to my happiness. I hope the just reasons you assign in the Introduction, for this undertaking, will always prevail to make you Continue it.[1] Besides the pleasure it will afford me, it may afterwards be no Small fund of Entertainment to yourself, to peruse these sheets, where you'll have your former conduct in full view, which neither reflexion nor any other method could supply; I am anxious to know further as to the Offence the Dedication of the C[ub] has Given.[2] Prevail on the Peer[3] to bring about an Interview with His R. H[ighness] and I have no doubt but your Address will soon Reinstate you in his favour: It is surely right to be in Good terms with the Noble Peer, it may be of great servi[c]e to you, and you must learn to Wink at the foibles of Great Men, when it's neither in your power, nor your bussiness to Correct them. When you have occassion to mention in these sheets, any incidents in which it's improper to name the real Character, Substitute a fictitious one. As you justly observe, there can be no absolute certainty of one's most private papers not falling into the hands of those who would make a bad use of them. Tho' I have no Suspicion of your Diffidence[4] in me, nor while I live shall you have

---

[1] "It will give me a habit of application and improve me in expression and knowing that I am to record my transactions will make me more carefull to do well. Or if I should go wrong, it will assist me in resolutions of doing better" (Journ. Nov. 1762, Introduction).

[2] *The Cub at Newmarket: a Tale*, JB's feebly humorous account of his introduction to the Newmarket spring races by Lord Eglinton during his first visit to London in 1760, had been published by Dodsley in Mar. 1762. The dedication to the Duke of York, to whom JB had been introduced by Eglinton, had been made without permission (*Lit. Car.*, pp. 16, 18; *post* 21 Dec. 1762; Journ. 27 Nov. 1762).

[3] Alexander Montgomerie (1723–69), 10th Earl of Eglinton (*ante* 22 Sept. 1760, n. 1).

[4] MS. orig. "Confidence". JJ is using "diffidence" in the correct but now rare sense of "want of confidence".

any cause for it, Yet who can be Surety, against the many unfore-
seen accidents that happen.

Nothing but your peremptor[5] orders to write by this nights
Post, could have made me comply, as I have been all day, and still
am throng about[6] bussiness that cannot admit of delay, and you
know I am under a Necessity of attending to it, and whenever I fail
in writing a Post, when I ought to do it, put no worse construction
upon it, than that it has not been in my power. Friday last I only
received a few lines from you dated 1st Decemr. concerning the
Boy. In my letter on Thursday last I wrote you fully on that
subject, nor can I add any more at present, having not seen him
since, but will call for him soon.

Davie calls for me sometimes. I like the Boy much, he is greatly
interested in your Wellfare, he told me that my Lord and Lady
were much pleased with a letter they received from you this day
Se'ennight.[7] Be active in procuring your Commission. I long to
hear of your success, as till then you'll appear to yourself Idle. My
Good Wishes attend you and I am Dear Sir Yours most sincerely while

JOHN JOHNSTON

To Johnston, Tuesday 14 December 1762

MS. Yale (L 685).

London, 14 December 1762

MY DEAR SIR: I sent you last week two parcels of Journal. I have
this week sent you three which bring it down to the 76 Page.[1]
I suppose C[airnie] has informed you particularly about my having
got what I wished for.[2] I am realy fond of the character of a Father.
I feel myself more dignified somehow. Pray my friend be carefull
of it. It is obliging me just now: and consider that perhaps you will
afterwards have the thanks of a fine honest clever fellow. God
bless him. C —— writes me that He had never seen you as then

[5] A synonym, now obsolete, for
"peremptory". The word was chiefly
used in Scots law (OED).

[6] Scots: much occupied with.

[7] Like JB's other letters home, this
does not appear to have been preserved.

[1] That is, to the end of the entry for
10 Dec.

[2] JB had not yet received JJ's letter of
9 Dec., which must have arrived later in
the day and caused him to write the
second letter of the same date, which
follows. He had heard of his son's birth
from Cairnie, but did not yet know
whether JJ had heard of it. The child was
presumably born about 7 Dec.

when he wrote. I am surprised at that. Pray don't neglect to see and talk with him often about my —— which he has taken much trouble about. I am very well and very happy at present. My Journal will show you fully all my proceedings. I have therefore little to say in my letters. I shall however sometimes write long ones. In the present political disturbance, I am told all letters are opened at the Post-Office.[3] I hope it is not true. Tell me if mine come safe. Yours ever

JAMES BOSWELL

To Johnston, Tuesday 14 December 1762

MS. Yale (L 686).

London, 14 Decr. 1762

DEAR SIR: I had this day the pleasure to receive your last, after my three packets were sealed. Your complaints of Antiquity give me much concern. Well can I imagine your distress, who have experienced it so much. Indeed it is very hard to have no friend to whom we can lay open our dejected minds, and by tender sympathy obtain releif. But pray my friend do this in your letters. Whenever you are in low spirits sit down and write to me all your thoughts, tho' never so gloomy: freely and without Study. This will do you good and by imagining that you are talking to your absent friend you will insensibly feel yourself lightened of the dreary burthen under which your fancy labours. It is realy a very strange disorder. Nothing can be more dreadfull we say when we have it. And yet stretch us on the rack but for a moment and we would be glad to have it back again. However this is not enough: that we may be worse. Why not be better. Why not be well? Why not be happy. Our beneficent Creator certainly intended us for felicity, altho'

---

[3] The suspicion that correspondence was being tampered with reflects the sense of insecurity in the country. The new king's party, unpopular throughout the country, had ousted Pitt's experienced and successful administration at a critical juncture in the war, soon after Spain's entry as France's ally. Lord Hardwicke in a letter to Lord President Dundas, dated 12 June 1763, refers to "the opinion which prevails of the infidelity of your post" and adds: "If one cannot write to a friend with that freedom which is requisite to let him into the writer's way of thinking on the subject in question, I am sure it cannot inform, and may possibly mislead" (*The Arniston Memoirs*, ed. G. W. T. Omond, 1887, pp. 174–75). An order to prevent tampering with the letters of Members of Parliament was made in the House of Commons on 17 Nov. 1763 (*Journals of the House of Commons* xxix. 671).

when antiquated we cannot comprehend this; and are apt to doubt of it. Just now (thank thee O God!) I am quite easy and chearfull. All my thoughts are pleasant. All my ideas are bright. I can imagine celestial joy I am perswaded that you and I shall enjoy lasting happiness in a future state of being when our souls are purified and refined from that dross which now occasions these gloomy clouds of Spleen. You are very kind to express so strong a concern for my happiness. I hope I shall do very well. You will see by my Journal how I go on. I am sure it must comfort you. I said that I had little to say in my letters. But I find that I must administer a little soothing speech particularly to you. Be assured my worthy friend that I shall do every thing I possibly can for your assistance and amusement. I hope I shall do you good. I value myself much on feeling that my freindship is firm and permanent and not confounded by the infinite variety of this Metropolis. Your account of the proceedings about Charles is very accurate and gave me much satisfaction. It was quite proper to have it done by Grant.[1] I shall send you a letter of thanks to him if you think it right. By all means let the Nurse give my child the sirname of Boswell immediatly. I am not ashamed of him And I am not affraid of it's being known. Besides the Kirk-Treasurer of the Cannongate noised it about.[2] Commissioner Cochrane[3] told me

---

[1] *Ante* 27 Oct. 1762, n. 2.

[2] The rigorous church discipline of the 17th century was giving place to a milder system whereby faults of the kind over which kirk sessions exercised jurisdiction could be expiated by the payment of a fine. When it became apparent that she was about to bear a child, JB had paid the necessary fine on behalf of Peggy Doig to the kirk treasurer of the Canongate parish in which she lived. His meeting for the purpose with the kirk treasurer (whose name appears to have been James Gentle) is recorded in his Notes, 23 July 1762.

Creech, contrasting the times in which he was writing with the Edinburgh of his youth, says: "In 1763—The fines collected by the kirk-treasurer for bastard children amounted to 154l. and, upon an average of ten succeeding years, they were 190l. In 1783—The fines for bastard children amounted to near 600l. N.B. It is to be remarked, that the repentance-stool,

and all church censure, for fornication and adultery, have been several years abolished" (William Creech, *Edinburgh Fugitive Pieces*, 1791, p. 79). Such relaxation of discipline was by no means universal even then. In 1786 and 1788, in Mauchline kirk, Robert Burns was publicly admonished for fornication by the Rev. William Auld (F. B. Snyder, *The Life of Robert Burns*, 1932, pp. 125–26, 303–04). Public compearances for rebuke were in fact not abolished in Mauchline parish till 1809 (Andrew Edgar, *Old Church Life in Scotland*, 1885, p. 301).

[3] Basil Cochrane (1701–1788), uncle of JB's mother, was a son of William Cochrane of Ochiltree and a brother of the 8th Earl of Dundonald. JB characterized him as "a Man of great common sense and Prudence" (Journ. 30 Oct. 1762). He had served as a captain in the 44th Infantry Regt. (Lee's Regt.) during the Forty-

every circumstance of it. Therefore I desire that this may be notified to the Nurse immediatly. I return you thanks for your care about this matter. Pray continue it.

As my Landlord here is in a public office, all his letters come free. Direct therefore To Mr. Terrie at the Plantation Office Whitehall London, and inclose my letters. Yours sincerely,

JAMES BOSWELL

To Johnston, Tuesday 21 December 1762

MS. Yale (L 687).

London, 21 December 1762

DEAR SIR: I had the pleasure of your last,[1] and received most sincere pleasure at knowing that my Journal gave you so much satisfaction. Indeed I do think it may entertain those who as Mcquhae says, *are affectionately attached to me.* You must know that to try if I could have attention and application enough to keep a journal when I got to London I promised to Mcquhae to write one during my jaunt thro' Scotland this harvest.[2] I did so. I never mist one day in it, but sent it to him, down to the night before I left Scotland. He has it. I am sure you will be fond to see it. I shall therefore write to him by and by, to send it in to Davie, who will deliver it to you; Poor Mcquhae he is just now in great Affliction on account of the death of his Pupil the only child of Mr. George Reid[3] a worthy old Clergyman and a most amiable Woman a cousin of my Father's and sister to the late Reverend Mr. Campbell

five, and had later acted as Deputy-Governor of the Isle of Man. In 1761 he had been appointed a Commissioner of Excise, and in 1764 a Commissioner of Customs in Scotland. He was a bachelor and was probably already living at Pinkie, near Musselburgh, where he certainly resided from 1769 to 1777 (*Scots Peer.* iii. 349; *Edinburgh Almanack,* 1770, pp. 123, 125; *Original Portraits,* i. 384–85; *Journ. passim*).

[1] *Ante* 13 Dec. 1762.

[2] This journal covers the period 14 Sept. to 14 Nov. 1762 (MS. Yale J 2). *Ante* 17 Aug. 1762, n. 3. "Harvest" (pronounced "harst" or "hairst") was the usual Scots word for autumn.

[3] George Reid (1696–1786), who had been tutor to Lord Auchinleck, was minister of the parish of Ochiltree, which included much of the estate of Auchinleck. He was 66 and was to continue in his charge for another twenty-four years. His wife Jane (or Jean), a daughter of George Campbell of Treesbank, was Lord Auchinleck's first cousin (James Paterson, *History of the Counties of Ayr and Wigton,* 1863, i. 656). On 7 Dec. they had lost their son, James, a boy of eight years old. *Fasti Scot.* iii. 62 lists James as the second of three sons, but gives no dates of birth or death for the other two, so that JB may still be right in calling him his parents' only child. One would expect him to know the facts in a matter concerning his own family.

the Nathaniel upon whom I wrote an Epitaph.[4] They were very fond of this Boy. He was a remarkable Genius. They are much to be pitied. Mcquhae was very comfortably situated in their family. They were all very fond of him, and he lived social and independent which is just the life that he likes. I have written to him to stay with them, for sometime. I hope to get a settlement for him soon.[5] I have his interest greatly at heart. Good heaven, what is this world? What Blockheads and Knaves do we see succeed. How many amiable pretty men in difficulties!

Now to the subject of my Journal again. I must insist that no Mortal see a word of it. You need not mention it, at all. You may tell any storys or anecdotes you think can entertain from it, and just say you had them from your friend Mr. Boswell, at London. Let it be carefully deposited at full quarto size and kept clean and safe. Perhaps at the year's end, we may think of binding it up. But I beleive it will be better to keep it in sheets. However, this can be settled time enough. My Dear Freind! I am glad you think yourself obliged to me. Indeed you are, for so much good entertainment For, I assure you, your happiness is a great motive to me. You must write much, and write how particular passages affected you. I have not been with Lord E[glinton] this ten days. I chuse to show him that I can do very well without him, and as to the Dedication, I think I did the D[uke] of Y[ork] a favour and am angry that he did not take it properly.[6] I will not forgive your

[4] John Campbell, Lord Auchinleck's first cousin, son of George Campbell of Treesbank, had been minister of Riccarton parish in Ayrshire from 1739 (*Fasti Scot.* iii. 64). JB's *Epitaph on the Rev. Mr. John Campbell, Minister of Rickarton* appeared first in *The Scots Mag.* Apr. 1761 (xxiii. 204) and was reprinted in Donaldson's *Collection* (ii. 86). It begins:

In quiet peaceful silence here repose
The bones of one who never could have foes:
For, in a line his character to draw,
Nathaniel once again on earth we saw.

For Nathaniel see *John* i. 47.

[5] McQuhae was ordained on 1 Mar. 1764 to the Ayrshire parish of St. Quivox, though it may be doubted whether JB's

influence had any part in placing him there (*ante* 17 Aug. 1762, n. 7).

[6] *Ante* 13 Dec. 1762. Of his disappointed hope of acquiring the Duke of York as a patron, JB later wrote: "A l'age de dix neuf ans, quand j'etois neuf et en reverie, certainement je n'avois pas tort d'etre enflé de Vanité parceque j'etois connu á un Prince. Mais á present quand j'ai quelque experience, et que je commence d'etre un vrai Philosophe combien me semble-t-il fou de se piquer d'une chose si frivole. Le Duc de Yorke n'etoit pas un homme de dignité ni de genie extraordinaire. Il etoit perdu en debauches et il etoit quelquefois le compagnon des plus vils du genre humain. Je ne le connois qu'un fort peu et il ne me rendut le moindre service" (French theme, c. 9 Nov. 1763).

delaying to write after monday's post. Write if it were but a line. Pray let me hear about Charles. Be kind to Davie. Give my kind service to Mr. Hay.[7] He is a worthy man. I remain yours sincerely

JAMES BOSWELL

To Johnston, Tuesday 28 December 1762

MS. Yale (L 688).

London, 28 Decr. 1762

DEAR SIR: I am surprised that I have had no letter from you these two post⟨s⟩. This day forthnight I sent you two packets of my Journal which should have gone to you, on the Saturday after, and of which I should have got an account last week or yesterday at farthest. I am uneasy lest they should be lost; or have been opened. You should be sure to write me every monday and let me know whether they come or not, as I regularly send you some parcels every tuesday. This day senight, I sent you three parcels. I hope to hear that they all came safe. I can make many excuses for you. You may be gone out of town. You may be sick and in that case to hear so particularly of your freind may releive you. However my good freind You must give me a sufficient excuse for this seeming neglect. I do think that my regular attention is to be admired and demands a regular return from[1] you. I hope you will kindly excuse this peremptory method of talking. Consider it is in the way of Business, where the greatest regularity is absolutely necessary even between intimate freinds.

I am going on very happily. I am pleased to view London at this time of hearty festivity. According to the custom of England I wish you the compliments of the season. Many a merry Christmass may you see my honest Johnston.[2] I am writing this beside Miss

---

[7] Presumably James Hay of Cocklaw, W.S. (*ante* 11 Jan. 1760, n. 1).

[1] MS. "for".

[2] In Scotland Christmas was not widely held as a festival, its celebration having come to be popularly associated with Catholicism and Episcopalianism. The general holiday of the season was New Year's Day. The observance of Christmas as a public holiday had been forbidden in England in 1652 by an Act of the Puritan parliament, but it had been revived in the time of Charles II. In Scotland the revival was much slower in coming. "A merry Christmas" seemed to JB a typically English wish, where the typical Scottish greeting of the season would have been "a happy New Year" (T. G. Crippen, *Christmas and Christmas Lore* [1923], pp. 88–91, 181–82; W. F. Dawson, *Christmas: Its Origin and Associations*, 1902, pp. 284–85).

Dempster[3] who is realy a charming Woman. She has an elegant Person and a fine countenance, a sweet disposition black hair a lovely white skin, a lively imagination a great deal of wit and agreable cleverness. She has good sense She admires me. O Johnston do not thou smile at this my amorous Rhapsody. Altho' a Laird yet thou art also a Writer[4] which is not a Profession very subject to the delicate influence of the tender Passions. Captions and Hornings[5] avail not in the court of love; nor does Cupid pay any regard to a Macer of the High Court of Justiciary. I love Miss Dempster warmly, Altho' it is now very hard frost. In short she is quite a Goddess etc I remain yours sincerely

JAMES BOSWELL

I have sent you one packet just now which brings my Journal down to the 152 Page.[6] You must take it (to use the words of Tim) *more or less*.[7] Yours etc.

[3] Jean Dempster (b. 1736), second daughter and fifth child of John Dempster of Dunnichen in Forfarshire (Dundee Register of Baptisms), was a sister of JB's friend George Dempster, who had recently been elected member for the Perth burghs. In *Letters of George Dempster to Sir Adam Fergusson, 1756–1813* (ed. Sir James Fergusson, 1934), four other sisters are mentioned. Jean, though not mentioned by name, may have been the sister referred to as being in a decline in 1770: "My sister, who has daily declined since you left us, I have brought down here by Sir John Pringle's advice to try the effects of goat's whey &c. I am sorry to say she appears hitherto to have reaped very little benefit from the experiment" (Dempster at Abergavenny to Fergusson, 17 July 1770, p. 69). Jeanie Dempster is frequently mentioned in JB's London journal of 1762–63, but his views of her tended to vary with his own state of mind. They range from the panegyric of this letter to the despairing: "I thought ... her an ugly disagreable wretch, and myself the silliest and most dreary of mankind" of the journal entry of 17 July

1763, recording a visit to the Dempsters on a miserable rainy Sunday.

[4] "'A solicitor, attorney, proctor, agent, or procurator.' ... While in England the name of attorney is selected, in Scotland they receive more commonly the title of 'writer,' or Solicitor at Law" (William Chambers, *Book of Scotland*, 1830, p. 137).

[5] Scots legal terms: *captions*, letters of apprehension or arrest for debt; *hornings*, letters charging a debtor to pay his debt, under penalty of being put to the horn, or outlawed (Robert Bell, *A Dictionary of the Law of Scotland*, 1807).

[6] That is, to the beginning of the entry for 23 Dec.

[7] JB is referring to the character Tim, son of Sir Gregory Gazette, in Samuel Foote's *The Knights*, a very popular afterpiece, originally introduced as a mainpiece at the Haymarket in Apr. 1749. From Tim's first appearance in the play his tag line is "more or less", just as his father's is "good now, good now! ay, ay". (Information furnished by Professor George Winchester Stone, Jr.)

From Johnston, January 1763

Missing. Sent from Edinburgh to London, acknowledging receipt of journal instalments, and giving some news of Charles and of JB's brother David. Commenting on a passage he had read in JB's journal, JJ described Thomas Sheridan as "malevolent".

To Johnston, Tuesday 4 January 1763

MS. Yale (L 689).

London, 4 Janry. 1763

MY DEAR JOHNSTON: Your last letter gave me much satisfaction as it releived me from a good deal of anxiety having realy been apprehensive that some of my packets had been lost or opened, either of which would have been very dissagreable. I could wish to hear regularly from you. But as you are sometimes busy and out of order I must excuse you. I am sorry to find that you have been worse this winter. Pray take exercise. It is the best thing for you. Diversion too for the mind is quite necessary. I flatter myself that my Journal contributes greatly to releive you. Indeed you tell me so. I can assure you my freind that I am very mindfull of you. I took a kind of a dreary fear lately that you was dead which made me very unhappy. And yet certain it is that one or other of us *must* hear of his freind's death. I am glad that Davie and you are well together. He is a fine Boy. I hope to see him a pretty man. Your accounts of Charles please me much. Pray be mindfull of him at all times. You will see by my Journal that the Duke has given up the pursuit of my Commission in the Guards, and that Lady Northumberland now has taken the charge of me.[1] I beg that you would give me your best advice whether to take a Cornetcy in the Blues a[2] prodigious fine corps and great pay. My objection is that I don't like the horse service, that I would be quartered in Country

[1] Charles Douglas, 3rd Duke of Queensberry, had written on 22 Dec. (MS. Yale C 2334) to say that he could not obtain a commission in the Foot Guards for JB and that he advised him to turn his thoughts to a civilian career. Lady Northumberland, however, had held out hopes that she might get for him, through her connexion by marriage Lord Granby, commander-in-chief of the British forces in Germany, the commission he wanted, or, failing that, a cornetcy in the Horse Guards which might serve as a step towards realizing his ambition to become an officer in the Foot Guards (Journ. 26 Dec. 1762; 10 Jan. 1763). The Horse Guards were called the "Blues" because of the colour of their uniform, which distinguished them from the scarlet-clad Life Guards.

[2] MS. "&".

towns and that I would be discontent, not having just the thing that I wished for. But then I am amongst the first People in England, in rich spots of country, can get to London some months every year and I am told can easily change for an Ensigncy in the Guards. I do think that since Lady N—— has been so kind as to undertake to do for me, that I should do as she directs. Indeed I may wait sometime before I get any. I can assure you my freind that waiting for a Commission is a very sad thing. However I am a Man who can *soap his beard* in all situations. I thank you for your remarks. I agree with you in thinking S[heridan] malevolent.[3] Give my service to C[airnie.] I will write him soon. I hope you like him better than you imagin'd. God bless you My dear Sir. A good new year and all happiness to you. This Packet makes 176 Pages.[4] I remain yours sincerely

JAMES BOSWELL

To Johnston, Tuesday 11 January 1763

MS. Yale (L 690).

London, 11 Janry. 1763

DEAR SIR: I stand much in the same light to you My Dear Johnston, that the great Dryden did to the Managers of the Theatre. He obliged himself to furnish them with Six plays (I beleive that was the number) every year.[1] And I begin to think myself obliged to

[3] Thomas Sheridan (1719–88), the dramatist's father. JB had reported Sheridan as declaring (Journ. 28 Nov.) that he could no longer bear Dr. Johnson, and as criticizing Garrick adversely (Journ. 30 Nov.). He himself speaks of Sheridan's "malevolence" in the entry for 18 Jan. In 1762 Sheridan had taken offence at a hasty remark of Dr. Johnson's, and JB later described the quarrel in full (*Life* i. 385–89). Long afterwards Sheridan took his revenge on Johnson in a harsh attack on him in his *Life of Swift*, 1784, pp. 520 ff.

[4] Which carried the journal to the beginning of the entry for 31 Dec.

[1] Dryden's successes in 1667, *Secret Love, or the Maiden Queen* and *Sir Martin Mar-all*, established his reputation as a playwright. "He was therefore in an excellent position to bargain for his services, and probably it was at this time, the spring of 1668, that he entered into a formal agreement with the King's Company. By the terms of this agreement Dryden contracted to provide the company with three plays a year, in return for which he received one and one-quarter shares of the company's profits" (J. M. Osborn, *John Dryden: Some Biographical Facts and Problems*, 1940, p. 186). Dryden drew his share of the profits for ten years, during which he provided the players with nine new plays. When in 1678 he offered his *Oedipus* to the rival company (the Duke's), his own company submitted a petition of complaint to the Lord Chamberlain in which they laid claim to the new play and pointed out how far short of fulfilling the original agreement Dryden had fallen (Edmond Malone, *Life of Dryden*, 1800, i. 73, n. 4; J. M. Osborn *op. cit.*, p. 188).

furnish you with Six Sheets of Journal every week. Indeed the task tho' now and then a little opposite to my indolent humour is a good one, and as it gives pleasure to my honest freind it is of very substantial Utility. I think I might venture to challenge all the young men of life and spirit about town at steadiness and exact perseverance. Not a Tuesday do I ever let slip without loading the Post with a heavy Packet with which he trotts over hills and dales thro' frost and Snow and wet and dry till he arrives at old Edina and deposits it safe in the Post Office; from thence the Letter-carrier swift as the winged messenger of Jove the lively Mercury runs with it to Forrest's Coffeehouse. Then it is called for with pleasing expectation by Mr. John Johnston who has a pleasant tho' small inheritance in Annandale, but whose views of life and love of social happiness lead him while the courts of Justice sit, to the Metropolis of his native country. Home does he hie with the wish'd for prize to his comfortable lodging from which he can view the Lomond hills these sublime representatives of Lady Betty Macfarlan's Bubbies which he used to gaze with strong desire at when painted by Lindo[2] all swelling to the sight. Should his buxom Landlady oppose his passage thro' the trance[3] he drives her over in the impetuosity of his haste nor should the children unfortunately be in his way, they meet with no better fate. So when a stately Man of War comes gallantly into Leith road she over-turns a Kinghorn Boat[4] or two Newhaven Wherrys. To his room he runs, down he sits with his face opposite to the Cupboard which

[2] This portrait-painter signed himself F. Lindo. Nothing appears to be known of his life except that he worked mainly in the north-east of Scotland and was in demand among the landed families of that area between 1750 and 1765. He painted five family portraits now in the Rose of Kilravock collection, and there are por-traits by him in the Erskine–Murray, Maxtone Graham, and Newbattle Abbey collections. The Scottish National Portrait Gallery has a list of paintings by him which includes portraits of members of the families of Ogilvy of Inchmartin, Erskine of Alva, Gordon of Gordonstoun, Campbell of Glenure, and Dalyell of Barncrosh, but the present location of these is uncertain. The portrait of Lady Betty which Boswell here refers to may be one of two portraits of her now in the possession of Sir Ralph Anstruther of Balcaskie, who has inherited many of the pictures and papers of the Erskines of Kellie. Of the six Erskine children, only Lady Betty and Lady Janet married, and only Lady Janet (m. 1763 Sir Robert Anstruther of Balcaskie) had children. *Gent. Mag.* for Mar. 1767, p. 144, records the death of Francis Lindo, Esq., at Isle-worth on 8 Mar. 1767. This may not refer to the painter, but it may be noted that no portraits by him of later date than 1765 have been traced by the Scottish National Portrait Gallery.

[3] Scots: corridor or passage-way.

[4] Ferryboat plying between Leith and Kinghorn on the coast of Fife.

holds the Currant Jelly[5] which with delicate milk-bakes[6] has often regaled his freind. He reads, He laughs, He is pleased. Age flies off. Youth succeeds. He is all contentment and Joy. Yours ever

JAMES BOSWELL

I insist that you lay by all my letters. They will amuse me. Write me if you have done and will do so.

From Johnston, January 1763

Missing. It appears from JB's letter below, that JJ wrote in answer to his request for advice (4 Jan.) and urged him to accept Lady Northumberland's offer to get him a cornetcy in the Horse Guards. He may also have told him that their mutual friend Robert Irving was in London. This letter was received on 14 Jan. as appears from JB's phrase "forthnight past yesterday" in his letter of 29 Jan.

To Johnston, Tuesday 18 January 1763

MS. Yale (L 691).

London, 18 Janry. 1763

MY DEAR SIR: Your kind and prudent advices did me much good. I shall certainly accept of a Commission in the Blues, if the Countess gets it first for me. But you will see by my Journal that I hope to get into my favourite Guards. You will also see that I am passing my time extremely agreably, so cannot be very uneasy at waiting a little till my Commission shall be procured. Altho' I am no doubt somewhat anxious about it. I heard of honest Mr. Robert Irvine's[1] being in town, from his freind Mr. Charles Douglas.[2] I shall

---

[5] JB had a particular liking for currant jelly. *Currant-Jelly. A Poem* is one of his contributions to Donaldson's *Collection* (ii. 88–90).

[6] Scots: milk biscuits.

---

[1] Robert Irving (1704–72), an Edinburgh Writer to the Signet, third son of William Irving of Bonshaw, was a member of an ancient Border family whose interests had been for generations closely allied with those of the Annandale Johnstons (Burke, *Landed Gentry*, 1894, ii. 1050; *Writers to the Signet*, p. 204). JB had met him in Dumfries during his

tour of the south of Scotland in the autumn of 1762, and had travelled with him to Kelhead, and thence to Bonshaw Tower, where he dined with the Irvings before proceeding on his way to Springkell (Journ. 6–7 Oct. 1762).

[2] Charles Douglas (d. 1770) was a brother of Sir John Douglas of Kelhead, and JB's cousin, for their mothers were half-sisters. He had come home, after twenty-five years in India, with a fortune of £20,000, and now lived in London. JB had met him at Kelhead in the previous October when visiting the Douglases in the company of Robert Irving (Journ. 6 Oct. 1762; *Scots Peer*. vii. 149).

certainly go and call for him this week. It will give you great
satisfaction to hear him tell that he has seen me very well. The
frost here has been quite intense for sometime past. It is likely to
be a most severe winter which is very hard on the poor people.[3] I
am this night a little out of spirits. I find writing a pain to me; and
yet I want much to talk to my freind, and want much to do all I
can to make him happy when I am at a distance, which I know my
letters do. Indeed I have a little business to mention which I just
now recollect. You may remember that you got me some Stocks
made. I want to have half a dozen more of the same and have
inclosed one as a Pattern. You may send them in little packets
addrest to Mr. Terrie. You must also take the trouble to call for
Orlando Hart Shoemaker in the Mint (or grays) close and ask
him if he has made the shoes and Pumps that I ordered being six
pair in all, and cause them be sent up by sea and let him know my
direction and let me know when and where they are to arrive. Pay
him for them and send me his receipt, and let me know how much
both the Stocks and the Shoes come to and I will remit you the
money by a sure hand. Pray write as much and as often as you can.
Let me know when you saw Charles, and how he is. I am anxious
that he be taken care of. Altho' I am happy that he has had so good
Guardians. This Packet brings down the Journal to Page 236.[4] I
ever am My Dear Sir yours most sincerely

JAMES BOSWELL

To Johnston, Tuesday 25 January 1763

MS. Yale (L 692).

London, 25 January 1763

MY DEAR JOHNSTON: You must take notice in a very particular
manner to this Letter. You must observe that it is written upon
mourning paper.[1] You will be anxious to know the reason of
this. I will not keep you long in suspence. I have reason to mourn

---

[3] "In London the severity of the cold
has been such that two soldiers were
frozen to their death on their duty; and
in other parts several that have lost their
way in the night have been found frozen
to death in the morning" (Historical
Chronicle, 20 Jan. 1763, in *Gent. Mag.*,
xxxiii. 44).

[4] That is, to the end of the entry for
12 Jan.

[1] The paper does not differ from that
used for the other letters, but the wrapper,
which has not been preserved, perhaps
had a black border, as well as being sealed
with black wax (*post* 1 Mar. 1763).

and to lament very sore. In short Sir the fair Louisa[2] has tip'd me a favour which I dread above every thing. You will see by my Journal how I traced it and you will hear further accounts of it next week. In the meantime, your poor freind is close confined and fed upon slender diet. I am determined to take the greatest care of myself, which is absolutely necessary in this severe Winter. The infection is not bad, so I would hope that I may get rid of it soon. It is realy a most unfortunate affair. However the reasonings about it will be found at length in my Journal. Pray my worthy freind sympathise with me. Write me consolation in your Epistles. Mention Mary Queen of Scots and Lord Darnley, and many more of our favourite topics. Try what you can to divert me. You may beleive I require it just now. And now My Dear Johnston our Bet of a Guinea is fairly lost and won. You have catched me at last. Now when I am got to the great Mart of Lewdness. Pray get honest Currie[3] into your room give him Bread and Cheese and Brisk Twopenny and inform him of this Affair, but caution him to Secrecy. I would not have it by any means known in Scotland. Tell him that I remember him kindly and love him for taking my part at Bonshaw in my Absence, and let him know that I am a fellow of such spirit, as to be able even in my distressed state of genitals, to look forward with pleasure to our Joyous evening at honest Thom's as you will see by the inclosed paper,[4] which preserve. Remember my compliments also to Gordon Abercrombie and Bailie[5]

---

[2] Mrs. Lewis, an actress, with whom JB had been having an affair, the progress of which is described in the journal.

[3] Either William Currie Carlyle (d. 1775), "the young Laird of Bridekirk" whom JB met at Bonshaw on 7 Oct. 1762 (Journ.), or (more probably) James Currie, an Edinburgh solicitor ("writer"), who appears to have been William's younger brother. James Currie was a close friend of JJ and is mentioned in conjunction with him several times later in JB's journal. In the entry for 9 July 1774 JB records how he paid a similar wager which he had lost to JJ and other cronies of his and JJ's: Erskine, Currie, Abercromby, and Loch. James Currie was closely connected by marriage with the Irvings of Bonshaw (Journ. 27 July 1776; Burke's *Genealogical and*

Heraldic History of the Colonial Gentry, 1895, i. 157).

[4] This paper, which has not been located, probably stated the terms of the wager and indicated JB's intention to pay his debt by entertaining his friends at Thom's tavern, the favourite Edinburgh haunt of JJ and his friends.

[5] John Gordon (d. 1789) of Balmoor was admitted a Writer to the Signet five months after the date of this letter. Alexander Abercrombie (d. 1804) was admitted to the same body in 1770 (*Writers to the Signet*, pp. 168, 55). James Baillie, an Edinburgh solicitor, is often mentioned in JB's journal in connexion both with social occasions and with legal affairs. All three were particular friends of JJ's, who named them all as trustees under the terms of his Will.

and tell them I am not such a kind of human being as to forget my old Acquaintances. I hope they will not forget me. My Journal now amounts to 276 Pages.[6] My Landlord is not at home. So I dont know if I get a letter from you last Post. I have sent you half a dozen franks One of them is by the oldest Viscount in England.[7] I shall send you more from time to time and I ever am My worthy freind yours with sincerity and Affection

JAMES BOSWELL

To Johnston, Saturday 29 January 1763

MS. Yale (L 693).

ADDRESS: To Mr. Johnston, Edinburgh.

NOTE ADDED BY CAIRNIE: Mr. Cairnie begs to see Mr. Johnston at Stewart and Lindesay's Shop on Monday at eleven o'clock.

London, Saturday 29[1] January 1763

MY DEAR JOHNSTON: I am realy uneasy at present. It is a forthnight past yesterday since I heard from you. This is realy hard. I must blame you. I assure you seriously that I cannot help being anxious and thinking that my letters are lost or opened. I am most scrupulously regular in sending my packets to you. Pray indulge me a little with a like return. I dont ask you to write a letter. I know you sometimes are not able. I shall be satisfied if you will only say, "I have received so many pages of Journal" Write just when you can. But I beseech you send such a receipt exactly. It will make me easy from time to time I beg your excuse for being so explicit about this matter. But realy I have been kept in so much pain that I allmost resolved to send no more journal till I heard of each packet being safe, and so continuing. But I am sure you can allways write three plain lines.

---

[6] That is, he had posted it to the end of the entry for 19 Jan.

[7] Anthony Browne (1686–1767), 6th Viscount Montagu, who succeeded to the title in 1717, was at this time, by a considerable margin, the oldest viscount in England (*Comp. Peer.* ix. 102). The oldest viscount in terms of creation was Edward Devereux (1741–83), 12th Viscount Hereford, a title dating from 1550 (*Comp. Peer.* vi. 482). Lord Hereford was an ensign in the 1st Regt. of Foot Guards. Lord Montagu's title was second in terms of creation (1554). The fact that JB used a sheet franked by one of these peers is not proof that he knew him personally for until the passing of the Act of 1764 (*ante* 20 Nov. 1762, n. 2) franked sheets were often passed on from hand to hand.

---

[1] MS. "28".

For fear of miscarriage I have inclosed this to Cairnie. I ever am yours sincerely

JAMES BOSWELL

From Johnston, February 1763

Missing. Sent from Edinburgh to London and received by JB on 8 Feb. The letter acknowledged receipt of further journal instalments and gave news of Charles and of David, as is shown in JB's reply below.

To Johnston, Tuesday 8 February 1763

MS. Yale (L 694).

London, 8 February 1763[1]

MY DEAR SIR: This morning I was relieved from a good deal of uneasiness which I have suffered for sometime, on account of my Journal. I had realy allmost laid my account with it's having been lost or what was still worse, opened. Consider with yourself how unhappy such apprehensions must make a man in close confinement when he has full time to ponder over every dissagreable circumstance. Indeed my freind I was unwilling, very unwilling to suspect that you could be so very neglectfull. I thought you would not make so ill a requital to my constant care for your entertainment. I could not help thinking that such uncommon regularity and attention in a young man of life and spirit, amidst all the hurry and gayety of the Metropolis, was much to be admired and ought to be encouraged as much as possible, and have the warmest returns made to it. I expostulated pretty sharply with you in my last letter. The Affair is now over. I trust I shall not again have so dissagreable a cause of Complaint. You require no frank;[2] and two minutes will serve to acknowledge the receipt of my Packets. This you must *never fail* (if in town) to write every Monday.

Your Sympathy with me in my misfortune sooths me much. Your kind anxiety makes me wish sincerely for your happiness.

I am now in a fine way of recovery. My freind Douglas attends me and I follow his directions most carefully. I have realy taken the utmost pains this time; as I have a very ticklish constitution,

---

[1] MS. "1762".   [2] *Ante*, second letter of 14 Dec. 1762.

and have formerly been so very bad. I am convinced that I was hurt and kept back in my former infections by exercise and cold. This time I have confined myself close and kept quite warm; and as I have observed the exactest cool regimen, I have made it easier in the mean time and will sooner get well. I am determined to be entirely rid of it, and to take still more care than ever against it. I want to keep a sound constitution. I have a regard to my future offspring. I rejoyce to hear that my little boy is so well your particular accounts of him gave me much satisfaction. I approve of Davie's seeing him. He will be fond of him. I hope Davie is often with you. He will be a fine man. Pray encourage him to be an active Banker and make a fortune.

My brother John was very bad this winter at Plymouth. He was confined by a severe disorder. He was quite delirious—Good God! how alarming. But it was occasioned by a fall from a Stair.[3] He is now quite well, is in London and goes to Scotland this week. He is more different from me than Davie. If you hear the story of his illness mentioned pray let the fall be known. Is it not surprising that during this confinement, I have kept charming spirits. I have been very little aged. I am now in glorious trim and shall go forth to the world again with a keen relish. I shall read Melvill:[4] it will do me good, and give me very agreable sensations. You have now a great portion of Journal. I sent none last week, fearing the worst. You see I am very good to you. Receive to the 348 Page.[5] Yours most sincerely

JAMES BOSWELL

[3] *Ante* 13 Sept. 1762, n. 11. The "disorder" was an acute attack of the form of insanity that was to affect John Boswell intermittently for the rest of his life. This attack, probably the first of its kind, had occurred at Plymouth in Sept. or Oct. 1762 and was said by John to have been "brought on by a fall he got one day on guard" (Lord Auchinleck to JB, 24 Dec. 1762). In this letter to JJ, JB is following instructions sent to him by his father shortly before that the distressing illness must be ascribed to the fall (From Lord Auchinleck, 13 Jan. 1763). This particular attack lasted some three months, but John made an apparent recovery and on 5 Jan. 1763 JB was "agreably surprised" at his arrival in London "in good health and spirits" (Journ.).

[4] Sir James Melville (1535–1617), diplomat, privy councillor, gentleman of the bedchamber to Mary Queen of Scots, and confidential adviser to James VI, wrote the autobiographical *Memoirs* which were published by his grandson in 1683. The book obviously became one of JJ's favourites, for it is referred to more than once in the correspondence, and JB records that, when toasts were being given one night, four years later, at Lady Betty Macfarlane's, JJ proposed "Sir James Melvill" (Notes, 20 Feb. 1767).

[5] That is, to the end of the entry for 7 Feb.

To Johnston, Thursday 10 February 1763

MS. Yale (L 695).

London, 10 Febry 1763

DEAR SIR: Immediatly upon receipt of this execute the Commission which it contains. I want to have the copies which I kept of my letters to Erskine.[1] They are in Parcel 1. Amongst some more papers. You must therefore break up that parcel and take them out. I am not sure if the other papers are separately sealed up in smaller parcels. But at any rate I have all confidence in your acting with honour and not opening or reading one of them: as some of them contain the secrets of other people as well as of myself. Seal up the other papers in a Parcel again, with the title of Parcel 1 as before: And by the very first post send the copies of the letters in separate parcels inclosed to Mr. Terrie. Remember not to lose a Post. I depend upon you. ever yours

JAMES BOSWELL

To Johnston, Tuesday 15 February 1763

MS. Yale (L 696).

London, 15 Febry 1763

DEAR SIR: My letters are to you what the two o'clock bell[1] used to be to me when in the days of my youth I lived at old Edina. They summon you to an intellectual or rather indeed a fancifull repast just as the Bell used to summon me to a hearty dinner. O Johnston! Johnston! Youth early youth is the season of joy.[2] then it is that we taste pleasure and relish the good things of this life. We never have such stomachs afterwards, as we had when at College. Never shall I forget with what rapacious haste I have sallied from the seat of erudition down the horse-Wynd, up Borthwic's Close,[3] rush'd

---

[1] *Ante* 13 Sept. 1762, n. 12; 24 Nov. 1762, n. 1.

[1] "In 1763—People of fashion dined at two o'clock, or a little after" (William Creech, *Edinburgh Fugitive Pieces*, 1791, p. 76). "The dinner-hour of people of fashion [until the promotion of Robert Dundas to be Lord President in 1760] was three o'clock, and that of writers, shopkeepers, etc., two, when the bell

rung; but his late and irregular hours made the ladies agree to postpone their meal till four" (*Scotland and Scotsmen* i. 337 n. 1).

[2] "Youth's the Season made for Joys", *Beggar's Opera*, Air 22.

[3] JB's direct route home from the Old College may be traced on William Edgar's map of 1765. Horse Wynd took him straight to the Cowgate, and Borthwick's Close direct from there to the

by the crowded cross,[4] regardless of Advocates, Writers, Scotch Hunters,[5] Cloth-merchants Presbyterian Ministers, Country Lairds, Captains both by land and by sea Porters chairmen and Cadies.[6] With what rapid steps or rather jumps did I ascend the Customhouse Stairs and with what a tremendous noise did I burst open the door of the House of my father making it shake to it's very foundations, while Lock and key sent forth a horrid clank as if the jarring elements had met in discord fell. With what amazing velocity did I scamper about, traversing the house, like a Lyon in search of his prey, how quickly did I run from the dining room to the Kitchen; and from the Kitchen to the diningroom. What multitudes of questions did I ask at every servant, in particular with what reiterated Interrogations did I harrass the ears of thee O John Bruce[7] thou surly Son of fidelity who whilst You carefully watched the interests and accurately obeyed the commands of thy

High Street, near the Cross. Turning left, he passed the Cross and entered Parliament Close, where his father lived in a building known as Blair's Land.

[4] "In those days it was the custom for the merchants and bankers in Edinburgh, to assemble regularly every day at one o'clock at the Cross, where they transacted business with each other, and talked over the news of the day; and as there were among the merchants at that time—I speak of the period before 1772—several gentlemen of a literary turn, and possessed of considerable powers of conversation, we were joined by many who had no concern in the mercantile world, such as physicians and lawyers, who frequented the Cross nearly with as much regularity as the others for the sake of gossiping and amusement merely" (Forbes, p. 26).

[5] "The Honourable Company of Scottish Hunters" held country meetings far afield in the hunting season, and gave annual balls at Holyrood, one of which is described by James Grant in *Old and New Edinburgh*, ii. 76.

[6] The caddies were an important institution in Edinburgh. They were organized as a society and had their headquarters round the "crowded cross". They maintained, as a body, high standards of honesty and courtesy, and were useful,

intelligent servants of the public (Edward Burt, *Letters from a Gentleman in the North of Scotland*, 1754, ed. R. Jamieson, 1876, i. 23–24). They were prepared to undertake any odd job—hold horses, sell pamphlets, guide strangers, or run errands to any part of the city for a penny. The name survives in connexion with only one of their many functions—the carrying of golf clubs.

[7] John Bruce, Lord Auchinleck's majordomo, is again mentioned in JB's journal for 19 Mar. 1767. It might be supposed that he was a member of that family of Bruces whose hereditary service so pleased JB's feudal fancy that he caused James Bruce, gardener and overseer, to be present with his four sons for the administering of the romantic oath of allegiance to the Family of Auchinleck which he drew up for David Boswell to sign before setting out for Valencia (*post* 9 Oct. 1767, n. 7). The documentary evidence, however, seems to indicate that John Bruce and James Bruce were not related. James never mentions John in any of his many surviving letters to JB, and a begging letter to JB from John's son John, cabinet-maker in London, 1 June 1785, makes no reference to James or to his children. From this letter we learn that John Bruce was later a "keeper" in the Parliament House.

beloved Master, yet thought it not unmeet to domineer over his Sons with tyrranic sway. To rule them with a rod of iron. But when at last the dear dinner was upon the table set, and when Mr. Joseph Fergusson[8] stiff as the lofty tree in the forrest had amply bestowed upon it his benediction in phrase correct as ever issued from the hall, where young Theologians learn us all to teach,[9] then did I mightily fall on, and make a meal most prodigious. O Johnston! if you devour my Journal with half the relish that I did dinner, you will wish my letter quickly at an end as I did the preparatory sound of the bell, that you may proceed to the delicious entertainment, which it ushers in. Yours sincerely

JAMES BOSWELL

There are now sent 372 Pages.[10]

From Johnston, February 1763

Missing. Sent from Edinburgh to London along with four parcels containing copies of JB's letters to Andrew Erskine. It expressed appreciation of the journal instalments, as is shown in JB's reply.

To Johnston, February 1763

Missing. Sent to Edinburgh from London along with enclosures addressed to Lord Auchinleck, Dr. John Boswell, David Boswell, and Jean White, and received 23 Feb., as is shown in JJ's reply dated 24 Feb.

To Johnston, Tuesday 22 February 1763

MS. Yale (L 697).

London, 22 Febry. 1763

DEAR SIR: Last Post brought the four Packets safe, and showed that you can execute a Commission very cleverly when you please. However, you had made the Packets directed to Mr. Terrie greatly too large. Remember never to put above two ounces under one cover. I thought indeed that this rule was only to be observed in the case of franks. But I find it is also necessary in packets directed to the Plantation Office. With a good deal of difficulty

---

[8] *Ante* 26 Sept. 1759, n. 2.
[9] The Divinity Hall (Divinity Faculty) of the University.

[10] That is, to the end of the entry for 14 Feb.

did my Landlord get me skreened from the payment of half a guinea Postage. This was no fault of yours. Only be cautious in time coming. You made me truly happy by telling me that my Journal relieved you. It is a tender expression. I love it. My worthy friend! I am sure I need not repeat my regard for you. I am sure that you entertain no doubt of it. My sending you my Journal is a strong proof of confidence and affection. Don't you think this a pretty good Winter for you? It is comfortable and fine to receive such a supply of entertainment every week: especialy as it comes on Saturday which is realy the most agreable day in the week. As it was our day of freedom when at school, our fondness of it still continues and men who are engaged in business continue to have it as a day of relaxation after the fatigues of the week. But even those who have little to do, with whom one should think all days alike, still retain a kindness for honest Saturday. I for instance have it very strong and you see in my Journal that I contrived some little amusing whims to add to it's pleasing efficacy; such as going for the *North-Briton*, myself, sauntering to comfortable child's[1] etc. I would beg my dear Johnston that you would sometimes on the Saturday forenoons if the day be good take a solitary walk to the King's Park, where we have so often strayed together and indulged warmth of heart and romantic feelings. Look up with awe to old Arthur'seat, with a sort of superstitious reverence to St. Anthony's Chappel,[2] let the milkwite sheep feeding on the green mountain give you sweet notions of rural simplicity and innocence and think the little creatures happy who wander on our favourite hill. View the firth of forth with elevated spirits or if it inspire any degree of harshness, by making you think of Kinghorn Boats,[3] turn your eyes to the fertile fields on the East and

---

[1] Child's Coffee-house, St. Paul's Churchyard, was a favourite resort of JB's at the time: "dusky comfortable and warm with a Society of Citizens and Physicians who talk politics very fully and are very sagacious and sometimes jocular" (Journ. 11 Dec. 1762). Addison's reference to Child's, which JB had in mind when he chose to frequent it, occurs in *The Spectator*, No. 1 (1 Mar. 1711): "Sometimes I smoak a Pipe at Child's; and whilst I seem attentive to nothing but the *Post-Man*, overhear the Conversation of every Table in the Room."

[2] The ruined chapel and hermitage of St. Anthony, on a knoll on the north slope of Arthur's Seat, beside the well of St. Anthony, a place of superstitious associations from the earliest times.

[3] The crossing by the busy ferry from Leith to Kinghorn in Fife, often crowded and sometimes rough, may well have been the longest sea-voyage ever taken by JJ, for though he visited Fife more than once, there is no record of his ever having been abroad. In 1794 there were nine passage-boats of about 50 or 60 tons each, as well as a few pinnaces engaged

mark the ancient Craigmillar.[4] That you may not fatigue yourself too much you may repose a little on the dry warm grass, provided that no breeze of wind disturb your placid meditation. Then take some good Author out of your pocket and read and muse. Turn your view to the Canopy of Heaven! adore the great Author of Nature. Bow your heart in his presence. Offer him your tribute of gratefull praise for his goodness, for his forming so many delightfull objects and for his giving you faculties to feel so much felicity. When you find your soul expand with noble sentiment, cherish the hopes of Immortality; cherish the hopes that God will surely preserve so glorious a work as the mind of man; that he will improve it in another scene of being; that there you will meet your freind Boswell and others whom you regard; that you will enjoy social bliss, be instructed in the ways of Providence which now seem dark, and ever love and praise your Creator. Consider that the gloom and weakness of mind which you sometimes experience in this imperfect state is necessary to compleat the great schemes of heaven, and that it will enhance your future felicity! O Johnston! these are encouraging these are transporting thoughts— (O God! o Author of our Beings impress them ever upon us! O let not our hopes perish!)—Now my friend you may quit your sacred retreat you may return homewards. As you walk along pray behold Edina's lofty towers the ancient Capital of your Country. What a grotesque heap of Building! What a Smoak. See how the City Stretches away to the Southeast while new houses are every day rising to increase it.[5] When you come to the Abbey of Holyrood-house that most beloved object of all Think on James the fifth— Think on Queen Mary. Be much of an Antiquarian. Look at old Lord Somerville.[6] Trace him in his younger days as a gay young

on this ferry. The town of Kinghorn was sometimes filled to overflowing with passengers waiting for fairer weather to make the crossing (*Statistical Account of Scotland*, ed. Sir John Sinclair, Bt., 1791–99, xii. 238, 242–43).

[4] Craigmillar Castle, to the south-east of Edinburgh, appealed to romantic tastes because of its various associations with Stuart sovereigns, and in particular with Queen Mary.

[5] JB is not referring to the New Town to the north of Edinburgh, which, though projected, had not yet been planned.

Craig's plans were not completed till 1767, and the first house was built in that year. Most of the extension to the city in the hundred years preceding the founding of the New Town was in the east, in the Canongate area, and in the south, along the main highways through the Newington district. See Bartholomew's chronological map of Edinburgh, reproduced in "Early Views and Maps of Edinburgh", *The Scottish Geographical Magazine*, Aug.–Oct., 1919.

[6] James Somerville (1698–1765), 12th Lord Somerville (*Comp. Peer.* xii. 104), a worldly nobleman who had restored the

officer and imagine what scenes he has run through and how they must amuse him now. Then think him like Sir Roger de Coverley and Reflect that he was the Patron of your friend in his most early years. As you walk up the Cannongate so called *a Cannonicis*, from the old monks, comfort yourself with thinking "I get a Packet of Journal to-night" and be pleased with your entire ignorance of what it will contain. Keep yourself in this fine frame till night and then you will read it with such pleasure that you will think your existence worth enjoying tho' it were for no other end. Thus my freind have I poured forth my genuine feelings to you. I hope you will like them. *The North-Briton* is a bold insolent paper. He lashes without reserve. The partys of Whig and Tory are again alive. To tell you the truth I am not sorry. you know why. I differ much from Mr. Wilkes the Author of the *N. B.* yet I love his cleverness. I have sent you last Saturday's paper.[7] Some ideas in it will please you. Pray show it to Cairnie. I remain with much affection ever yours

JAMES BOSWELL

From Johnston, Thursday 24 February 1763

MS. Yale (C 1616).

Ed[inburgh] 24th Febry 1763

DEAR SIR: This being a post night to the South Country I am So

fortunes of his family by judicious marriages to wealthy widows, was for JB the type and symbol of courtly, cultured, old-world grace, allied with *savoir-faire*. When dining with the Dutch Minister in Berlin, along with "a German Count who had great vivacity and *usage du monde*", JB had "old Abbey, Lord Somerville ideas" (Journ. 16 July 1764). Lord Somerville, who took an interest in the Edinburgh stage, had befriended JB when he frequented the theatre and dreamt of being a playwright, and JB thought of him as his "first noble Patron or encourager". Besides his house at Drum, he had apartments in the Palace of Holyroodhouse, and there he entertained JB, who ever afterwards connected him with the Abbey in his thoughts. JB had dined with Lord Somerville on 14 Nov. 1762, the day before he left Scotland. It was their last meeting, for Somerville died shortly before JB's return in 1766.

[7] *The North Briton*, No. 38 (Saturday, 19 Feb. 1763) attacks the government in Wilkes's most effectively sarcastic vein. It purports to be a letter from the Pretender to his "dear cousin" the Prime Minister (John Stuart, 3rd Earl of Bute) commending him for all his excellent work on behalf of the dispossessed Stuarts, the Jacobites, and the Scots, and giving him instructions how to proceed still further to undermine the stability of the country and the House of Hanover. Bute was not really vulnerable to the charge of veiled Jacobitism: his father, though a Stuart, had commanded the government troops in the west of Scotland during the Fifteen, and he himself had been at all times loyal to the House of Hanover. But he was unpopular as a Scot, a royal favourite, and a cat's-paw of the King, and his ministry was believed to be undoing all the good work done by Pitt's.

much hurried with writing Letters, That I have no more time than barely to mention the receipt of the Journal on Saturday's night now 372 pages[1] with your *Strictures on Elvira*,[2] and last night I also received a letter covering one to my Lord, one to the Doctor,[3]—Davie—and Jean White.[4] All but the last I Sealed and gave to Davie. My Worthy friend, I return you my most Sincere and Gratefull thanks for your Goodness to me. It's a great Comfort to think I have one person of so much merit and real worth, that is interested in my wellfare, Your leaving your Letters open for my perusal is a favour I am very Sensible off. I admire the easy method you have in writing in different Characters, particularly the Letter to my Lord,[5] it's Solemn, and yet like a man of Spirit,

[1] *Ante* 15 Feb. 1763, n. 10.

[2] *Elvira*, by David Mallet, a tragedy dedicated to Bute and supposed to have political implications, had been produced at Drury Lane on 19 Jan., and was having a fairly successful run. Mallet, son of an innkeeper at Crieff, had been for a time janitor to the Edinburgh High School before his appointment as tutor to the sons of the Duke of Montrose. Though a talented man, he was detested for his presumptuousness by JB and his friends. He had had a career of such blatant toadyism and opportunism that he had come to be regarded as the type of the unprincipled Scots careerist. Changing his name from Malloch, adopting an aristocratic air and a London accent, he had ingratiated himself with the ruling political leaders, but earned the contempt of most of his countrymen. JB, Erskine, and Dempster planned to damn his play before they had even seen it: "This was a day eagerly expected by Dempster Erskine and I as it was fixed as the period of our gratifying a whim proposed by me. Which was that on the first day of the new Tragedy called Elvira's being acted, we three should walk from the one end of London to the other, dine at Dolly's and be in the Theatre at night, and as the Play would probably be bad and as Mr. David Malloch the Author who has changed his name to David Mallet Esq was an arrant Puppy, we determined to exert ourselves in damning it" (Journ. 29 Jan. 1763). The pamphlet

which they combined to produce was published by Flexney towards the end of January and was called *Critical Strictures on the New Tragedy of Elvira, written by Mr. David Malloch* (*Lit. Car.*, p. 18; Journ. 27 Jan. 1763).

[3] Probably Dr. John Boswell (*post* 20 July 1763, n. 2).

[4] Perhaps the foster-mother in whose charge JB's natural son Charles had been placed.

[5] Neither JB's letter to Lord Auchinleck nor David's letter to JB has been recovered, and the journal is deliberately uninformative as to the worsening of relations between JB and his father. Since JB's protest, following David's revelation, was in a submissive strain, this disagreeable subject can hardly have been the violation of privacy that JB resented so fiercely a month later (*post* 22 Mar. 1763). It may be that Lord Auchinleck had only now learned of the existence of his natural grandson, but in view of the kirk-treasurer's loquacity and Commissioner Cochrane's knowledge of that matter (*ante*, second letter of 14 Dec. 1762), this too seems unlikely. The most plausible explanation perhaps would be that Lord Auchinleck had just learned that David had given JJ the four parcels of JB's private papers left with Lady Auchinleck, and, having some inkling of what dangerous matter they contained, had rated David and said unkind things about JJ. The references in JB's letter to JJ of 8 Mar. 1763 to his father's reply

at Same time in the Submissive Strain of a Son to a parent. I am Sorry you had cause to write on Such a Subject. Davie, poor Boy, came to me in great distress and told me what had happened. As he was to acquaint you of it, I thought it unnecessary to mention So disagreeable a Subject. Your Brother[6] has been Some days in Town. I want much to see him, and wish to meet him on the Street, as I am not So well acquainted as to call for him. I have sent you the copies of Capt. Erskines Letters which you'll have received by this time. The Stocks are made. I will Send them under cover to Mr. Terrie, if you continue to think it right to send them in that way;[7] Mr. Irving[8] returned about 4 weeks ago, he regretted much not having seen you. I am My Dear Sir yours most affectionately

JOHN JOHNSTON

To Johnston, Tuesday 1 March 1763

MS. Yale (L 698). Received by JJ on Saturday 5 March.

London, 1 March 1763

MY DEAR SIR: I have this moment received your last, which gave me as much satisfaction as usual. I have now the pleasure to write to you, as a free Man. The dismal black wax no longer seals my Epistles.[1] The gay red resumes the office; O that my coat were of that colour. I had a letter from Cairnie last week. He tells me that Mr. Hart is to discharge the debt to Mossman and is to draw a bill upon me payable for the £40 and interest from the time the debt was contracted till the first of April. This I am to accept, and am to take Love's bill in the same terms to me. I have no doubt of

to his solemn and spirited letter support this guess. Also, it can be seen from Lord Auchinleck's letter to JB of 30 May 1763 that Lord Auchinleck was much more alarmed by JB's willingness to trust his friends with matter prejudicial to his reputation than he was by his debaucheries.

[6] That is, John Boswell, who had left London for Edinburgh on 10 Feb. (*ante* 8 Feb. 1763, n. 3).

[7] It is rare to find a scruple being expressed, by anyone in a position to benefit from it (*ante* 20 Nov. 1762, n. 2), about the abuse of the privilege of franking. Evidence that it was felt as a serious infliction by the Post Office is shown by the sixpenny pamphlet *A Letter from a Porter in the City, to the Lords and Commons of Great Britain* (Dec. 1757) reviewed in *The Monthly Review* xvii. 563.

[8] *Ante* 18 Jan. 1763, n. 1.

[1] *Ante* 25 Jan. 1763.

getting it easily settled. But you know I gave Mr. Hart a bond of relief for £40 of the £60 which we borrowed jointly from Mossman's friend. Now I suppose you must see both these papers cancelled. Would not that bond stand against me? or will the sum in the bill be mentioned to be the same with that in the Bond?[2] I am but recovering yet. The severe shock I have had will require time to be got the better of entirely. But I am in a fine way, and Cardinal Richilieu could not have been a better patient.[3] My Journal will inform you most particularly of all my transactions. Indeed you know better how I have gone on, than I do myself. Many things must slip through my memory, but you have the papers before you. I have a whimsical request to make to you. And that is when my Journal comes to 500 pages, you shall not read that division of it any more but let it remain unlooked into till you and I meet and then it will be equaly new to us both. This

---

[2] What had happened was presumably this: JB had been in debt to Hart, his Edinburgh shoemaker (*ante* 18 Jan. 1763), and as Hart had needed the money, and JB, far from being in a position to settle at once, had also been in need of cash, they had jointly borrowed £60, through an agent named Mossman. Of this sum JB had taken two-thirds, out of which, no doubt, he had paid what he owed for boots and shoes, and given Hart a bond of relief which absolved him from responsibility for that fraction of their joint debt. When the bond became due for payment, Mossman had claimed the money, and Hart, in JB's absence, had agreed to pay the whole £60, but had at the same time drawn a bill on JB to recover the two-thirds due from him. As James Love, in London, had borrowed from JB as much money as would clear him, JB decides to cover his debt to Hart by drawing up his bill on Love in precisely the same terms. He is concerned only lest Hart should not have made it clear that the £40 in the bill is the same sum as that mentioned in the bond of relief, as he is afraid these two documents might be taken to represent two separate debts. He asks JJ to make sure that both the original bond and the bond of relief have been cancelled.

Orlando Hart (d. 1793), who carried on his shoemaking business in a shop in the High Street, Edinburgh, opposite the city guard-house, was for many years prominent in civic politics. Besides being Deacon of his own Guild (the Cordwainers), he frequently served on the Town Council as a representative of his own or other trades and more than once held the important office of Convener of the Trades. (See *Original Portraits*, i. 223 for an account of him, with a "portrait".) Mossman has not been precisely identified, but he was probably John Mossman (d. 1787), merchant in the Lawnmarket, who served with Hart on the Town Council (*Scots Mag.*, 1773, xxv. 504; 1787, xlix. 518; Williamson's *Directory*, 1773).

[3] Richelieu is said to have been a lifelong invalid, subject to boils, neuralgia, and various other disorders of the blood and nerves; even, perhaps, from time to time, to attacks of epilepsy and insanity. His whole energetic career has been represented as the product of an indomitable will which enabled him almost to the last moment of his life to carry on the high business of the state. As a patient he was exemplary. "Jamais un murmure, ni même une plainte" (G. Hanotaux, *Hist. du Card. de Richelieu*, 1947, vi. 432).

rule you are to observe in each division by which I mean 500 pages. You may read the division as many times as you please while it is unfinished but when once the number is compleat it[4] must not be any more read. Can you understand this? and can you have command enough over yourself to comply with it? Pray tell me honestly how do you preserve my Journal   I am affraid you have neglected to get a box made, and that you do not keep it fairly spread out and clean and unsullied. I beg it of you tell me particularly how you do in every respect. Dont write on an Annandale Postnight; but take full time. I am affraid my Journal will grow too bulky, if I go on at this rate.[5] I beg it of you give your opinion freely. 24 pages a week is an immense deal. We had better have a few pages more correctly done. My attention to stated rules and forms is great. I have somehow fixed it that 24 pages a week is absolutely necessary. I consider it as a duty upon me. And I will eke it out any way rather than want my complement. It would oblige me much if you would sit down and write a character of my Journal, just as it would appear to you, if written by an indifferent Person. It would als[o] oblige me if you would make out a sort of index to each division as you go along, and send me a copy of it. You need not do it Alphabeticaly nor you need not be nice. But just mention some of the principal things in their order. I have given you many charges in this letter. I wish you may observe them. You are realy too indolent. I would particularly beg your advice about the quantity of Journal I should write a week and whether you think I follow a right method. Tell me too when I inadvertently insert things that ought not to be written. My Journal is a most candid history. You will there see that I am apt to waver about plans of life when I see the difficulties of getting into the Guards. O had I you to talk to me. Write strongly in behalf of my steadily pushing. You will give me life and spirit to go on. I suppose you will be leaving Edinburgh soon. I will send you no Journal till you return to town. I will not trust it to private posts. When June comes, you will have a vast treasure to receive. I shall constantly write to you, wherever you are and I remain your most warmhearted friend

JAMES BOSWELL

[4] MS. "compleat. It".
[5] The entry for the previous day, 28 Feb., ends at the bottom of p. 424. JJ's letter of 10 Mar. shows that JB now sent him the portion of journal up to that point.

To Johnston, Tuesday 8 March 1763

MS. Yale (L 699).

London, 8 March[1] 1763

DEAR SIR: I hope you will read this with attention. I am going to talk to you cooly and seriously, and I expect what I say will have some weight with you. You and I have been long friends. My regard for you has been strong and constant, and I appeal to your own breast, if I have not at all times done what I could for your happiness.

I realy could not doubt of having an equal return from you. Yet sorry I am to be obliged to tell you, that your behaviour to me has given me the greatest uneasiness. You know very well that between friends the slightest neglect cannot fail to hurt. You also know that I am most particularly delicate in every point. Why then will you use me so ill as to refuse complying with a request which I have very earnestly made you?

The promise which I gave you to send weekly a parcel of my Journal, seemed highly valued by you, at the time when it was given. All I asked in return, was only regular information that my Packets arrive safe, to keep my temper free from anxiety. This you neglected, some time ago; and I wrote you about it in the strongest terms. I pointed out a very easy method to give me satisfaction. You receive a packet every Saturday; and writing two lines, on the Monday after, of a bare receipt, was what I required; and surely this is not much. I have notwithstanding the mortification to find that this small request is not complied with. I received this day a letter from my Father,[2] which I inclose for your perusal and beg you may immediatly return to me. It is in answer to my letter to him which you saw and praised so much.[3] You will observe how severe he is upon me. How he treats my scheme of keeping a Journal and sending it down and in what a light he considers you. When he mentions *Persons* in the Plural, he certainly means to include Mcquhae, for he would not insinuate your reading it to

---

[1] MS. "Febry." Reference to the letters of 10 and 22 Mar. clearly indicates the place of this one in the sequence.

[2] Neither this letter nor JB's reply has been preserved, but both are mentioned in Lord Auchinleck's of 30 May, which opens: "My last Letter which was wrote in Febry let you know how much I was displeased with some particulars of your conduct which had come to my knowledge. The Answer you wrote me was telling me in pretty plain language you contemnd what I coud say or do."

[3] *Ante* 24 Feb. 1763, n. 5.

others. You will observe in what a light he considers you and "how cheap" he thinks "my correspondence is held" by you. Now, Sir, consider how very galling it must be to me, that at the very time when I received this letter I should have a fresh proof of your neglect. Upon my honour, I cannot help imagining that you don't care for my Journal. But it would be better to tell me so in direct terms. You may plead Business or Dissipation. But I am sure no man is so busy or dissipated but he may literaly write two lines. This is a thing which I consider of importance and which (if we are to continue our corespondence) I must absolutely insist upon. O man! how terrible is this! You vex my very heart! and allow me to say in so silly a manner.—I am quite unhappy at present. I am doubtfull if there be such a thing as friendship. I am upon my soul. For God's sake, if you are alive and if you are not totaly changed think and act properly. I cannot bear to be so horridly slighted— Yet (in better hopes) I still remain your affectionate friend

JAMES BOSWELL

From Johnston, Thursday 10 March 1763

MS. Yale (C 1617).
ADDRESS: To James Boswell Esqr., London.

Edinr. 10th March 1763

DEAR SIR: I ought to have wrote you last week, but could not do it, many things occurr to Baulk one's intentions.[1] The Letter of the 22d feby. which I received alongst with the Journal, merits particular thanks. I cannot tell you how much it pleased me. I read it often, it's full of tenderness and sincere friendship;—Indeed, My Dear Sir, I firmly believe your Letters and Journal are become one of the necessarys of life to me. If any unlucky accident should ever deprive me of this Comfort, I must feel the loss most sensibly; The Journal I received on Saturday (424 p's) informs me of your recovery. Thank God for it, and be Cautious for the future; The pleasure you had upon going abroad, and from every things appearing new after your Confinement, in Some measure makes up for it: Yesterday I met Capt. Blair.[2] He enquired kindly for you; he had heard of your illness, and asked me the nature of it. I informed him, and that you was now quite well. He is your friend

---

[1] This letter would cross the one of 8 Mar. in which JB complains of JJ's neglect.   [2] *Ante* 13 Sept. 1762, n. 8.

and a Gentleman, I could not Equivocate to him. Let me know If
you think I did right: Your Whim of returning to Edinr. is only
the Effects of Confinement and antiquity. By no means Indulge it,
reflect how often you was unhappy here. Your intention of Writing
your father about returning here alarmed me much, as I well know
you would Soon come to your former way of thinking, and then
your unsteadiness would be unpardonable, and place you in a most
ridiculous light. By all Means push your friends for your Commission, with that address you are capable off. I am now Convinced your Relations here heartily wish that you may not
Succeed, and would readily Stop any from Serving you in this
affair. No Doubt it proceeds from a good motive. But They do not
know you; Let them See in Spite of that, what you can do for
yourself. Do not reject the Horse Guards, if a Commission in the
Foot cannot be obtained. This way of life you know I have often
disswaded you from, but I find it is the only one you have most
Steadily adhered to, and if you Should not meet with Success, or
wantonly give it up, would hurt you much, as you could not say
with the least degree of certainty, that you would pursue any other
Scheme proper for you. Many things I am inclined to Say to you,
but the hazard of one's letters appearing afterwards restrains me;
The observations you desire me to make on the Journal, tho' an
agreeable Task, is impracticable at present. I dread your reflections
against Saturday for not writing Sooner. You often Call me
indolent, but you wrong me, I have no more of it than is necessary
to make me happy. I never neglect Business nor my friends. When
Antiquity seizes me, I cannot do much, but that is my misfortune,
not my fault. I would have Sent the Stocks this night, but have
Some hopes of Sending them by Mr. Orr[3] who will See you in a
few days if he continues his resolution of going to London. I thank
you for Wilks's paper,[4] it is indeed very impudent, but Clever
enough. On Tuesday I met your Brother John by accident, we
Spoke a little, he went to Ayrshire yesterday with Logan.[5] Davie

---

[3] Probably Alexander Orr of Waterside, a Writer to the Signet. There is no
record of his having met JB in London
at this time, nor is there any mention in
the Journal of a meeting with him at any
time, but JB attended his funeral in
Edinburgh in 1774 (Journ. 29 Nov.
1774).

[4] *The North Briton*, No. 38 (*ante*
22 Feb. 1763, n. 7.)

[5] Hugh Logan (d. 1802) of Logan, an
Ayrshire neighbour of the Boswells, celebrated for his racy humour and lavish
hospitality (James Paterson, *History of
the Counties of Ayr and Wigton*, 1863, i.
346). He spent so freely that he had

is a fine Boy, he comes frequently to me, he is to be Bound this week.[6] I showed him the *Strictures*[7] I never See Cairnie, tho he promised to call for me Adieu My Dear Sir. I always am yours Sincerly

JOHN JOHNSTON

Since writing the above I saw Cap. Blair, he desired me to offer his Compts. to you, and that he is to be in London in 3 weeks with 40 recruits, and that you'll probably hear of General Blair and his Little Army passing thro Duncaster etc. in their way to the Great City. Let this Enliven you, and figure yourself in the Same way. Blair is a fine fellow, I like him much, keep him your friend.

From Johnston, c. 15 March 1763

Missing. Sent from Edinburgh to London and received on 21 Mar. JJ comments on Lord Auchinleck's letter to JB and complains of the severity of JB's last letter to him. He is prepared to forgo the pleasure of receiving the weekly instalments of Journal, since JB is upset by his frequent delays in acknowledging their receipt and also, it would seem, because Lord Auchinleck has cast doubt on his reliability as a confidant. He reveals what he has hitherto kept tactfully secret—that the sealed letter-packets had been broken open before they were brought to his lodgings from Lord Auchinleck's house (*ante* 24 Nov. 1762; 10 Feb. 1763; 24 Feb. 1763, n. 5).

To Johnston, Tuesday 22 March 1763

MS. Yale (L 700).

London, 22 March[1] 1763

MY DEAREST FRIEND: Last night I had the pleasure to receive your last, which is a manly spirited and generous letter. Your feelings on account of the suspicions entertained or thrown out to your disadvantage, are very proper. When I sent you My Lord's letter,[2]

to sell much of his estate, and the secret report on him in 1788 was: "A good-humoured man. A bad manager, but has still an estate of £400 or £500. A batchelor" (*View of the Political State of Scotland [in 1788]*, ed. Sir Charles E. Adam, 1887, p. 32).

[6] David Boswell was about to be apprenticed to the Edinburgh banking firm of John Coutts & Co. (*post* 4 Aug. 1763, n. 2).

[7] *Critical Strictures on the New Tragedy of Elvira (ante* 24 Feb. 1763, n. 2).

[1] MS. "April". JB says he sent no letter "last week", but in the week before 22 Apr. he sent two letters. JJ's letter, referred to at the beginning, though it has not been preserved, was plainly written in reply to that of 8 Mar.

[2] *Ante* 8 Mar. 1763, n. 2.

I declined giving my own opinion of it. I thought it improper in me to censure one to whom I stand in such a light; therefore I was silent. But, my worthy friend be assured that I am confident of your worth and that my regard for you is most sincere most strong, and most permanent. Friendship is a most supreme blessing to a mind endowed with fine feelings, which I will venture to say, You and I posess in a great degree. We have long enjoyed this comfort; and I trust we shall more and more while our Beings continue, which I hope will be for ever. Do not therefore o! my friend indulge the least fear of my becoming cold and careless with respect to you. My last letter I own was a very severe one. I do not remember it particularly; but the general tenor of it, I have in my mind. However, My Dear Sir! you must consider that I was realy chagrined at your neglect; when you could so very easily satisfy me. It is a dissagreable Subject. I mention it, no more. Only for God's sake never let me be fretted again. I admire your generous spirit in offering to lose so much satisfaction for my interest. But My dear Johnston You will not have such a sacrifice to make. What! should you be deprived of what you kindly say are become like the necessaries of life to You? Indeed Sir I have very proper notions of keeping well with my Father but the comforts of friendship I will never give up. Besides, my connection with you is not considered as a heinous offence; but only as a folly; therefore can never be made a matter of vehement dispute. But altho' it were, I declare to you upon my honour that Interest should not make me give up my intimate corespondence with a man whom I regard from my heart. Therefore make your mind easy, and let us just go on as we set out in the beginning of this Winter, which I consider as one of the most perfect plans of sincere and tender regard. The unhappy fact which you have disclosed to me of my packets having been broke open, shocked me a good deal. However it was right to inform me of it. I would willingly impute all that my parents do, to a real tho' mistaken concern about me: But realy this was so very un-genteel and realy so very hard that it pains me exceedingly. It was doing what no Parent has a right to do, In the case of a Son who is a Man, and therefore an independent Individual. It is equaly unjust to steal his secrets, as his money; especialy when we consider that secrets cannot be restored; and that perhaps those of other people may be connected with them. Happily they could not possibly know the hands of some of the letters written to me;

otherwise there might have been sad mischief. Indeed People ought to be very cautious what papers they preserve. When you can get a trusty hand, pray send me up all the packets. I will look them over; and destroy any thing that ought not to be kept. But from many circumstances, you must see my friend, how very terrible a situation I should be in were I to live as young Laird in my Father's Family.

I sent you no Journal nor letter last week; just to let you feel what it is to be dissapointed. If I mistake not, you must have had some uneasiness. But this next Saturday makes all right again. And I must *puff* like a Publisher of a new book and tell you that the Journal is now written upon a much better paper. I got into a very odd habit of writing it upon most pitifull paper. It now comes to 460 Pages.[3] Pray let me know how you take care of it. Let me know too, when you go to Annandale and whether your estate is spelt Grainge or Grange.[4] I am serious. I have a particular reason for wishing to know.

As to my Commission, I find the Duke of Queensberry will do nothing. He has certainly had instructions.[5] Lady Northumberland I am doubtfull of. Lord Eglintoune with all his dissipation is yet my best friend   o Johnston are you not glad? you allways regretted our differing last summer as he first brought me into life. He has presented a letter from me to Lord Bute; who said that at present to give me an Ensigncy in the Guards was impossible. But at My Lord's desire he has promised me one in another Regiment, which My Lord insists that I shall accept of, as it will either be in a Regiment that is to be broke, or I can exchange it with such a one; so that I shall [get] £30 a year half-pay,[6] have no sort of trouble as I will not join my Corps and then it will be a step to my getting into the Guards. It is a matter of some consequence once

---

[3] That is, to the end of the entry for 18 Mar.

[4] It is fairly clear that JB's reason for asking for the exact spelling of the name cf JJ's estate was that it is mentioned in the volume of his correspondence with Andrew Erskine, then being printed (From Andrew Erskine, 5 July 1762). He could not now give the reason to JJ, for JJ as yet knew nothing of the project, JB having deliberately excluded any mention of it from the journal he was

sending to Scotland in instalments. JJ thus first heard of it when he received JB's letter of 16 Apr. 1763 (*post*).

[5] That is, instructions from Lord Auchinleck. See Journ. 26 Dec. 1762: "I imagined my Father was at the bottom of it."

[6] The Seven Years War being over, all infantry regiments junior to the 70th Foot were being broke and their officers transferred to others or put on half-pay.

to fix myself fairly out of my Father's reach as he still imagines he is to have me under his eye, as you may judge from a letter of my mother's[7] which I send you, and beg it may be returned. You will see mention made of taking away my allowance, in order I suppose to force me back, but you know,[8] by a transaction last Summer with my father, I have a settlement of £100 a year lying by me in form;[9] so I am realy my own master. He little thinks of my stealing this half-pay March. Dont mention a word of it; and pray write me your opinion of the Scheme. I use you truly as a friend. If you have my vivacity and whim and humour; You have also all my affairs to hear. I think the plan is a good one; and one thing is certain it can do no harm; as I can throw it up every hour after I am tired of it; or find that it will not forward my scheme.

I am glad you like the *North-Briton*. I send you another of his papers. Erskine and I added the lines[10] which you will see, and were

[7] "I Supos you have no Expectations new [i.e. now] of a Comision in the Gaurds and as you are folowing no other Busness I belive no Body woud thinck it reasonable or advice your Father after your year is out to Continou your Alouance to live idely at London I know no young Gentelman of this Country that lives ther in that way your poor Father is stil in great distress about you your showing A dislike at this Country is a thing very disagreabl to him however I hope you will Come to See that it is both your duty and intrest to Setel hear befor the End of this year" (From Euphemia Boswell, 7 Mar. 1763).

[8] MS. "know. By".

[9] This document, dated 2 Apr. 1762 (MS. Yale C 210), entirely in the hand of Lord Auchinleck, binds him and his heirs male to pay to JB "by way of alimentary provision only The sum of One hundred pounds sterling yearly during his Life", in equal portions at Martinmas and Whitsunday. This unconditional allowance appears to have been the inducement offered by Lord Auchinleck to persuade his son to sign a deed dated 7 Mar. 1762 (MS. Yale M 16, a copy in JB's hand) under which JB agreed to vary his rights of inheritance under his parents' marriage contract in such a way as to permit his father, if he thought fit, to vest the

entailed Auchinleck estate in trustees after his death. JB, in this case, would have been paid for the rest of his life half the free rents of the estate and would have had the right to reside at Auchinleck, but would have had no say in the management of the property. In later years he was bitterly to regret this "renunciation of my birthright, which I *madly* granted to him" (To W. J. Temple, 2 Sept. 1775; Journ. 21 Mar. 1772; see *post* 27 June 1763 for a reference by JJ to the deed). On 31 Oct. 1780 (Journ.) JB was able to inspect the marriage contract for the first time and concluded that his worries about his father's disinheriting him had been needless, as such action was outside his power. But the trusteeship allowed under the "Deed of Renunciation" was another matter, and JB was still concerned about this possibility as late as 7 Jan. 1780 (Journ.). Only after his father's death did he learn that his fears had been groundless and that no use had been made of the deed.

[10] The paper sent was probably No. 41, 12 Mar. 1763, which ends with eight riddling couplets imitating the speech of the Fool in *King Lear*, III. ii. 81–95. In the original *North Briton* (a small folio of six pages) there is a considerable blank space between these lines and the imprint at the foot of the last page. JB perhaps

to have sent it to the Gentlewoman who is very narrow,[11] without a frank: But we recollected that Lord Prestongrange is subject to low-spirits, and our hearts relented. So it comes to you. Pray be kind to Davie.[12] He is a charming little fellow. Go to Hart and get up my bond. I have accepted his bill. Write me about Charles. Go and see him. My shoes are arrived. I shall have them in a day or two; And now My most worthy friend I commit you to God.

JAMES BOSWELL

To Johnston, Tuesday 29 March 1763

MS. Yale (L 701).

London, 29 March 1763[1]

MY DEAR SIR: This morning I received the Packets with the stocks which I am very well pleased with. But the Packets were so heavy that they were charged ten shillings which I beleive I must pay; so, for the future, make any packets you send very small. You see I am allways under weight in my packets of Journal.

My brother John owes me a guinea and Digges will soon owe me half a Guinea for Pamphlets etc.[2] These debts you will receive for me by and by. Or I can return you the money for the Shoes and

means that he and Erskine have entered in this blank space, with pen and ink, certain additional verses which they have composed. For discussion of the possibility that the eight couplets of *North Briton*, No. 41 were also composed by JB and Erskine, see Appendix 3.

[11] There is no overt reference in *The North Briton*, No. 41, or in the verses appended to it, to a gentlewoman, other than the "Margaret" who represents Scotland: "When *John* leaves *Marg'ret* in the lurch". If "the Gentlewoman" was a nickname applied by JB and JJ to William Grant (c. 1701–64), Lord Prestongrange, the attribution of narrowness is apt, for though he was generally liked, and admired as a judge in the courts of Session and Justiciary, he had an established reputation for parsimony (*Scotland and Scotsmen* i. 125–26).

[12] Now that David Boswell had entered on his apprenticeship in Edinburgh, he would be separated from his family during the part of the year they regularly spent in Ayrshire. Bankers and other merchants then combined their living and business premises, and it was customary for apprentices to become members of the household and thus remain under the supervision of their principals. That this was no mere formality is proved by Sir William Forbes's account of his own experience in the same banking-house a few years earlier: "So strict was Mr. John Coutts in the discipline of the counting-house, that I slept but one night out of Edinburgh from the commencement of my apprenticeship in May 1754 till the month of September 1760, when I obtained leave to go to Aberdeenshire with my mother to pay a visit to our relations" (Forbes, p. 14 n.).

[1] MS. "22 March 1762": cf. Journ. 29 Mar. 1763 and the reference in the letter of 5 Apr. to this one having been written "This day senight".

[2] West Digges (d. 1786), the actor who had so fired JB's imagination in

Stocks by some of the Edinburgh Gentry now in London. Some days ago I accepted Mr. Hart's bill which is indorsed to a Mr. Fell Chinaman[3] in Cornhill London. I am to pay it on Tuesday next. I wish I may get Love to muster up the money, as his benefit does not come on till the 15 of April.[4] However, he has promised to let me have it. You must know my friend that I am at present very antiquated: I don't know for what. I would give a great deal for your consoling company. I hope I shall get rid of my antiquity soon. My mind has a strange mixture of vivacity and gloominess. I set apart this forenoon for bringing up my Journal to the end of last week; but am so listless and so uneasy that I realy cannot write. You must sympathise with me, and take the inclosed eight pages[5] kindly, as all that I can give you. The Spleen is a most unaccountable thing. It comes and goes like the Wind sudden and unperceived. I have just now a distaste of every pursuit and every pleasure. I am to dine with Captain Webster[6] and a parcel of young lively english fellows at the Tilt-yard.[7] I have an aversion to think

Edinburgh, was in correspondence with him and was receiving a copy of *The North Briton* from him each week (Journ. 11 Dec. 1762). This, however, was a gift, and the pamphlets referred to were publications which he had bought and sent to Edinburgh at Digges's request. On 9 Dec. 1762 Digges wrote to JB thanking him for his "care about My little bundle of pamphlets"; on 29 Dec. 1762 he asked for "the two Gentln. of Verona"; and on 31 Jan. 1763 for "the Citizen lately published—I have some thoughts of playing it here". *The Monthly Review* notices both these shilling pamphlets, the former in Jan. 1763, p. 75, and the latter in Feb., p. 166: "*The Citizen, A Farce as it is performed at the Theatre-Royal in Covent-Garden.*, By Arthur Murphy, Esq." Digges acknowledged receipt of *The Citizen* on 18 Feb.

[3] A merchant dealing in porcelain, or "China-ware".

[4] At Love's benefit performance at Drury Lane on 15 Apr., the plays given were Shakespeare's *2 Henry IV* and *The Witches, or Harlequin Cherokee*, written by Love himself (*Drury Lane Calendar, 1747–76*, ed. Dougald MacMillan, 1938, p. 95).

[5] That is, to p. 468, which terminates with the end of the entry for 21 Mar.

[6] James Webster (1740–81), JB's cousin, second son of Dr. Alexander Webster, minister of the Tolbooth Church, Edinburgh, had been commissioned Captain in the 33rd Regt. of Foot two months earlier, on 14 Jan. 1763. He enjoyed a successful military career, becoming Lt.-Col. of his regiment at the early age of 34, but was fatally wounded in action during the American War of Independence.

[7] The Tilt-yard Coffee House, off Whitehall, was much frequented by army officers (Edward Walford, *Old and New London*, n.d., c. 1876, iii. 344, 364; iv. 82). Andrew Erskine's elder brother, Lt. Archibald, had the previous year sung its praises to JB (To Andrew Erskine, 16 Feb. 1762). "I dined with Webster, who treated me as his guest at a military mess at the Tilt-yard. . . . I had this day the satisfaction of a very good dinner, genteely served up in an elegant room, and a good company round me. Yet was I melancholy. . . . I disliked the idea of being a Soldier. I thought of refusing a Commission" (Journ. 29 Mar. 1763).

of it yet it will probably relieve me. You will see what effect it has, when you get my next parcel of Journal. Let me know when you go to the Country. I hope Davie will do well. I rejoyce to hear good accounts of Charles. Farewell my worthy friend; and beleive me ever your most faithfull friend

JAMES BOSWELL

To Johnston, Tuesday 5 April 1763

MS. Yale (L 702).

ADDRESS: To Mr. John Johnston, to be left at Forrest's Coffeehouse, Edinburgh.

FRANK: Eglinton.

POSTMARK: 5 AP

London, 5 April 1763

DEAR SIR: How very unaccountable how very changeable is the mind of your friend. This day senight I wrote to you from my cell in the Newgate of Melancholy. This day I write to you from my elegant Apartment in the Palace of felicity. This day I present my mind to you under one appearance. Tomorrow I cry whip Jack and be gone, and you behold as different a picture as Guido Rheni's Mary Magdalene[1] is from the portly print of Mr. Edward Bright the renowned fat Man of Essex,[2] whose Effigies adorns many a house of entertainment. Surely O Johnston thou must well remember this wonderfull Exhibition. Have not thy eyes beheld it on a Saturday afternoon at Mussleburgh, or at Leith? Has it not served to amuse thee at Lintoun, after a long day's ride from Annandale, in thy way to the ancient Edina? Has it not struck thy view in the house of thy kinsman Mungo Johnston at Lockerbie on the great occasion of a Lammas fair, when the honest Laird has come jogging down from the Hass upon his sturdy nag got his purse filled from receipt of Custom and given a hearty entertain-

---

[1] Guido Reni (1575–1642) of Bologna has several Mary Magdalenes to his name. Characteristically he depicts them as gaunt, tearful, and penitent. He was a popular painter in his own day, and highly esteemed in Britain in JB's time, when his paintings were in high demand (*Dictionary of Painters and Engravers*, ed. Michael Bryan, 1903).

[2] Edmund Bright (1721–50) of Malden, the fair-booth prodigy, weighed about 600 lb. His portrait by David Ogborne was engraved by James MacArdell and, soon after Bright's death (10 Nov. 1750, *Gent. Mag.*, xx. 525), reproductions appeared in *Lond. Mag.*, Feb. 1751, xx, facing p. 82, and *Universal Mag.*, Feb. 1751, viii. 69.

ment to all his friends?[3] Amongst these friends you o Johnston could not fail to make one. Much would you eat and drink, and much would you laugh. The Spirit of Wantoness would posess you, and all the Lasses would dread your prowess. Clergymen would tremble for their Wives and their Daughters, and every farmer would hide his *joe*[4] from the fury of the *ramp*[5] *Laird of the Grange*. Wearied at last with these fruitless pursuits, the Maid of the Inn would attract your amorous affections. Pleasing words of flattery would you whisper in her ears and a gay ell of ribband would you tie round her head. Then would you gently hurry her down to the Cellar and like the lively James the fifth lay her *owr* the *gantrees*, and do it again and again.[6]

I am now resolved to accept of an Ensigncy in a marching Regiment, and to exchange it immediatly with a half-pay one, and so have that pretence to push for the Guards. Lord Eglintoune advised me to take it. I am sure of having it. I inclose you Lord Bute's card,[7] sealed with his own large seal. His mention of his Majesty is only a form. it means the secretary at war. I inclose

---

[3] Lockerbie House stands on the skirts of a hill named the Hass. From there William Johnstone of Lockerbie would ride down, at the close of the great Lammas lamb-fair (which was the largest in Scotland and was constantly growing throughout the century) to collect, as due to the proprietor of the fairground, a fee from each salesman proportionate to the amount made by the sale of his lambs.

Mungo Johnstone (d. 1783), wine-merchant at Lockerbie, was a man of substance and probably a near relative of the laird (in whose family Mungo, the name of the local patron saint, was common). In 1753 his first wife, Henrietta Carruthers, had inherited the property of her uncle John Carruthers of Butterwhat, and shortly afterwards he had leased from William Johnstone "an eighth part of the innfield land of the town of Lockerby lying on the south end of the west side of the town" (Register of Deeds, Dal. 211, p. 444; Register of Testaments, Dumfries, 30 Nov. 1785).

[4] Scots: sweetheart (literally joy).
[5] Wanton, riotous (OED).
[6] Many racy popular poems, like *Peblis*

to the Play, *Christ's Kirk on the Green*, *The Gaberlunzie Man*, and *The Jollie Beggar*, have been ascribed to James V, the "Gudeman of Ballengeich". Since no such phrase occurs in any of the poems usually associated with his name, JB may have had in mind some ballad or chapbook song which has been lost since his day, or a suppressed stanza from one which has survived. A *gantree* is a stand or frame on which barrels are stored, and a reference to its occasional use for the purpose suggested by JB occurs in the lines (almost certainly familiar to him) from Ramsay's *Tea-Table Miscellany*:

> The malt-man comes on Munday,
> He craves wonder fair,
> Cries, "Dame, come gi'e me my siller,
> Or malt ye sall ne'er get mair."
>   I took him into the pantry,
>   And gave him some good cock-
>   broo,
>   Syne paid him upon a gantree
>   As hostler-wives should do.

[7] A photographic reproduction is given in the limited edition of *Boswell's London Journal*, Heinemann, 1951, facing p. 297.

you Hart's Bill which I payed this morning. Love cannot give me the money till his benefit is over. It is on friday senight. Lazy dog that he is. I wish I had my money. But there is little fear of it. I shall be glad to hear of your safe arrival at Grange; I shall write you often and I ever shall be your affectionate friend

JAMES BOSWELL

The Journal is now 492 pages.[8]

Pray show Hart the Bill and get the Bond cancelled. Return me the letter from Lord Bute. I suppose you may burn the Bill.

INTENDED ENCLOSURE[9]: Lord Bute to Lord Eglinton, Saturday 26 March 1763.

MS. Yale (C 710).

ADDRESS: To The Earl of Eglinton.

FRANK: Bute.

ENDORSEMENT: The Prime Minister's Note that I was to have an Ensigncy. But as I liked only the Guards I declined it.

Lord Bute presents His Compts. to Lord Eglinton, and acquaints His Lordship that He mentioned to the King Mr. Boswell's Case, and that His Majesty will not fail to order that He should have a pair Colours.

South Aud[ley] Street, March 26th 1763

From Johnston, Thursday 7 April 1763

MS. Yale (C 1618).

Edinr. 7th April 1763

DEAR SIR: I am now thinking of going to the Country, which has kept me very busy for some days putting all my affairs in order, and packing up my Books and papers, as I do not return to my present Lodging, which you alwise disliked so much.[1] Where I lodge when I return, is uncertain, as I have found no place to my

---

[8] That is, it had been posted to the end of the entry for 3 Apr.

[9] JB actually forgot to enclose this, as JJ's letter of 18 Apr. shows, but he may have sent it later.

---

[1] JJ was moving out of his Don's Close lodgings, of which JB had written: "Donaldson the Painter . . . reminded me of former days at Edinburgh, when he drew Johnston's Picture in the Lawn Market, where my friend then lived and where I could wish he still had lived, rather than down in Don's close; tho' indeed his having an agreable buxom Landlady, and having a view of the Lomond hills from his windows are very great inducements" (Journ. 4 Mar. 1763).

liking. I received the packet Safe on Saturday. To write even so much, when in such humour, shows great Command of yourself. God help me! When I am ill I can do nothing but with the greatest reluctance and trouble. Since Sunday Evening I have been and still am very ill. And do you know it afforded me Some relief to think, that from your Letter,[2] it was probable you was Suffering at the same time. There is Something very absurd in this, but I am Sure there is no Malevolence in it: The Story of Sitting up all night, and calling on the Watch to light your Candle,[3] was very Romantick. But I Blame you for imposing such hardships on yourself, when you had been guilty of no neglect but what could easily have been made up the next day. You ought to take particular care of your health, as the mind suffers alongst with the body; I am not fond of your accepting of a Commission in a Regiment which is to be broke, it has a queer appearance[4] unless your being in half pay will forward your Commission in the Guards; It's surprizing how you are charged Postage for the 3 packets, when I weighed them, and found each Severall drops under 2 oz. after put under Mr. Terries cover. Since you wrote me of it, I thought the 2 oz. I had weighed the packets with, might be Dutch weight and So misled.[5]

---

[2] *Ante* 29 Mar. 1763.

[3] "When I went home in the evening, I felt myself quite dissipated by running about so much. I was indolent and careless and could not fix to any thing. Even this my Journal was in danger of being neglected. Near a whole week had elapsed without my writing a single page of it. By way therefore of pennance for my idleness, and by way of making up for the time lost, and bringing up my business I determined to sit up all this night; which I accordingly did, and wrote a great deal. About two o'clock in the morning I inadvertently snuffed out my candle, and as my fire was long before that black and cold, I was in a great dilemma how to proceed. Down stairs did I softly and silently step to the Kitchen. But alas, there was as little fire there as upon the icy mountains of Greenland. With a tinder-box is a light struck every morning to kindle the fire which is put out at night. But this tinder-box I could not see, nor knew where to find. I was now filled with gloomy ideas of the terrors of the night. I was also apprehensive that my Landlord, who allways keeps a pair of loaded pistols by him, might fire at me, as a thief. I went up to my room sat quietly till I heard the Watchman calling, 'Past three o'clock'. I then called to him to knock at the door of the house where I lodged; He did so; and I opened it to him and got my candle relumed without danger. Thus was I relieved, and continued busy till eight next day" (Journ. 21 Mar. 1763).

[4] It is a theme of complaint in *The North Briton* that regiments about to be disbanded were being filled up at the last moment with needy and unscrupulous Scotsmen who had given no war-service but were hoping to live on half-pay at the nation's expense. There is a possible allusion to this in *North Briton*, No. 38 (19 Feb. 1763); it is handled at length in No. 42 (19 Mar. 1763); and the complaint is repeated in No. 45 (23 Apr. 1763).

[5] Several different standards of weight were in use in Scotland till the Imperial

I have now compared it with English and find it is no more. I wish Mr. Terrie may not think too much freedom is used with his name, and intends to check it in this way. Pray weigh 2 of the stocks, and 2 pieces of paper equal to Mr. Terries cover and your own, and you'll be satisfied. The Journal is now 468 ps.[6] I have put it and your four parcels of private papers into a Box and Lock'd it up, so every thing will remain Safe. I will write you a few lines on Monday, as I Sett off on Tuesday morning. You'll receive this on Tuesday, so will Stop your sending any more Journal untill I return here. Do not neglect to write it, tho' you keep it by you, nor forget to write me when in Annandale, by the direction I gave you in my last. A Report has prevailed here for Several weeks and seems to gain credit. That the Marq[ui]s of Annandale is reconvalesced, and freed from his Confinement.[7] I Sincerely wish it may prove true, but doubt it much, pray inform yourself, and acquaint me. Put Mr. Scots Letter[8] into the penny Post or General Post Office. Adieu My Dear Sir and I always am yours most sincerely

JOHN JOHNSTON

system was introduced in 1826. By an Act of 1618 the Scottish Parliament attempted to establish a standard based on the French Troy, which came to be known as Lanark weight, because the standard stone-weight was by old tradition in custody of the burgh of Lanark. It was also popularly known as Dutch, or Amsterdam weight, since the Dutch standard was similar and it was used in the trade between Scotland and the Continent, most of which passed through Holland. The Act was not generally effective and, except for purposes of export, most districts retained their own local systems. By article 17 of the Act of Union, a further attempt was made in 1707 to standardize Scottish weights in conformity with the English practice, but this was no more successful. The cost of parcel postage to England was, of course, reckoned in English pounds and ounces. JJ, on learning of the surcharge on the package sent to London, was afraid he might have calculated its weight by the Dutch, or Lanark scale, according to which one English ounce would have

weighed little more than three-quarters of an ounce (John Swinton, Lord Swinton, *A Proposal for the Uniformity of Weights and Measures in Scotland*, 1779; R. W. Cochran-Patrick, *Mediaeval Scotland*, 1892, pp. 151 ff.).

6 *Ante* 29 Mar. 1763, n. 5.

7 George Johnstone (1720–92), 3rd Marquis of Annandale, hereditary chief of the great Border clan of which JJ was a member, had been declared insane in 1748, and the management of his estates had been vested in trustees. He never re-covered sufficiently to resume respon-sibility for his affairs (*Scots Peer.* i. 269).

8 Another letter had been enclosed in the cover addressed to JB, and JJ asks him to send it on by the Penny Post, which operated only in London and its imme-diate neighbourhood. It was probably addressed to JJ's relative Patrick Scott, a London merchant. He was the son of Francis Scott of Johnston, an Edinburgh solicitor who had died on 28 Apr. 1761 in his 76th year (*Scots Mag.*, 1761, xxiii. 249), leaving JJ to wind up his estate as executor of his will (Grange MSS.).

To Johnston, Saturday 16 April 1763

MS. Yale (L 703).

London, 16 April 1763

MY DEAR FRIEND: I imagine this will find you safely arrived at the place of your Nativity; at that Grange about which we have had so much gentle good-humoured altercation. You know the title of Laird was allways offensive to your ears. You took it as much amiss as an Ensign does when People call him Captain. And yet Johnston You and The Ensign would both repine a good deal if the one should lose his estate, and the other his Commission.

I suppose you will expect that I must adapt my letters to the place where you chance to be when I write to you. When you are at Edinburgh I must talk of nothing but the Parliament House, the Lords' Boxes,[1] Infeftments[2] Memorials Deeds, Bottles of two-penny rolls and rum-punch.[3] And now when you are got to the Grange my whole letter must be full of Sheep and tar and clasped confessions of faith[4] and brown-boarded New-testaments and plows and Harrows and Dung-carts and Boston's *Four-fold State* and Vincent's *Catechism*[5] and a comb without many teeth lying on the dusty chimney-piece.

There now Johnston I have painted ideas proper for Edinburgh and Grange, in one way; and to show my liveliness of imagination, I will paint you a set of each in another way, or rather taste.

When you are at Edinburgh, I must talk to you of the warmth and Society of a comfortable City; of the Church-of-England Chapels and organs which inspire exalted Devotion; of the noble Palace of Holyroodhouse, and the wild grandeur of the King's

---

[1] The receptacle for legal petitions, memorials, and such other official documents as were addressed to the Lords of Session.

[2] Scots legal term: The deed or instrument by which a person is infeft (or enfeoffed), i.e. put in possession of heritable property.

[3] The bottles of twopenny ale and the rolls are probably associated in JB's mind with the regular mid-morning snack which lawyers took in one or other of the many taverns round about Parliament Close; the rum-punch with their festive evening gatherings.

[4] Possibly the *Westminster Confession,* but more probably the two-volume "Dunlop's Collection": William Dunlop, *A Collection of Confessions of Faith, Catechisms. Directories, Books of Discipline, etc. Of Public Authority in the Church of Scotland,* 1719–22.

[5] Among the grim symbols of Scottish rural life in this list are two favourite documents of 18th-century Presbyterianism: Thomas Boston's *Human Nature in its Fourfold Estate,* 1720, and Nathaniel Vincent's *The Principles of the Doctrine of Christ: a Catechism,* 1691.

park; of brilliant Assemblys and a crowded Theatre and an elegant Concert of Music.

When you are at Grange, I must talk to you of the pleasing retirement of the Country; shady walks among your own trees; lying upon the green grass; seeing the ewes milked, and kissing the Maids; visiting your neighbours, and entertaining them in your turn.

And now Johnston, I must inform you that Captain Erskine and I have published a Collection of our letters, with the utmost boldness too, as we have printed our names at length.[6] The narrowminded and censorious Scotch rail at us. The goodhumoured jolly English like and praise us. To be sure it is a whimsical enough Experiment. I am affraid only of my Father's displeasure.[7] He will think it terribly imprudent. Pick us up what you hear about us, and send [it] me. I ever am yours sincerely

JAMES BOSWELL

From Johnston, Monday 18 April 1763

MS. Yale (C 1619).

Edinr. 18th April 1763

MY DEAR SIR: You'll be Surprized not to have heard from me Since I received your last letter with the Journal and Bill, But untill this day I never could get up the Bond from Mossman,[1] who always Said it was in the Country. However he at last Sent for it,

[6] *Letters between the Honourable Andrew Erskine, and James Boswell, Esq.*, was published on 12 Apr. by Flexney. It was the first of JB's publications to bear his name (*Lit. Car.*, pp. 19–24).

[7] Lord Auchinleck was duly dismayed. A friend at Jedburgh showed him a review of the *Letters* in which one was inserted as a specimen. "I read it and found that tho' it might pass between t[w]o intimate young Lads in the Same Way that people over a bottle will be vastly entertained with one anothers Rant, It was extreamly odd to Send Such a piece to the press to be perused by all and Sundry. The Gentlemen at Jedburgh imagined and indeavoured to perswade me that it had been some body who put in that Article in the news by way of Jest for they coud not sus-

pect the Letter to be genuine, At the same time They said it was a cruel Jest as it was exposing you" (From Lord Auchinleck, 30 May 1763). Though JB's family pride was no less than Lord Auchinleck's, his sense of humour was different, and such a remark as this was unlikely to amuse his father: "The Boswells, you know, came over from Normandy, with William the Conqueror, and some of us possess the spirit of our ancestors the French. I do for one. A pleasant spirit it is. *Vive la Bagatelle*, is the maxim" (*Letters between The Honourable Andrew Erskine, and James Boswell, Esq.*, 1763, No. 1).

[1] *Ante* 1 Mar. 1763.

and it is now in my Custody retired. Mr. Hart was this day to have given me up your Letter of Relief,[2] but has mislaid the key of the Desk where it lyes, and if he does not find it this night[3] will break it up and Send the Letter to me in the Country, tho' its no great matter, as it cannot affect you since the prin[cip]le Bond is retired. I was really vext at the Body[4] Mossman who has keept me in Town Since Thursday purposely waiting to get up the Bond; I wish Love may have paid you the money. If he has, keep Clear of him, and such persons for the future. I was greatly dissappointed at not finding Lord Butes Letter enclosed, as you intended.[5] You have mislaid it, and by this time will be Sensible of your Mistake, pray be So good as to Send it to me, and I will return it. Tomorrow I leave Edr. and hope to be regaled with a Letter from you, lying at Grange, when I go there. It will do me much good after my Journey. The Journal 492 pages[6] is Lockd up in a Strong Box, with your private papers. I have been very Low Spirited for a long time, God help me, for it increases every day. Farewell My Dear Sir and I ever am your sincere friend

JOHN JOHNSTON

Davie is well; Good Boy, he calls frequently for me. He is much Shagreened[7] at your not writing to him. You ought to do it, it will please the Boy, he may afterwards be your friend and an usefull one.

To Johnston, Monday 25 April 1763

MS. Yale (L 704).

Oxford, April 25. 1763

MY DEAR SIR: By the date of this letter you will see that I have at last made out my intended jaunt to Oxford. You know what high ideas we have allways conceived of this venerable seat of learning. I assure you that the reality comes up to the idea. The magnificence of the buildings the elegance of the Gardens and walks the number of Academics are all very noble circumstances: And

[2] The bond of relief referred to *ante* 1 Mar. 1763, n. 2.

[3] MS. orig. "soon".

[4] In Scots usage the term carries a sense of mild contempt and here serves to emphasize JJ's annoyance with Mossman.

[5] *Ante* 5 Apr. 1763, n. 9.

[6] That is, to the end of the entry for 3 Apr.

[7] At that time an alternative spelling for *chagrin*. The latter has since become specialized for the metaphorical sense, and *shagreen* for the literal (OED).

when we reflect that so many great men have been brought up here our reverence for it, borders on Superstition. I yesterday looked at the Windows of Mr. Locke's room, and of Mr. Addison's room[1] in which he wrote the most of his Saturday's papers; which were originaly intended for the Pulpit.[2]

And yet Johnston I am so very unfortunate as to labour under a load of Antiquity. I am realy an instrument very easily put out of tune. Before I got here, my spirits had become torpid and my mind gloomy. I require the nicest and most delicate management. Change of circumstances tho trifling puts me out of order. I have at present no relish for the noble scenes arround me. The entertainments and civilitys which I receive are a burthen to me; and I am anxious till tomorrow morning comes when I shall get into the Coach and drive back to dear comfortable London. Beleive me ever yours most sincerely

JAMES BOSWELL

From Johnston, Thursday 28 April 1763

MS. Yale (C 1620).

Schaw 28th April 1763

My DEAR SIR, I had the pleasure of receiving your Letter Yesterday,[1] which gave me great comfort in this bleak Country, where the Snow is just now falling in great flakes, attended with a violent East wind. Consider the quick transition from the Warm and Comfortable City, Surrounded with Lothians fertile fields, now in full verdure, when compared with this place, and you'll easily find out my Situation not to be very agreeable at present. I am just now with our friends at Schaw,[2] where I stay 3 days till a

[1] JB gives a fuller account of this visit in his Journal (23 to 26 Apr.), but though he mentions the colleges of Whitefield and Hervey (Pembroke and Lincoln), he says nothing about those of Locke and Addison (Christ Church and Magdalen).

[2] JB's statement, which probably reports what some guide or caretaker told him, may not be entirely without foundation. In order to provide his clientele with good week-end reading, Addison tended to present more serious topics in his Saturday papers. He is known to have revised earlier work for *The Spectator*, and some of these reworked

pieces may date from his Oxford days. See John Nichols's edition, 1789, vi. 92 n., vii. 21 n., &c. A manuscript book of early essays, all "of formidable solemnity," was recently acquired by the Bodleian Library. See M. C. Crum, "A Manuscript of Essays by Addison", *Bodleian Library Record*, v (1954–56), 98–103. (Information supplied by Professor Richmond P. Bond.)

[1] *Ante* 16 Apr. 1763.

[2] William Graham (d. 1773) of Shaw, an estate in Dryfesdale near JJ's own farm of Heithat, belonged to a family long

friend of theirs (who died here) is buried. It is one Mrs. Anderson[3] who you'll remember used to Sit opposite to you in the new Church[4] at Edinr. The gloomy Scene of death, a funeral etc. hurts me much, even tho' it is a person I had no friendship for. I believe it arises from the Selfish consideration, That one day or other, it will be my own fate, and that of my best friends. If you are in high Spirits when you receive this, you'll think these dreary reflexions ridiculous, but I always Speak to you without reserve, and never dread your Censure.

I came to the knowledge of publishing your Letters from Some Body who had Seen the publication advertised in one of the London papers, and acquainted me of it, before I received your letter. You know I am now in a place of the world where Such Topicks are Seldom introduced, and can hear only the Opinion and Sentiments of those, whose Judgement is not much to be relied on. I am affraid of my Lords displeasure, which you Seem to dread. It Surely ought in a great measure to Influence your Conduct. Tho' he has not indulged you So much as Some parents would have done, Yet the Duty you owe, and the Expectations you have from him, Ought to restrain you from doing any thing which may appear to him very imprudent, even though laudable in the Eyes of the World, especially at this time, when you are So much dependent on him. His Character is So well Established, That in any dispute betwixt you, he would have a Majority on his Side. What I have Said is the dictates of my Sincere friendship for you,

settled in Dumfriesshire and long associated with the Johnston clan. He and JJ's father had been principal heritors of Hutton parish, and may have been related through Graham's grandmother, Anna Johnston, wife of James Graham of Shaw. JJ was a frequent visitor to Shaw, where the family consisted of William Graham and his wife, a daughter of Michael Anderson of Tushielaw; George, their only son, whom JJ named along with JB as one of the trustees under his will; George's wife Margaret, only daughter of Robert Johnston, surgeon at Moffat; and two of George's sisters, Janet and Margaret (Register of Sasines, Dumfries; Dumfries Testaments; W. R. Rogerson, *Hutton under the Muir*, 1908, p. 7).

[3] Almost certainly Janet, widow of Michael Anderson of Tushielaw (1710-

62), sister-in-law of Graham's wife. She was the daughter of Sir James Naesmyth of Posso, 1st Bt., by his third wife, Barbara Pringle, d. 1768 (J. W. Buchan and Henry Paton, *A History of Peeblesshire* iii. 568–69; Thomas Craig-Brown, *The History of Selkirkshire* i. 334). Her testament dative (Edinburgh Testaments xii, pt. i, 3 Sept. 1765), though it does not give the precise date of her death, indicates that it took place in 1763.

[4] The New Church, otherwise known as the High Church, was one of the four sections into which St. Giles Cathedral was divided, and the official kirking-place of the Edinburgh magistrates. It had "a sort of dignified aristocratic character, approaching somewhat to prelacy" (Robert Chambers, *Traditions of Edinburgh*, 1912, p. 114). The Auchinleck family attended regularly when in town.

without regard to the merit of the Letters, or the reception they may meet with from the World. I return to Grange on Monday, will Stay a few days there and write from that place, and date my Letter below a tree of my own planting. It is very agreeable to retire a few days now and then from the World in this way. Your Country and City Scenes are very humorous. They Entertained me much. Continue to Write me frequently while I am in the country. Your Letters will come Safe to me thro' Provost Graham's care.[5] Tell me always what you are doing, and omit nothing relating to your happiness and Success. Let me know if you write the Journal, and if Love has repaid you the money. I always am My Dear Sir Your most Sincere friend while

JOHN JOHNSTON

Let me have a copy of the Letters when published if an opportunity offers of sending it, unless a copy can be had from any of the Booksellers in Edinr. Tho' I rather wish to have it from your own hand.

To Johnston, Tuesday 17 May 1763

MS. Yale (L 705).

ADDRESS: To John Johnston Esq: at Grange, to the care of Provost Graham, Dumfries, Scotland.

FRANK: Free G. Dempster.

POSTMARK: 19 MA.

ENDORSEMENT: London 17th May 1763.

London, 17 May 1763

MY DEAR SIR: Do not imagine because I have not written you so frequently since your[1] being in the country, that I am in the least forgetfull of you. You may rest satisfy'd of the permanence of my friendship altho' Dissipation[2] may now and then turn me giddy.

---

[5] John Graham of Kinharvie, a former provost of Dumfries, had played a notable part in the history of the town. At the time of the political riots of 1759 he had been the unsuccessful candidate for the provostship, whose defeat through the machinations of Provost Corbet (representing the party of the landowners and wealthy merchants) had so incensed the craftsmen and common people of the town that violence had broken out on several occasions (William McDowall, *History of the Burgh of Dumfries*, 2nd ed., 1873, pp. 556–68).

JJ's letters were directed to his care, no doubt, because Graham, who was a merchant in Dumfries, was in the way of making regular country deliveries of goods.

---

[1] MS. "your'e".

[2] That is, irregularity and lack of concentration, not, as now, being dissolute.

I have of late been rather too dissipated. It is a very unhappy situation of mind. It debases the soul; deprives it of sollid Enjoyment, and feeds it only with frivolous amusement. And yet a Man[3] on whom the gloomy Dæmon of Melancholy takes strong effect is often glad to fly to Dissipation for relief. This is much my case, and when groaning under the pressure of dark despair, I give up all my high ideas of propriety and of dignity and am glad to compound for humble ease and undistinguished forgetfullness of care. I have indeed a tollerable cause of low spirits. I find myself in an uncertain and idle situation. My Father's displeasure hangs over me; the airy forms of gayety and pleasure that glittered before my fancy are vanished or hid in clouds of discontent; and wherever I turn my thoughts I can find no certain joy. Let me however retract this. For in the comforts of friendship I surely have a certain and a permanent joy. I have not yet got my Commission in a marching Regiment: But expect it soon. The difference between that and one in the Guards is £600 and Doctor Pringle[4] says he imagines my Father may be brought to advance that Sum. I have written a most warm letter to my Father and told him that if he can have no peace of mind unless I return to Scotland that I will make that sacrifice, but have beg'd him to allow me some years in my own way, and then I may more effectualy settle. Doctor Pringle is to write to him to let me try the Army. My Dear friend! you must be sorry at my situation. However, I hope the best. You talk sensibly about the publication of our letters. I hope My Father will not take it highly amiss. Donaldson[5] has sent a parcel to Edinburgh. So you may get them there. We resolved not to make one present of the first Edition. Your situation at

---

[3] MS. "And yet to a Man" (The construction of the sentence alters midway because at "on" JB turned the leaf to write on the other side.)

[4] John Pringle (1707–82), the reformer of British military medicine and hygiene, later physician to George III, President of the Royal Society, and a Baronet. He had long since resigned from the army and settled in practice in London. The Pringles were old friends of the Boswells, and Pringle, though likeminded with Lord Auchinleck rather than with JB, was sufficiently kindly disposed to serve as a useful go-between. JB calls

him "my father's great friend" and in his Mem. for 16 May, makes the resolution: "At night see Pringle . . . bid him settle all but not too fast."

[5] Alexander Donaldson, though he figures largely in the book as an intimate friend of Erskine and JB, was not the publisher of the *Letters*, which were printed for Flexney. But Donaldson had interests in book-selling businesses in both capitals, and often undertook the distribution of London publications in Scotland. He had taken "a parcel of the *Letters*" to distribute in Scotland (Journ. 13 Apr.).

Schaw was gloomy.[6] You are now I suppose stretched beneath a shade raised by yourself. I continue to write my Journal. You may look forward with pleasure to the middle of June, when you will get many a Packet. Yours ever

JAMES BOSWELL

From Johnston, May 1763

Missing. JJ asked JB for his opinion of his conduct in a matter the nature of which it is impossible to conjecture from the comment in JB's letter below.

To Johnston, Saturday 28 May 1763

MS. Yale (L 706).

London, 28 May 1763

MY DEAR SIR: Our Corespondence is not now so frequent and regular, as when you was at Edinburgh. To account for this, I call in the aid of Simile. You must suppose that I resemble a Fowler. When you was in town, I had a full view of my game; I knew the exact place where you was. But now you are in the Country, I fire at Random into the Wood. You may be basking below an Oak at the Grange, or hopping about among the branches of a Plaintree at the Schaw. Nay who knows but what Miss Jenny in a benevolent and frolicsom humour may have taken you into the house, tenderly fed you, scratched your head, and laid you upon her bosom to enjoy soft repose. Indeed if that be the case, her benevolence must be very great; for her inducements to use you so kindly, are surely not owing to any perfections in you, which are discernible by the common run of Mankind. The Beauty of your shape and gay colour of your feathers are what I never yet could discover; altho' my senses are far from being dull. Neither have I been able to perceive any peculiar sweetness and delicate melody in your notes. Miss Graham is to be sure a Poetess,[1] and has a creative Imagina-

---

[6] *Ante* 28 Apr. 1763.

[1] Janet Graham (? 1724–1805), eldest daughter of William Graham of Shaw, wrote Scots dialect verse, "pieces of humour not to be sung but to be recited", according to Alexander Young of Harburn, whose father was minister of Hut-

ton parish and knew her well. But her best-known composition, *The Wayward Wife*, which Burns admired, was set to music and included in Herd's *Ancient and Modern Scottish Songs*, 1776, ii. 120–21. On the strength of it she finds her way into Joseph Irving's *Book of Scotsmen*, 1881 (p. 179), Frank Miller's *Poets of*

tion; So that she may fancy a thousand endearing qualitys in you, which neither Christopher Caruthers[2] nor I have ever had the happiness to discern. And thus my worthy friend have I indulged myself in fantastical Similitude, and if I began with making myself a fowler, I have not ended without making you a Bird.

Your Conduct in the affair about which you ask my opinion, was highly proper. I rejoyce to know that Matters turned out as you could wish. The Gratification of your Vanity was no trifling pleasure; altho' indeed I am not a fair judge, as I posess so great a share of that Passion.

By the time that this reaches you, I suppose you will be preparing for your return to Edinburgh. I wish you a good journey. All happiness attend you my honest friend, and ever believe me yours most sincerely

JAMES BOSWELL

To Johnston, Thursday 16 June 1763

MS. Yale (L 707).

London, 16 June 1763

MY DEAR FRIEND: I wrote to you some time ago, since I had your's from Shaw.[1] I hope you received it. I have expected a letter dated below a tree of your own planting; which was a pleasing romantic idea that you mentioned some time since.

Dumfriesshire, 1910 (pp. 159–60), and the DNB. By those who had known her personally, she was remembered for her "sprightly conversation, good humour, fine dancing, playful wit, and genuine humour" (W. R. Rogerson, *Hutton under the Muir,* 1908, p. 38).

On some occasion when JB was at Moffat, probably in May 1766 when he and JJ stayed there together (*post* 10, 21 May 1766), Janet Graham was also on a visit there. JB called on her and she later wrote to him "to express the gratitude I feel for your kind visit and friendly behaviour, it gave me great pleasure bothe on enjoyment and reflection. . . . I found a Strong inclination to Stay a day or two longer at Moffat but . . . I Suspected it was my duty to go home So you See how I have profited by your Sense of duty-

Doctrine I should certainly be ane adept in your reasonable System had I the happiness to be Some times with you, but I can see no chance for that till you come to Moffat again" (From Janet Graham, [?9] June [?1766]).

[2] Probably the eldest son of John Carruthers of Hardriggs. Christopher Carruthers, younger of Hardriggs, married Elizabeth Graham, and may have been connected through her with the Grahams of Shaw (A. S. Carruthers and R. C. Reid, *Records of the Carruthers Family,* 1934, p. 26). JJ employed JB as advocate on behalf of John Carruthers on at least two occasions (*post* 14 Jan. 1768; Journ. 3 Apr. 1777, 10 July 1779).

[1] *Ante* 28 Apr. 1763.

I fancy you are by this time returned to Edinburgh. However I have inclosed this to my Brother Davie to be delivered to you by himself. Pray take a charge of him; and pray go soon and see Charles, and let me know very particularly about him.

And now my friend I am to inform you that I have laid aside all thoughts of going into the army. I am disgusted with the neglect and hollowness of these great People from whom I expected great cordiality. Besides, I have lately had a most affectionate letter from my Father.[2] He is truly a worthy Man. I assure you he is. All his little mistakes are owing to a confined and narrow Education. He has set before me, both schemes, and he seems so very anxious to have me in a civil capacity, as his eldest Son, and in a creditable way in my own country; and he promises to give me all encouragement and mentions my getting into Parliament, as a noble Incitement.

When I think seriously and weigh all these considerations, I am fairly convinced that my pushing my Army Scheme, against so Many Obstacles, would be very hard, and as I would most certainly tire of it, in a few years, it would be very imprudent to run dissagreable hazards and to have the mortification of rendering my Father unhappy, for the transient indulgence of whim. I realy am of opinion that by putting on the gown and being in that proper way, I have the best chance for sollid and lasting satisfaction and for being able to serve my friends. However I have begged first to go abroad which I hope will be allowed as I could not well come down immediatly.[3] I may, after travelling come back a decent grave

[2] The letter is severe at the start. Lord Auchinleck reproaches JB for having kept the journal of his Harvest Jaunt and entrusted it to McQuhae, for having mimicked certain men of established position during his visits to the houses of friends in the south of Scotland, and for bringing, by his way of life, shame and distress to his parents. It ends with a piece of advice which, though partly aimed against McQuhae, must have appealed to JB, for he tried to follow it all his life: "I woud further recommend to you, to indeavour to find out some person of worth who may be a Friend, not one who will say as you say when with you and when he is away will make a Jest of you as much as of any other" (From Lord Auchinleck, 30 May 1763). Lord Auchinleck disclaims any desire to exert undue authority over JB, advises him to take the ensigncy offered him if he is still bent on an army career, and if on the other hand he is willing to take the wiser course of studying law, makes no objection to his going abroad for a time. Beneath its severity, the letter reveals the writer's affection for his son, and a remarkable understanding of JB's nature. For the full text, see *Lond. Journ.*, Appendix II.

[3] That JB had long been considering what his aim should be if he failed to obtain the coveted commission in the Guards is proved by his memorandum for 19 Feb. 1763: "Let your scheme be study and push Guards in the meantime

Man. My dear friend! I dare say you will be glad at my views, and glad to think that we shall sometime hence have our Saturday's Walks on Arthurseat. Write soon and full and believe me ever yours sincerely

JAMES BOSWELL

From Johnston, Monday 20 June 1763

MS. Yale (C 1621).

Edinr. 20th June 1763

MY DEAR SIR: Last week I called at Schaw in my way to Edinr. and there received your letter.[1] It diverted me not a little to receive it at the very place which you humorously introduce as the Scene of Action. Your former letter[2] was quite in the antiquarian Style which affected me much. I felt Sensibly for you; as I was altogether depressed at the time I received it, and often Since; I now begin to think it is better to Endeavour to reconcile ones Self to it,[3] than to get free of it; I came here on friday, and am not as yet fixed in a proper lodging, which makes me unhappy. I could not ornit acquainting you of my return to Edr. tho' I cannot write Seriously upon any Subject. Your Brother has just now called for me and delivered your letter.[4] I had only time to read it over in a hurry, will write you more fully in a few days and expect to hear from you on Saturday as usual and I am My Dear Sir Yours most Sincerely

JOHN JOHNSTON

From Johnston, Monday 27 June 1763

MS. Yale (C 1622).

Edinr. 27th June 1763

DEAR SIR: I have reflected Seriously upon your last letter,[1] acquainting me of your resolution to fix upon that plan of life, which you know I always wished you to pursue, but the many

---

as it is the most agreable to your inclinations. If it does not do, you can go to Holland etc. and push law—In the meantime be retenue and keep counsel."

[1] *Ante* 28 May 1763. JJ had just returned to town for the opening of

the Session, which was on Tuesday, 14 June.

[2] *Ante* 17 May 1763.
[3] That is, to hypochondria.
[4] *Ante* 16 June 1763.

[1] *Ante* 16 June 1763.

objections that you So Strongly Urged against it, rendered it impracticable for your friends to remove them. I do not think it will be any force upon your inclination to give up the thoughts of a Military life, as it was only that way of it, which could permit you to live in London, tha[t] you liked; You are now Convinced, That to procure a Com[missio]n in time of peace, will be very difficult, even tho' your friends were keen to Serve you, and to purchase one will require a Sum, which I am affraid you could not advance without my Lords assistance, and this you cannot expect he will ever Comply with; To Continue in London without any plan of life, must Shagreen him much, and might even force him in a short time to withdraw £100 of your annuity, which would render your living Scanty and uncomfortable, Besides the risque you run of his using that power he has now in his hands to your disadvantage.[2] In this Situation you ought not to reject My Lords proposal, as he has generously consented to your going abroad for two years, which I learned last night from your Brother John. You was extremely right to make that a Condition of your Complying with my Lords Scheme. It would never have answered to come down directly to Settle, after leaving this place so lately with a different view. My Dear Sir, let me not only Suggest, but advise you in the Strongest terms, Steadily to adhere to this plan, otherwise never embrace it. If you should fail, it is deceiving your father, and undoubtedly must Confirm the World of your unsteadiness and want of Resolution; The opinion of the World must not be despised. Whenever one Sinks in it's esteem, he must be unhappy, and rendered useless to his Country and friends; I Suppose the time will Soon be fixt for your leaving London, to have an Interview before you go away is what I cannot expect. It is with regrete I think of it. Our Correspondence in a great measure must Stop, the distance will not admit of it's being frequent, but I hope neither absence, nor Silence will ever cause indifference.

I have not Seen Cairnie, So can give no account of Charles. I will See him Soon. No doubt you'll leave orders for paying his Board etc. and wherein I can be usefull Command it; Did I write you formerly that I paid Mr. Hart's Acco[un]t before I went out of Town. Let me know if Love has repaid you the money; I always am My Dear Sir Yours Sincerely

JOHN JOHNSTON

[2] *Ante* 22 March 1763.

To Johnston, Thursday 30 June 1763

MS. Hyde Collection.

London, 30 June 1763

MY DEAR FRIEND: I have been dissapointed in not hearing from you, a second time, before now, and as I intended to answer that expected letter, I have delayed writing for a Post, or two.

I hope you approve of my plan of going abroad. I never could be able to make any thing of my Army schemes. My Father's rooted Aversion would have allways prevented me from rising in that way. By falling in with his schemes I make him easy and happy, and I have a better prospect of doing well in the World: As I will have no up hill work; but all will go smooth. I have had a letter[1] from my Father in which he expresses much Affection, and declares that he has not had so much satisfaction these four years. I wish from my heart that I may be able to make myself a Man, and to become steady and sensible in my Conduct. But alas this miserable melancholy is allways weighing me down, and rendering me indifferent to all pursuits. For these two days past, I have been very bad (owing to thick rainy weather) and have been viewing all things in the most dissagreable light. I have now got relief and am pretty easy and chearfull. I sympathise very heartily with your distress. It is indeed a most severe Affliction. You are right in thinking that we cannot drive it away. I advise you to study it carefully. Observe it's effects, and find out by what methods to render yourself tollerably easy while it lasts. What I want to do is to bring myself to that aequality of behaviour that whether my spirits are high or low, People may see little odds upon[2] me. I am perswaded that when I can restrain my flightiness, and keep an even external tenor, that my mind will attain a settled serenity. My Dear Friend! do all you can to keep free of it. Mix business and amusement, so that your mind may be allways employed and no time left for the gloomy broodings of a distempered fancy. My Father inclines that I should pass next Winter at Utrecht and after-

---

[1] The letter, dated 18 June 1763, written in his usual firm style with its Biblical inflections, reflects Lord Auchinleck's relief and delight at JB's decision. He and Sir David Dalrymple have planned that JB shall do as he himself proposes— go abroad at once and resume his studies at Utrecht. He commends Dalrymple and Pringle to JB as good friends on whose advice he may rely, and suggests that he should write to the Lord Advocate and to the Lord President and tell them of his new resolve.

[2] That is, difference in.

wards proceed thro' the south of Europe. At Utrecht I am told that I shall have a most beautifull City to live in. Very genteel People to be acquainted with; an opportunity of learning the french language and easy opportunity of jaunting about to the Hague, Roterdam and in short up and down all the seven Provinces. I am also to hear the lectures on civil law and put myself on the plan of acquiring a habit of Study and application. Too much of that would be bad for me. But Idleness is still worse. And now my friend Dont you think that I am upon a better plan than forcing myself into the Guards in time of peace where I should be continaly fighting—not against the french—but against my Father's Inclination? Don't you think too that I am now upon a more independent and extensive Plan; and that a Man with such a mind as I have, should rather embrace soft measures. My dear Johnston! you may figure the many spirited gay ideas which I entertain when I consider that I am now a young man of fortune just going to set out on his travels. That time which I have often at a distance looked forward to, is arrived. My Father wants to have me go as soon as possible. So that I shall set out in a Forthnight or less. As to my affairs, Love has payed me £10 and still owes me £30 which I believe I must allow to lie over a little. My Boy's maintenance I imagine will come to £10 a year.[3] I have a notion to make out three Bills each of that Sum which I will cause Love sign payable at different future terms and these I will indorse to you; so that you can be supplied from time to time. I am anxious to hear of Charles. Meet with Cairnie and get his accounts of him. I shall send you some Journal next Tuesday. You shall hear every Post from me now till I leave Britain. I ever am Your sincere friend,

JAMES BOSWELL

To Johnston, Saturday 2 July 1763

MS. Yale (L 708).

London, 2 July 1763

DEAR SIR: It gives me much Satisfaction to find by your letter of last Post,[1] that you are pleased with my embracing the sober prudent plan which my Father has allway been so anxiously bent

[3] C. B. Tinker notes: "In the good old days of Samuel Pepys, the care of an illegitimate child 'for ever' cost a man £5. Moll Flanders, it may be recalled, got rid of her child by an initial expense of £10" (*Young Boswell*, 1922, p. 24).

[1] *Ante* 27 June 1763.

on my pursuing. Indeed Johnston I found, by carefully making observations for a Winter in London, that the constant Repetition of gayety and dissipation would soon pall upon me. Some People are formed for nothing else, and so have ideas of nothing better. But I have got (as you know from being intimate with me) a mind that must have something more substantial. By following my Father's plan, I have the best chance for rational permanent felicity. And indeed, considering all the circumstances of my situation, I could not embrace any other, upon a respectable footing. My going abroad is a matter of great importance. To return to Scotland immediatly, would have appeared odd, and with all my easy assurance, I should have found it hard to have stood the ridicule which would have fall'n upon such inconsistent desultory conduct. I hope to return from abroad, a settled decent Man. I hope then to take a meditative walk with my friend upon Arthur's lofty Brow with infinite serenity and calm content. In the mean time, I shall study steadiness: and I don't despair of attaining it. Habit is all in all. When I am abroad, I will not have such temptations to foolish extravagant conduct; as I will be among Strangers, and so may take what character I chuse, and persist in it.

You have often asked after the Noble Lord of Annandale.[2] Poor Man! he is just in the same melancholy situation that he has been in for years. He is more calm; but there are no hopes of his Recovery. My friend Douglas[3] attends him, as Surgeon. I am in your debt for Hart's account and for the Stocks[4] which I think came to half a Guinea. I will take care that you be payed before I leave England. I ever am your affectionate Friend

JAMES BOSWELL

To Johnston, Tuesday 5 July 1763

MS. Yale (L 709).
ADDRESS: To Mr. John Johnston, to be left at Forrest's Coffeehouse, Edinburgh.
FRANK: Eglinton.
POSTMARK: 5 IY.
ENDORSEMENT: London 5th July 1763.

London, 5 July 1763

MY DEAR FRIEND: I am allways as good as my word. I said I would write to you, every post, while I remained in Britain; and

[2] *Ante* 7 Apr. 1763, n. 7.   [4] *Ante* 18 Jan. 1763.
[3] *Ante* 20 Nov. 1762, n. 3.

lo! have I something to say, or have I nothing to say, away goes a letter.

You must know that I am a good deal uneasy at hearing that Utrecht is a dull stiff starched place. I am affraid of growing melancholy there;[1] But to shift going to it, may vex my Father. I would hope that I may contrive to jaunt thro' the Provinces in Autumn; and pass the winter at Berlin. Alas my friend! I fear I am born to misery. I am at present dull to a severe degree. However, I hope allways the best. I ever am your's sincerely

JAMES BOSWELL

I send you a great quantity of Journal; even to the 610 Page.[2] You will be glad to have the usual entertainment renewed. I am affraid our Corespondence by and by, must be but seldom. However I am allways getting more Ideas.

To Johnston, Thursday 7 July 1763

MS. Yale (L 710).

London, 7 July 1763

DEAR SIR: If Ministers of State were as honest and as exact in fullfilling their engagements as I am, instead of being the detestation of mankind, they might be loved and esteemed. Some Posts ago I gave a promise of writing to you every time that he blew his horn with his face to the North, during my stay in Britain. And must you not own with that candour for which you have so long been conspicuous, and on account of which the eyes of the whole Nation are turned upon you, holding you up for a pattern as it were for universal Imitation; I say must you not own that I have kept, and am keeping my promise with the utmost exactness?

I have had a curious Adventure since I wrote you last. My Landlord has been very impertinent, and I have quitted his house.[1] My

---

[1] JB's resolution had rapidly weakened and already, by 29 June, he had been rendered gloomy by the mere mention of Utrecht. He heard "a dreary account of it" from the Judge Advocate, William Cochrane, who had just returned from Holland (Journ. 3 July 1763).

[2] The entry for 15 June ends at the bottom of p. 610. JB had been withholding the journal instalments until JJ should return to Edinburgh (ante 1 Mar. 1763).

---

[1] The Journal explains what had happened. Terrie had interrupted JB, on the evening of 5 July, while he was noisily entertaining Temple and his brother, Bob Temple, in his lodgings, and wrongly accusing them of having the maid with

friend Temple is gone to Cambridge, today for the Summer and has kindly insisted on my living in his Chambers; and accordingly I am now a *Master Ranger* a lively Templar.[2] I shall be here till I leave London.

You must now direct for me thus. "To James Boswell Esq: Inner Temple No. 10 opposite the Church, to the care of Mr. Edwards Stationer London." I ever am My Dear Sir your's sincerely

JAMES BOSWELL

Please meet with Cairnie, and give him my Address, and tell him I wish to hear from him.

I am now in charming spirits. All is gay and pleasant and happy. Would I could make the tour of Europe in such a frame!

To Johnston, Saturday 9 July 1763

MS. Yale (L 710).

Inner Temple, 9 July 1763

DEAR SIR: My Letters will now come upon you with a successive velocity equal to the rattling hail,[1] or the words of a talkative woman. Before you have read one, or at least before you have got it by heart, another will demand your attention. When you call at the Coffeehouse every Post night and ask, if there are any letters for you, the waiter's answer will be "O yes to be sure Sir. There is one from the person that allways writes." Such will be the answer which the waiter at Forrest's Coffeehouse will make to the question of John Johnston Esq: of Grange, when he enquireth for the letters of his friend James Boswell a Sojourner in foreign Countrys during the days of his Youth.

Many different views have I had of my schemes of travelling, within these few weeks. I have been told that Utrecht is a dull, formal, dissagreable place; and that I shall grow very melancholy

them, had called out the watch. JB had calmed him, but had been unable to take as strong a line of injured innocence as he would have liked, because he was using the parlour of the house, which, by agreement with Terrie, he had the right to occupy only in the mornings.

[2] "A *Master Ranger* a lively Templar" refers to the character Ranger in Hoadly's *The Suspicious Husband*; the play opens in his chambers in the Temple. See also *post* 23 July 1763, n. 1.

[1] Seventeen letters written by JB to JJ between 30 June and 4 Aug. have been preserved, 16 at Yale, one in the Hyde Collection.

there. I am also told that it is a pleasant City chearfull and polite, and much in the french taste. No wonder then that I have been fluctuating in my views of travelling. Doctor Pringle at first proposed that I should go to Berlin, which will undoubtedly be very agreable. But my Father wants to have me at Utrecht as a Place more grave and fit for Study. At Berlin I would have the advantages of being amongst men of Literature, and at the same time, the *Beau Monde* which allways must be where a court is. In short, I cannot as yet determine what I shall do. In the mean time, I shall go over to Holland, jaunt up and down the Low Countries, and if I can stay comfortably at Utrecht, I shall pass the Winter there. But if it is very horrid, I shall proceed to Berlin and there pass the Winter. I can settle matters easier, when abroad than when in England. I ever am yours sincerely

JAMES BOSWELL

I send you an excellent new song called *The Barber*[2] with which the Streets of this great City are at present loudly resounding. It is as popular as Wilkes himself.[3] If you can find out it's meaning, the

---

[2] A copy of this broadside ballad of six eight-line stanzas (perhaps the copy here referred to) is among the Boswell papers at Yale (P 5). The refrain "to be the barber" (repeated with variations twice in each stanza) illustrates Francis Grose's definition in *A Classical Dictionary of the Vulgar Tongue*, 1785: "A ridiculous and unmeaning phrase, in the mouths of the common people about the year 1760, signifying their approbation of any action, measure, or thing."

> Let all true Britons with me pray,
> That George may bear the regal sway,
> Old England he will give fair play,
>   For that will be the Barber.
> That harmony may still remain,
> And put each Briton out of pain,
> Defiance bid to France and Spain.
> Which always was the Barber.

The ballad, apart from the refrain, appears merely to combine conventional popular anti-Bute sentiment with equally conventional praise of Pitt and Wilkes. It is harder to explain the woodcut at the top, which shows a man with a saw amputating the legs of a bearded man strapped into a high-backed arm-chair. Perhaps the "barber" of the woodcut is Pitt and the bearded gentleman is Louis XV of France or Charles III of Spain; perhaps the cut has no real relation to the verses, being (as the costumes would suggest) an old one pressed into service merely because it shows a "barber". JB was so captivated by the piece that he soon afterwards composed a stanza on young Robert Temple in imitation of it (To W. J. Temple, 23 July 1763). In this he records the air ("Nancy Dawson"), which does not appear in the broadside itself.

[3] *The North Briton*, No. 45, in which Wilkes attacked the Speech from the Throne, had appeared on 23 Apr. The two Secretaries of State, Halifax and Egremont, had issued warrants for the arrest of the printers, and on their information had had Wilkes committed to the Tower, his house ransacked, and his papers seized. There was widespread doubt about the legality of a general warrant (i.e. a warrant which did not name the person or object required). Such proceedings against a member of Parliament were in any case irregular, and when

price viz 1/2 shall not be charged. It makes a hearty english laugh
I can assure you.

To Johnston, Tuesday 12 July 1763

MS. Yale (L 712).

Inner Temple, 12 July 1763

MY DEAR SIR: I dare say there are very few people who would
beleive that I am so exact a Corespondent. They would imagine
that if I resolved to write on the third day of the month, it would at
least be the thirteenth before I would put pen to paper. But my
writing every Post would appear as great an Impossibility as a
man's drinking up the firth of forth or eating up Arthur-Seat, or
the Castle of Edinburgh which in the year 1745 General Guest
bravely defended against five hundred highlanders with small
arms; for which act of valourous Conduct a noble monument is
erected to his memory in Westminster Abbey.[1]

Indeed my freind! you may testify that I am a man of exceeding
Accuracy and, that any Writer might take me as his Clerk, or any
merchant as his Bookkeeper.

Wilkes was released from the Tower on a habeas corpus, he instituted legal actions against Halifax and his under-secretary Wood. This affair, in which Wilkes met with such spirit the hostility of an unpopular government, made him the hero of the moment (Horace Bleackley, *Life of John Wilkes*, 1917, pp. 91 ff.).

[1] JB is probably ironical in his reference to the part played by Lt.-Gen. Joshua Guest (1660–1747) in the defence of Edinburgh Castle against Prince Charles's army. Guest, who was commander of the military forces in Edinburgh, received high commendation from the King at the time of his death, two years after the siege, when he was buried in Westminster Abbey. But there was a widespread popular belief in Scotland that the credit was due, not to Guest, but to his subordinate, Lt.-Gen. George Preston (?1659–1748) who had long been Deputy Governor of the Castle, but had been superseded by Guest in 1745, possibly because of some doubts about his loyalty if there were a Jacobite uprising. He remained in the Castle, however, as a volunteer.

In the event, when the Jacobite army reached Edinburgh, it was Guest, so the story went, who was lukewarm in his adherence to the Hanoverian cause and anxious to surrender the Castle, which he considered too weak to hold out, and Preston whose enthusiasm prevailed. Though he was 87 years old and had to be carried in his arm-chair, he is said to have visited the sentries and gun posts every two hours throughout the siege to strengthen the morale of his men (Robert Chambers, *History of the Rebellion in Scotland in 1745, 1746*, 1827, i. 191–95; James Grant, *Memorials of the Castle of Edinburgh*, 1850, pp. 221–39). Whatever the truth, Chambers records (p. 298 n. 3) that his information came partly from a member of the Preston family, so it was perhaps not entirely impartial. JB would naturally be inclined to accept the story current among his cousins the Prestons of Valleyfield, for General Preston had been a great-uncle of Sir George Preston.

Surely o Johnston thou hast discernment enough to perceive just now that I am not in the humour of writing: That I would fain write; and yet cannot do so with any ease. How unlike is this hammering to the free lively flow of many of those Epistles which you have received from me, since I left old Caledonia (for it is an elder Kingdom still than Old England itself)[2] which Letters I hope are laid up in safe Custody till I return to my native land. I have been patroling the City this forenoon. I have been upon the top of St. Paul's: And I have been buying a travelling trunk, from the famous trunk-maker at the corner of St. Paul's Churchyard. Sir William Maxwell of Springkell[3] is in town. He is just going abroad, but will not stay long. He and I are to pass the evening quietly by ourselves. He is a genteel man. He is an Annandale Knight. He will recall to me many pleasing ideas of his worthy Mother,[4] the English Border, diet loaf[5] and nonjurant Clergymen.[6] I remain your sincere friend

JAMES BOSWELL

To Johnston, Thursday 14 July 1763

MS. Yale (L 713).

Inner Temple, 14 July 1763

DEAR JOHNSTON: How curious is the Situation of a man who writes a letter every post! Perhaps indeed your honour may reply, Equaly curious is the Situation of a man who eats a Breakfast every

---

[2] The unification of Scotland took place under Kenneth MacAlpin, King of Scots, in 844; that of England during the Danish supremacy of the 11th century. But the reference is probably to dynasties rather than to territories, and the succession of Scottish kings, historical and legendary, is, of course, many centuries older than that of the kings of England. That this Scottish boast was a common subject of ridicule among the English at the time is suggested by the mocking references to it in *The North Briton*, No. 2 (12 June 1762) and No. 4 (26 June 1762).

[3] Sir William Maxwell of Springkell (1739–1804), 3rd Bt., one year older than JB, had succeeded to the baronetcy in 1760.

[4] Maxwell's mother, Catherine Doug-

las (c. 1707–61), daughter of Sir William Douglas of Kelhead, had been JB's first cousin. Her mother, Helen Erskine, was the half-sister of JB's mother, Euphemia Erskine.

[5] A light and wholesome Scots delicacy very like what is nowadays called Madeira cake, or sponge cake.

[6] After 1748, and until 1792, all clergy of the Episcopal Church in Scotland necessarily "non-jurant" because by statute they were declared incapable of qualifying. The Springkell family were Jacobite in sympathy, and Dr. William Garioch, who had been tutor to the family for two generations, was an uncompromising non-juror and high churchman (Journ. 7 Oct. 1762).

morning. Judicious indeed tho' you are in the highest degree, yet I must be forgiven for differing in opinion from you upon this occasion, nor could any thing convince me that you are in the right, except my seeing you in a full-bottomed Periwig, like a Lord Chief Baron of his Majesty's Exchecquer.[1] Till that happy time arrives, I must remain as confident upon the one side, as you are upon the other.

Indeed Johnston, bottling small beer is not so frivolous a matter as some People of shallow understandings imagine. Corks must be had my friend. Those Corks must be nicely cut, and well adjusted to the mouths of the Bottles; and I can assure you that no mean degree of strength is required in order to fix them properly. If then bottling small beer, be so difficult a matter, how much more so, o Johnston! is the writing of a Letter. Many a sermon have I heard preached by Presbyterian Ministers. Many have been their allusions, and many their Conclusions. In imitation of those reverend Guides have I diligently penn-ed[2] these two pages which thou hast just now read. I realy don't know whether or not it is right in me to indulge myself in writing in this stile of ludicrous extravagance, now when I am resolved to become a grave composed prudent man; An A.M. and an I.C.[3] However, among friends, *Dulce est desipere*;[4] and while I can restrain folly, except when with my freinds, or when writing to them, I shall have a very good opinion of myself.

Farewell My Dear Johnston and beleive me ever your's with much Sincerity

JAMES BOSWELL

[1] The judges of the Court of Exchequer were known as Barons. In Scotland there was a Lord Chief Baron, at this time Robert Ord (d. 1778), a Newcastle-born man, and four puisne-Barons (*Universal Scots Almanack*, 1763, p. 57).

[2] JB here introduces the hyphen to imitate the minister's manner of speaking. Cf. Journ. 6 Apr. 1772.

[3] *Artium Magister* and *Iuris consultus*. JB states in his biographical *Memoirs* (*Europ. Mag.*, 1791, p. 323; *Lit. Car.*,

p. xxix) that he "went through the regular course of the College of Edinburgh". As was very usual in his day, he did not go through the formality of graduating A.M., but he may now have been thinking of taking his degree, as well as being admitted advocate, on his return to Scotland.

[4] Horace, *Odes* IV. xii. 28. *Dulce est desipere in loco* ("It is pleasant to play the fool on a proper occasion").

To Johnston, Saturday 16 July 1763

MS. Yale (L 714).

Inner Temple, 16 July 1763

DEAR SIR: My last letter was of the humourous kind. This must not be so. It would be like forcing two Syllabubs[1] down a man's throat when he had only a mind for one; or perhaps it would be like forcing a man to marry two Wives, when he would gladly be free from them both. This last likeness I must retract, for indeed Johnston I beleive you have no aversion at receiving a letter from me, and were you sure that a wife would give you as much entertainment and as little trouble, I am perswaded that you would marry tomorrow. But indeed my friend there is a very great difference between a Letter and a Wife. A Letter may be transported from one end of the Kingdom to another, in the slight vehicle of a piece of paper; and if we know a member of Parliament, it will cost us nothing. But a Wife cannot be moved even a few miles without a Post-Chaise, or some other wheel Carriage; and altho' we are intimate with both the houses of Lords and Commons, we can never have our Spouses to travel gratis. A Letter is a silent Companion. A Wife a noisy one. If a Letter displeases us, we can tear it in pieces, or throw it into the fire, or apply it to other purposes; But should we tear even the hair of a Wife, or burn one of her fingers, a terrible uproar would immediatly ensue. The peace of the family is broke, would be the dolefull cry. and perhaps a criminal Prosecution might be commenced and a severe Judge might oblige us to pay costs and damages. A Letter allways remains of the same size and is never known to multiply. But a Wife swells to an enormous magnitude, and brings forth many more Beings of her own species. A Letter neither requires meat nor Cloaths. But a Wife must have a sufficient share of both; especialy of the Latter. They have indeed some circumstances in common. A Letter is of a frail contexture. So is a Wife. We are jealous of another man's reading our Letters: And we are jealous of another man's kissing our Wives. When we first receive a Letter, we are fondest of it, and see most Beauties in it: And when we first marry a Wife, we like her best, and see most charms about her. A Wife indeed may have a very substantial advantage over a Letter. A

---

[1] A dish, or a drink, made of cream or milk curdled with wine or some other acid, and sweetened and flavoured (OED).

Letter can never posess a handsom fortune in it's own Person and convey it to us. But a Wife may. When such a Wife shall present herself, with tollerable qualifications besides, then o Johnston! do you enter into the honourable estate of Matrimony, till which happy time I remain your most sincere friend

JAMES BOSWELL

To Johnston, Tuesday 19 July 1763

MS. Yale (L 715).

Inner Temple, 19 July 1763

MY HONEST JOHNSTON: I am going to recall a chain of curious ideas. I am going back to the time when I was first acquainted with you, when you had a straw-coloured lining to your coat and I thought you quite the genteel Gentleman. When you used to walk to Lieth with Mr. Dun[1] and me on a Saturday come in by the

---

[1] This passage presents a baffling problem in chronology, important for the present correspondence because it may have a bearing on the question as to when JB and JJ first became acquainted. It appears to refer to repeated Saturday excursions by JB, JJ, and Dun at a time when Dun was domiciled with the Boswells ("go home with us . . . our room") and the intimacy between JB and JJ was in its earliest stages ("when I was first acquainted with you"). John Dun (b. 1724) was domestic tutor to JB for four years, apparently from the autumn of 1748 to the autumn of 1752, and may well have shared a room with him (see Journ. 7 Nov. 1762). In the "Ébauche de ma vie" (L 1107) which JB wrote for Rousseau, 5 Dec. 1764, JB says he was under Dun's tuition "de huit a douze"; also, "Quand J'avois douze ans mon premier Gouverneur recut le charge de Ministre, et on me donnoit un autre Gouverneur". Dun was ordained minister of Auchinleck 9 Nov. 1752 and held the charge till his death in 1792 (*Fasti Scot.* iii. 4). Consequently, if JB and JJ became acquainted while Dun was still JB's tutor, their acquaintance must have gone back to at least the summer of 1752, when JB was not yet twelve years old. But all the other evidence we have indicates that their intimacy, at least, did not begin before the autumn of 1755. The "Ébauche de ma vie", in the section specifically devoted to the years at Edinburgh University, speaks of JB's slowness in forming friendships, and continues, "Á la fin, Je me suis lié avec un Anglois nommé Temple . . . et avec un Ecossois nommé Johnston". JB undoubtedly met Temple in Robert Hunter's Greek class, 1755–56, and the John Johnston whose signature appears in the roll of that class was almost certainly JJ. Also, in the published Erskine correspondence, JB remarks that his intimacy with JJ has endured "more years than the Egyptian famine lasted" (p. 107). The phrase is not in the original letter (9 May 1762), but it was probably accurate for the date in early 1763 when JB wrote it, and points again (though admittedly more vaguely) to the year 1755. The easiest solution to the problem would be to assume that JB wrote "Dun" when he really meant "Fergusson", but this is not very plau-

Abbeyclose and eat Mrs. Bird's tarts,[2] and then go home with us, set yourself down in an easy chair in our room and stretching out your legs with a pleasing languor look out at the Window to the lofty Arthur-Seat on which the silver moon would softly shine; while a pleasing mixture of Edinburgh and Annandale ideas would fill your mind. You would call up the old Scotch Kings in your Imagination, and you would think of their courts and guards stately Men and lovely Women with lines of black hair down their backs like Lady Mary Douglas.[3] You would also think of the Lochwood[4] and the *auld Lairds* of Johnston; of fine buxom lasses milking their ewes on the banks of the Water of the Milk.[5] In short you was a very happy being.

My Dear Johnston! A Gentleman of Lincoln's Inn is just come in.[6] I must entertain him; and so you must excuse my not giving

sible, for Dun clearly did know JJ quite well (*post* 20 Oct. 1771, n. 11). Perhaps in the early years of his ministry Dun paid the Boswells extended visits in Edinburgh. An appropriate time for such visits would have been the meetings of the General Assembly in May.

JB's general attitude towards Dun after boyhood was rather one of esteem than of affection. He paid tribute to him for awakening his love of literature and for mitigating the harsh and gloomy ideas of religion which he had acquired from the services of the Kirk and his mother's earnestly Calvinistic instruction, but he deplored the coarseness of Dun's breeding and his consequent limitations as a preceptor of manners ("Ébauche de ma vie").

[2] In quite incongruous surroundings, at a spectacular firework-display in a Berlin park, JB, who was feeling flat and a little homesick, had the sudden association of ideas: "Cannongate—Johnston—Mrs. Bird's Tarts" (Journ. 9 Sept 1764). Mrs. Bird has not been further identified.

[3] JB does not record having met Lady Mary Douglas at any time, but he mentions that he heard her spoken of at Kames: "A sudden scheme gleamed upon me of marrying this Lady whom, by the by, I never have seen. She is daughter to the Earl of Morton, is about five and twenty, well-look'd sensible and polite,

with a fortune of £15,000. I considered, that by marrying her, I should gain an acquisition to the family of Auchinleck; that I should have opulence and respect, and that my children Should have some of the blood of the Douglasses. . . . Lady Mary is to be in London with her Father in Winter. I may then have an eye upon her" (Journ. 24 Oct. 1762). She married in 1774 Charles Gordon, 4th Earl of Aboyne, and died in 1816.

[4] The Tower of Lochwood, surrounded by a wood of old oak-trees, had been formerly the family seat of JJ's forbears, the ancestors of the Marquess of Annandale. It had been abandoned in 1724 for the house of Raehills nearby, and had become a ruin.

[5] The estate of Grange is skirted by the Water of Milk, a small tributary of the Annan which forms part of the boundary of Tundergarth parish.

[6] "I sat in all the afternoon at french, and writing letters. Claxton came and past the evening with me" (Journ. 19 July 1763). John Claxton was a friend of Temple's. He was admitted to Lincoln's Inn in 1758 as "of Great Ormond Street, son of Brown Claxton, deceased" (*Lincoln's Inn Admission Register, 1420-1893*). Subsequently, in 1772, he was made a Fellow of the Society of Antiquaries.

you some more curious ideas. But next post you may depend on having a Bushel of them. I ever am your's sincerely

JAMES BOSWELL

Pray write me particularly if my letters are kept and if you have 'em neatly lay'd up in their order.

To Johnston, Wednesday 20 July 1763

MS. Yale (L 716).

ADDRESS: To Mr. John Johnston, Writer in Edinburgh.

NOTE BY JB: With £2.7.

ENDORSEMENTS: Inner Temple 20th July 1763. 25th Aug. 1763. Recd. the within Sum of £2.7. Sh. from Mr. Boswell.

Inner Temple, 20 July 1763

MY DEAR SIR: You have heard of extraordinary gazettes, and extraordinary *North-Britons*,[1] This then is an extraordinary Letter. It comes by my Uncle Doctor Boswell,[2] who came up to London, some weeks ago, by sea, and is now about to return on the surface of the same Element. He is a worthy amiable man, altho' it must be owned that he has very near as much levity as your humble Servant. However, I could wish that you and he were acquainted. He and I are quite hand and Glove. That to you may be some recommendation of him. He is a great Virtuoso. His collection of Shells and Pebbles will amuse you greatly.[3] He is hospitable, and affectionate, and generous, and worth a thousand of your cold-blooded prudent cunning people who have done much better in the world.

[1] *A North Briton Extraordinary, which was Printed, but never Published* was dated 7 Apr. 1763. It was followed by such pamphlets as *A North Briton Singular and Extraordinary*, Apr. 16, *An Extraordinary North Briton*, May 12, *The North Briton Extraordinary*, May 17 (*The Polit. Controversy or Weekly Mag.*, 1763, iv. 46, 172, 211).

[2] John Boswell (1710–80), a doctor in Edinburgh, was Lord Auchinleck's younger brother. He took the degree M.D. at Leyden and was later President of the Royal College of Physicians in Edinburgh. The close now known as Boswell's Court, on the south side of the Castle Hill, owes its name to the fact that he had a house there (*Book of the Old Edinburgh Club*, 1923, xii. 52). In his sociability, and a certain waywardness of character, he resembled JB, who found his company congenial.

[3] Dr. Boswell showed "his curious museum" to Dr. Johnson when he was in Edinburgh in Nov. 1773 (*Tour*, p. 385). Three years later, when he had fallen upon hard times, he told JB that he had been offered £200 for his "curiosities" (To Dr. John Boswell, 30 Aug. 1776).

	£	s
I owe you for Shoes	1–	16
and for Stocks——	–	11
	£2–	7

I have sent the money by the Doctor, who will pay it you.[4] This is quite a letter of Business, and so (as the King says) we bid you heartily farewell. Your's with much truth

JAMES BOSWELL

To Johnston, Thursday 21 July 1763

MS. Yale (L 717).

Inner Temple, 21 July 1763

MY DEAR JOHNSTON: I promised thee in my last interrupted Epistle,[1] a Bushel more of curious ideas. I don't know if I shall be able to give you full measure; But I shall give you what I have; and as most dealers do, I may perhaps mix up a good deal of chaff with my Wheat. However, take them as they come.

The ideas which you and I like best are not your lofty and your pompous matters. We are fond of recalling such circumstances as have marked our Seasons of happiness of any kind. And sure it is that happiness is often produced by casual and inconsiderable little Affairs.

I would therefore Oh! my friend! remind you of the many tea-drinking afternoons which we have past both in your room and mine, both in the Lawn market Don's Close and the Parliament Close.[2] I would remind you of Mr. Joseph Fergusson, of his velvet bretches, his grizly Wig and his Speech concerning Kate Straton:[3] Of his systematical morality which he learnt from Professor

[4] Three months later Dr. Boswell wrote to JB in Holland: "I deliver'd your Letter and pd the money mention'd to your Friend Mr. Johnston and finde him a Man according to our own hearts after the Flesh. and hope to have him for an agreeable Friend so long as I shall stay here. He is now att Annandale. I bid him send his letters either to me (for you) or to direct them for you as I've done this" (From Dr. John Boswell, 17 Oct. 1763).

[1] *Ante* 19 July 1763.

[2] When JB first knew him, JJ had had lodgings in the Lawnmarket (*ante* 7 Apr. 1763, n. 1). Later he had lived in Don's Close, which ran north from the High Street, near the Luckenbooths (Edgar's Map of Edinburgh, 1765; *The Book of the Old Edinburgh Club*, 1923, xii. 26–27). Parliament Close, otherwise Parliament Square, was where Lord Auchinleck had his town house in the tenement known as Blair's Land.

[3] Kate Straton has not been identified

Hutchison,[4] his excellent Equivocations, and his bawdy narrations. I would remind you of your being at Auchinleck,[5] of your jaunting about thro' the miry clay to My Lord Dumfries's[6] and to Mr. Whitefoord's,[7] of our comfortable evenings over negoes[8] with that great Philosopher and Divine, Doctor William Mcquhae, and of our merry and humourous flights with that most renowned Naturalist Mr. James Bruce.[9] I would remind you of the loud laughs, the serious romantic conversations, and the indolent luxurious morning Slumbers which we then enjoyed. I would remind you, of the many wild reveries which you have heard me utter; of the dreary marriages which I have escaped,[10] of the many

[4] Francis Hutcheson (1694–1746) delivered his influential lectures on religion and morals while occupying the Chair of Moral Philosophy at Glasgow University between 1729 and 1746. Fergusson was a student at Edinburgh University but is not known to have studied in Glasgow. He was no doubt influenced by Hutcheson's publications, and JB seems here to hint in particular at *A System of Moral Philosophy*, which was published posthumously in 1755.

[5] *Ante* 22 Sept. 1760, 21 Aug. 1761.

[6] William Dalrymple-Crichton (d. 1768), 4th Earl of Dumfries and Stair, lived at Dumfries House in Ayrshire, between two and three miles SE. of Auchinleck House. The Notes record their dining with Lord Dumfries on 11 Sept. 1761: "I was very happy to see Johnston in the grand magnificent hall with the pompous Earl."

[7] Allan Whitefoord (d. 1766), of Ballochmyle, which is about 2½ miles to the NE. of Auchinleck House, entertained JB and JJ to breakfast on 11 Sept. 1761 and to dinner, "genteelly and hospitably", the next day (Notes). Second son of Sir Adam Whitefoord of Blairquhan, 1st Bt., he was a close friend of Lord Auchinleck, to whom he was distantly related through his mother, a daughter of the 7th Lord Cathcart. On the day of JB's birth, 18 Oct. 1740, O.S., his baptism was witnessed by three of his father's special friends, Dr. John Pringle, Walter Macfarlane of that ilk, and Allan Whitefoord (Edinburgh Baptismal Register,

as quoted in *Notes & Queries*, 3rd series, vii. 197). Whitefoord had achieved worldly success as an executive officer of the Royal Bank of Scotland and also for many years held the Crown office of Receiver-General of the Land Tax of Scotland. About the year 1750 he bought the estate of Ballochmyle, which he left, on his death, unmarried, to his nephew, Sir John Whitefoord, 3rd Bt. (*post* 22 Mar. 1780; *Whitefoord Papers*, ed. Hewins, 1898, xv; James Paterson, *Hist. of . . . Ayr and Wigton*, 1864, ii. 469; *Comp. Bar.* iv. 400).

[8] Usually spelt *negus*: a drink made of hot sweetened wine and water.

[9] Mr. McQuhae is not mentioned anywhere in the record of JJ's visit to Auchinleck in 1761, but he was probably there, for he would naturally have accompanied David, his pupil, to Auchinleck with the family as soon as the Session rose in August. JB's note for 3 Oct. 1761 (following a gap, 27 Sept.–2 Oct.) reads "At Grange. Rode with Mr. McQuhae"—i.e. JB and McQuhae had ridden over to repay JJ's visit.

James Bruce was gardener and later overseer at Auchinleck (*ante* 15 Feb. 1763, n. 7). JB had a great respect and affection for him and referred to him after his death as "a kind of friend and tutor" (Journ. 23 Aug. 1790).

[10] In several letters written in the autumn of 1761 (To the Earl of [Eglinton], 25 Sept. 1761, *Scots Mag.*, xxiii. 469–71; To Andrew Erskine, 17 Nov. 1761, 22 Jan. 1762), JB jests about

plans for life which have played upon my Imagination and which I have with unreserved confidence disclosed to You. I would remind you of my various mad projects to get back to London; of my leaving Scotland at last; of your coming to Edinburgh after I was gone; and of all that you have heard of me since.

My Dear friend you can scarcely imagine how happy I am at present. The Temple is a Residence worthy of an Addison of a genuine Spectator.

I am enjoying perfect felicity. But the time is fast approaching, when I must leave dear London, and embark for distant Regions. However, I shall comfort myself that I am getting more ideas on which I may feast my mind thro' the whole of after life. I send you a couple of *North Britons* No. 51.[11] I beleive the Scandal on the President and Justice Clerk is very false.[12] I remain yours most sincerely

JAMES BOSWELL

schemes, not of his own making, for getting him married. The young lady he was referring to was Katharine Colquhoun (1742–1804), eldest daughter of Sir James Colquhoun of Luss, 1st Bt., and at least one of the poems he was then writing is addressed to her: "To Miss Kitty C——" (Donaldson's *Collection*, ii. 81; Bodleian Douce MS. 193, folios 39, 39 verso). In his journal a year later JB adds another name: "I considered how much happier I was than if I had been married last year to Miss Colquhoun or Miss Bruce and been a poor regular animal tied down to one. I thanked Johnston for his kind advices" (Journ. 30 Nov. 1762). If the marriages were as practicable as this sounds, they must have had Lord Auchinleck's approval, not to say backing. Miss Bruce is not yet identified from among several eligible young ladies of that name, but Lord Auchinleck certainly knew Miss Colquhoun, for he was one of the trustees under her mother's marriage contract (William Fraser, *The Chiefs of Colquhoun and their Country*, 1869, i. 349). The diary jottings made between Nov. 1761 and Apr. 1762 show JB in frequent attendance, not only on Miss Colquhoun and Miss Bruce, but also on Miss Isabella

Thomson and (to a lesser extent) on Miss Margaret Stewart. He perhaps saw more of Miss Thomson, daughter of Dr. David Thomson, than of any of the others, but he appears nowhere to have recorded matrimonial inclinations towards her. On 28 Nov. 1762 she married Captain Frederick Bridges Schaw (*Edinburgh Marriage Register, 1751–1800*, p. 702); JB's journal of 15 Mar. 1763 records their meeting again in London a few months later and gives a short sketch of her character. Miss Margaret Stewart (c. 1742–1816) was the eldest daughter of Sir Michael Stewart of Blackhall, 3rd Bt. In a later letter in the present series (23 Sept. 1763) JB professes to have considered her the woman he would marry, if he were to marry. Both she and Miss Colquhoun were married in 1764, while JB was at Utrecht (*post* 11 May 1765, n. 11).

[11] Published 2 July 1763: one of the series which Sumpter brought out without Wilkes's assent, as a continuation of Wilkes's *North Briton*.

[12] *The North Briton*, No. 51, attacks Scottish institutions, in particular the Court of Session and the Faculty of Advocates, and accuses the Scottish legal

To Johnston, Saturday 23 July 1763

MS. Yale (L 718).

Inner Temple, 23 July 1763

MY DEAR SIR: The Imagination of a man is not like his Purse, which when you have taken so much out of it, is empty and of itself can yield no more. It rather resembles the Blood-Vessels which are no sooner sufficiently empty'd than they begin a-filling again, and in a short time, are as ready to yield up the stream of life as they were before. I think I have rather hit upon a bad allusion, at present; however as it is fairly down, let it go; Perhaps, Johnston, it may do as well as a Better. My writing you a letter of more than one page, every post, is a pretty strong proof of the fertility of *my* Imagination. Indeed it may be a fertility of weeds; a fertility which I believe I may presume (without offence) is sometimes to be observed upon the lands of Grange, altho' it is never found in the imagination of it's Laird.

profession of Jacobite tendencies. It alleges that, towards the end of Queen Anne's reign, the Faculty of Advocates ordered a medal to be struck, representing the restoration of the Pretender, which was offered to the Queen as a pledge of loyalty to the House of Stuart; and by naming as the then Dean of Faculty Robert Dundas, later (1748–53) Lord President and father of the Lord President of the day, singles him out for special "scandal". As further proof of the Faculty's disaffection, it tells an anecdote about James Erskine, Lord Justice-Clerk from 1710 to 1714, who lived "in the North of Scotland, by the shore of the narrow seas which wash the eastern coast of that kingdom, and the western of Sweden and Denmark", and who is said to have been seen by his neighbours eagerly scanning the ocean for signs of an invading fleet in order that he might be the first to welcome it.

A letter from Sir David Dalrymple (7 July 1763) which JB had received shortly before writing the present one, comments adequately on these charges: "Have you seen the North Briton No. 51. If it is the composition of Mr. Wilkes he has exposed himself beyond emendation. The two storys of President Arniston and of

the late Justice Clerk are ridiculously false, and occasion much mirth here." An anonymous pamphlet later pointed out that the medal, with the Pretender's head on it, had been presented as a gift to the Faculty by the Dowager Duchess of Gordon, daughter of the Duke of Norfolk, but that its reception by the Faculty had been opposed by the Dean (Robert Bennet) and many others, and agreed to only because it came from "the first Englishwoman of the nation". "All you write of Mr. Erskine, the late Lord Justice Clerk", it continues, "and of the narrow seas which wash the eastern coast of Scotland, betrays ignorance of him, and ignorance of geography" (*A Second Letter to the Author of the North Briton*, 1763). See also G. W. T. Omond, *The Lord Advocates of Scotland*, 1883, i. 291–95 for details of this affair. The year was 1711. Robert Dundas was not Dean. The Dundas concerned (he was not Dean either) was his elder brother, James Dundas, younger of Arniston. James's part in favouring the acceptance of the medal led to his prosecution on a charge of sedition. The prosecution was ultimately abandoned, but his career was ruined.

I am still living in my calm and pleasing chambers in the Inner Temple. I have a thousand agreable ideas which I have formed in my youth of this ancient Seat of Retirement, where so many of the brave Knights of Jerusalem have whilome dwelt[1] and where the Spectator's ingenious friend[2] fixed his Residence. Indeed I can figure no place better fitted for Study and Meditation. Then how great an Advantage have we that after conversing with the silent Sages of Antiquity we can immediatly be with the Literati of modern times; after forming agreable Theorys, we can enter into the great world of London, and have all opportunitys of practice. Indeed Johnston this is so very comfortable a life, that I question if I shall ever be happier in any stage of my present Existence. Had I but you and Temple near me, my felicity would be rather too great for mortality.

I have had letters from Scotland last Post; but my time for leaving London is not-yet fixed. However it cannot be long now before I breathe the air of another Climate. Sir David Dalrymple[3] tells me that I have got very false ideas of Utrecht. So that I hope to be very happy there, and to reap a good deal of Advantage.

My good friend! many an hour will you think of me and many an amusive idea will you feast upon. You will be thinking of my realy seeing those scenes which We have heard so much of, and you will be thinking of the rich fund of materials which I will bring home to entertain you with. I shall certainly take *Addison's Travels*[4] with me, as you hint. I shall read them abroad, with high relish.

The mother of Charles is in town. I have seen her and have got fine accounts of my little Boy.[5] God bless him. I hope he shall be

---

[1] *Ante* 7 July 1763, n. 2. The property known as the Temple had formerly belonged to, and derived its name from, the medieval Order of Knights Templar, founded in Jerusalem to protect pilgrims to the Holy Sepulchre.

[2] "The Gentleman next in Esteem and Authority among us, is another Batchelour, who is a Member of the *Inner Temple*; a Man of great Probity, Wit, and Understanding . . ." (*Spectator*, No. 2, 2 Mar. 1711).

[3] Sir David Dalrymple (1726–92), who took a sympathetic interest in the son of his friend Lord Auchinleck, had

himself studied law at Utrecht. It was a common thing for Scottish students to take a further course at a Dutch university after completing their law studies at home, and Lord Auchinleck had himself been at Leyden. Dalrymple's letter, dated 18 July, is extant.

[4] Joseph Addison, *Remarks on Several Parts of Italy, etc. in the Years 1701, 1702, 1703*, first appeared in 1705; there were at least nine printings in England before 1763.

[5] "Peggy Doig the Mother of my little boy is in town. I have seen her and advised her not to fall into such a scrape

happy. I wish I could but see him. Remember me kindly to Mr. Cairnie. Beleive me My Dear Johnston ever your's with much sincerity of affection

JAMES BOSWELL

To Johnston, Tuesday 26 July 1763

MS. Yale (L 719).

Inner Temple, 26 July 1763

MY DEAR JOHNSTON: Were your indolent Personage in my place just now, you would scarcely sit down to write a letter even to your most intimate friend. I shall briefly tell you the circumstances. I sat up all last night writing Epistles of an uncommon kind—for me—that is to say to my Lord President, my Lord Advocate, Mr. Fergusson of Pitfour,[1] all about my important self; and indeed Johnston since I have taken it into my head to prefer the rational plan, I may, without joking, turn out a man of some importance. But only think of a man who has written these Epistles; besides several more to Lord Kames,[2] Commissioner Cochrane[3] and my Mother; and who has been wandering all day up and down the

again. I realy don't know how to talk on such a Subject, when I consider that I led her into the Scrape. However, it was not the first time; and she has been well taken care of" (Journ. 28 July 1763).

---

[1] The Lord President at the time was Robert Dundas of Arniston (1713–87), who had himself studied at Utrecht. The Lord Advocate was Thomas Miller (1717–89). James Ferguson of Pitfour (c. 1701–77) was to be promoted to the bench in the following year as Lord Pitfour (*College of Justice*, pp. 523, 527, 530).

It was Lord Auchinleck himself who had advised his son that it would be proper for him to inform the first two legal dignitaries of the change in his plans for his future (From Lord Auchinleck, 18 June and 23 July 1763). The letter to James Ferguson of Pitfour was to similar purpose, for he had been Dean of Faculty since 1760. See Journal 29 July 1763 for some particulars of the contents of these three letters.

[2] Since coming to London, JB had kept in correspondence with Lord and Lady Kames (*ante* 27 Oct. 1762, n. 4). His journal notes for 1761 and 1762 show that he had spent much time with them at their Edinburgh house, and Lady Kames wrote, soon after he left Edinburgh, how much he was missed by all at their Sunday night parties. In fact, the company present had dwindled so much that "I begin to think they have formerly come for you". Her husband's surviving letters are friendly and contain good advice to JB on his behaviour and future, conveyed in a manner which shows the sympathy felt by the old eccentric for the young one (From Lady Kames, 28 Dec. 1762; from Lord Kames, 5 Dec. 1762, 27 Mar., 16 July 1763). Their attitude towards JB changed somewhat after his return to Scotland in 1766, but he remained on reasonably friendly terms with them until the death of Lord Kames in 1782.

[3] *Ante* n. 3 of second letter of 14 Dec. 1762.

Citys of London and Westminster in quest of French Servants and English Poets,[4] can such a man with any colour of reason, be called upon to write a fresh letter not altogether stupid, at seven oclock in the evening. Why at seven in the evening you would have been stretched at full length upon the soft featherbed, with your warm tea, your milk-bakes and your currant jelly on a little table before you, while Abercrombie's *Scots Warriors*[5] and Goodal's *Queen Mary*[6] would have been cordialy placed upon your pillow. It is not improbable but what little Mr. Duchat the popish priest[7] might have come in, layd by his hat and his Stick, taken his chair close by the fire, and drank a dish of good green[8] well sweetned, to chear his heart and then told you many amusive anecdotes of his travels abroad, interrupting his narration now and then with tother pinch of well-scented Rapee a sure sign of a sound high churchman.

While he talk'd of foreign parts, you would think with the warmth of affectionate friendship on him who now writes to you one of the last letters which you will receive from me before I leave England. I send you your usual allowance of Journal for a

[4] "English poets" probably refers to a copy of Gray's *Poems* for which Temple had asked in response to JB's proposal to give him a parting gift (From W. J. Temple, 24 July 1763).

[5] *The Martial Atchievements of the Scots Nation. Being an Account of the Lives, Characters, and memorable Actions, of such Scotsmen as have signaliz'd themselves by the Sword at Home and Abroad. And a Survey of the Military Transactions wherein Scotland or Scotsmen have been remarkably concern'd, from the first Establishment of the Scots Monarchy to the present Time*, Patrick Abercromby's monumental work, appeared in two large folio volumes in 1711 and 1715.

[6] *An Examination of the Letters said to be written by Mary Queen of Scots to James, Earl of Bothwell*, by Walter Goodall (c. 1706–66), was published in two volumes in 1754. By adopting an apologist attitude towards Queen Mary, Goodall inaugurated the phase of romantic writing about her character and career which produced in time the popular conceptions of her as a martyred saint or tragic heroine.

[7] This is the only mention of M.

Duchat in JB's extant writings, and it suggests a vivid memory shared with JJ. There may here be a glimpse into something connected with the shadowy episode of JB's short-lived conversion to Catholicism, which led him to run away to London in 1760 and directed his mind at that time towards a monastic life in France. In the published lists of the Catholic missionaries in Edinburgh during the 1750's, and among the Scots College MSS. preserved at St. Mary's College, Blairs, the name does not occur, but many of the priests of the time were obliged to adopt aliases. A guess may be hazarded that M. Duchat was Joseph Duguid (1713–75), who studied at Douai, in Spain, and at Rome. He joined the Jesuit order in 1731, studied further at Douai, and joined the Scottish mission in 1742. He became a Professed Father in 1747. In 1763 he was one of three Roman Catholic missionaries assigned to the region of Edinburgh, where he and his two associates ministered to a total congregation of about 310 persons (J. F. S. Gordon, *Ecclesiastical Chronicle for Scotland*, 1867, iv. 542, 636).

[8] That is, a dish of green tea.

week: 24 good pages. It is now up at 678.[9] I shall leave it exactly 700 pages when I set out upon my travels. I am angry at you, Johnston, for not giving me a particular enough account how you have layd it up. You know my foolish anxiety about these little matters. Pray humour me. And now Johnston once more I subscribe myself what I hope to do a thousand times before I die, your affectionate Friend

JAMES BOSWELL

To Johnston, Thursday 28 July 1763

MS. Yale (L 720).

Inner Temple, 28 July 1763

MY DEAR SIR: However lightly you may think of the matter, I can assure you that I am seriously angry with you for not having written to me, for many Posts. I give you my word that I am much more angry than if you had cut the button and loop off my hat,[1] and broken all the four tongues of my Stock-buckle. Here now is the misery of being a man of some humour. No sooner do I begin to grow angry, than up bounces a ludicrous image or two; I cannot help laughing. I cannot help being pleased. And thus my anger which I fondly imagined to be hot as an Alchymist's or rather a Brazier's furnace is blown out as easily as a bit of lighted paper; This is truly severe.

Indeed, my friend, this Indolence of yours, when carried to such excess, is a real fault. I wish you would try to amend it. Activity will make you relish your favourite ease, much more. Consider now my present Situation. I have been expecting every Post, a fullfillment of your promise of a particular letter informing me all about my little Boy. You know how happy such a letter would make me, and how uneasy I must be at the want of it; and yet you will not rouse yourself up from your lethargy. Take my opinion, that writing a letter to a friend will allways give satisfaction. It relieves one from distress of mind, and it enhances our joy when we are communicating it to a Person for whom we have a sincere regard and affection. But I cannot help concluding from experience that

[9] The entry for 17 July starts at the top of this page.

[1] Fashionable men's hats at this time were cocked, the raised portion of the brim being held in place by a loop or lace attached to a button in the centre of the crown (A. S. Turberville, *Johnson's England*, 1933, i. 390–91).

most certain of all teachers, that such Reflections as these must be thrown away upon you; as you have so often been told of your neglect and yet have been and still are so very neglectfull. There is but one other week to elapse before the time that you will be set free from these upbraidings; For when you hear from me at very long Intervals, you will not grudge that much trouble of answering them in the same way. You may smile at my talking so strongly upon this Subject; But I assure you I am serious and I declare to you, that upon my honour, your neglect vexes me. Did not I send you some franks to inclose your letters to me, in? But—no more of this.—I hope you are sorry.

I have now fixed tomorrow senight friday the fifth of August, for my setting out. My heart beats with a mixed kind of anxiety when I write this. On Saturday the Sixth, I shall be upon the Channel. However you will hear from me, thrice more yet, before I leave my dear dear London, and my sweet, calm Recess, in the Temple. Alas my heart grows tender.—I wish I may ever be so happy. This is weakness to be so affected. Adieu my friend Your's Sincerely

JAMES BOSWELL

From Johnston, July 1763

Missing. Sent from Edinburgh to London and received on 29 July. JJ wrote an account of a visit to Charles and described him as resembling his father, as appears from JB's reply below.

To Johnston, Saturday 30 July 1763

MS. Yale (L 721).

London, 30 July 1763

MY DEAR FRIEND: Had the last Post but whip'd his horse a little more, and got to London a day sooner, I should have received your most agreable letter on Thursday giving a particular account of my dear little Son; and consequently should not have written my chiding Epistle to you. However, upon second thoughts, considering how long it would have been, even then since I had heard from you, you well deserved a Reprimand, and as you would have wanted it had your letter arrived on Thursday, it is much better on account of the great principle of Justice, that it did not. You can scarcely beleive what pleasure I received from the description of your Sunday's visit at the Residence of Charles. The Circumstances delight my romantic Imagination. Fancy herself could not form finer ideas of the Scene, the time, the Persons, the Situation. And then your taking my Boy in your arms, and feeling your heart warm to him, is an exquisite Stroke. Poor little creature! I wish from my heart, that I had seen him, before I left England.[1] His resembling me is a most agreable thing. I am positive that he is my own. He shall allways find me an affectionate Father, and I must indulge many fond—perhaps foolish—ideas of his making a figure in life. I am determined that nothing shall be wanting to accomplish him for whatever his Genius leads him to. I am much obliged to you, My Dear Friend, for your kind concern about him. It is the greatest kindness to his father, and it is a kindness for which the namesake of our Martyr'd Sovereign may be in a situation to show his gratitude. Think my friend what joy it will give us both if he lives and rises in the World. I suppose he may remain where he is, for a year or two longer, as his nurse is a good creature and loves him. After that time I shall send him to some School at a pleasant Village in England, where his Parentage shall not be known; as the scoffing of his Companions might break his spirit. I shall send you an order upon Sir David Dalrymple for the twenty Shillings which you have layd out for me on his account.

Doctor Boswell has taken down my other debts to you. I shall leave orders for money to be transmitted to you, from time to time. You are affectionate in asking to have my picture. I dont know of any cheap miniature Painter, here. But I shall get it done either in London, or in Holland and send it to you.[2] I am surprised that Cairnie never writes. I ever am—yours most sincerely

JAMES BOSWELL

From Johnston, Monday 1 August 1763

MS. Yale (C 1623). Received 20 Oct. (Reg. Let.).

Forrests Coffeehouse Edr. 1st Augt. 1763

MY DEAR SIR: This is probably the last letter that I shall have the Pleasure of writing to you while in Brittain, for a Considerable

[1] He never saw Charles, who died in Scotland in 1764, while JB was still in Utrecht (*post* 9 Apr. 1764).

[2] The promise was fulfilled two years later when JB was in Rome. He com-missioned James Alves to paint a miniature portrait which he sent back to Scotland by Robert Strange (*post* 19 July 1765).

time. I am much inclined to write you a long one; but I am affraid that you'll have left London before the Post arrives, and in this uncertainty, it is surely right to Say little.

I received your packet on Saturday, and this Evening a very Smart Letter,[1] which roused me not a little. In return I shall only say, That you are Sometimes too keen, and throw reflexions before you allow yourself to think Seriously how far they are well founded. I believe it is only your friends that you treat in this way, and I can easily account for it, a Warmness of Heart will often cause one blame his friend for indifference, when no such thing is intended. You accuse me of the fault in too Strong terms, especially when I can honestly tell you, that my not writing you Sooner about our young friend was not owing to that. It's true, three post nights intervened between my Seeing him and writing you, but every one of those nights I was employed in business. My time is not wholly my own, I must attend to what I am engaged in, Tho' scarce any thing So material could occurr, that would cause me neglect what tended to your happiness or wellfare. I referr you to my last for an acco[un]t of our young friend. Nothing on my part Shall be wanting as to him.

May kind Heaven take you under its protection and return you Safe to your own Country, where, may you live long, happy with yourself, and an ornament to your Country and friends. Farewell my Dear Sir, and I always remain your most affectionate friend while

JOHN JOHNSTON

If by any means you can let me know of your receiving this, do it.

To Johnston, Tuesday 2 August 1763

MS. Yale (L 722).

Inner Temple, 2 August 1763

MY DEAR JOHNSTON: I am a man whom nature has endowed with a love of forms and Ceremonies. When once I fix on a time *when*, and a method *how* any thing is to be done, I observe my plan as religiously as a Turk does the prescriptions of his Prophet. No

---

[1] *Ante* 28 July 1763.

inconvenience is admitted as an excuse. I boldly surmount every obstacle, even that of Indolence, which I believe you would allow as the greatest in the World.

As an instance of this my attachment to forms, Tuesday's is the Post by which I fixed to send off my weekly packet of Journal, and I dare affirm that during the time that I have been in London, I have never once sent it by any other Post. This night is Tuesday night. I am much hurried very confused and very unfit for writing, and yet home I am come like lightning to my chambers and am writing away as if I were to [be] broke upon the wheel, if I did not. Methinks the Executioner with a look most horrid urges me on, and on I go, like a frighted horse without consideration.

Hurried and confused as I am, I cannot help thinking how very curious this method of keeping a Journal is, and how very naturaly you will by this time look for a Saturday's Packet, as we used to do in my Father's family for a Saturday's Roll; for, my Mother honest Woman had but one Whim. She had toast for breakfast Six days in the week, but allways on Saturday, were we regaled with hot Rolls; every man his bird,[1] and so it was called Bird-day.

Your receiving a letter every third day must be another diverting circumstance. It is very wonderfull to think that all these great matters are of this year's growth. But it is grievous to think that the crop will not continue. The fertile Tree itself is to be transported into other climates where it may perhaps bear as well, but from whence the fruit cannot be so easily transported. However, you may depend upon it, they shall be *preserved*. I see now Johnston that human calculation is vain. I limited my Journal while in London, to 700 pages.[2] It allready exceeds that number. Beleive me ever your's most sincerely

JAMES BOSWELL

To Johnston, 3 August 1763

Missing. A brief note referred to as written earlier on the same evening as the letter dated 4 Aug.

[1] The *Scottish National Dictionary* records no instance of such a use of the word. Breakfast rolls were called 'birds' in the Boswell household, perhaps, because they were bought at Mrs. Bird's shop (*ante* 19 July 1763, n. 2).

[2] Page 700 is occupied by an early portion of the long journal entry for 22 July.

To Johnston, Thursday 4 August 1763

MS. Yale (L 723).

Inner Temple, 4 August 1763

MY DEAR JOHNSTON: In the former part of this evening, I wrote you a short line. I now intend to give you a letter of decent length; and yet it is very late, and I am very much hurried,[1] so cannot write so easily as I could wish.

I am now to leave London in a few hours, and in a few days shall be in a foreign country, and it may be very long before you and I shall meet again.

I leave you in the first place a strict charge to look diligently after my little Boy. See him from time, to time, and see that he have every thing that is proper for him. You will call upon Sir David Dalrymple, and receive 20 Shillings. I have left £20 in bills upon Love with Cochrane & Herreis Merchants[2] the one bill due in Twelve, the other in Sixteen months after the 28 of July 1763. They have given me money for a third due in five months. My friend Temple owes me £7 – 7s which he will transmit to you, when there is occasion. I will write to him that you are to have it for my use and you must fix how it is to be sent down whether by a bill, or by any other way. And now my good friend! I have an easy mind with respect to Charles; which you may beleive I consider as a matter of much consequence.

You will receive along with this, a packet of Journal, till the last night of my stay in London, making it 734 Pages.[3] Whether you will get any sent from abroad I cannot say; but I imagine the expence and hazard would be too great. However I shall continue to keep it regularly, and you shall see it when I return.

And now my friend I have a demand to make, and I insist that

[1] MS. orig. "flurried".

[2] Herries Cochrane & Co. (the correct style), the London bankers who paid JB the allowance made him by his father, carried on their business in Jeffrey's Square, St. Mary Axe. They were at this time the London branch of John Coutts & Co., the Edinburgh firm to which David Boswell had been apprenticed (*ante* 10, 22 Mar. 1763). By an agreement signed on 25 Dec. 1762, Sir William Forbes and James Hunter (later Hunter-Blair) had become the active partners in Edinburgh, while the management of the London branch had been assumed by Robert Herries (?1730–1815), an experienced banker, and William Cochrane, a former woollen-draper from Edinburgh, related to the Coutts family. John Coutts's sons James and Thomas had by this time left the firm and were carrying on their own banking business in the Strand (Forbes, pp. 15–18).

[3] The last entry, that for 4 Aug., ends on p. 734.

you comply with it. I beg you may, with my last wishes while here. You have now a great deal of Journal and Letters. I insist that you allow them to lye by and that you never read a word of them, after this month, till my return, so that then they will be quite new allmost to us both. I think my diligence in writing and sending it may entitle me to demand this, and I expect to have your solemn promise to comply with it, in the first letter that you write to me at Utrecht. You will get my foreign letters to amuse you, tho' not very frequently. Now, my good friend make no Objections to this. It is now near two o clock, and I am to rise at half an hour after three.[4] Farewell, once more, my friend and beleive me your's ever

JAMES BOSWELL

[4] JB's unreadiness for setting out on a journey was chronic, and regularly resulted in his spending all or most of the previous night packing and writing letters (see Journ. 28 Aug. 1769). In his earlier years he also had a practice of occasionally sitting up for the whole night when no journey was involved, merely to bring his correspondence and journal up to date and to exhaust his superabundant energy (e.g. *ante* 7 Apr. 1763, n. 3). He had been up writing two nights within the present week (Journ. 30 July, 3 Aug. 1763), and had recorded a rare resolve to mend his ways—"I last night sat up again, but I shall do so, no more, for I was very stupid today and had a kind of feverish headach"—but immediately had to sit up again in order to get everything ready for leaving London.

III

September 1763–June 1764

Boswell spent this period, in his twenty-third and twenty-fourth years, in Holland as a student of law at the University of Utrecht.

III

September 1763–June 1764

To Johnston, Friday 23 September 1763

MS. Yale (L 724).

ADDRESS: To John Johnston Esq: of Grange, to the care of Provost Graham, Dumfries, North-Britain.

Utrecht, 23 Septr. 1763

MY DEAR JOHNSTON: I find myself at a loss how to begin this letter. As it is my first to you, from a foreign country, I should perhaps break off with a pompous Exordium: But a pompous Exordium will not offer me it's services. Perhaps too, I should begin with an Apology for not writing sooner: But this I imagine you will own is hardly necessary, after you have read this page. I am now fairly begun, and shall say no more on the Subject.

I shall give you my history since I set out from London, as well as I can. I tell you beforehand, that it is strange and affecting; so do not be suddenly shocked.

I set out upon my travels, with a kind of gloom upon my Mind. My enthusiastic love of London made me leave it with a heavy heart. It might not have been the case, had I been setting out on an immediate tour thro' the gay regions of Italy and france. But to comply with my Father's inclinations, I had agreed to pass my first Winter at Utrecht a dutch University town of which I had received the most dissagreable preposessions. Mr. Samuel Johnson honoured me with his company to Harwich, where he saw me embark and set sail from Britain. I was sick and filled with a crowd of different ideas. But we had a good passage and landed on Sunday the 7 of August at 12 at noon. I shall not be tedious with particulars; But give you the great lines of my Story. I went to Rotterdam, where I met with Mr. Archibald Stewart (Sir Michael's youngest son)[1] who is settled a Merchant there. I was not much acquainted

---

[1] Sir Michael Stewart of Blackhall (?1712–96) in Renfrewshire, 3rd Bt. Archibald, his youngest son, left Rotter- dam later on to go to Tobago, where he had come into possession of a fortune of about £20,000, as he told JB in London

111

with him. But he insisted that I should stay in his house, where I met with every civility. Noveltys entertained me for a day or two; and then I went to Leyden, and past some days. I began to turn low-spirited and set out for Utrecht. I travelled between Leyden and Utrecht nine hours in a sluggish *Treck Schuyt*[2] without any companion so that I brooded over my own dismal imaginations. I arrived at Utrecht, on a Saturday Evening. I went to the *Nouveau Chateau d'Anvers*.[3] I was shown up to a high bedroom with old furniture where I had to sit and be fed by myself. At every hour the bells of the great tower played a dreary psalm tune. A deep melancholy seised upon me. I groaned with the idea of living all winter in so shocking a place. I thought myself old and wretched and forlorn. I was worse and worse next day. All the horrid ideas that you can imagine, recurred upon me. I was quite unemployed and had not a soul to speak to but the Clerk of the english Meeting[4] who could do me no good. I sunk quite into despair. I thought that at length the time was come that I should grow mad. I actualy beleived myself so. I went out to the streets, and even in public could not refrain from groaning and weeping bitterly. I said allways "Poor Boswell! is it come to this? Miserable wretch that I am! what shall I do?"—O my friend pause here a little; and figure to yourself what I endured. I took general speculative views of things; all seemed full of darkness and woe. Tortured in this manner, I determined to leave Utrecht and next day returned to Rotterdam in a condition that I shudder to recollect. I sent for Stewart, and in the best way I could, trusted him with my dreadfull situation. He behaved like a humane and a generous Man; took me to his house, and did every thing in his power to amuse me. But alas, how could I be amused? My worthy

(Journ. 29 Mar. 1772). He was killed there in 1779, while trying to repel an attack by some American privateers who had landed on the island and were laying parts of it waste (Burke, *Peerage and Baronetage*, 1899, p. 1375; *Comp. Bar.* iv. 261).

[2] *Trekschuit*, a horse-drawn barge.

[3] There were two hotels named Château d'Anvers, the "Old" and the "New".

[4] The English-speaking (Presbyterian) congregation in Utrecht had been founded in 1622, by agreement be-

tween the States of Holland, the Corporation of Utrecht, and the British residents. For a century and a half it had provided a minister and a religious meeting-place for the British colony in the town (William Steven, *History of the Scottish Church at Rotterdam*, 1832, p. 338). At this time the minister was Robert Brown (d. 1777). The clerk's name was Caron. His father was French, his mother English, and JB later engaged him as a French teacher (French Themes, p. 17, c. 7 Oct. 1763; Mem. 30 Sept. 1763, 15 Oct. 1763).

Father was pleased thinking that I was now upon a prudent plan according to his inclination; whereas, I had given up all schemes of doing any good. I had quitted Utrecht. I was now in Rotterdam. But what should I do next? Good God! what distracted horrors did I now endure. Sometimes I thought of going to Berlin, sometimes to Geneva, sometimes to Paris; but above all of returning to London and my dear calm retreat in the Inner Temple. I recollected that Dempster was in Paris. I wrote to him my situation and begged he would meet me at Brussels. Irresolute and fickle every hour I was for writing a new letter. Mr. Morgan a Northamerican[5] who had just taken his degrees in Physic, at Edinburgh was making a tour of Holland. I agreed to go with him. We went to Gouda Amsterdam Haarlem etc. I remembered an advice of your's and did not go, but was taken. We then came round by Utrecht, where we stayed a day or two. But it still appeared so terrible that I could not stay. So we returned to Rotterdam. I was now a little better, and began to think that I might put up at Leyden. In the mean time I got a letter from Dempster[6] who had come from Paris to Brussels, 62 leagues in 30 hours a strong proof of his regard for me, and generosity of soul. It was hard to think that he had set out before my letter bidding him write first, could reach Paris and so had missed seeing me. I received a letter from Temple[7] imputing my misery to idleness and beseeching me to act a part worthy of a Man. I met with several papers in the *Rambler* describing the wretchedness of a mind unemployed, a peevish and gloomy fancy indulged.[8] I began to think that I had no title to shelter myself from blame under the excuse of Madness which was perhaps but a suggestion of idle Imagination. I read another of his papers where he talks of Patience as the noble duty of a Man and

[5] John Morgan (1735–89) of Philadelphia was founder and first professor of the Medical College in the University of Pennsylvania. He was physician-in-chief of the American Army in 1775–76. Like JB, he made the Grand Tour and visited Voltaire (on 16 Sept. 1764). His journal for part of the tour has been published (*The Journal of Dr. John Morgan of Philadelphia from the City of Rome to the City of London, 1764*, 1907), but no journal of his tour of Holland is known to exist. He refers to JB in a letter of 1 Nov. 1763 to Sir Alexander Dick: "I made the Tour of Holland in Company with Mr. Boswell Lord Augenleck's Son, whose spirited and agreeable Conversation gave me more Pleasure than any other I met with in Holland" (from a photostat in the Library of the American Philosophical Society, Philadelphia, of the original letter in the possession of the Dick-Cunyngham family).

[6] Dempster had written JB two letters from Brussels, 22 and 23 Aug.

[7] This letter is dated 23 Aug.

[8] See *Ramblers* 47, 74, 85, 134.

of a Christian and he pushes fortitude of mind so far as to doubt if "a Mind well principled will not be separated before it is subdued"[9] I was roused with so noble an idea of human Nature: I met with another paper on the power that a Man has over his ideas and how he may harden himself against being unhinged by little evils; with another where he shows how much happiness is gained by cherishing good humour, and with another where he shows that Mental Employment and bodily exercise are absolutely necessary to keep our frame easy and well.[10] Thus prepared I resolutely determined to return to Utrecht to fix myself down to a regular plan and to persist with firmness and spirit and combat the foul fiend. I have done so; and thanks to Mr. Johnson whose precepts (with the favour of God to whom I earnestly prayed to assist me) I am quite well. I have taken a neat house, and have a good Servant. I hear a College[11] upon Civil law. I read Greek, latin french and English. I find that in Winter we shall have a number of *Noblesse* with whom I shall be acquainted. Count Nassau[12] is an amiable and polite Man. I view myself here, improving myself in learning and fitting myself for making the tour of Europe with advantage; and consider my friend what a noble discovery I have made, that Melancholy can be got the better of. I dont say entirely. But by vigourously opposing it, I have a conscious satisfaction even in my dark hours and when I have the sunshine of the soul[13] then I am doubly blest. My Dear Johnston! this is a strange letter. I had not room to be full enough. But from what I have said you may by the assistance of your fancy have matter of thought for some time. Pray let my victory have a proper effect upon you. I shall think this late shock a fortunate affair if it help us both to a method of preserving constant satisfaction of soul. I shall write more to you on the subject. I continue my Journal and much entertainment will it afford. I shall transmit it to Temple; and when I return, we shall read it together. Oh my dear Johnston! felicitate your poor friend restored to comfort. This last affair appears now allmost incredible.

[9] *Rambler* 32: "I think there is some reason for questioning whether the body and mind are not so proportioned, that the one can bear all that can be inflicted on the other, whether virtue cannot stand its ground as long as life, and whether a soul well principled will not be separated sooner than subdued."

[10] Respectively, Nos. 29, 72, 85.

[11] Attend a course of lectures.

[12] Jan Nicolaas Floris (1709–82), Count of Nassau La Lecq, was chief magistrate at Utrecht. JB had been commended to him by Sir David Dalrymple.

[13] Pope's *Essay on Man* iv. 168: "The soul's calm sun-shine, and the heart-felt joy."

Luckily I did not write all the time to my Father. I hope now to be in no danger. Pray take care of Charles. Temple will send you a Bill for some money soon. Write immediatly, before you leave Grange for old Edina. And now Johnston! I must consult you as I have often done. Miss Peggy Stewart[14] (daughter to Sir Michael) is a woman every way accomplished. When I was in Scotland, I thought her the woman that I would marry, had I any such intention. But you know I was then upon a roving and dissipated plan. I am now fixed to be a worthy Laird of Auchinleck, and a man of the law, perhaps in Parliament. I have heard more in Miss Stewart's favour from her Brother. I admire her, without the passion of romantic love. Do you think that I might make advances to her by Postscripts in Stewart's letters, and see how it would relish without a direct proposal. Should I let a Woman who would be my amiable Companion and entertain my friends be taken off by some body who does not deserve her so well. Would not having this scheme in view please me on my travels and keep me fixed to Scotland. Is this a whim or not? I ever am My Dear Johnston affectionately yours

JAMES BOSWELL

Address: A Monsieur Monsieur Boswell á la Cour de l'Empereur á Utrecht. Write fully your thoughts about my schemes of Miss S——
    Take care and open this letter nicely, or you'll tear the writing; especialy the two little seals on the sides.[15]
    P.S. Write freely on S. Scheme. It is the only Scots one I can think of. For I have allways thought of some fine english one. Should I banish this whim, and have a run of several more years?

[14] *Ante* 21 July 1763, n. 10; *post* 11 May 1765, n. 11. In a letter written on the same day, JB says of Margaret Stewart (1742–1816), Archibald Stewart's sister: "Stewart's Sister is sensible amiable, has been several winters in London is perfectly accomplished. She is not handsom but is extremely agreable and what you would call a woman of fashion. She and I were allways good friends and when I was in Scotland she was the only woman I could think of for a Wife" (To W. J. Temple, 23 Sept. 1763). JB's fragmentary diary for early 1762 showed that he danced three times with Miss Stewart in Jan. and Feb., and that he took her once to a concert and once to a play (*Venice Preserved*). He admitted (in cipher) to being "afraid of love and confounded domestic notions", but does not in the diary accord her the special preference he mentions here. On 20 Feb. 1762 he wrote of Miss Bruce, "tea Miss Bruce perfectly desperate thought of composed life—walking out and in Post-Chaise and red slippers".
[15] Written, with the final postscript, on the outside of the letter, at the back, after folding.

From Johnston, ? December 1763

Missing. Recd. 17 Jan. 1764. "Mr. Johnston" (Reg. Let.). As it was written at Grange, lost in the post and rewritten from a copy JJ had kept, this letter was probably sent in its first draft as early as September, in response to JB's first letter from Utrecht. It contained JJ's comments on the suggestion that JB should "make advances" to Margaret Stewart with a view to proposing marriage, as is shown in JB's reply below.

To Johnston, Friday 20 January 1764

MS. Yale (L 725). Sent 20 Jan. 1764 (Reg. Let.).

ADDRESS: To Mr. John Johnston, to be left at Forrest's Coffeehouse, Edinburgh, By London, Great Britain.

POSTMARK: IA 24.

Utrecht, 20 January 1764

MY DEAR SIR: You may be assured that my surprise and uneasiness at the long intermission of our Corespondence, has not been less than yours. As I am at present at a great distance from you I have not sent one letter after another, as I used to do from London; but have waited week after week, for an answer to my first. My conjectures began to be exhausted, and I was just going to write to Davie, begging to have some accounts of you, when your letter arrived, and fully cleared up what before appeared so dark. It was lucky that you kept a copy of your letter; tho' it is dissagreable to think of it's having been miscarried and perhaps opened by people who we would not wish should know the contents, yet it is written in so guarded a manner, that much could not be discovered from it, by strangers. Had I not seen it, I should have been very much vexed at it's falling into strange hands as it is the Answer of my worthy freind to the most important letter that I ever wrote to him, and consequently might have been supposed to contain my most intimate secrets. The whole of your letter shows me the continuance of that warm freindship, which I hope shall never cease to fill the hearts of us both. Your complying with my request in writing from Grange pleases me much. Such little agreable circumstances are not to be neglected. We should think no innocent gratification however small, beneath our enjoying. Let us lighten our moments in this state of existence, every lawfull way we can. You have given me the advice which I expected from you, with regard to my matrimonial scheme. Often and often have I consulted you, upon such projects; and I realy beleive that had it not

116

been for your prudent counsel, I should have been a Husband two winters ago, and by that means, should have e'er this time been a very unhappy man.[1] This last scheme was founded on the same principles with my former ones; and now I am equally glad at my not having attempted to realise it. My freind Temple[2] advised me by all means not to think of it; and to please my gay fancy told me that I must marry an english Lady of family and fortune. This may perhaps be the case. At any rate, what you say is very just, that it will be time enough to think of matrimony, when I return from my travels.

If I remember right, I gave you in my last a very full recital of the severe fit of melancholy which I was seised with, upon my first coming to Utrecht, as also of my having taken a manly resolution to conquer it and of my having succeeded. Indeed my freind, it was the crisis of my distemper. I had allways yeilded to spleen as to an invincible foe. He at last pushed the oppression of a Conqueror so hard that I turned upon him and fairly obtained a victory. Observe my freind that I never before attempted to oppose the foul fiend so never before enjoyed happiness on any sure foundation. I told you that my honoured freind Mr. Samuel Johnson had supplied me with the weapons of philosophy. It was in the *Rambler* that I found the causes of my woe described, and cures pointed out. I beg you may get that Book. It costs twelve shillings. But it is worth much more. Study it, and endeavour to preserve the noble sentiments which it inspires. It is the best book that england has produced for such people as you and me. It proceeds upon the supposition that we are here in a state where there is much gloom and fortifys the mind to enable it to support the evils which attack it. I have got so much to say to you that I should not dwell too long on any one topic; and yet again, I find I have much to say on every topic; I must do my best, and give you as much as I can, till my paper be filled. Would you beleive that for these four Months, I have never resigned myself to *age* one day. I have had gloomy fits, but have never yielded. I wish I could get you to understand this clearly, and to try the same vigorous regimen. The great point, is not to brood over the suggestions of a dreary disposition. Reasoning cannot remove them. But employment will; therefore even at the time

---

[1] *Ante* 21 July 1763, n. 10; 23 Sept. 1763, n. 14.

[2] This particular letter from Temple has not been recovered. JB received it on 20 Oct. (Reg. Let.) and answered it on 9 Nov. 1763.

that all employments seem insipid, let the *Antiquarian* force himself to do something briskly and his rusty ideas will vanish. I hear
a college on Civil law. I study greek and french and dutch, besides
what I read of other books, and I assure you I am doing very well.
I feel my mind composing itself more and more. I continue steady
to my resolution of being a good member of society in civil life.
I shall return to Scotland and put on the gown as an Advocate.
After that I shall either continue at the Scots Bar, or perhaps get
into parliament. But, my general plan shall be that of a decent
attentive Man, a worthy Laird of Auchinleck. I have read, this
winter, Dr. Clarke's *Evidences of natural and revealed Religion*[3] a
Book which I would earnestly reccommend to you. It has given me
very strong conviction of the truth of Christianity, which is a continual support to the soul. When a man has once the hope of
celestial Joy, he is above the little vexations of this state: At least
he supports them with patience. I have found Utrecht to be a most
excellent place. I have here excellent opportunity to study, and at
the same time, to see foreign company. There are a number of
noble familys who reside here in the winter. I have been received
into their Assemblys where I pass two or three evenings a week
improving in french, and in politeness. At Christmas we had a
month of vacation. I then went to the Hague where I past three
weeks in the most brilliant gayety. The stile of living there is
much in the manner of paris. I found my Relations there to be
people of the first rank[4] and was received by them with the utmost
civility. I had recommendations to a variety of people. I was presented to the Prince of Orange and the other Princes there to all
the foreign Embassadors in short, to every body. I past a couple of
days at Leyden where I supt twice with the young Prince of
Strelitz our Queen's Brother[5] once at his own house once at the

---

[3] Samuel Clarke's Boyle sermons,
preached at St. Paul's in 1704–05, had
been recommended to Dr. Johnson by his
friend, William Adams of Pembroke
College, Oxford. The volume was published under the title, *A Discourse Concerning the Being and Attributes of God, the
Obligations of Natural Religion, and the
Truth and Certainty of the Christian Revelation*, 1705–06. Though Johnson considered its defence of Christianity not
wholly orthodox, he had recommended it,
with some reservations, to JB (*Life* iv.

416 n. 2).

[4] JB's great-grandmother Veronica,
Countess of Kincardine, was Dutch. She
was a daughter of Cornelius van Aerssen
van Sommelsdyck (1600–62), whose
grandson, Francis Cornelius van Aerssen
van Sommelsdyck, Lord Auchinleck's
second cousin, was the representative of
the family at the time of JB's visit to
Holland.

[5] Charlotte Sophia, who married
George III in 1761, was the youngest
daughter of Charles Lewis, Duke of

house of Mr. Gordon Lord Aberdeen's Brother:[6] And now I am returned to this seat of the dutch muses and have resumed my studious regularity with much satisfaction. Formerly such a change of life used to unhinge me quite. Now I am firm and keep my post. I shall ever reverence Utrecht, for it was there that I first began to act upon steady and manly principles. I am allready not a little altered. But, altered for the better. However I must guard against extremes. No longer ago than last winter, I was the ardent votary of pleasure, a gay sceptic who never looked beyond the present hour, a heroe and Philosopher in Dissipation and Vice. Now I am all devoted to Prudence and to Morality. I am ⟨full⟩ of the dignity of human Nature; and so far am I from indulging myself in mimicry and ludicrous jocularity, that I must allways have some grave or some usefull Subject. Perhaps, I am too much an enthusiast in Rectitude. But candour makes me own that Rectitude has to me all the charms of novelty. You see then in what situation your freind now is. Are you not happy to be informed of it. On Christmas day I was at the Hague and received the blessed sacrament in the Embassador's Chapel.[7] His Chaplain[8] is just that genteel amiable, church of england Clergyman, whom I have heard you say that you would like to have in your house, were you a man of great fortune. I have no room to write you remarks on this country. I must refer[9] them till meeting when you will be entertained with my *foreign Journal* which contains allready 310 pages. In the mean time, I would have you read Sir William Temple's *Observations on the Netherlands*. They are short and entertaining, and will give you some idea of the country where your freind is. Into whatever

---

Mecklenburg-Strelitz. Her youngest brother George Augustus, at this time aged 15, was a student at the University of Leyden.

[6] Charles Gordon (1745–71), son of the 2nd Earl of Aberdeen, like the Prince a student at Leyden, was later a captain in the 66th Regt. of Foot (*Town and Country Magazine*, 1771, iii. 717, second numbering; see also *Scots Peer.* i. 92).

[7] Though JB had not previously made his communion in an Episcopalian chapel, he and JJ had often attended Episcopalian services in Edinburgh, and (though they retained their connexion with the Church of Scotland) continued to do

so after JB's return. "I have observed with satisfaction that his [JJ's] religious principles have of late grown stronger, and it pleases me that by having a seat for myself by the year in the old English Chapel I accommodate him, so that his attendance upon publick worship is more frequent" (Journ. 15 Feb. 1784).

[8] Robert Richardson, chaplain to the Ambassador, Sir Joseph Yorke, subsequently became a close friend of JB during his stay in Holland.

[9] "Refer. v. 7. To defer, postpone, put off (something) *to, unto, till, until* another time or season. *Obs.*" (OED).

nation I shall go, I must have you to read an account of it. Sir William Temple in his *Observations* says something particularly applicable to you and me.[10] You cannot miss it; so your mentioning it to me will show me that you have read the book. I think it is a pity to take off the embargo on my papers. However, I indulge you with liberty to read my letters: but let the Journal be reserved till I am sitting at your fire-side. I hope my papers are safely preserved. Lest they should grow damp, I would wish to have them taken out of the box sometimes and exposed to the air in a room where there is a good fire. By the by, my Father's opening my 4 Bundles dwelt so in my mind, that I took the liberty to mention it to him in my last letter. I have not as yet had his answer. My intention was that he should ask pardon as a freind, which I hope he will do. I have not passed so *sound* a winter these six years. Yet I am not quite content; for I do not enjoy enough, I am affraid to resign myself to pleasing sensations lest I should be too susceptible of uneasy ones. I am realy of too anxious a temper for, I dare say you will think I have no reason to fear my having too hardened a soul. My Dear Johnston never allow yourself to doubt of my freindship for you. Go to Arthur-seat where we have often walk'd and where I hope we shall walk yet oftener. Recall every agreable hour, and be assured that as long as that old Mountain stands, so long shall my freindship last. You give me great comfort by your accounts of Charles. I trust him entirely to you. I left £20 in the hands of Herries & Cochrane.[11] I shall write to them soon so as that they may answer your draught for £10. I shall write in a week or two; so that you may have the money before you go to Annandale. I am happy to find that you are so well with the worthy Doctor.[12] He was the great freind of Lady Limekilns.[13] He writes me much good of you. Davie gives me

[10] *Observations upon the United Provinces of The Netherlands*, 1673. The passage referred to here is perhaps an account in chapter IV of the nature of spleen, in which Temple expresses JB's own opinion that hypochondria is best countered by activity.

[11] *Ante* 4 Aug. 1763, n. 2.

[12] The reference is to JB's uncle, Dr. John Boswell.

[13] "Old Limekilns, my Grandfather's great freind" (Journ. 21 Aug. 1778)

was John Carlyle of Lymekilns, Dumfriesshire, an Edinburgh "writer" who died in 1741. He had married in 1713 Christian, daughter of Michael Anderson of Tushielaw, who is presumably the lady here referred to. The wife of JJ's friend, William Graham of Shaw, came of the same family (*ante* 28 Apr. 1763, n. 2). Dr. George Carlyle (1715–84), nephew of John, had studied medicine at the University of Leyden at the same time as Dr. John Boswell.

uncommon satisfaction. He will be a Man. Tell him I shall write to him soon. Let me hear from you often and send your letters to your freind[14] in London. I ever remain My Dear Sir your most affectionate freind

James Boswell[15]

Dic mihi ubi habitas hoc anno. An florret Theatrum Edinburgense? An Dominus Digges adhuc in scenam prodit? Amicos nostros communes meo nomine saluta. Solus sum Anglus in hac Academia et igitur cum exteris consortium diurnum habeo. Spero noctes hilares tecum terere apud Thomam hospitem illum excellentem.

From Johnston, 1 February 1764

Missing. Sent from Edinburgh on 1 Feb. and received in Utrecht on 8 Mar., this letter told JB of the death of his son Charles. It is acknowledged in his reply of 9 Apr. and referred to again in his letter of 11 June.

To Johnston, Monday 9 April 1764

MS. Yale (L 726).

ADDRESS: To John Johnston Esq: of Grange, to the care of Provost Graham, Dumfries, North Britain, By London.

POSTMARK: AP 20.

ENDORSEMENT: Utrecht 9th. April 1764.

Utrecht, 9 April 1764

My Dear Freind: On the eight of March, I received your last letter, which contained the melancholy news of my poor Boy's death.[1] It has affected me more than you could have imagined. I had cherished a fond idea. I had warmed my heart with parental

---

[14] Possibly Patrick Scott, a London merchant, with whom JJ was at this time in correspondence over the estate of his father, Francis Scott of Johnston, JJ's cousin, who had died in 1761 (Grange MSS.).

[15] JB wrote what follows in Latin because, as it was written on the outside of the letter, he wished to foil the curiosity of postmen. The sense is: "Tell me where you are living this year, whether the Edinburgh theatre prospers, whether Mr. Digges still appears on the stage.

Greet our mutual friends for me. I am the only Englishman in this university, so my days are passed among foreigners. I look forward to whiling away happy evenings with you at the tavern of our good host Thom."

---

[1] "Yesterday you rose well—after breakfast you received a letter from Johnston with accounts of the death of the poor little Child. Alas what is the world. You was distrest & sunk" (Mem. 9 Mar. 1764).

affection. I had formed many agreable plans for the young Charles. All is now wrapped in darkness. All is gone. My Dear Sir! let me repeat my sincere sentiments of freindship. Let me again assure you that you are ever dear to me. Your care of my child while he lived, was allways tender. It showed your attachment to his Father. I much approve of your having given him a decent interrment[2] and of the company that you selected. Cairnie is a worthy fellow. I have been very much obliged to him. I retain a very gratefull sense of his kindness, and wish much for an opportunity of being of use to him. I have not written to him since I came abroad. I did not chuse to put him to the expence of Postage. Pray assure him fully of my sentiments towards him. Let me know what his schemes are, and find out if my writing to him, is expected. Abercrombie and Currie[3] are excellent lads. Give my kind service to them.

And now, my freind, I must give you an account of myself since my last. Our Corespondence is now upon a very different footing from what it was a year ago. While I remained in London you had a regular Saturday's Pacquet. You could trace me from day to day in my Journal, nor was there ever a forthnight of my life beyond your knowledge. But, since I crost the seas, months of silence intervene between my Epistles. I may be sick, I may be dead, long before the report can reach You. You must be satisfied with now and then receiving an abstract of my life, during a stretch of time. You may depend on periodical narrations. You shall never want the great lines. The minute circumstances will furnish entertainment to us, when We shall have again the happiness to be together.

My jaunt during the Christmas Vacation, produced some alteration on my mind. When I returned to Utrecht, I had not the same internal firmness that I had carried from it. I began to think that my resolute Philosophy was a mere Imagination which I had formed in the sober Retreat of a Provincial town, that I had indeed acted from this Imagination and might have continued to do so, had I remained in the same uniform circumstances as when I first framed the Idea. But, alas! a short change, a transient view of the brilliant Hague, a little tumble in the real world shook off the fascination and showed me that I was still the same weak-minded

---

[2] The place of Charles's burial is unknown.   [3] *Ante* 25 Jan. 1763, nn. 3, 5.

Being as ever. I fell desperately in love with a young beautifull amiable and rich Widow.[4] This Passion tore and hurt my Mind. I was seised with a severe cold. My Nerves were relaxed, my blood was thickened. Low-spirits approached. I heard of Charles's death. It shocked me. It filled me with gloomy reflections on the uncertainty of life, and that every Post might bring me accounts of the departure of those whom I most regarded. I saw all things as so precarious and vain that I had no relish of them, no views to fill my mind, no motives to incite me to action. I groaned under those dismal Truths, which nothing but a lucky oblivion prevents from weighing down the most vivacious Souls. Black Melancholy again took dominion over me. All my old dreary and fretfull feelings recurred. I was much worse on this account that after my first severe fit on coming to Utrecht, I realy beleived that I had conquered Spleen for ever; and that I should never again be overcome by it. I lived in this perswasion for four Months. I had my dull hours. But I considered myself as a Soldier. I endured such hardships: But I kept my post. You may conceive what I felt on the sad conviction that my hopes were fancifull. O how I was galled! O how did I despise myself. I must mention one circumstance which is very hard. When I am attacked by Melancholy, I seldom enjoy the comforts of Religion. A future state seems so clouded, and my attempts toward devotion are so unsuitable, that I often withdraw my mind from divine subjects, lest I should communicate to the most sublime and chearing Doctrines my own imbecillity and sadness. In short, for some weeks past, I have suffered much. However, I can now inform you that I am greatly better. That I have resumed my military Metaphor, and that I again am on vigorous service. Certain it is that the Hypochondriac disease may be in a great measure cured. Certain it is that a man has it much in his power to fill his mind with what ideas he pleases. Hence it is that he may allways have so much happiness. I am sorry that I mentioned my Uneasiness to my Father. Melancholy is timorous, and wishes for the Counsel of the wise. It is amazing how spleen makes sport of the mind of man; how it

---

[4] Catharina Elisabeth van Geelvinck (1738–92), née Hasselaer, was an intimate friend of Zélide's (*post* 11 May 1765, n. 12). After one year of married life she had been left a widow in 1757 by the death of Lieve Geelvinck. She married François Gabriel Joseph, Marquis de Chasteler et de Courcelles, in 1767, and after his death married for the third time, in 1790, George, Graf von Schlitz (J. E. Elias, *De Vroedschap van Amsterdam 1578–1795*, 1903–05, ii. 809).

represents distant objects as agreable. However, I have gone regularly on with my Plan here, and I have certainly proffited a good deal. I have increased my knowledge of law and History, I have learn't french and some dutch. I have seen foreign manners. Now when I am easy, I can be sensible of these advantages. You must know I have learned the important art of Reserve. I can chat for whole evenings, without giving a hint of my Malady. Come, my ⟨worthy⟩ freind, encourage me. Remind me that I have past the winter with a high character: that this last distress has been just a temporary fit; that it is now over and that I am to proceed anew with real spirit. I shall be here till July or August. My rout after that, is not yet fixed. You shall hear it particularly. Come, my freind, let us both determine to be manly; let us "resist the devil and he will flee far from us."[5] Here is my plan. I am to travel. I am to return to Scotland, put on the gown, remain Advocate or get into Parliament and at last be comfortably settled in a good office. I hope also to do good at Auchinleck. The great point is to be allways employed as my worthy Father says. Upon this principle, he has allways been happy. Long may he be so. I have now proper ideas of Religion. That is the most important Article indeed. I am determined to act my part with vigour, and I doubt not to have a reward. My mind will go allways stronger, by discipline; Even this last attack has not been unrepelled by me. I realy beleive that these grievous complaints should not be vented; they should be considered as absurd Chimæras, whose reality should not be allowed in words. One thing I am sure of that if a man can beleive himself well, he will be realy so. The dignity of human Nature is a noble preservative of the soul. Let us consider ourselves as immortal Beings, who tho' now in a state inferior to their faculties, may one day hope to exult in the regions of light and glory. My Dear Johnston let us retain this splendid sentiment. Let us take all opportunitys of elevating our minds by devotion, and let us indulge the expectation of meeting in Heaven. But, at the same time, let us do our best in the state where God has placed us. Let us imitate the amiable Pitfour. Who is a better member of Society? yet who is a greater Saint?[6] Write to me very

---

[5] *James* iv. 7: "Resist the devil, and he will flee from you."

[6] Though JB could not yet know it, James Ferguson of Pitfour, then Dean of the Faculty of Advocates, was about to be promoted to the bench, where he took his seat on 14 June as Lord Pitfour (*College of Justice*, p. 527).

fully. I will disdain to own that the melancholy fiend can get the better of me. I even hesitated if I should inform you of this last conflict. But to my freind I will own every weakness. My great loss is an inconstancy of mind. I never view things in the same light, for a month together. Are you so? I am sincerely happy at the success of honest Baillie[7] to whom remember me cordially. This letter carrys it's own Appology. Write soon and give me full advices and put my future life in Britain in agreable colours. I have need of your assistance. May God bless you My Dear Freind prays your's ever

JAMES BOSWELL

To Johnston, Monday 11 June 1764

MS. Yale (L 727).

ADDRESS: To Mr. John Johnston, to be left at Forrest's Coffeehouse, Edinburgh, Great-Britain, By London.

POSTMARK: IV 22.

ENDORSEMENT: Utrecht June 11th. 1764.

Utrecht, 11 June 1764

MY DEAR FRIEND: More than two months ago, I sent you a long letter to the care of Provost Graham. If it has been lost or miscarried, I am very sorry. Yet I think at any rate you might have written to me again, before this time. I hope you are well, at least in your ordinary state. Since I received your last, I have had most dreadfull returns of the blackest Melancholy. I have endured more than I ever did. To tell you my sufferings from a horrid Imagination, is scarcely possible; for I have had ideas of which to describe the frightfull effects, no language has words sufficient. God preserve me from returns of the dire distemper for indeed of late it had allmost crushed me. My mind was tortured in a thousand ways. I realy was not myself. O Johnston how unfortunate am I to have such a Mind! However, let me console myself. Let me view the agreable side. I have bright parts. I have generous sentiments. I have warm affections. When I am well, I am supremely blest. No more of this. 'Tis all chimæra. Let me talk plain matter of fact, plain common sense. I have now completed my winter at Utrecht, have improved in knowledge and have made the most of

---

[7] *Ante* 25 Jan. 1763, n. 5.

the Company here. I have been several times at the brilliant Hague, and have established a freindship with my Dutch Relations, and obtained the Acquaintance of other People of distinction. In short, I have past nine months in Holland to rational purpose, and to the satisfaction of my worthy Father.

And now Johnston as a reward for my behaviour behold me enjoying uncommon good fortune. My Lord Marischal is so good as to take me with him to Germany.[1] I expect him here every day. We are to go to Lunenbourg, to Brunswic and at last to Berlin. My Father is highly pleased with the scheme, and has given me a genteel credit. All is well; and if I am not happy it must be owing to a disturbed mind. This unexpected felicity has made me quite a new Man, has given new life to me. Not three weeks ago the whole Creation and all the events of life seemed equal and in-different. All was jumbled in one dreary chaos. You have no notion how bad I was. However I have had such a conduct here as to leave a character which will allways do me honour.

Think only of my happiness now to travel with the ancient Scot-tish nobleman who has seen so much of the world in all it's grandeur and all it's pleasure, who is at Courts as I am in the houses of Ayr-shire Lairds and who is with all this a freindly easy Man. Such a change as I now feel makes me more and more convinced of im-

---

[1] George Keith (c. 1693–1778), 10th Earl Marischal, elder brother of Frederick the Great's field-marshal, had been attainted for his active participation in the Jacobite rebellion of 1715 and had also been one of the leaders of the abortive Jacobite invasion of 1719. Escaping capture, he spent the next 40 years on the Continent, furthering the Jacobite cause whenever possible, but taking no active part in the attempt of 1745. In 1747 he declined any official appointment in the Pretender's service and went to Prussia to join his brother. Frederick appointed him Prussian ambassador at Paris, and later Prussian ambassador to Spain. While holding the latter post he discovered the secret Bourbon "Family Compact" and disclosed it to the British Government, for which service he re-ceived in 1759 a royal pardon for his former high treason. In 1760, after an Act of Parliament had removed the legal disabilities consequent upon his attainder, he returned to Scotland with the intention of remaining there (*Scots Peer*. vi. 62–64). However, Frederick, who was fond of his company, urged him to make his home at Potsdam, and it was in response to this entreaty that he was now returning to Germany. There he was to remain till his death, much admired and loved, but always retaining the simplicity of man-ner which made JB describe him as a "plain old Scots nobleman" (Journ. 13 June 1764). JB wrote: "This Morning was indeed a Morning of Joy. I received a large Pacquet of letters, one from my Lord Marischal, informing me that I was to accompany him to Berlin, one from my Father to the same purpose, and letters from my Scots and London Bankers with a credit upon Berlin, of £30 a month. Never was Man happier than I this morn-ing" (Journ. 4 June 1764).

mortality: For I see how a Man can be quite extinguished and yet can revive. Go my freind by yourself to Arthur-Seat think of me in distant Regions. Love me ever and let us hope for many many happy days together. God bless and preserve you my worthy Sir. I ever remain your most affectionate friend

JAMES BOSWELL

Pray recollect the conversations which we have had on travelling. I shall, while abroad, lay up a store of pleasing ideas. I shall return composed and put on the gown and be a usefull Member of Society as well as an agreable private friend: Be as happy as you can, and think that you contribute to make me so; as indeed you certainly will, when you relate to me your complacent days during my absence. Remember me kindly to Cairnie and to our other good common Acquaintances. Farewell.

IV

September 1764–January 1766

During this period, from his twenty-fourth to his twenty-sixth year, Boswell toured the Continent, passing through Germany, Switzerland, Italy, Corsica, and France.

IV

September 1764–January 1766

To Johnston, Monday 10 September 1764

MS. Yale (L 728).

ADDRESS: To John Johnston Esq: of Grange, to the care of Provost Graham, Dumfries, North-Britain. By London. Par Hollande.

NOTE (in another hand): Fr. Amsterdam.

POSTMARK: SE 28.

ENDORSEMENT: Berlin 10th. Septr. 1764.

Berlin, 10 Septr. 1764

MY DEAR SIR: Why have you not written to me, since I left Utrecht? Davie would have given you my address. But, I excuse you; for, although I wrote you the last letter, you are waiting for a letter from Berlin.

How do our minds alter with the times! How easily do we submit ourselves with contentment, to Circumstances! While I was in London, you would have been very uneasy if you had been a week without hearing from me; and when you now and then neglected a Post, you was sure to receive from me a very warm letter, in which anger, anxiety and affection were mingled, so as to show the heart of a most sincere freind, who suffered so much from the apprehensions of a tender and gloomy mind, as realy to upbraid Him whose innocent neglect caused his Uneasiness. Now our situation is very different. We are at such a distance from each other, that frequent Corespondence cannot be carried on, but at a great expence. We have therefore set our minds at ease, and as we have no fixed time of expectation, we are never dissappointed. Yet my freind, beleive me, three months is a long time. I think we might corespond once in two months. What say you?

To give you my history since I emerged from Holland, would be to transcribe or abridge my Journal, neither of which would I wish to do. For, I hope to have the satisfaction of reading it with you at length. I shall therefore give you a sort of Index to the later part of my Journal, by giving you the principal lines of my

Story since I left Utrecht. I had a most agreable Journey with My worthy Lord Marischal. You can scarcely imagine what satisfaction I felt in the company of the venerable old Earl, a true Scottish Chieftain, I do assure you. He has an[1] infinite fund of good storys, and tells them to great Advantage. The Turkish Lady[2] was indolent, but now and then very amusing. My Lord presented me at the court of Brunswic, where we stayed two days. We next came to Potzdam where I saw the King's Palace, as also Sans Souci, which is hard by. I then came to Berlin, where I saw a large and beautifull City. I enjoyed for some time the instructive and agreable conversation of Mr. Mitchell the British Envoy[3] who is now gone. He is a worthy and a very pretty man. I was presented to the Queen, and to many Princes and Princesses. But I found the Court very dull. I returned to Brunswic and past a forthnight during the Fair. I dined every day at Court and supped every evening but two. We had public diversions every day in the week, Sunday not excepted, on which we had a concert, or a grand court and cards. I was well received. I lived well. I was quite happy; and I assure you my Brunswic forthnight will ever supply me with pleasing recollection, which you and I have both agreed is often finer than present enjoyment. At Berlin I am lodged in the house of the *President de Police* whose family is extremely agreable.[4] I have got a pretty numerous Acquaintance among the rich Bourgeois, who live like Princes. When I quitted Utrecht, I

---

[1] MS. "in".

[2] Mme de Froment (c. 1725–1820), the Earl Marischal's adopted daughter, whose name had been Emet-Ulla, was the daughter of a Turkish captain of Janissaries and had been rescued by the Earl Marischal's brother at the siege of Ochakov in 1737. She had been converted to Christianity, and in 1763 had married Colonel Denis-Daniel de Froment of the Sardinian army. This marriage was shortly (in 1765) to be dissolved, and she was to make her home with the Earl Marischal till his death (E. E. Cuthell, *The Scottish Friend of Frederic the Great*, 1915, i. 186; ii. 158–59, 249, 310).

[3] Andrew Mitchell (1708–71), the son of a minister of the Edinburgh High Church, had studied law at Edinburgh University and subsequently at Leyden.

He was Under-Secretary of State for Scotland from 1742 to 1747 and afterwards sat in Parliament as M.P. for Aberdeenshire and later for the Elgin burghs. In 1756 he was sent as British Envoy to the court of Frederick, and accompanied him as a confidential friend on his campaigns during the Seven Years War. At the restoration of peace he returned to England, but was shortly afterwards reappointed Envoy to Berlin, where he stayed till his death.

[4] JB lodged with Carl David Kircheisen, President of the City Council of Berlin, his wife, son, and daughter, and fitted into the household as if he had himself been a member of the family: "Never was a fellow so kindly used as I am here" (Journ. 4 Aug. 1764).

beleived it impossible to remove the clouds which hung over my Mind. I was allmost sunk with despair: And yet, Johnston, variety, good company, the exercises of the Academy[5] and regular living restored me to health and Joy. I have had such a strong instance that Melancholy may be overcome that you would think it impossible for me to despair, if I retain my memory and my Judgment. And yet, this very morning was I bad, and began to think I never should be well. I remembered my former woe, and I remembered that it was cured. I judged too from all probability of reasoning that my present woe must also be cured. And yet my imagination was so strong, that reason bowed before it. What shall we say of the human mind, my dear freind? Every man must judge in a great measure from what he has experienced. You know what sort of experience mine has been.

As to the course which I am next to steer, I cannot as yet exactly inform you. I would wish to pass four months in Italy; But, my Father is averse to my going to that intoxicating Region. He wishes to have me pass the winter at Geneva, and go to Paris in the spring. I however still beg to be allowed to see Rome. My Lord Marischal and Mr. Mitchell have both written in my favour, so that I am not without hopes that my request may be granted. In the mean time, I am to leave this in ten days, make a tour by Dessau, Dresden, Gotha, Maanheim and some more courts to Geneva, where I shall receive my Father's final determination, and from whence I have a plain passage into France, or a mountainous one into Italy. If my Father is absolutely against my going to Italy, I shall see how I like Geneva. If it is agreable, I shall stay there till the spring. If otherwise, I shall go to some University town in france. I shall however have an opportunity of seeing Voltaire and Rousseau. I hope to be very well amused in the German Courts which I intend to visit. You shall hear from me when I get to Geneva. In the mean time do you write me a long letter proving that you are alive, that you have not forgot me your absent freind, and that you have no Antipathy at the Abbey of Holyroodhouse, or at the noble mountain of Arthur-seat. Let your letter be sent to the care of Messrs. Splitzerber et Daum,[6] á Berlin.

---

[5] The "Academy" was a riding school: "At seven in the Morning I go to the Manège and ride the great horse" (To W. J. Temple, 23 July 1764).

[6] The firm of Splitgerber and Daum, bankers, merchants, and ship-owners, was a famous one. They were financial agents of Frederick the Great himself

I pray you Johnston give me consolation against the hour of Antiquity. Both you and I must lay our account to suffer such hours. Let us assist each other. I study Hypochondria as a Science.[7] I am allways picking up more knowledge with regard to it. My Dear freind I feel sincerely the want of you to talk with. God grant that we may yet be much together. Encourage me in my plan of following the law in Scotland. May I not do pretty well between the Session-House and Auchinleck with now and then a jaunt into England? You know my sad changeable humour. Help me to get the better of it.

You are now at Grange. Walk out on a sunny day and indulge pleasing Meditation. One thing is most sure that after the blackest gloom we may be quite happy. Strange is our existence. Let us hope for a better world and do as well as we can in this. Pray be kind to Davie. Make my kind compliments to the family of Schaw, to worthy Mr. Irvine, to Currie and to all our other freinds.

Give me any material news that is passing in the country. Your Lords of Session have died fast of late. Poor Lord Edgefield's death[8] shock'd me very much. Pray do not forget to give my best compliments to Mr. Fergusson. Is he married? What is he doing? Remember me in the best manner to Provost Graham Mr. Orr and Mr. Hay and ever beleive me My Dear Johnston your affectionate freind

JAMES BOSWELL

and played an important role in the question of the Silesian Loan, as their ships were molested by English pirates, and this offence, among others, was used by Frederick as an excuse not to pay the amount due on the Loan (Ernest Satow, *The Silesian Loan and Frederick the Great*, 1915, pp. 225–26, 254–61). JB's *z* in "Splitzerber" is probably the Scots character with the value *y*, and represents an attempt to record the Berlin pronunciation with fronted *g*.

[7] In the series of seventy essays by "the Hypochondriack" which JB contributed to *The London Magazine* between Oct. 1777 and Aug. 1783, several are directly concerned with the topic of hypochondria, and many make observations on it. In Nos. 5 and 6 the symptoms of the disease are described in some detail; in No. 39 he writes himself out of a fit by discussing it; in No. 63 he shows his attitude towards

it to be partly scientific, partly superstitious: "All the modes of cure—exercise — medicine — amusement — study — must be tried. Sometimes one will be successful, sometimes another. I have in a former paper earnestly recommended piety in a particular manner to those who are afflicted with *Hypochondria*. And I would now enforce my counsel by the consideration that I have a belief that the malady is sometimes owing to the influence of evil spirits" (*Lond. Mag.*, Dec. 1782, li. 551).

[8] Robert Pringle, Lord Edgefield, had died on 8 Apr. and been succeeded by James Ferguson of Pitfour. Two other Lords of Session had died within seven weeks of him: George Sinclair, Lord Woodhall on 5 May, and William Grant, Lord Prestongrange on 23 May (*College of Justice*, pp. 515, 519, 520).

To Johnston, Monday 1 October 1764

MS. Yale (L 729).

ADDRESS: No. 1. To John Johnston Esq: of Grange.

Anhalt Dessau, 1 October 1764

MY DEAR JOHNSTON: Behold a new Project for the entertainment of our hours of freindly Sociality. I am now upon my travels. I cannot hear from you often, as you know not how to direct for me. Nor would I chuse to put you to the expence of hearing often from me. Yet as freindship is kept alive by continued by repeated exercise of the kind affections, I have formed a very excellent Scheme. At every city or Court where I reside three days I shall write you a letter and if I find time I shall even write where my stay is very short. These Letters I shall regularly seal and direct so that they shall be to me as if I had sent them to you. I shall put them up in a Bundle which I shall keep till I return to Scotland.[1] Then Johnston shall you and I open these letters and read them in their order. The pleasure will be mutual. I shall be pleased to see my freind pleased. Besides I shall have forgotten the contents of the letters and they will appear as new to myself as to you.

This first letter is written from Anhalt Dessau where I have past a week with much pleasure as will appear from my Journal.[2]

[1] The numbered series of letters, of which this is the first (not sent, but kept by JB to be given to JJ in a single packet on his return), forms a supplement, of a summary sort, to the Journal of his continental tour. Years later JB lent this batch of letters to his friend Sir Alexander Dick, who replied with a curiously florid, involved, and flattering letter of thanks: ". . . I could easily perceive the different effects and degrees of vivacity and humourous philosophy which prevaild in your mind suited to the different climates and purity of the air and countries and people throw which you passd, and must own to you, you have drawn a more naive and truer family picture of your self than Rhaphael coud have done if you had sat to him and fitter to be deposited in your family Library at Auchinleck in memory of you to the latest future times for the instruction of your posterity and the true friends, of your ancient house and particular[l]y the honest Johnstons, of hundreds of years yet to come. you have immortalizd, with your self the worthy Johnston of the present age and indeed as it were embaulm'd your selves both in one catacomb for the Boswells entertainment and instruction, yet to come, as a true *family* piece—If you are so kind as to allow this Letter of mine to accompany them, I shall proudly consider my self as having contributed as it were some of the frankincense and odoriferous gums anciently so neccessary together with the surrounding Vittas that preservd and keept so well together the embaulmd figures of the Human bodies we now see which have subsisted some thousand of years before our time. . . ." (From Sir Alexander Dick, 10 Aug. 1782).

[2] JB arrived at Anhalt-Dessau on 24 Sept. and was immediately received at the court of Prince Leopold Friedrich Franz, where, in that Prince's absence,

I have delayed writing till my Trunks are gone to the Post Waggon. I must set out immediatly. In time coming I shall write with more composure. In the mean time my scheme gives me great satisfaction. I ever remain your affectionate freind

JAMES BOSWELL

To Johnston, Saturday 6 October 1764

MS. Yale (L 730).
ADDRESS: No. 2. To John Johnston Esq: of Grange.

Leipsic, 6 Octr. 1764

MY DEAR JOHNSTON: I find myself perfectly well in this City which is much larger than I imagined. It is fair time; so that there is here an immense concourse of all nations. The hurry the variety the novelty agitate my spirits and leave no entrance for the gloomy fiend. If he shows his black visage on the frontiers of my Mind a detachment of brisk animal spirits like a Corps of light troops give him a reception so smart that he is glad to retreat with grumbling precipitation.

Do you know I past a week at Dessau in perfect happiness. So much was I employed, so well was I amused that during seven days I am sure I had not seven hours of Melancholy. I shall ever remember this agreable court with gay regard. Where We have been admitted to the embraces of fair felicity we feel an instantaneous joy spring up in our Souls. You know the famous story of the horse of Darius whose neighing made his Master a King.[1] Did My Sovereign wish to hear me express my gladness he must cause me be led to the noble forrests of Anhalt Dessau.

I have come here without any letters of recommendation; so have had a fair tryal of my real Merit. And what have I found think you? I have found Johnston that your vaunting freind has not

his brothers, his sisters, and his uncle, Prince Dietrich, made JB welcome. He was shown over the palace, its stables and its cattle-farm; taken out stag-hunting; entertained repeatedly to dinner and supper, to cards and music; and invited to a reception and ball given in honour of Prince Charles of Saxony (Journ. 24 Sept. to 1 Oct. 1764).

---

[1] In the story told by Herodotus (iii.

84–86) seven aspirants to be king of Persia agreed to admit the claim of the one whose horse neighed first after sunrise on the following day. Oebares, Darius's groom, tethered a mare specially favoured by Darius's horse by the road-side, in such a position that the horse should recognize her and whinny to her as the seven candidates rode past at break of day. This was taken as a sign from heaven and Darius was immediately elected.

half the Pride that he ought to have. Sir I am one of the most engaging Men that ever lived. Amidst the innumerable multitude of Existences that have past thro' this World I beleive upon my honour that very few have been blest with more agreable talents. I have made acquaintance with Professors[2] here who have shown me an attention and a cordiality that would charm thy benevolent soul. Leipsic has ever been a distinguished Seat of learning. It still preserves it's reputation. I have seen two very noble Librarys, and some very elegant Gardens.[3] Tomorrow morning I set out for Dresden. Congratulate with me Thou old and faithfull freind of Boswell thou firm Borderer who hast allways stood by him in fair weather and foul. Live long and long be happy. I ever remain My Dear Sir your most sincere freind

JAMES BOSWELL

To Johnston, Friday 12 October 1764

MS. Yale (L 731).

ADDRESS: No. 3. To John Johnston Esq: of Grange.

Dresden, 12 Octr. 1764

MY DEAR JOHNSTON: The Capital of Saxony now contains your freind. I wish with all my heart that I had you here. Dresden is the most beautifull City that I ever saw. The houses are generally built of free Stone so that the Streets have a most elegant look. The Catholic Church and some other public edifices are very fine; very splendid I should say. There is a fine river here, over which is built a magnificent bridge. The Country on each side of the river is prettily varied with hill and dale and often ornamented with Vineyards.[1] It fills me with agreable ideas and refreshes in

[2] JB had met Johann Christoph Gottsched (1700–66), Professor of Logic and Metaphysics ("a big stately comely Man, with an ease of manners like a Man of the world"); Karl Andreas Bel (1717–82), Professor of Poetry and University Librarian ("a lively Hungarian, with a degree of french manners"); and Christian Fürchtegott Gellert (1715–69), Extraordinary Professor ("a poor sickly creature") (Journ. 4, 5 Oct. 1764).

[3] JB had been much impressed by the University Library, and he had also

visited the Magistrates' Library. The gardens he saw that morning he says he "liked much. One of them is noble and extensive. It has the dutch taste improved. There are in it four large Stone statues of excellent Workmanship; Indeed the best of the kind that I ever saw" (Journ. 5, 6 Oct. 1764).

[1] "This day I had a pleasant drive between Meissen and Dresden. We went along the side of the Elbe. On each side of the river were Beautifull rising grounds

my mind the fading pictures of my gay sensations in the days of Youth. But why talk so? Am I not young still? Am I not healthy? Am I not joyous? Yes I am. Without doubt I am so this afternoon. Well, and shall I not be so tomorrow? Ah! Johnston my worthy freind! Thou who knowest my gloomy as well as my gay disposition, thou knowest that eer the Sun has gone another round I shall probably be old, be sickly and be sad. What a strange temperament have I got! And pray My freind have not all mankind the same in a certain degree? Yes; all Mankind are more or less Hypochondriack. What think you of this method of entertaining you? Notwithstanding of all the Objects arround me, I cannot help reflecting on myself. O Johnston forgive me for harping upon this string which one would think must e'er now have been thrummed to pieces. What will you have Man? Will you have Poetry? Well the whim seises me and I will give thee at all events two or four lines. This is a true Whim as much as if a Man who had an empty house should say, "Come Johnston You shall sup with me, and I'll give you two or four dishes." Never was honest man's house emptier than is my head just now, and never did any man know worse where to find Victuals than I just now know where to find rhimes.

However Come on.

> Thou freind of Boswell! and thou Laird of Grange
> Preserve thy Lands, let not thy freindship change,
> Write not too much, lye not too long abed,
> Nor let strong liquors knock thee on the head.
> Hire a stout Nag and on the sands of Leith[2]
> Ride like an English Rogue on Hounslow heath.[3]
> Thus mayst thou purchase all the joys of health
> And laugh at Hopetoun with his heaps of wealth.[4]

covered with Vines. Pray may we not have the same in Scotland? Surely our climate differs little from that of Saxony. I saw too here and there old Castles *Heerschaften*'s houses, seats of Gentlemen. It pleased me. It was Scottish" (Journ. 8 Oct. 1764).

[2] Horse-races were held regularly during the summer on the sands at Leith.

[3] Hounslow Heath in the 18th century was the nearest stretch of really wild country to London, and across it the two main roads from the west of England converged towards Hounslow. It was con-

sequently a favourite resort of highwaymen, and along the roadside in that area the bodies of hanged robbers were exposed on gibbets as a warning to others.

[4] John Hope (1704–81), 2nd Earl of Hopetoun, owned, with other property, the productive mines of Leadhills. He was wealthy enough to be able to give away in charity the whole salary of his public office as a Lord of Police, and yet raise an exceedingly large family. By his three successive wives he had eighteen children, fifteen of whom survived to maturity (*Scots Peer*. iv. 497).

Thus to my freind may vigrous Sons be born
And future Granges Annandale adorn.

Adieu My dear freind and beleive me ever yours
JAMES BOSWELL

To Johnston, Saturday 20 October 1764

MS. Yale (L 732). The date and the first five words of this letter are also found as a fragment (MS. Yale L 733) on a leaf containing JB's German and Swiss Memoranda, 26 Oct. to 1 Nov. 1764 (MS. Yale J 5).

ADDRESS: No. 4. To John Johnston Esq: of Grange.

Saxe-Gotha, 20 Octr. 1764

MY DEAR JOHNSTON: Let not thy curious Imagination be put in Motion, or rather be set aworking by the name of Saxe-Gotha. Think not to have a Royal letter, because I am writing at the Place from whence came the Mother of our Royal Sovereign.[1] No Johnston. Human Beings and the Epistles of human beings are very different things. Nor ought one to expect a good letter from the Place whence sprung a good Princess. I am this day a very dull Mortal, not melancholy, but realy stupid. You may judge from my manner of writing. What clumsy attempts am I making to entertain You! I beg you may not laugh at me. At least laugh as gently as you can. Make not the whole Neighbourhood ring with thy unrestrained bursts of merriment. There is a certain kind respect due to a freind in his moments of Dullness. He is in a certain degree dead: And the Dead allways have a claim to our reverence. To be dead is a sufficient plea for obtaining regard. But when he who is dead has been distinguished in life, surely we may pay him extraordinary honour. Upon this principle Johnston, I this day demand thy serious tenderness. Thou mayst smile; But it must be with reluctance; and thou must say to thyself, "My poor freind! is it so with thee? Is this the vivacious the romantic Boswell with whom I have past such hours as Angels might have past with pleasure. Alas! but I say no more. Yet a few days, perhaps a few hours and we shall have him again."

What think you Johnston of writing my Epitaph? In these enlightened days when the arts are advanced to a degree allmost incredible, when calculation reigns, and a Man builds a house for

[1] The mother of George III was Augusta, daughter of Frederick II, Duke of Saxe-Gotha.

139

thirty years, as exactly as a Cook makes a dinner for thirty People, what think you of writing an Epitaph for a man who is to be dead only two days? It must neither have the sadness of one upon a man who is dead for good and all; nor must it be so liberal in Eulogiums; as our dead man is to get up again very soon, and may probably give them the lie. It must be a short, decent Composition as Thus.

Epitaph on Mr. Boswell dead from Saturday to Monday.
Ye who the generous lively Boswell knew
With kind regret this gloomy Object view
But let not hopeless grief your bosoms pain
For, in two days he'll be alive again.

I ever remain My Dear Freind yours with all Affection
JAMES BOSWELL

To Johnston, Saturday 27 October 1764

MS. Yale (L 734).
ADDRESS: No. 5. To John Johnston Esq: of Grange.

Werkle, 27 Octr. 1764
MY DEAR JOHNSTON: You will no doubt be surprised to find me dating a letter from a place not mentioned in any history,[1] seldom to be met with in a News-paper; and hardly to be distinguished upon a Map. The truth of the matter is, I forgot to write to you from Cassel where I have past two or three days. My forgetfullness galls me. Shakespear says "a galled horse will wince,"[2] and you see Johnston, a galled freind will write. At the first stage I sit down to attone for my Neglect. I am in a little dirty village, and wearied is my body.[3] My mind bears it company. So I am a pretty

[1] Werkel is a small village at a road junction, fourteen miles from Kassel on the way to Marburg and Frankfurt.

[2] "Let the gall'd jade winch; our withers are unwrung" (*Hamlet* III. ii. 253).

[3] He was travelling as cheaply as possible and had passed the day in an uncomfortable closed wagon, along with his own servant and a French servant whom he describes as "a Blackguard, impudent dog". He also tried to sleep beside them on the straw-strewn floor of the inn, but found this impossible: "It was terrible. The heat of an Iron Stove rendered the straw Musty and the air hot and this joined to the breaths of a good many people by no means of the most clean race, rendered the room most abominable. I could not sleep. One sad circumstance in the *Stube* or common room of a German Inn is being obliged to sleep with a tallow candle or a coarse lamp a-burning. I had recourse to the *Stall Knecht* and got a place in the Hay loft, where I slept sound tho' cold" (Journ. 27 Oct. 1764).

sort of a fellow. However Johnston I greet you well. I send you the kind wishes of a sleepy freind, and the affectionate sentiments of a stupified companion. Mayst thou ever be independent, and of good report. Mayst thou have a wife of distinguished merit. And mayst thou never be made a Cuckold. If however thy head should unhappily shoot forth horny excrescences, may they be of noble size, such as Kings and Princes have borne upon their elevated brows.

Forgive this attempt towards a letter, and ever beleive me My Dear Sir Your Affectionate Freind

JAMES BOSWELL

To Johnston, Wednesday 7 November 1764

MS. Yale (L 735).

ADDRESS: No. 6. To John Johnston Esq: of Grange.

ENDORSEMENT: Manheim 7th Novemr. 1764.

Manheim, 7 Novr. 1764

MY DEAR JOHNSTON: To find Boswell in bad humour is no new thing for you. You have seen him sulky as a Welchman who has been rejected in the Herald's court,[1] as an Englishman who has had his dinner spoiled, as an Irishman who has been detected in uttering five Bulls, and in forming a project to carry off a rich widow, and as a Scotsman who has lost an Election, or who has got a younger officer put over his head. I could give you many comparrisons as excellent as these, should I come upon the continent. But, at present I would not chuse to go out of his Majesty's dominions. If you ask me in a respectfull manner why I am in bad humour, I shall tell you. I say in a respectfull manner, because when a man is sulky he is also proud, and requires particular attention to be payed him, even by his best freinds. Well do you know this, Johnston. Well may you remember how I begged of you one evening at Thom's not to lean upon the table, because it gave me pain.

I am in bad humour at Manheim because I have found here a very bad court. The Elector wants forsooth to be a prodigious great man. He gives an Opera and a French Comedy and a Concert or an academy of Music as he calls it, all which entertainments are realy magnificent. But then he treats Strangers with a distance

---

[1] A reference to the proverbial Welsh pride of family and pedigree.

which makes some of them laugh at him, and others curse him, according to their temperaments. For my own part I have had an inclination to do both. As to his table I can say nothing. Strangers are very seldom invited to dine there. I have not been asked once. What an inhospitable dog![2] I have been obliged to dine at an Ordinary amongst fellows of all sorts and sizes. It was one of the best tables in town: But the company disgusted me sadly. O British take warning from me and shun the dominions of the Elector Palatine. I remain My Dear Johnston ever yours

JAMES BOSWELL

To Johnston, Friday 9 November 1764

MS. Yale (L 736).
ADDRESS: No. 7. To John Johnston Esq: of Grange.
ENDORSEMENT: Carlsrus 9th. Novemr. 1764.

Carlsrus, 9 Novr. 1764

MY DEAR JOHNSTON: I shall not here repeat the old song that The World is full of changes. But I shall not delay to inform you of a most agreable one for your freind. Instead of fretting at the Court of Manheim, I am now carousing at the court of Baden-Dourlach. The Marcgrave is a sensible, polite man. He has travelled a great deal, which one may soon find out from his Conversation and Address. He has been in England twice, and has liked it much, for he talks the language realy well, knows the history of Britain, and is even acquainted with the particular genius of the different parts of the Kingdom. His highness remembers the names of Streets

[2] On his arrival, JB had sent in his letter of introduction to General de Fürstenberg, Governor of Mannheim, who had referred him to M. Harold, an Irish Gentleman of the Chamber at the Elector's court. For various reasons he was not presented until two days later: "Harold talked of not presenting me till tomorrow. After having allready waited two days, this piqued me not a little; and had I not been presented this day, I should have bluntly set out next morning. However the Grand Chambellan presented me to the Elector. His Highness asked me from whence I came. He was very swarthy, and very high and mighty. I was presented to the Electrice, who was much painted, and also exceedingly lofty" (Journ. 5 Nov. 1764). The Elector was Karl Theodor (1724–99), who later succeeded to the Electorate of Bavaria. JB was so piqued by his reception and so unfavourably impressed by the insolent hauteur of the Elector that he wrote of him:

"Burnt be his palace to the very ground
And let no vestige where it stood be found.
For Hospitality ne'er enter'd there
But studied grandeur to make Blockheads stare."

(Ten Lines a Day, Verses, 7 Nov. 1764, MS. Yale M 281).

and Squares and a thousand little particulars with regard to London, which prove that he has entered into the spirit of the Place. I have allready had the honour of talking a long time with him, and since dinner he has done me the honour to send me a parcel of English Newspapers. Ay Johnston this is treating a Stranger with politeness. And do you imagine that a Prince loses any thing by such a conduct? Have I not as much respect for his Highness as if he had held up his head and looked at me as a Bashaw looks at a Slave? Indeed I respect him more much more than the silent Negroe at Manheim. You must know that the Elector Palatine is exceedingly swarthy. I wish he was well drubbed.[1]

And now Johnston I am contented and chearfull. My Servant a good Suiss[2] is not a little pleased to find me so; for, when I am vexed and consequently gloomy it is not a very agreable post to put my hair in papers.

All good things attend you My Dear Johnston. I ever remain Your Most Affectionate Freind

JAMES BOSWELL

To Johnston, Thursday 22 November 1764

MS. Yale (L 737).
ADDRESS: No. 8. To John Johnston Esq: of Grange.
ENDORSEMENT: Strasbourg 22d. Novemr. 1764.

Strasbourg, 22 Novr. 1764

MY DEAR JOHNSTON: You must have often seen in an Edinburgh

[1] JB's chagrin at his treatment by the Elector, which had fermented in his mind for three days, was completely mollified by the courteous reception he received from the Margrave of Baden-Durlach, and by the prominence given him at supper with Eberhard Friedrich von Stetten, the Margrave's Maréchal, and "a good jovial company", when he was placed at the head of the table.

Karl Friedrich (1728–1811), the Margrave, is remembered for his friendship with Voltaire and for his attempt to found a German Academy. Later, by alliance with Napoleon, he greatly enlarged the area of his principality, and held successively the titles of Prince Elector and Grand Duke.

[2] Jacob Hänni, JB's Bernese servant, had been engaged at The Hague to accompany him on his tour, as he spoke both French and German. He was a useful, active, intelligent servant, though he had a Swiss independence which made him unprepared to suffer with docility JB's occasional bouts of ill temper. He criticized JB to his face and accused him of inferior breeding, stinginess, and a taste for low company: he reproached him, too, for cruelty towards the dog Jachone which Paoli gave him as a parting gift: but he stayed with JB throughout the Corsican expedition, and left him only when he reached Lyons on his homeward way (Journ. *passim*).

Advertisement the City of Strasbourg. "Strasbourg and St. Domingo Snuff."[1] Who has not read this? In the City of Strasbourg am I now writing. Lest I should forget an anecdote of importance I will tell it you immediatly. The Tobacco trade here employs Six thousand hands. I must ask your pardon, My Dear Johnston, for having neglected to write to you from Ratstat where I past three days at the court of Baden Baden. The Prince[2] is Catholic, so we had high Mass in his Chappel, which pleased my solemn humour very much. It is the court in Germany where a man is most at his ease. You would have loved it dearly. You would have been hand and Glove with his Highness. He would have called you Grange. You can scarcely beleive how simple and free he is, without Affectation, quite natural. If he does not make you respect him I defy you not to like him. We had a very excellent table both at dinner and Supper. The Court is numerous, and there are some very handsom women there, Again, for you Johnston. Methinks I see your honest eyes glittering with delight to behold the sweet Mademoiselle de Geismar.[3] So tall! so genteel! so loving! Come come Johnston, compose yourself: Be upon your good behaviour. Consider where you are. You must not think to get up and take the charming Creature in your arms and give her a kiss as you do to a bonny Lass on your *ain braes*. I know a little the manners of courts: So be counselled by your freind. If you had her with you in the Garden, or in your Bedchamber, I should not oppose your tasting her delicious lips. But at present, taste something else. The Marcgrave's Rhenish and Burgundy are both excellent. Call for a couple of glasses of any of the two, and we'll drink your Mistress's health. You see Johnston how Imagination carrys me back from Strasbourg to Ratstat.[4] That may be true. But tomorrow morning early a coach comes to carry me forward to Basle; and that will be truer. So, my good Johnston good night. I am ever your true freind

JAMES BOSWELL

[1] The tobacco industry was then, and still is, important in Strasbourg.

[2] August Georg (1706–71), Margrave of Baden-Baden. On his death the principality was merged with Baden-Durlach.

[3] Presumably a daughter of Baron von Geismar, Chief Privy Councillor of Baden-Baden.

[4] He had taken leave of the Margrave at Rastatt on 19 Nov. and come on next day to Strasbourg.

To Johnston, Monday 26 November 1764

MS. Yale (L 738).

ADDRESS: No. 9. To John Johnston Esq: of Grange.

ENDORSEMENT: Basle 26th. Novr. 1764.

Basle, 26 Novr. 1764

MY DEAR JOHNSTON: Germany is now behind me. I am now fairly entered into Switzerland. I have very little to say to you at present   Only this that my Father formed me early to be an antiquarian and hence I view this Town with a venerable pleasure. Holbens was born here.[1] The great Erasmus lived long here,[2] founded a College for poor Students died here and is buried in the Cathedral Church. In latter times the great Maupertuis died here attended by four Capuchins to support his soul in the last moments. Why not? If this served but to compose his mind by pleasing his Imagination, was it not of Advantage.[3] Frobenius lived here.[4] You may have seen at the end of Ancient Editions of the Roman Authours *Basileæ typis Frobenii*. I remain My Dear Johnston ever yours

JAMES BOSWELL

[1] Hans Holbein (1497–1543), the younger, was born at Augsburg and lived chiefly at Basle from 1515 to 1532. The best known of his works in Basle is the altar-piece in eight small canvas panels, depicting the Passion of Christ, which was preserved until 1777 in the town hall and then transferred to the museum.

[2] Desiderius Erasmus (c. 1466–1536), having completed his researches in Holland, France, Italy, and England, settled in Basle about 1514 to supervise the publication of his writings by Johann Froben, the printer. Though he left Basle at intervals to go to England, the Netherlands, and elsewhere, it remained from that time his headquarters, and Froben's press the main instrument of his propaganda for the new classical learning. The residue of his considerable estate he left for the benefit, among others, of promising young scholars (R. B. Drummond, *Erasmus*, 1873, ii. 340; E. Bonjour, *Die Universität Basel*, 1960, p. 104).

[3] The death of Pierre Louis Moreau de Maupertuis (1698–1759), the French mathematician and philosopher, was not, according to La Beaumelle, so dignified and peaceful as JB suggests. Worn out and ill, he had retired to Basle in 1758 and there lay in great weakness and suffering, tormented by the news that Voltaire, who hated him, intended to spread abroad a damaging scandal about him. La Beaumelle draws a pathetic picture of his helplessness on his deathbed, with the children of the house chasing the flies away from his face, and of his final delirium in which he ceaselessly talked of his mistress Eleonore, so that those about him were concerned only to keep his wife out of his presence (L. A. de La Beaumelle, *Vie de Maupertuis*, 1856, pp. 214–16).

[4] Johann Froben (c. 1460–1527), the printer whose press became for a time the most important in Europe because of his fruitful co-operation with Erasmus, who chose and edited the classics he published.

To Johnston, Wednesday 28 November 1764

MS. Yale (L 739).

ADDRESS: No. 10. To John Johnston Esq: of Grange.

ENDORSEMENT: Soleure 28th. Novr. 1764.

Soleure, 28 Novr. 1764

MY DEAR JOHNSTON: Man is a curious Animal: and I am not at all amazed that many Philosophers have tried to define him and Pope written a Poem upon him as the Philosophers as well as the Poet were men themselves. But whatever may be the essential nature of man, sure I am that his happiness or misery his Abilitys or his Weakness depend allmost entirely on his Position. This evening Johnston, you are shivering with cold at Edinburgh: While I bid defiance to Winter at Soleure. You are probably thoughtfull and gloomy. I am thoughtfull and gay. And whence comes this mighty difference between two men who in many hours of their existence have differed less than most men. Why from no other cause but Position. You are in a Scots Town. I am in a Suiss Town. You are in a dirty Town. I am in a clean Town. You have past the day in Uniformity. I have past the day in Variety.

I have walked the ramparts. I have viewed from a Tour the Environs. I have been in the Jesuits and Franciscan Churches.[1] I have been at a Card Assembly. I have kist (but no more) a comely healthy Maid at my Inn. I have dined and supt at the French Ambassador's. There is my day.

I must mention one circumstance as to Soleure which will please you much. It is the first town I have been in that Mr. Addison mentions in his travels.[2] Does not the Spectator's having been

[1] "Queen Berthe, wife of Rodolph II, King of Bourgogne, was the founder of a convent of monks, which she richly endowed, and which still exists. . . . The Jesuits also have a very splendid dwelling in this town. They first received permission to reside in it in the year 1646, on condition that they made no purchase, and did not augment their number beyond fifteen. As the people, however, rarely keep their promises, they soon increased their society to thirty, and ingratiated themselves so much into the favour of Louis the Fourteenth, that he purchased some land in the town, whereon they erected the present edifice. . . . In the centre of the town stands part of an old tower, which may be ranked amongst the monuments of antiquity, the stones that were employed in building it, are said to have been cemented together with the whites of eggs and wine; but whatever the composition was, the smallest portion cannot be detached without the greatest difficulty" (A. Yosy, *Switzerland, As now Divided into Nineteen Cantons*, 1815, ii. 151–53).

[2] "*Soleurre* is our next considerable Town, that seem'd to me to have a

ıere give a value to it. It is mighty agreable to read Mr. Addison's observations and then look at what he has described. I have
found many Alterations or more properly new works since his
time. With these my Journal shall be enriched.[3] With these my
worthy freind shall be feasted.

My Dear Johnston! "Live well" as the good German says, and
beleive me ever Your Most sincere Affectionate Freind

JAMES BOSWELL

To Johnston, Wednesday 5 December 1764

MS. Yale (L 740).
ADDRESS: No. 11. To John Johnston Esq: of Grange.
ENDORSEMENT: Vall. de Travers, 3d. Decemr. 1764.

[Môtiers] Vall de Travers, 5[1] Decr. 1764

MY DEAR JOHNSTON: Art thou alive o! my freind? or has thy
spirit quitted it's earthly habitation. To hear of thy death would
not now distress me. I would glory to think of thy exaltation.

Johnston I am in the Village which contains Rousseau. These
three days I have visited that Sublime Sage.[2] He has enlightened
my mind. He has kindled my Soul. Yes, we are Immortal. Yes.

greater Air of Politeness than any I saw in *Switzerland*. The *French* Ambassador has his Residence in this Place. His Master contributed a Noble Sum of Mony to the Jesuits' Church, which is not yet quite finish'd. It is the finest Modern Building in *Switzerland*. The old Cathedral Church stood not far from it. At the Ascent that leads to it are a couple of antique Pillars that belong'd to an old Heathen Temple, Dedicated to *Hermes*: They seem *Tuscan* by their Proportion. The whole Fortification of *Soleure* is fac'd with Marble. But its best Fortifications are the high Mountains that lye within its Neighbourhood, and separate it from the *Franche Compté*" (Joseph Addison, *Remarks on Several Parts of Italy, etc. in the Years 1701, 1702, 1703, 1705*, pp. 481–82).
[3] "I saw the Jesuits Church which was a building when Mr. Addison was here. As he was here more than Sixty years ago the Church does not seem new. . . .

Where the Old Cathedral stood they are now building a magnificent Church. When Mr. Addison was here there was a church a building. When Mr. Boswell is here, he finds the same thing. There is a stroke of real vanity. Mr. Addison mentions two tuscan Pillars which stood at the Ascent to the Cathedral. One of them is still standing. I mounted a Tower and saw the Town. It is not large. I took a walk on the Ramparts. Mr. Addison says 'the whole fortification of Soleure is faced with marble.' It is indeed faced with a hard stone which may be called Marble, but which is so coarse that the term marble should hardly be given to it" (Journ. 28 Nov. 1764).

[1] MS. "3".
[2] He had had at this time three meetings with Rousseau, on the 3rd, the 4th, and the 5th. Later he returned from Yverdon to Môtiers, and had two further meetings with Rousseau on 14 and 15 Dec.

147

Jesus has given us a Revelation. I feel an enthusiasm beyond expression. Good Heaven am I so elevated? Where is Gloom? Where is Discontent? Where are all the little vexations of the World? O Johnston! Wert thou but here![3] I am in a beautifull wild Valley surrounded by immense mountains. I am just setting out for Neufchatel. But I return to Rousseau. I am to be alone on Horseback in a dark Winter night, while the earth is covered with Snow.[4] My present Sentiments give me a force and a vigour like the Lion in the desert. Farewell My Dear Freind

JAMES BOSWELL

To Johnston, Sunday 9 December 1764

MS. Yale (L 741).

ADDRESS: No. 12. To John Johnston Esq: of Grange.

Neufchatel, 9 Decr. 1764

MY DEAR JOHNSTON: I am now at the old Government of My Lord Marischal,[1] where upon his Lordship's Recommendation I have been extremely well received. It is a fine healthy Place. The air is fresh. The beautifull lake yeilds most delicious large trout, and the Hills arround in vines abound. I have realy lived luxuriously. There is a great deal of good Company here very social very gay.

There is an English Captain of the Navy[2] here an amiable young fellow. He has the true grave composure of a John Bull of good temperature. He looks at a jolly Suiss Girl, and says: "That now is what we call in England *a good piece*," and he never alters his countenance, not he.

[3] This letter, written spontaneously to share a mood of exuberant high-spirits with an intimate friend, illustrates the way in which the unposted letters, though intended for the same reader, could serve an entirely different purpose for JB than that of the Journal, with its more consciously ordered narrative.

[4] He was about to return from Môtiers to Neuchâtel, spending a night on the way at Brot: "The night was such as Lady Randolp[h] describes—

it was dark December: Wind and rain
Had beat all night.

I was firm and bold and among the wild rocks had grand thought. About nine I arrived at *Bro*" (Journ. 5 Dec. 1764). Lady Randolph is the distressed mother in Home's *Douglas*.

[1] The Earl Marischal had been appointed Governor of Neuchâtel by Frederick the Great in 1752, and had lived there until 1759, when he went as Prussian Ambassador to Spain.

[2] George Bowyer (1739–99) was later an admiral, and doubly a baronet—first in 1794 (after he had distinguished himself in the naval victory off Ushant), by creation, and then in 1799 by succession to his elder brother's title (*Comp. Bar.* iii. 59; v. 289).

A Parcel of his Countrymen threatened this winter to take a house here. The whole train consisted of Five Gentlemen, Five Tutors, twelve Servants twelve Horses and thirty Dogs. Was there ever such a Set? Luckily no house could be had, tho' they wrote in the true english stile, "Never mind money. We grudge no expence."

I have obtained my Father's permission to make the tour of Italy. It is impossible for me to express my happiness. My Dear Freind! I shall have the richest enjoyment of all the fine arts. Live and prosper o Johnston! and continue to regard your most affectionate freind

JAMES BOSWELL

To Johnston, Wednesday 19 December 1764

MS. Yale (L 742).

ADDRESS: No. 13. To John Johnston Esq: of Grange.

Yverdun, 19 Decr. 1764

MY DEAR JOHNSTON: A plain man like your Honour cannot fail to marvel much at the diversity of dates of these my letters. Some of these dates are to you utterly unknown and I beleive you will wet your thumbs and turn the leaves of Gordon's *Geographical Grammar*[1] many many a time without being a whit the wiser as to the point in question. I say Gordon's *Grammar* because I know it is your Book altho' we have had twenty better since his time. But you are an Antiquarian and love what is old. I know no man on earth who would do so ill at Paris as you; for, you are never in the fashion.

When you see a date like the present, you will perhaps conclude that I am playing at Hide and Seek with you. And your black beard will begin awagging, and you will grumble pretty hoarsly that You do not understand such Jokes on an old freind. Come Johnston man. Keep your temper. As the Children say I'll give you three guesses to tell where I am. I see you are realy sulky. I must tell you then.

I am in Switzerland at a little Town in the Canton of Bern where there is a number of very easy chearfull People. Much have I

[1] *Geography Anatomized: or, A Compleat Geographical Grammar*, by Patrick Gordon, F.R.S., London, 1693, continued to appear in new enlarged editions until 1754, when the 20th was published.

heard of Yverdun from my good Mess-mates of Utrecht Madame Brown and Mademoiselle Kinloch.[2] Sir James their Father has been thirty years in this Country.[3] He is still the old Scot. He is ar East Lothian Suiss Laird. I have been to see him at his Country House about a league from this. I talked *braid Scots* with him, and sung him *Sherrifmuir*[4] and made him as merry, as if I had poured a bottle of whisky down his throat. He passes the winter at Yverdun. He has a fine family three Sons in the Portuguese Service and Six daughters. One of his daughters is married to the Baron de Brackel a Gentleman of Courland who was formerly in the frencl service and a great freind of the Marischal de Saxe.[5] He is a very pretty Man. I live in his house where I am treated like a near Relation. His Lady is a charming Woman. May You have such another My good old freind: so prayeth

JAMES BOSWELL

[2] Catharine Brown (b. 1736), the wife of Robert Brown, minister of the English Church at Utrecht, and Marguerite Susanne Kinloch (b. 1742), who had been staying with her when JB was in Utrecht, were both daughters of Sir James Kinloch, and natives of Switzerland. JB had seen much of them, and had improved his French by conversing with them ("Dialogues at the Hague", MS. Yale M 91). See Henry Wagner, "Descendants of Sir James Kinloch, Bart.", *The Genealogist*, n.s., xiv. 200–03; G. R. de Beer, "Anglais au Pays de Vaud", *Revue Historique vaudoise*, juin 1951, pp. 60–66.

[3] Sir James Kinloch (1705–78) of Gilmerton, 4th Bt., had married a Swiss wife and lived in summer at Giez, near Yverdon, and in winter at Yverdon. Four of his daughters were married, the second eldest, Louise Madeleine (b. 1733) to Frédéric Casimir, Baron de Brackel, a member of the nobility of Courland who had been exiled by the Russian government. Before leaving Scotland, Sir James had been married to a Scots wife, and the legality of his second marriage seems to have been dubious. His brother David, not his son, succeeded to the baronetcy (*The Genealogist*, n.s., xiv. 200 ff.; *Comp. Bar.* iv. 347, note c). "My compliments to Mr. Brown of whom I hear a mighty good character, His wifes Fathr is My

Lady Coalstouns Brother but poor mar he was unhappy having a Wife in this Country still alive to whom he was married before he married Mris Browr Mother. I mention this to you in confidence don't speak of it Mris Brown may be a good woman notwithstanding this Macula natalium so it should not be published" (From Lord Auchinleck, c 10 Dec. 1763).

[4] The famous song with the opening lines, "There's some say that we wan, Some say they wan", the authorship of which was ascribed by Burns to Murdoch McLennan, minister of Crathie from 1749 to 1783. It appears in David Herd's *Ancient and Modern Scottish Songs* 1776 (i. 104–08), and in many later collections.

[5] Maurice (1696–1750), Comte de Saxe, Marshal of France, one of the 354 acknowledged illegitimate children of Augustus the Strong, Elector of Saxony and King of Poland, had been elected Duke of Courland in 1726, at the instance of the hereditary Duchess, Anna Ivanovna, who had offered to marry him. He had accepted the dukedom, but declined her hand; whereupon her opposition had driven him out of Courland, in spite of an army he had succeeded in mustering for his defence.

To Johnston, Friday 21 December 1764

MS. Yale (L 743).
ADDRESS: No. 14. To John Johnston Esq: of Grange.

Lausanne, 21 Decr. 1764

MY DEAR JOHNSTON: Ignorance is the mother of Absurdity. This I recall a strong instance of in my own life. Some years ago Doctor Pringle proposed to my Father that I should go to Lausanne.[1] I would by no means hear of it, having formed some strange dissagreable idea of it merely because I knew nothing about it or of it to write good english. I am now at that very place; and I find it a most agreable healthy gay little Town.

I have found here a swarm of British, and amongst others the young Laird of Garthmore.[2] I imagined him to be in Turky and was most joyfully surprised to find him here. We have walked and have had the most excellent conversation. He is a fine bold Highlander learned lively cordial. I set out tomorrow for Geneva having past here only two nights. Adieu my ever cordial freind

JAMES BOSWELL

To Johnston, Tuesday 15 January 1765

MS. Yale (L 744).
ADDRESS: No. 15. To John Johnston Esq: of Grange.

Turin, 15 January 1765[1]

MY DEAR JOHNSTON: It is now many a week since I last wrote to you.[2]

[1] This may have been in 1760, when JB was bent on joining the Roman Catholic Church. When Gibbon was sixteen years old he was converted to Catholicism to the distress of his father, who arranged for him to be put for a time in the care of a Calvinist minister at Lausanne. There he was soon induced to abandon his Catholicism.

[2] William Graham (d. 1775), eldest son of Nicol Graham of Gartmore, had been a member of the Edinburgh Faculty of Advocates since 1756 (*Faculty of Advocates*, p. 87). His mother Lady Margaret Cunningham was a daughter of the 11th Earl of Glencairn (*Scots Peer*. iv. 250). He never became Laird of Gartmore, but died before his father, who

was succeeded by his younger son Robert (d. ?1797; later Cunninghame-Graham).

William Graham was making an extended visit to the Continent, and had spent some time in France before coming to Switzerland. JB was so pleased to have his company at Lausanne that he wrote: "I flew to see him and happy we were to meet. He was quite gay. It pleased me to see that an Advocate *may* be made a fine fellow. He raged against the Scots Parliament House and a Man's passing his whole life in writing d—mned *Papers*" (Journ. 21 Dec.).

[1] MS. "1764".
[2] On 6 Jan. he had crossed from Switzerland by Mont Cenis, and called

Since that time I have seen a great deal, but Dissipation has so overpowered me, that I have been a mere passive Existence driven along by a whirlwind of agitation. I have been at Geneva, I have been with Voltaire,[3] I have past the Alps. You see I have had enough to say, could my mind have possessed half an hour of calm. But, I must own to you my freind, that my mind requires a little more of the sober influence of Old Father Time to give it that settled serenity which constitutes the true felicity of a rational Man. You will wonder that I did not become composed during my residence at Geneva, where John Calvin preached his gloomy orthodoxy, and where my Scots Presbyterian ideas might be supposed to return. But my good freind must know that Geneva is much more changed than Edinburgh. The Ghost of John Calvin would not be half so much dreaded at their Market place, as would the Ghost of John Knox at our Cross. The Mutability of Mankind is every where to be observed. At Geneva I have seen a most remarkable proof of it.

And now Johnston I am in the City of Turin. I have found it different from what I expected. There is neither the elegance of taste nor the politeness of manners that I supposed. It contains a great many idle men, and a great many abandoned women. Gross gallantry is their occupation. They couple without sentiment, like the Beasts of the field, with this difference that the Beasts have some natural affection for their offspring and the People here have none. Yet among this good-for-nothing race have I been as dissipated as if I had been among the most gay agreable Society on earth. O Johnston! I have lost my time here. I have been present⟨ed at⟩ court. The King of Sardinia is ⟨quiet and⟩[4] has no grand air. I was glad t⟨o view⟩ him as a Relation of our Royal House.[5]

at the *hopital des pèlerins*. Of the priest in charge of the chapel there he wrote: "My Reverend Father had a kind of resemblance of My old freind Johnston" (Journ. 6 Jan. 1765). He had reached Turin in the evening of the 7th, and had there sought out Wilkes, and started at once to lead the gallant and rakish life which he thought suited to a visiting English aristocrat—laying siege without success to the hearts of three Italian countesses, Mmes. di San Gillio, Borgaretto, and Scarnafigi.

[3] The meetings with Voltaire had taken place at Ferney on 24, 27, and 28 Dec. 1764.

[4] The phrase in brackets has been supplied from the Journal, where JB calls him "just a little quiet Man" (11 Jan. 1765).

[5] Charles-Emmanuel III (1701–73) was a great-grandson of Charles I: his mother, Anna Maria, was a daughter of Charles's daughter Henrietta. According to the Jacobites, he was next in the succession to the British throne, after Henry Benedict Maria Clement Stuart, Cardinal York.

His Son the Duke of Savoy looks well. I can say no more to you here. After this I shall write to you more regularly.

I ever remain very sincerely yours.

JAMES BOSWELL

To Johnston, Friday 25 January 1765

MS. Yale (L 745).

ADDRESS: No. 16. To John Johnston Esq: of Grange.

Milan, 25 January 1765

MY DEAR JOHNSTON: My rule now is to write to you, the day on which I arrive at a town and thus dissipation shall never make me forget my regular tribute   How whimsical is my present suite of Epistles to You. Is it possible that they are to be composedly bundled up till we meet. I write every one of them as if my Servant waited to carry it to the Post directly. I imagine your happiness when you receive it, and if I omit to write at any place where I ought to do it, I fancy you very angry with me. Few People of any nation can boast an Imagination more lively than mine. Vivacity I am certain of; but for strength for justness for continuance I must send you somewhere else. Perhaps however you are content with me and indeed take me as I am this evening, and you are much in the right.

You see from the date of this that I am now at Milan. Pleasing and curious are my ideas when I find myself for the first time in a City described by a Latin Classic. Milan is described by Ausonius as Mr. Addison has remarked.[1] I have great satisfaction in comparing

---

[1] Addison's translation of the description of Milan by the 4th-century Latin poet Ausonius is as follows:

Milan with Plenty and with Wealth o'er-flows,
And num'rous Streets with cleanly Dwellings shows;
The People, bless'd with Nature's happy Force,
Are Eloquent and Chearful in Discourse;
A *Circus* and a Theatre invites
Th'unruly Mob to Races and to Fights;
Moneta consecrated Buildings grace,
And the whole Town redoubled Walls embrace:

Here spacious Baths and Palaces are seen,
And intermingled Temples rise between;
Here circling *Colonnades* the Ground enclose,
And here the Marble Statues breathe in Rows:
Profusely grac'd the happy Town appears,
Nor *Rome* it self, her beauteous Neighbour, fears.

(Joseph Addison, *Remarks on Several Parts of Italy, etc.*, 1705, pp. 50–51).

ancient and modern sentiments manners and Buildings. Let Ausonius be placed in Milan as it now is and it would appear more strange to him an old Italian than it does to me a distant Caledonian. What think you would be his notion of the pompous Mass and of the variety of Religious orders. I suppose he would take the City of Milan for a Place of immense commerce, and the Monks for Merchants of different nations who are come hither to trade. As he would be extremely curious in asking questions he would be amazed to find the language so changed. When the Milanese would answer him in Italian he would take them also to be foreigners and finding very few People who could talk to him in the Roman tongue he would be much embarrassed. Perhaps he and I might meet, and bad as my Latin is, I would contrive to entertain him so well, that he would embrace me as a Countryman. In short honest Ausonius and I would be hale fellow well met. My Dear Johnston I am ever yours

James Boswell

To Johnston, Tuesday 29 January 1765

MS. Yale (L 746).

ADDRESS: No. 17. To John Johnston Esq: of Grange.

Plaisance, 29 Janry. 1765[1]

My Dear Johnston: I desire that you may look upon this as an extraordinary letter and may receive it as a Counterballance in part to former omissions. It is written at Plaisance or Placentia. I suppose a zealous Scots Etymological Antiquary of the Laird of Macfarlane's sect[2] would suppose Plaisance to be just the same name with the Pleasants of Edinburgh.[3] But of this you may judge for yourself.

Plaisance is a very comely Town situated upon the Po. The

[1] MS. "1764."

[2] The reference is to Walter Macfarlane of Macfarlane (d. 1767), Lady Betty Erskine's husband, whom JB despised as an "old clumsy dotard" (Journ. 2 Dec. 1762). He was a doggedly nationalistic Scot. His interest in the etymology of the names of people and places appears in his *Genealogical* and *Geographical Collections* (published in 5

vols. by the Scottish Historical Society, 1900; 1906–08).

[3] Piacenza, called in former times Placentia, did give its name to the steep, narrow street in the south-east quarter of Edinburgh known as the Pleasance. It was so called after a religious house, St. Mary's of Placentia, which stood there in pre-Reformation days (*Old and New Edinburgh*, i. 382).

great street is spacious and airy. I have past half a day here and seen all that was mentioned to me as curious. I set out this morning at three for Parma. I have been up all night, which in the month of January is not very comfortable, and which I suppose very few upon this globe experience save Sentrys, Sickwatchers, Chymists, Monks and Lunatics. I am sure My good Johnston that you at least are in your warm nest. Lye still then my honest fellow and take you a good sound sleep. You'll be a good Boy at nine oclock and will neither throw your slippers at the maid, your Tea-kettle at the Barber, a Caption[4] at your Landlady nor a Penfull of Ink on some Brother of the South who comes capering into your room. Farewell My indolent Freind

JAMES BOSWELL

To Johnston, Thursday 31 January 1765

MS. Yale (L 747).

ADDRESS: No. 18. To John Johnston Esq: of Grange.

Parma, 31 January 1765

MY DEAR JOHNSTON: Can I leave Parma without writing to You? Indeed no, as the present proves. It was here that My Lord Strath-more lived two years enchanted by an amiable Italian Countess.[1] I have seen her twice at the Opera and once in the Royal Garden. She has a gay Roman countenance. Her soul shines in her lovely eyes. She has a noble air. Take her all together and she is a very fine woman. I am not at all surprised when I hear of those violent passions in Italy. Were I not clouded by gloom and fortified by Stoicism it is most certain that I should be the Heroe of romantic Intrigue if I found Beauty and Sentiment united, and this may surely be found. Perhaps it may not be impossible to find this in a Scots Lass some sweet daughter of the hill whom Ramsay should

---

[4] Legal document intimating arrest, or apprehension for debt.

[1] John Lyon (1737–76), 9th Earl of Strathmore, who later married Mary Eleanor Bowes, heiress of George Bowes, M.P., and by Act of Parliament assumed his wife's surname, had travelled to Italy in 1760 with Thomas Pitt, son of William Pitt's eldest brother. According to Horace Walpole he did not return until more than three years later, when he impressed Walpole unfavourably as being "too *doucereux* and Celadonian", i.e. too consciously charming and swainlike (Walpole to Mann, 30 June 1763). The lady was Costanza Scotti (c. 1736–94) who had married Count Alessandro Sanvitale in 1756 (cf. Mann to Walpole, 26 June 1762).

have seen and sweetly sung of. Adieu My honest freind I am ever sincerely yours

JAMES BOSWELL

From Johnston, 1 February 1765

Missing. Reçu 27 Mars 1765. "Mr. Johnston" (Reg. Let.). A long letter which gave JB "uncommon joy" (*post* 9 Apr.). That it was dated 1 Feb. is mentioned in JB's letter of 11 May. In it JJ excused himself for his long silence and asked forgiveness. It contained news of JB's brothers John and David, of his friend Andrew Erskine, and of affairs in the Edinburgh Parliament House.

To Johnston, Tuesday 5 February 1765

MS. Yale (L 748).

ADDRESS: No. 19. To John Johnston Esq: of Grange.

Bolonia, 5 February 1765

MY DEAR JOHNSTON: If Strasbourg is remarkable for it's snuff Bolonia is no less so for it's Sausages. During all my travels I meet with places whose celebrity is made known to many only by the back or the Belly. Strasbourg and this Bolonia are allready mentioned. But I can give you a list to prove the truth of my assertion.

Westphalia is renowned for it's hams, Brunswic for it's Mum,[1] Leipsic for it's Larks, Neufchatel for it's wine, Florence for it's oil, Venice for it's Poplins, Genoa for it's velvets Rome for it's Purl[2] if we may beleive the London signs, Parma for it's cheese and so on till your Larder and wardrobe are compleatly filled.

[1] An English form of the German word *Mumme*, the name of a beer originally brewed in Brunswick. It was imported into England in large quantities in the 17th and 18th centuries (OED).

[2] "A liquor made by infusing wormwood or other bitter herbs in ale or beer" (OED). The "London signs" referred to may be illustrated by No. 5531 of the British Museum's collection of satirical prints: "The Black and White Scuffle, or Barber and Chimney-Sweeper at Fisty-Cuffs", No. 221 of a series printed and sold by Carington Bowles, and probably engraved earlier than the date of publication, 1 Jan. 1778. On a tavern wall behind the combatants is inscribed "Punch in Large Quantities" and "Hollands Gin and Roman Purl" (Mary D. George, *Catalogue of Political and Personal Satires . . . in the British Museum*, Vol. 5, 1771–83; photostat of the print in the Lewis-Walpole Library, information supplied by Mrs. Genevieve B. Butterfield, Curator of Prints.)

My Dear Freind I am fatigued tonight. I have seen a great deal in this ancient city and it's environs, but for my account thereof you must be referred to that capacious Treatise my Journal and so we heartily bid you farewell.

JAMES BOSWELL

To Johnston, Sunday 10 February 1765

MS. Yale (L 749).

ADDRESS: No. 20. To John Johnston Esq: of Grange.

Loretto, 10 Febry. 1765

MY DEAR JOHNSTON: This Letter is short but precious for it is written in the Holy Church of Loretto where I have seen the immense riches of our Lady and the Holy House itself where the blessed Virgin Mary lived which house was transported hither from Nazareth by Angels.[1] I am in a most pleasing solemn frame and upon my soul I cannot refuse some devotion to this miraculous Habitation, without giving up my faith in human testimony. Such is the cloud of evidences for this History of the Holy House. Who knoweth the ways of God: or who can say what may be the interpositions of his supreme power. I am a Sceptic. But a devout one. The grandeur of the High Mass—The crowd of Pilgrims and the various sacred appearances now arround me have made a strong impression upon my mind and fill me with a serious awe which I greatly preferr to all the levity of mirth. Farewell my Freind. This

---

[1] According to legend, the Santa Casa, reputed home of the Holy Virgin, was conveyed by supernatural means from Nazareth to Loreto when the Christians lost their last foothold in the Holy Land. It is said to have been transported to its present site in 1295, after experiencing lack of veneration at two other spots (near Fiume, and near Recanati) during the previous four years (*Encyclopaedia of Religion and Ethics*, ed. James Hastings, 1961, s.v. Loreto). "The holy house, or chapel of our Lady, stands in the middle of the church. It is an oblong room, 31 feet 9 inches in length, 13 feet 3 inches in breadth, and 18 feet 9 inches in height; incrusted with Carrara marble, of beauti-ful architecture, designed by Bramante; and ornamented with sculptures by Sansovino, San Gallo, Bandinelli, etc. representing the history of the blessed Virgin. . . . The sanctuary is perfectly crouded with sixty-two great lamps of gold and silver; one of the golden ones, which was presented by the republic of Venice, weighs thirty-seven pounds. There are also Angels waiting about the holy image, one of massive gold, and two of silver: and the walls are covered with plates of silver. The sacred bowl, out of which the holy family used to eat, is preserved here" (Thomas Martyn, *The Gentleman's Guide in his Tour through Italy*, 1787, pp. 119–20).

Letter will be valuable to you. I ever remain yours with much
Affection

JAMES BOSWELL

I write on the confessional of the english Jesuit[2] who has shown me
every civility.

To Johnston, Tuesday 12 February 1765

MS. Yale (L 750).

ADDRESS: No. 21. To John Johnston Esq: of Grange.

Spoleto, 12 Febry. 1765

MY DEAR JOHNSTON: Had the Scots Militia taken place,[1] and you
been a Colonel in the Annandale Battallion, this Letter would
have highly suited you. I now write from a City whose gallant
Inhabitants drove off the victorious Annibal when he was marching
with flying colours to Rome after having defeated the Romans at
Thrasymene.[2] Little did he expect that Spoleto would oppose him;
but he found himself much mistaken, and received such a shock,
that he fled like Sir John Cope from the field of Falkirk.[3] This

---

[2] R. Gillibrand, who wrote to JB on
13 Feb. 1765. He is further referred to
in Mem., 17 and 18 June 1765.

[1] The English Militia had been re-
organized on a national basis in 1757,
and by the Act then passed, all able-
bodied men were liable, if chosen by bal-
lot, to serve in person or by substitute in
county regiments officered by gentlemen
of property chosen by the Lord-Lieutenants
of the counties. As disaffection had been
more widespread in Scotland than in
England during the Jacobite risings, the
scheme had not been extended to Scotland.
There was a renewed agitation for a militia
in Scotland in 1760, after the failure of
Thurot's expedition, which was believed
to have been intended against Scotland
(Scots Mag., 1760, xxii. 44–45). A bill,
supported by the Tories and a majority
of Scots Members of Parliament, was
introduced, but it was defeated by the
Newcastle party, who were accused of
bribing Lord Advocate Dundas to be

their principal speaker with the promise
of the Lord Presidentship to which he was
appointed soon after (Scotland and Scotsmen i. 333). Even as late as 1782, when
Scottish Members of Parliament were
again stressing the defencelessness of
Scotland, Parliament refused to agree to
the establishment of a militia there
(Journals of the House of Commons xxxviii.
1007, 1043, 1045, 1048), and it was not
until 1797, when danger of a French
invasion seemed imminent, that the Scots
Militia Act was passed.

[2] Hannibal, having led his Carthaginian
army through Spain and Gaul and across
the Alps, advanced in the spring of
217 B.C. to the shores of Lake Trasi-
menus, where he destroyed the main
Roman army. Though he did not attack
Rome itself, but marched over Italy experiencing varying fortunes in different
places, Rome remained his objective until
his ultimate recall to Carthage.

[3] JB is obviously thinking of the
battle of Prestonpans. Cope was not in

People are surely of the same constitution as the Scots High-landers. They are in the heart of the Appenines, and their City is built upon a Mountain. I have been patroling it this evening, and figuring to myself the spirited courage with which the Old Spoletti rushed down against the foe. I have also viewed the remains of a noble Aqueduct which has been a work of immense labour.[4] Johnston I am now Romanising every day. My Patriotism is inflamed, and every spark of generous sentiment which I contain is kindling. Adieu My Old freind worthy to be so were I as great as any Roman that ever dignified Humanity. I am ever Affec-tionately Your's

JAMES BOSWELL

To Johnston, Tuesday 19 March 1765

MS. Yale (L 751).
ADDRESS: No. 22. To John Johnston Esq: of Grange.

Naples, 19 March 1765

MY DEAR JOHNSTON: If a Man's Mind never failed to catch the spirit of the Climate in which he breathes I ought now to write you a most delicious letter: For Naples is indeed a delicious Spot *præter omnes ridet*.[1] I have been near three weeks here and have been constantly employed in seeing the Classical Places all arround. Is it possible to conceive a richer scene than the finest Bay diversi-fied with Islands and bordered by feilds where Virgil's Muses charmed the Creation, where the renowned of ancient Rome enjoyed the luxury of glorious retreat, and the true flow of Soul which they valued as much as triumphs. But My Dear Freind modern Naples has nothing of the ancient Parthenope except it's heat and it's idleness. The People are the most shocking race

---

command at the battle of Falkirk, which took place on 17 Jan. 1746, while the Jaco-bite forces were retreating to the north. At Prestonpans Cope's army was completely routed by a surprise dawn-attack and he had to make a headlong retreat—the vic-tory celebrated in the Jacobite song "Hey, Johnny Cope, are ye waukin' yet?"
[4] The Ponte delle Torri spans the valley between the hill on which Spoleto stands and an adjacent height.

[1] Horace, *Odes* II. vi. 13:

Ille terrarum mihi praeter omnes
Angulus ridet

("That corner of the earth [Tarentum] charms me beyond all others.") Horace was born at Venusia (Venosa) in Apulia, about 80 miles E. of Naples and the same distance N.W. of Tarentum (Taranto).

eaters of garlic and catchers of vermin an exercise which they scruple not to perform on the public Streets. Swift's Dermot and Sheelah[2] would make a true Naples Eclogue. I owe this conceit to the famous John Wilkes who is now here and is to settle for some time in the Environs.[3] I am so full of ideas that I cannot write. Swift's allusion to a Churchdoor is most applicable to my mouth this evening.[4]

The warmth of the air here has extracted the vicious humours from my blood, and covered my chin and neck with a prodigious scurvy which plagues me much. But as it probably has saved me a fever I do not complain tho' allmost certain that no Woman under fifty would give me a kiss without being payd for it as you have been payed for being the *Doer*[5] of some old Lady. Go on and Prosper. Ever your's

JAMES BOSWELL

To Johnston, Tuesday 9 April 1765

MS. Yale (L 752).

ADDRESS: No. 23. To John Johnston Esq: of Grange.

Frescati, 9 April 1765

MY DEAR JOHNSTON: You must surely be convinced of my having

[2] In *A Pastoral Dialogue*, Dermot and Sheelah, Irish peasants, are depicted in mock-pastoral manner, as carrying on a far from idyllic love-affair, while engaged in weeding a paved court with stubbed knives (Swift's *Poems*, ed. Harold Williams, 1937, iii. 879–82).

[3] After *The North Briton*, No. 45, had been consigned to burning by the House of Commons as a seditious libel, Wilkes had gone to Paris in Dec. 1763. In his absence the House had expelled him; and after the charges against him (of sedition, for *The North Briton*, and of obscenity, for the *Essay on Woman*) had been heard, he was outlawed on 1 Nov. 1764. He had stayed in Paris until Oct. 1764, when he had gone to join Charles Churchill in Boulogne. Churchill had died there on 4 Nov., leaving Wilkes as his literary executor. Wilkes had moved to Italy, and had paused in Turin and Rome before coming to Naples, where JB soon afterwards arrived. Wilkes was to remain abroad until Feb. 1768, when he went back to London to seek a reversal of his outlawry.

[4] "The common Fluency of Speech in many Men, and most Women, is owing to a Scarcity of Matter, and Scarcity of Words; for whoever is a Master of Language, and hath a Mind full of Ideas, will be apt in speaking to hesitate upon the Choice of both: Whereas common Speakers have only one Set of Ideas, and one Set of Words to cloath them in; and these are always ready at the Mouth. So People come faster out of a Church when it is almost empty, than when a Crowd is at the Door" ("Thoughts on Various Subjects" in Swift's *Prose Works*, ed. Herbert Davis, iv. 244).

[5] Literally, according to Scots usage, *agent* or *factor*: in the normal course of his legal business it would fall to JJ to look after the affairs of persons unable to attend to them.

a very steady freindship for you when I tell you that during your ten months silence I wrote you 22 letters. I wrote to you without knowing that you was alive. But I cherished my Affection for an old freind, and Consoled myself that your shade would be pleased with what I did. A forthnight ago I received a long letter from you which gave me uncommon joy. I shall answer it soon in the ordinary way. This is the first of my singular suite of letters since I had the comfort of hearing from you And it is written from a Place which I might have chosen as a *Locus sacer* to date a particular Epistle from.[1] Frescati is the Tusculum of old where the great Cicero past the hours for which I regard him most. He was here the Philosopher in which character he is dearer to me than when haranguing from the Rostrum with all his Eloquence. You may beleive that I feel the enthusiasm of the Place; So much indeed that I am writing a *Tusculan Question*.[2] I know not how it may turn out, but I am very fond of the idea. You must know too that the Bishop of Frescati is no less a Man than Cardinal Stuart Grandson to King James the second of Britain and Seventh of Scotland.[3] Does not this touch your old heart? I am at the country-house of Mr. Hamilton[4] whose merit as a Painter will ever do

[1] It was a whim of JB's to write letters to his friends from solemn or sacred places. At Wittenberg in 1764 he wrote a letter to Dr. Johnson using the tomb of Melanchthon as a table (Journ. 30 Sept. 1764). See also *post* 20 Oct. 1773.

[2] With Cicero's *Tusculanarum Quaestionum libri quinque* in mind, JB wrote a four-page essay: "Happiness: a Tusculan Question" (MS. Yale M 104).

[3] Henry Benedict Maria Clement Stuart (1725–1807), brother of Prince Charles Edward and last legitimate male descendant of King James II (VII), was known when a boy as the Duke of York, and when made a cardinal in 1747, at the age of 22, assumed the title Cardinal York. After his brother's death in 1788 he claimed also the title of Henry IX of Great Britain. On 26 May JB attended a Pentecostal mass at Frascati at which the Cardinal pontificated: "Came to Function; Mass, Jesuits—then grand Card[i-nal] Yorke. British arms—old Scots Royal blood majest[ic] and eleg[ant]— all the assemb[ly] face as face of Ang

—fine voice—quite noble smild as he pass'd" (Notes 27 May 1765). The passage of Scripture indicated is: "And all that sat in the council, looking steadfastly on him, saw his face as it had been the face of an angel" (*Acts* vi. 15).

[4] Gavin Hamilton (1723–98), a Scots-born painter, lived in Italy for most of his active life. He painted mainly classical heroic subjects, and had a very profitable sideline in the sale of ancient statues, busts, and reliefs excavated from Hadrian's villa below Tivoli, at Prima Porta, at Monte Cagnuolo, and elsewhere. JB commissioned a painting from him on a Scottish subject, which, when completed and sent to England, proved a disappointment: "I then carried the two young men to Sir Joshua Reynolds's, and shewed them my picture of Mary Queen of Scots being forced to resign her crown, painted by Hamilton. I saw from Sir Joshua's manner of speaking before the picture was produced, that he was not pleased with it. Indeed I was disappointed when I now saw it for the first time. All the figures were

honour to cold Caledonia. His worth as a Man is not less. Farewell My Dear Sir. Yours, ever

JAMES BOSWELL

To Johnston, Saturday 11 May 1765

MS. Yale (L 753). Envoyé 11 Mai 1765 (Reg. Let.).

ADDRESS: To Mr. John Johnston, to be left at Forrest's Coffeehouse, Edinburgh, Great Britain (One Sheet).

POSTMARK: MA 28.

ENDORSEMENT: Rome 11th. May 1765.

Rome, 11 May 1765

MY DEAR SIR: Your letter of the 1st of February has given me so much pleasure, that I have allmost forgot your eight months silence: That, Johnston is a long time between old freinds: But you excuse yourself so well, and so much in your own natural stile, that I see your honest countenance full in my view, and as you ask me to do, I "forgive you frankly." When I look back to the day on which I wrote you last, what a variety fills up the space between that day and this! I left Berlin in September, and made a very agreable and improving tour through a good many of the German Courts, where I lived with Princes, and had the most advantageous opportunity of forming my manners, while, at the same time, I saw a great extent of country and many places worthy of attention. I then went into Switzerland, where I past some weeks with satisfaction. I went and visited the celebrated Rousseau in his wild retreat, and had some conversations with him which will have an influence on the whole of my future existence, for we talked much both of this world and of the next. I also past four days at the Country Seat of M. De Voltaire whose name carries lustre with it over Europe. I had much conversation with him too, and as you know how very faithfully I can record what I hear from Men of eminence, you may well beleive that my Papers contain a rich foreign treasure. I was a very short time at Geneva, from whence I certainly intended to have written to you, as I thought myself sure of having a letter from you lying there under my Brother David's cover. But finding no such letter, I delayed writing till it should

well, but the Queen herself who had neither beauty in a high degree nor grace in any degree" (Journ. 18 Mar.

1776). It is now in the possession of Sir Arthur Eliott of Stobs.

come, and so put it off from month to month till I did not well know what to think.[1] The very day that your last arrived I had written to David begging that he would give me some account of you. I had sealed my letter to him and on receipt of yours, I burnt the one I had written and wrote him another. On the first of January I set out from Geneva and at the most rigorous season of the year, I had an excellent passage over the Alps. I stayed a fortnight at Turin, and then went by Milan, Placentia, Parma, Bologna, and the Holy House of Loretto to Rome. I stayed a few days and saw some of the principal things, and then went to Naples, where I past three weeks in viewing that City and it's classical environs. I past many an hour there with the famous Mr. Wilkes, who has chosen that Paradise as the Place of his Exile. He has hired an old Castle overlooking the delicious Bay, and has with him a beautifull Italian Girl.[2] He is as gay in his Exile, as when he used to make Aylesbury ring with his jovial mirth.[3] He is publishing Churchill's Works with notes, and is writing a History of England from the Revolution to the fourth year of his present Majesty.[4] Wilkes is a most extraordinary Man. He has constant flow of health and spirits, and is allmost the only instance of a man of genius who enjoys continual happiness in this strange World. Upon my return from Naples to Rome, I employed an Antiquary,[5] and in a regular course viewed the Remains of ancient grandeur, the Statues, and the Pictures. I give you my word that without

[1] The preceding letters, twenty-three in number, though written to JJ had not been sent. JB had not sent him a single letter since leaving Berlin the previous September, though he had continued, in imagination, to communicate with him at frequent intervals by means of the unposted letters, while at the same time preparing the daily journal for his reading.

[2] Gertrude Maria Corradini (b. 1745), the Italian courtesan with whom Wilkes had been living in Paris. The "Castle" was the Villa Pietracatella, about a mile from Naples (Horace Bleackley, *Life of John Wilkes*, 1917, pp. 163, 169).

[3] Wilkes had come into possession of the manor of Aylesbury through his marriage to the heiress Mary Meade, and had retained it after their separation in 1756. At Aylesbury and at Medmenham Abbey, about fifteen miles away, which

was rented by Sir Francis Dashwood, the revels were held of the self-consciously profane and profligate society known as the Monks of St. Francis or the Hell Fire Club, which included Wilkes and Dashwood, Robert Lloyd, Charles Churchill, and Paul Whitehead.

[4] *Ante* 19 Mar. 1765, n. 3. Wilkes never published the annotated edition of Charles Churchill's works on which he was engaged. His projected History was not carried so far as he intended, but was published in 1768 as *The History of England, from the Revolution to the Accession of the Brunswick Line*.

[5] His guide, of whom he writes more fully in the Memoranda, was Colin Morison, an Aberdeenshire man. JB describes him as large in body and solemn in demeanour (To Gavin Hamilton, 15 Dec. 1765).

affecting to be a *Virtuoso*, I have had great satisfaction from this course, and have formed a taste for the arts which will contribute to calm my mind while I live. I regret only that my time of elegant Study at Rome is so short. However, I shall continue to study, with the assistance of Books and Prints, in the Library at Auchinleck. While I tell you what I have been doing, during my travels, I must not neglect to give you some account how I have been thinking. My natural sensibility and Anxiety of Mind has ever kept me exposed to the attacks of Hypochondria. By the great exercise and entertainment which I have had, the foul fiend has been often chaced away; but I have never been able to promise myself any long continuance of felicity. I have experienced, during this last half year, such changes of sentiment as would hardly be conceived to arise in a Mind where Judgment was not totally overthrown. I shall not enter into particulars, but leave you to imagine all the wild ideas which your gloomy fancy can suggest, on the wettest Sunday, while the Bell is ringing for the Tolbooth Kirk, and all the gay ideas which cheer your mind when the air is pure, and the Sun is bright, and you are lying luxuriously upon Arthur Seat, or calmly musing in your wood at Grange. My great comfort is that I am ever firm in my attachment to the old Family of Auchinleck, to my worthy Parents, and to my Bosom Freinds. Were it not for Melancholy, I am one of the most fortunate young Men alive, for I know none who has more real advantages than I have. I must however own that I am uneasy when I think of returning to Scotland. My Father is very well satisfyd with me at present; But I much fear he will not be so when he finds me at home with him. By his way of writing I can discover that he expects me to be a sollid steady Man who shall apply to Business with persevering assiduity. But my Dear Freind You know that there is hardly any probability that I shall ever be such a Man. Years indeed may render me steady, but I despair of having application. God bestows his gifts as he thinks fit, and long study of myself has convinced me that my Constitution was never intended for great labour of Mind. I can pore over books as long as any Man. I did so at Utrecht. But the effect was not improvement but sickness and perturbation. I swear to you that I seriously think it my truest Philosophy to be content with the Powers which my Maker has assigned me, and not to torment myself by inefectual struggles to change my Nature. I find myself an amiable pretty

Man of moderate abilitys, but a Soul truly noble, a Soul which in reality sets me higher in the scale of being than if I had attained to the first honours which superiour talents procure, and been without such a Soul. I would however do what I can to promote the happiness of my fellow-creatures. I shall put on the gown as an Advocate and endeavour to acquit myself faithfully towards those who entrust me with their causes. But I shall not lay myself out for very much employment. If I can get a seat in the house for a Parliament, I shall like it much, but shall not absolutely set my heart upon it. I shall at all events hope to have a good Exchequer Gown,[6] and so enjoy *Otium cum dignitate*,[7] and have plenty of time to give to the cultivating our old Estate and following out the Studies which please me the most. The great point will be to begin properly when I return, and get My Father to see me as I realy am. Come, my good freind, encourage me. Who knows but I may yet rejoice my Father's heart. I call God to witness that I wish most earnestly to do so. His civilitys to you in my absence touch me sensibly. I hope to shew him that I am gratefull. I am just now quite well and happy, and storing my memory with rich ideas which will give much pleasure to us both many years hence. To be in illustrious Rome itself and to walk the scenes of classical enthusiasm is indeed noble. When I give you my warm account of all this, you will enjoy it very near as much as if you had been here. I know how to make your Soul feel joy. My Journal will be a treasure to us. Were you but with me this evening what store of entertainment would I pour forth! In a letter I can only give you a few ideas half-coloured. You must know I have travelled through Italy under the Protection of the Dominican Friers. The King of Sardinia's Antiquary[8] recommended me to a Father of that order at Milan. I found him a learned pretty man, and after having had some conversation with him I discovered a very curious circumstance. This was the Father who converted to the Romish Faith Sir Alexander Jardine.[9] You may be sure I had a full account of that singular

[6] Whether elected to Parliament or not, he hopes to be appointed one of the judges, or barons, of the Court of Exchequer. Their duties were less onerous than those of Ordinary Lords of Session, but the salaries (£700 p.a. at this time) were the same.

[7] "Dignified leisure" (altered from Cicero, *Pro P. Sestio* xlv. 98).

[8] Giuseppe Bartoli (b. 1717), Antiquary to the King of Sardinia and Professor of Belles-Lettres in the University of Turin (*Biographie Universelle*, ed. L. G. Michaud, 1811, s.v. Bartoli, Joseph).

[9] Padre Giuseppe Allegranza (1730–85), a Dominican of the Convent of Saint-Eustorgue, had the credit of this

affair. This Reverend Monk recommended me to the Convent at Bolonia, and from thence I have had letters from Convent to Convent, and been treated with great distinction. The dress of this order is White with a black gown. This, Johnston is being quite in my own romantic stile. I have now been more than two months in Rome. I shall stay just a week longer. I have been presented to two Cardinals, and on Monday I am to kiss the Pope's toe.[10] I go from hence to Florence, then to Venice, and afterwards come round by Parma to Genoa, where I am to embark for France. How long I shall yet be abroad I cannot say. My Father will no doubt expect to see me before winter. But I am very desirous to pass some time in France the country of gayety, and afterwards intend to travel through Flanders, where are a great many places well worth seeing, and so return to Holland and see my good Dutch Relations and Freinds.

I am by no means displeased to hear that Miss Stewart and Miss Colquhoun are both married.[11] My Matrimonial schemes were transient flights of restless fancy. You must know that I am very fond of the daughter of one of the Nobles of Utrecht.[12] She is well looked and has £8000. But she is an universal Genius and rather too learned. She is very amiable, but is too much of my own

conversion. Sir Alexander Jardine of Applegirth (1712–90) in Dumfriesshire, 4th Bt., after a military career, joined the Roman Catholic Church and was elected a Knight of Malta (*Nouvelle biographie générale*, Paris, 1855–56; *Comp. Bar.* iv. 290).

[10] "Yesterday morning at 10 went with Abbé [Grant] etc. to Monte Cavallo. waited—In Antichamber off sword etc. Then in and kneelings—and kiss of Slipper —rich with Gold. 'Sigr Baron Boswell'" (Notes, 14 May 1765).

[11] *Ante* 21 July 1763, n. 10; 23 Sept. 1763, n. 14. JB had seen a newspaper notice of Miss Stewart's marriage while he was still at Utrecht, 12 Apr. 1764, and in spite of what he says here had confessed that it "galled" him (Notes, 13 Apr. 1764). Two days later (Reg. Let.) he received a letter from his father repeating the news as to Miss Stewart and announcing that Miss Colquhoun's marriage was imminent (From Lord Auchinleck, 2 Apr. 1764). Margaret

Stewart had married JB's cousin, Sir William Maxwell of Springkell, 3rd Bt., on 24 Mar. 1764; Katharine Colquhoun had married Sir Roderick Mackenzie of Scatwell, 4th Bt., on 7 Apr. 1764 (*Comp. Bar.* iv. 409, 320).

[12] Isabella Agneta Elisabeth (1740–1805), "Belle de Zuylen", the daughter of Diederik van Tuyll van Serooskerken, Heer van Zuylen, a landowner in the neighbourhood of Utrecht, who was one of the governors of the province. The circumstances of this protracted love-affair are recorded intermittently in journal entries and correspondence over a period of four years, and the project was not finally abandoned until 1768 (*post* 25 Apr. 1768, n. 3). Zélide (as JB called her) married her brother's former tutor, M. de Charrière, in 1772. *Lettres de Belle de Zuylen (Mme de Charrière) à Constant d'Hermenches*, edited by Philippe Godet, appeared in 1909; see also Godet, *Madame de Charrière et ses amis*, 2 vols., 1906.

constitution being subject to inequality of spirits. I know not how two such lively souls could unite. And yet if I take a plain sensible woman it will look aukward to me. At any rate I shall be in no hurry to *yoke* as my Father calls it. Mademoiselle De [Zuylen] likes me, and coresponds with me, as does her Father a sensible worthy Gentleman.[13] Johnston what say you to my foreign Lady? You must go back to the dancing School and brush up your bows. My Brother John's conduct has given me much uneasiness.[14] But from the knowledge which I have of human nature I can only pity him. David is a fine fellow. I glory in him. Between ourselves, He will make the best figure of any of us. I am pleased to hear of your Interview with Erskine. I hope he shall be provided for. He ought to have been born a Laird. Your Parliament house news entertained me. You may depend on having a miniature picture of me,[15] which I shall either send to you or bring over when I return. I realy long to see you again and to enjoy with you such cordial evenings as make us thank God for our existence. In the mean time let us write pretty often. My Address is now Aux soins de Messieurs Vautier et Delarue á Gênes. My Dear Freind Farewell.

JAMES BOSWELL

To Johnston, Friday 24 May 1765

MS. Yale (L 754).
ADDRESS: No. 24. To John Johnston Esq: of Grange.

Horace's Farm,[1] May 24 1765

MY DEAR JOHNSTON: Can you read the date of this letter without

[13] Heer van Zuylen still appears to have thought JB quite a desirable son-in-law, and even continued to treat his proposal as still under consideration after receiving JB's letter of 16 Jan. 1766, which contains a long and intimate account of his scruples concerning Zélide.

[14] *Post* 31 Mar. 1769, n. 1.

[15] *Ante* 30 July 1763, n. 2; *post* 19 July 1765. If JB had not already commissioned the miniature, he did so shortly after writing the present letter. Willison had begun his portrait on 6 May, and JB had sat to him most of the 9th. On 31 May and 7 and 13 June JB made a memorandum to send to

Alves, and on 3 and 4 June sat to him also (Mem. 7, 10, 31 May; 4, 5, 7, 13 June 1765). Alves had probably by that time carried his miniature well towards completion from Willison, but wanted some sittings in order to verify the likeness.

[1] In spite of very persuasive evidence advanced more than a century earlier that Horace's Varia (*Epist.* I. xiv. 3) was Vicovaro, 8 miles north-east of Tivoli, and his Digentia (*Epist.* I. xviii. 104) the modern Licenza, popular topography continued to place Horace's villa at Tivoli till past the middle of the 18th

being rapt into Classical enthusiasm by supposing yourself where I now am. Divine Horace whose Poetry has charmed my youthfull Soul I am now on the very spot which was your delightfull Retreat. Johnston beleive me I would give much to have you here at this moment. I am viewing the Villa of the Philosophic Bard with a pleasure allmost equal to what he has felt from it   I see the very Nature from which he drew. The Romantic Sabine Hills, the sacred fountains the verdant trees are full before me and wherever I cast my eyes I perceive the scattered beauties of Horace's finest odes. *Mihi me reddentis agelli*[2] is again experienced by your freind, for from one of my fits of dismal despondency this enchanting scene has restored me to contentment and Joy.

I am not alone. I am sharing the Classical Satisfaction with an exiled Countryman Mr. Andrew Lumisden Secretary to the Son and Heir of King James the Seventh.[3] Let cool Politicians dispute as they may I shall love and esteem the Man who is generous who acts from what he beleives to be right, who exposed his life in the most dangerous Civil war to support his Prince and who continues ever faithfull to his old Master. I want no abstract reasonings I beleive everything noble and great may be annalysed to nothing by nice Sophistry and I suppose a Metaphys[i]cian might prove Regulus and Scaurus to be fools.[4] But he who has a

century. The discovery in 1757 of an inscription proving that the hamlet Bardela or Cantalupo, near Vicovaro, had borne the name Mandela (*Epist.* I. xviii. 105) well down into the Christian era, finally won general assent to the view that the Sabine farm given to Horace by his friend Maecenas lay somewhere in the Licenza valley. Ruins on a site answering to Horace's description, about 6 miles up the Licenza from Vicovaro, had been located and described only four years before the date of the present letter (Domenico De Sanctis, *Dissertazione sopra la villa di Orazio Flacco,* 1761; see also Giuseppe Lugli, *La villa sabina di Orazio, Monumenti antichi* xxxi, 1926, Eng. trans. *Horace's Sabine Farm,* 1930; E. K. Rand, *A Walk to Horace's Farm,* 1930). JB and Lumisden must have been among the first Britons to visit the site.

[2] Horace, *Epistles* I. xiv. 1: "The little

farm that makes me feel myself again."

[3] Andrew Lumisden (1720–1801) was a second cousin of JB's friend Sir Alexander Dick, and the son of an Edinburgh lawyer. Soon after the arrival of the Jacobite forces in Edinburgh in 1745 he had been chosen by the Prince to be his secretary. After the Act of Attainder he had escaped abroad and was now living in Rome as secretary to the Chevalier de St. George. He was the centre of the colony of Scots *émigrés,* and his friendship meant to JB the freedom of that circle. On the death of the Chevalier in 1766 he became secretary and general factotum to Charles Edward, but in 1768 was dismissed for refusing to allow Charles to go to an oratorio when drunk. In spite of an invitation to return, he retired to Paris, where he lived for most of the rest of his life.

[4] Marcus Atilius Regulus and Marcus Æmilius Scaurus were types of the noble

real soul is not to be thus talked with. Mr. Lumisden is learned
ingenious and chearfull. He knows your character and wishes to
see you. I have surely said enough to make you think me very
happy. Adieu My Dear Freind. May the day yet come when we
shall fancy this Villa at Grange or at Auchinleck and enjoy the
superiour felicity of refined taste and true freindship. Ever yours.

JAMES BOSWELL

To Johnston, Wednesday 26 June 1765

MS. Yale (L 755).

ADDRESS: No. 25. To John Johnston Esq: of Grange.

Padua, 26 June 1765

MY DEAR JOHNSTON: Were you to make the tour of Italy, I am
certain you would stay some time at Padua. For surely you must
have read of it, and if you have, must like it. What think you of
a venerable City founded by Antenor the Brother of King Priam,[1]
and besides it's antiquity renowned for learning and sanctity. It's
university has been famous and has procured it the title of Padova
la dotta: And the celebrated Saint Anthony must ever keep up it's
holy reputation. It has truly an ancient look, and were I here alone,
or in grave company, I should feel myself much of the Student
and much of the Monk. But I am here with Lord Mount-Stuart[2]

and incorruptible Roman. According to a
legend of the 3rd century B.C. (Livy,
Epit. xviii.), the former, when a prisoner
of the Carthaginians, was sent to Rome
on parole to negotiate peace-terms, which
he urged the Senate to decline. As in
honour bound, he returned to captivity,
and was tortured to death for failing in
his mission. Scaurus was repeatedly
praised by Cicero for his citizenship (*Ad
Brutum 29, 30, 33*; *de Oratore* i. 49; *Pro
Murena* 17, etc.) although he seems to
have been a clever political opportunist.
JB perhaps has in mind Sallust's character-
ization, that he was one of those to
whom right and justice were more
precious than riches (Sallust, *Jug.* 15),
but elsewhere Sallust condemns him as
avaricious (William Smith, *Dict. of
Greek and Roman Biog. and Mythology*,
s.v. Scaurus).

[1] According to a Roman tradition,
Antenor, the upright old Trojan who
would have had Paris return Helen to the
Greeks, and who was spared by the vic-
tors at the sack of Troy, settled in
Venetia and founded the city of Padua
(Servius, *Commentary on Aeneid* i. 247;
Livy i. 1).

[2] John Stuart (1744–1814), Viscount
Mountstuart, the eldest son of the Earl
of Bute, was then completing his education by making the Grand Tour in the
company of Colonel Edmondstone, his
governor, and M. Mallet, his tutor.
Subsequently, through succession and by
marriage, he was to acquire a huge ac-
cumulation of dignities and fortune. He
was created Baron Cardiff in 1776, succeeded his father as 4th Earl of Bute in
1792, and on the death of his mother, Lady
Mary Wortley Montagu's daughter,

whose ideas have no similarity with those which Padua ought to
give. A young handsom Nobleman of the highest fashion ha.
thoughts more light and more gay. Besides it is now fairtime, and
the town is full of Venetian Nobility. We have an elegant Opera
and genteel Coffeehouses; and so the hours run on as in all other
places of dissipation.

My good Edinburgh old freind, you have no notion of the
Coffeehouses of this country, in which you see crowds of Ladies
and Gentlemen in full dress, some walking about, some set down
to Card tables, and some making love in convenient corners
Johnston it will be long before you see such doings in the Forrest's
Coffeehouse to which your letters are addressed. My Dear
Freind, be assured that I am ever yours,

JAMES BOSWELL

To Johnston, Saturday 13 July 1765

MS. Yale (L 756).

ADDRESS: No. 26. To John Johnston Esq: of Grange.

Venice, 13 July 1765

MY DEAR JOHNSTON: *Venice preserved or a Plot discovered*[1] has often
roused our souls in the good Theatre of Edinburgh. To find myself
in the City where Pierre and Jaffier lived is what my enthusiasm
cannot fail to exult in; for you know Johnston that enthusiasm can
build a great deal on a very small foundation.

> On the Rialto every night at twelve
> I take my evening's walk of meditation.

Dont you remember with what solemnity Digges used to speak
this? I have walked the Rialto at noon; but never went there at

became in 1794 Baron Mount Stuart of
Wortley. He was also, in 1796, created
Viscount Mountjoy, Earl of Windsor,
and Marquis of Bute. He married in
1766 Charlotte, eldest daughter of Herbert Windsor, Viscount Windsor and
Baron Mountjoy; and soon after her death
married again, in 1800, Frances, daughter of the banker Thomas Coutts. He was
British Envoy to Turin from 1779 to 1783;
and from March to Dec. 1783, Ambassador to Spain (*Scots. Peer.* ii. 305–06).

[1] Otway's *Venice Preserv'd* was a
favourite play throughout the century. In
his Journal JB records seeing Digges and
Mrs. Bellamy act in it in Edinburgh on
13 Nov. 1762; and he also mentions
attending a later Edinburgh performance,
on 23 Jan. 1768, when the parts of Jaffier
and Pierre were taken by Ross and
Sowdon.

170

night. I hope however you wont suspect me of being affraid of *meeting the foe of mankind in his walk.*[2]

Venice is the most curious town in the world. I have been here a forthnight and am yet wondering to see immense Buildings in the water, and cannot but think it very strange to sail about from house to house.

I am now in company with Lord Mountstuart Colonel Edmondstoune and M. Mallet a Savant of Geneva.[3] Every thing in this world has advantages and disadvantages and so has my travelling in this set; however, upon the whole it is a good thing. I shall explain myself at more length in my next. I am just setting out, and my ideas are confused. We live here in the house of General Graeme Brother to Bucklivie.[4] He is Commander in Chief of the troops of this Republic and is a most polite old Gentleman as I ever met with. I know Johnston how you would like to see a good Scotsman a gallant Graeme advanced to high trust in the service

---

[2] The sinister lines spoken by Pierre, as he makes an assignation with Jaffier to plot against the state of Venice, are these:

> On the *Ryalto* every Night at Twelve
> I take my Evening's walk of Meditation,
> There we two will meet, and talk of pretious
> Mischief.
>
> (*Venice Preserv'd* I. i).

In Act II, as Jaffier waits at midnight on the Rialto, he mutters in great perturbation:

> For every Step I tread, methinks some Fiend
> Knocks at my Breast, and bids it not be quiet:
> I've heard, how desperate Wretches, like myself,
> Have wander'd out at this dead time of Night
> To meet the Foe of Mankind in his walk.

[3] Lt-Col. James Edmondstone (d. 1793) of Newton in Clackmannanshire, a close friend of David Hume, was acting at this time as governor to Lord Mountstuart. As his colleague he had Paul Henri Mallet (1730–1807), the Swiss historian and student of Scandinavian antiquities, who was acting as Lord Mountstuart's tutor. Thomas Percy's influential *Northern Antiquities,* 1770, was a translation of a work of Mallet's published in 1755.

[4] In 1753 William Græme, then an officer in the Dutch Brigade, bought the family estate of Bucklyvie from his elder brothers James and Hugh. James, who was still by courtesy styled "Græme of Bucklyvie", was chosen to be one of the four commissaries of Edinburgh. William was appointed to the Venetian command in 1756, according to *The Scots Magazine* (xviii. 137) which reported: "General Graeme, a Scotsman, and brother to Mr. Græme of Bucklyvie lately appointed commander of the land-forces of Venice is inspecting the military establishment there, in order to put the troops of the republic on a more regular footing, and to introduce the best method of discipline adopted by other powers." When he died in 1767, the Venetian government sent a vote of thanks to his family for his distinguished services and ordered his bust to be placed in the arsenal at Venice (Louisa G. Græme, *Or and Sable,* 1903, pp. 427–30).

of a foreign state. I am so hurried I can hardly write at all and yet it is with reluctance I leave off; for I am not quite in spirits and it consoles me to talk to my worthy freind. God preserve us to meet happily again My ever dear Johnston for after all there is nothing equal to warm freindship. Adieu. ever your's

JAMES BOSWELL

To Johnston, Friday 19 July 1765

MS. Yale (L 757). Envoyé 20 Juillet 1765 (Reg. Let.).

ADDRESS: To Mr. John Johnston, to be left at Forrest's Coffeehouse, Edinburgh, Great Britain, *Inghilterra*.

POSTMARK: AV 19.

ENDORSEMENT: Monigo (near Venice) 19th July 1765.

Monigo, 19 July 1765

MY DEAR JOHNSTON: It is not my fault if you have not received a very long letter written from Rome[1] in answer to the excellent one which I had the pleasure to receive from you in that City. I could hardly expect a return before this time, and therefore have nothing to say against you. If you have been indolent it has been but for a few days, and that you know is not to be minded in you. It is sometimes of advantage to have a great fault: a man's freinds become accustomed to it, and overlook little offences of the same kind. Were you a very regular Man, I should be in a passion with you for neglecting me a Post. But as you are you may e'en indulge your goodhumoured ease, Post after Post, and not have a word said to you.

I intended to have left Rome before the middle of May; but I formed a great intimacy with Lord Mountstuart, who kept me on from week to week, and at last insisted with me to accompany him in the rest of his tour of Italy. He removed the objections which I made on my Father's account, by assuring me that he would take care to have my conduct represented to him in such a manner, that instead of being offended he should be highly satisfyd with me.[2]

[1] *Ante* 11 May 1765.

[2] Lord Mountstuart did exert himself on JB's behalf. He wrote from Rome to William Mure, one of the Barons of Exchequer in Scotland: "Having got acquainted with Mr. Boswell, here at Rome, our acquaintance soon grew into a strong intimacy—so much so, that I have desir'd him to go on with me in my tour through Italy, as long as it would be agreeable to him. He liked the scheme much, as well as Colonel

You may be sure this made me very happy and on the fourteenth of June I set out with pride and pleasure as the distinguished Freind of an amiable young Nobleman son to the favourite of our Sovereign. I promised myself a sure interest for life, and I felt my heart warm with affection to a branch of the loyal house of Stuart. My Lord Mountstuart has with him Colonel Edmondstoune a worthy Scotsman who has attended him from the time that he left England, and M. Mallet of Geneva who was Preceptor to the Prince Royal of Denmark and has a handsom pension from My Lord Bute for instructing his Son in History.[3] My Dear Freind can you conceive any thing more agreable? We had a good journey to Venice, where we past a forthnight. We lived at the house of General Graeme Brother to Bucklivie. He is Commander in Chief of the troops of this Republic; and being an old freind of Lord Bute's, and a very sensible polite man, we have been entertained by him with the greatest cordiality and ease. We are now at his seat in the Country where fine air regular living and moderate amusement keep us in a state like what you have proved in your simple summer days at Schaw. This is a new strong proof to me that a man ought never to despair; for, after all my tossings in the

Edmonstoune, but says he is so much press'd by his father to go home, that he durst not take such a step without his leave; but that you, being a great friend of my Lord's, might easily obtain permission. Boswell is an excellent lad, full of spirit and noble sentiments; and (as the world goes) it ought to be reckoned a fortunate thing for him going with me, and indeed fortunate for myself, as he goes on in the same studies as I do, and, if possible, rouses me up whether I will or no" (Lord Mountstuart to Baron Mure, 5 June 1765. *Selections from the Family Papers Preserved at Caldwell*, ed. William Mure, 1853–54, pt. II. ii. 38, 39).

[3] The life pension is confirmed by Hélène Stadler, *Paul-Henri Mallet*, 1924, p. 168. The handsomeness of Bute's provision for Mallet seems somewhat to refute the contemporary charge that Bute did not adequately reward his children's tutors for their services: "When a friend expressed his surprize to Dr. Warton, that none of the gentlemen concerned in the education of Lord B—te's children had been provided for in a manner adequate to their fair expectations, he replied—in fact, my dear Sir, the Premier's ideas reach not beyond Scotland; his mind therefore naturally places us on a footing with the clergy of that kingdom; and to no higher affluence does he think we have a claim" (John Wooll, *Biographical Memoirs of . . . Joseph Warton*, 1806, p. 54 note 1). But what was at issue in this criticism was preferment in the Church of England, for which Mallet was not eligible. An English clergyman accepting a position as tutor to the children of a prime minister might well assume that he would eventually receive a deanery or even a bishopric, though nothing of the sort had ever been promised, whereas an eminent foreigner would expect his reward to be fully stated and fixed at the start. And Bute would undoubtedly have had to make a substantial offer to obtain the services of a man who had been preceptor to royalty.

variety of life, after all my dismal days of horrid gloom I am now clear as when my mind was rural, young, and undisturbed except one day in seven. And yet Johnston, I have reason to be unhappy for my conduct of late has not been that of a Sage. At Rome I ran about among the Prostitutes till I was interrupted by that distemper which scourges vice in this world. When I got to Venice I had still some small remains of disease, but strange gay ideas which I had formed of the Venetian Courtesans turned my head, and away I went to an Opera-Dancer, and took Lord Mountstuart with me. We both had her; and we both found ourselves taken in for the punishment which I had met with at Rome. Pretty doings! Our evil has been recompensed but moderately; but we are as much to blame as if we had suffered most sadly. I have blamed myself so much, and repented so sincerely, that I am now no more distrest. Besides I do assure you the climate of Italy affects me much. It inflamed my hot desires, and now it keeps my blood so warm, that I have all day long such spirits as a man has after having taken a chearfull glass.

Before I left Rome I took care to execute your Commission of having my Picture done in miniature. I had it painted by a Mr. Alves an Inverness Lad who is studying in Italy.[4] It is thought like and well-painted. I wish it may please you   It has been sent off

---

[4] James Alves (c. 1738–1808) seems in 1758 to have been a pupil of Joseph Marie Vien (1716–1809) in Paris. He had left Rome before Vien received his appointment as Director of the French Academy there in 1775, for JB met him at Inverness in 1773. He settled in London as a painter of miniatures and portraits in crayon, exhibiting at the Royal Academy in the years 1775–79. JB records meeting him in London in 1776. He seems to have retired at last to Inverness, for he died there in 1808 (Samuel Redgrave, *Dictionary of Artists of the English School*, 1878; Emanuel Bénézit, *Dictionnaire critique et documentaire des peintres, sculpteurs, dessinateurs, et graveurs*, 1948; Algernon Graves, *The Royal Academy Exhibitors, 1769–1804*, 1905; Journ. 29 Aug. 1773, 16 Mar. 1776).

The miniature, the present location of which is unknown, was painted from a portrait done by George Willison, a first cousin of JB's friend George Dempster, who was then an art-pupil at Rome. "In my last I mentioned to you Mr. Boswell of Auchenleck. He was much with me whilst here, and I have a particular esteem for him. He left with me the enclosed miniature of himself, painted by Alves from a large portrait done by Willison: it is exceeding like" (Andrew Lumisden to Robert Strange, 3 July 1765, James Dennistoun, *Memoirs of Sir Robert Strange . . . and . . . Andrew Lumisden*, 1855, ii. 33). The portrait is now in the Scottish National Portrait Gallery, to which it was bequeathed in 1913 by Capt. James John Wood, whose wife Jessie Blanche Adelaide (d. 1898), third daughter of Sir William Francis Elliott of Stobs, 7th Bt., had been, on her mother's side, a great-granddaughter of JB.

some weeks ago to Mr. Strange the Engraver,[5] who is to convey it to Mr. Thomas Boswell,[6] from whom you will receive it upon asking for it. I left it at Rome to the care of a very worthy Exile,[7] who is Secretary to a Scots Gentleman of a very ancient Family who is obliged to live abroad for particular reasons. You see there is something romantic in the history of this same miniature.

I leave this in a day or two, and after going with My Lord as far as Verona, I shall separate from him, and go to Parma, where I have an amiable French Acquaintance[8] a Man of knowledge and taste and sensibility to whom I was recommended by M. Rousseau. I may perhaps [spend] a little time at the court of Parma and then go straight to Florence, and after seeing the curiositys there, jaunt thro' the rest of Tuscany, embark at Leghorn and sail to Genoa where I shall embark for France. You must know I ⟨have⟩ been longer in Italy than my Father intended and have spent £440 since the month of January. I hope my worthy Father will not be uneasy; for I am determined ⟨to⟩ do what he inclines as far as may lye in my power. I think Johns[t]on you have here a pretty full account of me. Let me add that my regard and Affection for you is just as when we walked upon Arthur Seat and that I will convince you of when we meet. Pray see Davie from time to time. My heart is bound up in him. He is the *flower of the flock.* I am uneasy to

[5] Robert Strange (1721–92), a native of Orkney, after serving his apprenticeship as an engraver in Edinburgh, fought in the Jacobite army at Prestonpans, Falkirk, and Culloden. He escaped abroad and studied art in Rouen and Paris, returning in 1750 to set up business in London as an engraver. He left England again in 1760 and spent several years in Italy copying pictures to engrave for publication before returning once more to London. Among his patrons was King George III, who knighted him in 1787.

[6] Thomas Boswall (?1724–76), an accountant, who was employed in the Edinburgh post office, was no near relative of JB, though he may have shared distant ancestors with him. His brother, Alexander Boswall (1728–1812) of Blackadder, made a fortune in the service of the Nabob of Arcot in India (Journ. 5 Nov. 1776).

[7] Andrew Lumisden, whose sister Isabella was the wife of Robert Strange. There was a close friendship between the two men.

[8] Alexandre Deleyre (1726–97), a radical thinker who later came to prominence in the French Revolution (V. D. de Musset-Pathay, *Histoire de la vie et des œuvrages de J.-J. Rousseau,* 1821, ii. 54–55). He was librarian to the Duke of Parma. "I got to Parma at night. I sent to M. De Leyre Bibliothecaire du Jeune Prince a letter which M. Rousseau had given me for him, in which the illustrious Philosopher praised me, and at the same time painted my melancholy disposition. M. De Leyre came to me immediatly. I found him a genteel, amiable Frenchman with a simplicity of manners that charmed me. We were at once acquainted, and talked with unreserved gayety" (Journ. 29 Jan. 1765).

think that I am not yet Master of Myself; but I allways hope to
be better. Remember me kindly to all freinds, and pray write soon.
Adieu My Dear Freind I am ever your's

JAMES BOSWELL

My Address is now Chez Messieurs Vautier et Delarue á Gênes.

To Johnston, Tuesday 23 July 1765

MS. Yale (L 758).

ADDRESS: No. 27. To John Johnston Esq: of Grange.

Verona, 23 July 1765

MY DEAR JOHNSTON: Would you beleive that I have been just now
gravely studying how to write you this letter. I would needs have
it a good one because forsooth Verona was the City of Romeo and
Juliet, and because Shakespeare has a Comedy called *The Two
Gentlemen of Verona.* I say nothing of the younger Pliny[1] and other
great men of Antiquity[2] who were born here but I think I ought
at least to remember one pretty quotation from either of these
Plays of Shakespear which I have mentioned.

I have seen here some good pictures,[3] and a Portico of the

[1] The younger Pliny was born not at
Verona, but at Novum Comum, the
modern Como. JB was thinking of his
uncle, Pliny the elder, whose statue by
Alberto da Milano, with those of other
famous sons of Verona in Roman times,
he had just seen on the front of the
Loggia, above the cornice. Pliny the
elder seems to have been claimed for
Verona through misinterpretation of his
own statement ("Catullum conterraneum
meum", *Naturalis Historia,* pref. 1) that
he was "a fellow countryman" of Catullus.
By this, assuming "conterraneum" is
the word he wrote, he could have meant
that, like Catullus, he was born in the
region north of the Po, then not officially
a part of Italy and denominated Trans-
padane Gaul. In the *Life of Pliny* ascribed
to Suetonius, he is styled "Novocomen-
sis", indicating that he was, like his
nephew, a native of Como.

[2] For example, Catullus, Vitruvius,
Cornelius Nepos.

[3] The Memoranda (24 July 1765) record dinner with "Count Bevilacqua" and
tours of "St. George's Church" and an
unnamed palazzo (JB left a blank, having
forgotten the name). Since the party slept
in Vicenza, more than thirty miles from
Verona, the night before, two collections
of pictures, besides those of the Palazzo
Bevilacqua, may well have been all they
would have had time for. The pictures
in San Giorgio were clearly considered
the finest group in the city. The Marchese
di Maffei gives a complete list in *Verona
illustrata,* 1732 (iii. 175–76); two that
he and other contemporary commentators
considered worthy of special mention
were the martyrdom of St. George,
above the high altar, and St. Barnabas
blessing the rich, in a side-chapel, both
by Paolo Veronese (*ibid.*; M. de Blainville,
*Travels through Holland, Germany, Switzer-
land . . . Italy,* 1757, i. 434; John Northall, *Travels through Italy,* 1766, p. 448;
J. J. Le F. de Lalande, *Voyage d'un*

Museum Philarmonicum in which are collected a number of ancient inscriptions,[4] some of which can no longer be read, as the language in which they are written is lost. Nothing appears more striking to me than the loss of a language. A stately edifice may be repaired when ruined, or rebuilt from Plans or from exact Memory; A City may be swallowed up and after remaining for ages in the heart of the earth may be discovered; but a Language if once forgotten is never to be recalled. Words are arbitrary[5] marks and have seldom any original connection with the ideas which they represent. If therefore the meaning annexed to particular characters slips into desuetude, a language is for ever destroyed. Were the learned to put significations upon the old Tuscan characters, perhaps in ten thousand words they would not hit upon three significations the same with those which the characters formerly stood for.

I have viewed the magnificent Amp[h]itheatre of Verona[6] the inside of which is surprisingly entire. I have seen it put to a whimsical use this evening. In the *Arena* was erected a little Stage on which was acted an Opera Bouffé while the ancient rising seats were occupied by degenerate Italians. What a sad alteration has time made![7] Blackguards and effeminate Signori sit where the wise and brave and virtous[8] of old bestowed their valuable applause,

françois en Italie, fait dans les années 1765 et 1766, 1770, viii. 221). The Palazzo Bevilacqua had a fine collection of pictures: Northall (pp. 447–48) singles out three by Paolo Veronese, one by Tintoretto, and one by Titian. A plausible choice for JB's unnamed palazzo would be the Palazzo del Consiglio (town hall), now commonly called the Loggia, which receives prominent mention for its paintings in Maffei (iii. 183) and Blainville (p. 439).

[4] The Museo Maffeiano, founded in 1714, in the Via del Teatro Filarmonico, contains a collection of these ancient sculptures and inscriptions in the old Tuscan language (i.e. Etruscan).

[5] MS. "arbritary".

[6] The largest Roman amphitheatre, after the Colosseum at Rome, it can seat nearly 24,000 in comfort. "In this amphitheatre there are plays during the summer" (Thomas Martyn, *The Gentleman's Guide in his Tour through Italy*, 1787, p. 387).

[7] Compare Goldsmith's lines on Italy, which had just been published:

Yet still the loss of wealth is here supplied
By arts, the splendid wrecks of former pride;
From these the feeble heart and long-fall'n mind
An easy compensation seem to find.
Here may be seen, in bloodless pomp arrayed,
The pasteboard triumph and the cavalcade. . . .
Each nobler aim, represt by long control,
Now sinks at last, or feebly mans the soul;
While low delights, succeeding fast behind,
In happier meanness occupy the mind
(*The Traveller*, 145–50; 155–58).

[8] Not an inadvertency, but JB's usual spelling for this word and certain other adjectives in *-uous* (conspicous,

and on the spot where was formerly a fight with wild beasts, or a combat of Gladiators, a low *Scurra* a ludicrous wretch of a Harlequin cuts aukward capers and rattles out Infamous attempts at wit. My Dear Johnston, I am in a Passion; but not with you. So honest freind shake hands. Were there more such Men as your honour this age would be less despicable. I ever remain with strong Affection Your sincere Freind

JAMES BOSWELL

To Johnston, Wednesday 24 July 1765

MS. Yale (L 759).

ADDRESS: No. 28. To John Johnston Esq: of Grange.

Brescia, 24 July 1765

MY DEAR JOHNSTON: All that Addison says of this Town is only "Brescia is famous for it's iron works."[1] and as Addison is my Classic while I travel in Italy, and the least expression of so favourite an Authour valued by me like the least bits of the precious diamond, iron has run in my head since ever I arrived and I could not rest till I had seen the firearms which are the works mostly esteemed. They are indeed excellent for they make vast quantitys of them; This is the country where assassination is most frequent and Men and Women go often armed. I have bought a gun for three zechins as a little specimen of Brescia ingenuity, and have been allready not a little amused with it. So young is still this fancifull head of mine that I had no sooner bought my Gun than the ideas returned which used to stir my blood at Auchinleck when I was eager to be a Soldier; I brandished my Gun (if the

contemptous, presumptous). It indicates a variant pronunciation [vɜ(r)təs] or possibly [vɑ(r)təs] apparently not uncommon in 18th-century speech, though the corresponding shortened spelling is not recorded by the OED after the 15th century. See John Jones, *Practical Phonography*, 1701, edited by Eilert Ekwall, 1907, pp. 88, 115.

---

[1] Joseph Addison, *Remarks on Several Parts of Italy, etc.* 1705, p. 53. In mentioning only its iron-works and manufacture of fire-arms, Addison did scant justice to Brescia. It was a curious myopia which could make him overlook the white marble Duomo Nuovo, the Palazzo della Loggia, and the Broletto. And Brescia, as the former seat of a famous school of artists, had many notable paintings to show, as well as the so-called Temple of Vespasian and a variety of fragmentary remains of the Roman city. JB saw rather more than his mentor: "Arriv'd Brescia saw fine walk Ramparts —Dome" (Mem. 26 July), though he had travelled forty miles that day from Verona and did not have much time.

sword will permit me for once that expression) I slung it carelessly over my left arm like a handsom fowler or a Captain of a marching Regiment and I must own that I even shoulder'd my firelock like any bold Brother Soldier in his Majesty King George's service; all these motions I performed to an English march which I whistled and upon the honour of a Man who is not ashamed to discover the simplicity of his sentiments at times I do declare I was as happy as I could wish and giving my broad gold-lac'd hat a gracefull turn to one side of my head I thought myself a very great Man. My Dear Johnston I give you leave to smile. But let me tell you that in whatever way we can enjoy an innocent happiness in this sad world let us not disdain to enjoy it. The illustrious Johnson once cured me of haughty pride which despised small amusements. He told me "Sir, nothing is too little for so little a creature as man."[2] We are all little at periods of our lives and if we were all as candid Philosophers as I am would just march as I have done. My Dear Freind adieu

JAMES BOSWELL

To Johnston, Saturday 27 July 1765

MS. Yale (L 760).

ADDRESS: No. 29. To John Johnston Esq: of Grange.

Pavia, 27 July 1765

MY DEAR JOHNSTON: This has been a day of dissappointments to me. I left Milan early in the morning very much pleased with the thoughts of having a curious conversation with one of the Fathers of the famous Carthusian Convent[1] about five miles from this City. He was a very gay young man but of a religous turn of mind and

[2] The remark was made when JB told Dr. Johnson that he was keeping a journal: "He said indeed that I should keep it private, and that I might surely have a friend who would burn it in case of my death. For my own part, I have at present such an Affection for this my Journal, that it shocks me to think of burning it. I rather encourage the idea of having it carefully laid up among the Archives of Auchinleck. However, I cannot judge fairly of it, now. Some years hence I may. I told Mr. Johnson that I put down all sorts of little incidents in it. 'Sir (said he) there is nothing too little for so little a Creature as Man. It is by studying little things that we attain the great knowledge of having as little misery, and as much happiness as possible'" (Journ. 16 July 1763).

[1] The Certosa di Pavia is now a national monument and is in process of restoration. A few monks are still housed there, but not of the Carthusian order.

at the age of sixteen he felt himself strongly inclined to the severe monastic life. He went to the Convent where he now is and past eight days in all the strictness of the Order. He then returned to Milan and lived a year in the world during which time his inclination still continued so at the end of the year, He began his Noviciate through the whole of which he preserved a calm and firm resolution to follow the hard precepts of Saint Bruno and thus being perswaded that he had a true Vocation from God he took the vows and has now been a Religious above fifteen years full of peace and hope of celestial happiness. His name is Padre Serafina Grassi,[2] and as I had a letter to him from his Brother a very ingenious engraver, I promised myself an uncommon satisfaction from the study of a mind so much warmed with Piety. But on my arrival at the Convent I found that this was a day of silent retirement and that the Prior would not permit the Father to receive me. I however saw the excellent Convent and magnificent Gothic Church. My next dissappointment has been my not seeing the field of Battle where Francis the first was taken Prisoner by the army of Charles the Fifth. I hoped to have viewed with accuracy and enthusiasm this celebrated Scene and as Doctor Robertson in his *History of Charles the Fifth* will in all probability give some description of the Battel of Pavia[3] I rejoyced forsooth in the prospect of some mistakes which I supposed him to make and which I should correct with an air of importance and if he should insist on his being right I thought of giving him a grave reply, "You'll excuse me, Doctor. I have been upon the spot." But I find that nobody can give any distinct account of the situation of this field which must have been chang'd in many different ways since the Battel was fought; so that I pass on my way just as wise to the point which I intended to pique myself upon, just as wise as any honest Tradesman who

[2] The contents of the library of the Certosa are now in the Biblioteca Ambrosiana at Milan, but no information has been obtained from them or from the state archives in the public library at Milan concerning Father Serafino Grassi. A number of engravers named Grassi are known to have practised in Milan at various times during the century, but without more knowledge of him than can be derived from JB's letter it is impossible to gather additional information about Serafino Grassi's brother.

[3] William Robertson's *History of Scotland during the Reigns of Queen Mary and of King James VI* had been published in 1759 and had already gone into five editions. He was now, as JB was aware, preparing his *History of the Reign of the Emperor Charles V*, which was to appear in 1769. His account of the battle of Pavia in 1525, between Francis I of France and Charles, Duke of Bourbon, is in Book IV.

never travelled above four miles round his shop. However I have seen two curious Cells one ornamented with bones of the Pavians and one with bones of the french. Sculls and shin-bones and shoulder blades and other parts are arranged with singular art as you have seen pebbles in the grotto of a Virtuoso.[4] I have never seen a Conceit that struck me more. It is the first time that I have look'd on dead mens bones without horror. I find my freind that in this world all depends upon the imagination which may be affected very different ways by very small circumstances. I speak for myself. Farewell. Yours with much Affection

JAMES BOSWELL

To Johnston, Monday 29 July 1765

MS. Yale (L 761).

ADDRESS: No. 30. To John Johnston Esq: of Grange.

Cremona, 29 July 1765

MY DEAR JOHNSTON: Hardly will you have read the date of this letter till you have exclaimed, "Mantua væ misera! nimium vicina Cremonæ!"[1] This quotation makes a figure; does it not? But I will let myself down as much as Tommy Fitzmaurice[2] could wish. Such is my ignorance that I cannot tell why Mantua was unlucky in being near Cremona: And such is my inattention that

---

[4] These ossuary chapels no longer exist, but an inscription now preserved in the Museo Civico seems to indicate that they were located in the church of S. Pietro in Ciel d'Oro (information furnished by S. Gerevini, Director of the University Library, Pavia).

[1] Virgil, *Eclogues* ix. 28, properly *miserae*: "Mantua, alas! too near ill-fated Cremona." In 41 B.C., after the battle of Philippi, confiscations of land were made by Octavian for the benefit of the soldiers of the triumvirs. Mantua, because of its vicinity to Cremona, which had been faithful to the cause of the republic, shared its fate, and among those whose land was taken away from them was the father of Virgil.

That JB's unmetrical *misera* was not a slip of the pen is shown by his paraphrase of the passage two sentences further on. Though he had an excellent practical command of Latin and had read and could quote a good deal of Horace and Ovid (see J. G. Winter, "A Point in Boswell's Favor", *Michigan Alumnus*, lviii, 1952, 236–46), he gives no indication of ever having studied the rules of scansion.

[2] The Hon. Thomas Fitzmaurice, second son of the 1st Earl of Shelburne, had been a fellow student with JB at the University of Glasgow, 1759–60 (W. I. Addison, *The Matriculation Albums of the University of Glasgow*, 1913, p. 59; W. R. Scott, *Adam Smith as Student and Professor*, 1937, pp. 67–70, 239–54).

altho' I have recollected the famous pun on this same quotation[3] I have not been to look at Cremona Fiddles in the very town where they are made;[4] And yet Johnston no man can harangue more sollidly than I on the proper improvement of travelling and how we ought allways to visit the most celebrated Manufactorys of every kind as there are none where we may not pick up some usefull hints. So ill does my practice agree with my Theory. But of this the instances are so numerous *ut delassare valent Fabium*.[5] Does it not make you sick to hear a Man tell you all his follies. I would as soon hear him tell me how much he is obliged to scratch with the Itch, and how often he has had the misfortune to piss the bed. Follies are defects as nauseous to the moral mind as bodily weaknesses are to the sensual. And to think to be excused for our follies by telling them is now a stale fancy which no man who has any sense or who converses with those that have, can any longer entertain. I have found at Mantua Captain Keith Stuart[6] who has his ship at Genoa. He revived in my mind of nice sensibility many Scots ideas which have given me a simple pleasure. He presented me to the Contessa Masserati[7] whose Husband is in the Regiment doing duty here. She is a sweet pretty woman. Both her father and

[3] Sometimes ascribed to Swift, who is said to have declaimed this line on seeing the corner of a lady's cloak whisk a violin off a table: *Mantua*, in this case standing for mantle, and *Cremona* for violin (Patrick Delany, *Observations . . . on . . . Swift*, 1754, pp. 212–13).

[4] Though various followers and imitators of Antonio Stradivari were active in Cremona in 1765, one could no longer meet a Stradivari or Guarnieri there. Pietro Guarnieri II may still have been alive, but he had moved to Venice (W. L. von Lütgendorff, *Die Geigen und Lautenmacher vom Mittelalter bis zur Gegenwart*, 2 vols. 1922–26; Giovanni de Piccolellis, *Liutai antichi e moderni*, 1885).

[5] Horace, *Satires* I. i. 14: *. . . loquacem delassare valent Fabium* (. . . enough to exhaust even the loquacious Fabius).

[6] "Mantua" must be a mistake for "Cremona", for JB did not reach Mantua until 30 July and from everything in the present letter it appears that it was at Cremona that he met Stewart. Keith Stewart (c. 1739–95), later a vice-

admiral, was a son of Alexander Stewart, 6th Earl of Galloway. He tried to dissuade JB from going to Corsica: "An officer of rank in the British navy, who had been in several ports of the island, told me that I run the risque of my life in going among these barbarians; for, that his surgeon's mate went ashore to take the diversion of shooting, and every moment was alarmed by some of the natives, who started from the bushes with loaded guns, and if he had not been protected by Corsican guides, would have certainly blown out his brains" (*An Account of Corsica*, 1768, p. 266). When JB met him again in December of this year, at Toulon, on his return from Corsica, Stewart continued to belittle his expedition and treat it as a joke (*post*, n. 3 to first letter of 20 Dec. 1765).

[7] A group of wits and savants called the *Caffè*, which met at the house of Giovanni Verri in Milan, included "the beautiful Countess Masserati, who knew eight languages" (Giulio Natali, *I Settecento*, 1950, i. 132).

mother are irish but she has entirely the foreign air. She has some resemblance to Lady Katie Murray[8] but is a finer woman if I may be allowed to say so to a bold Borderer whom I have often heard sing

> To Katie's health let's fill a glass
> For She's a bonny blooming Lass.[9]

I hope tho' you will not maintain that there are none bonnier. This Charming Countess is not yet three and twenty but this Count is her second Husband allready. I told her she must like marriage much to have try'd it twice, and that for my part I was affraid to try it once. She is clever to a certain degree, and speaks english french italian German. Upon the whole I am very glad to get away from this. I know not how long such a Lady as this might make me stay. There is an old Castle[10] here which Keith Stuart said might be the Castle where Virgil defended himself. I invented upon this a wild popular tradition. The Swans of Mantua becoming very numerous and very large began to be jealous that a Man should sing as well as they. Upon which they attacked Virgil who made his escape to Cremona, and in this old Castle did he guard himself against the fury of his winged and noisy foes. My Dear Freind adieu

JAMES BOSWELL

To Johnston, Tuesday 30 July 1765

MS. Yale (L 762).
ADDRESS: No. 31. To John Johnston Esq: of Grange.

Mantua, 30 July 1765

MY DEAR JOHNSTON: If I go on journeying at this rate from one classical town to another, my letters will resemble the pages of a

---

[8] Lady Catherine Murray, Captain Keith Stewart's sister, was the wife of James Murray of Broughton. JB met her during his Harvest Jaunt of 1762 when she took a liking to him. She told the Herons that she hoped he would often visit her in London during the winter (Journ. 22, 24 Sept. 1762). He mentions only one occasion, however, when he called at Murray's house in London, and speaks only of seeing her husband and brother, not herself (Journ. 19 Dec. 1762).

[9] Lines typical of such drinking choruses as were probably improvised by the company at Thom's tavern to suit the toast of the moment.

[10] The fortifications of Cremona survive from medieval times when it was of peculiar military importance as a key position, a great road-junction at the northern end of the bridge across the Po. The commune was engaged in many wars during the 12th and 13th centuries.

German Commentator, where quotations come so thick upon one another that half the Book is brown with Italics. Can I be here without introducing *Mantua me genuit?*[1] I have come forty miles out of my road in order to see this City, which I find much larger and handsomer than I had any notion of. The Princess of Spain who is to be married to the new Grand Duke of Tuscany[2] past two days here in her way to Inspruck. They entertained her with a pretty little Pastoral opera, and now she is gone, it has been repeated twice to do a courtesy to the People who are all gay upon this occasion. I saw it tonight, and I assure you the Theatre[3] is a very handsom one. It was agreable to see an Italian Pastoral played in the Town where Virgil wrote his Eclogues. But Virgil's Birth-place[4] is two miles out of town. I shall go out to it tomorrow

---

[1] The ancient lives of Virgil say that he was buried beside the road from Naples to Puteoli, his tomb bearing the inscription (ascribed by Donatus to Virgil himself):

Mantua me genuit, Calabri rapuere, tenet nunc
Parthenope; cecini pascua, rura, duces.

(Mantua bore me, the Calabrian winds carried me off; now Naples has me. I sang of pastures, fields, and heroes.)

[2] Leopold (1747–92), Archduke of Austria, was about to be married to the Infanta Maria Luisa, daughter of Charles III of Spain. He became Grand Duke of Tuscany on the death of his father in 1765. In Feb. 1790 he succeeded his brother as reigning Archduke of Austria, and in October of the same year was crowned Holy Roman Emperor.

[3] The Teatro di Corte of Mantua, forming a wing of the Ducal Palace on the Piazza Castello, stood on the space now occupied by the covered vegetable market. The building that JB saw had been completed at great expense in 1731, and was widely praised for its magnificence. It was very richly furnished, and had a famous crystal salon by the Venetian architect Antonio Codognato, though this was not finished till 1767. It was completely destroyed by fire on 29 May 1781 and was replaced by another which followed, on a smaller scale, the design of La Scala, Milan. This last was demolished in recent times (Vasco Restori, *Mantova e d'intorni, guida storica, artistica, topographica*, 1937, pp. 116–17). The "Italian Pastoral" has not yet been identified.

[4] The ancient biographers say that Virgil was born at a village called Andes, which from the time of Dante, if not earlier, has been generally identified as Pietole, not the modern village of Pietole, 5 m. S.W. of Mantua, but an area in the vicinity of Pietole vecchia, an ancient village razed in the 19th century, which stood a mile north of modern Pietole, on the bank of the Mincio, and much nearer to Mantua than modern Pietole. Old Pietole had a harbour and (at least in earlier days) a regular ferry and transport service. "From Mantoa", wrote Sir Thomas Hoby in 1549, "we went by water downe the river Meltio, and afterwarde we entred into the Poo. . . . Within ij or iij miles of Mantoa there is a village called Pietola, where Virgile was born: and upon the hill there, there is a little bricke house which th'inhabitants of the countrey call casetta de Vergilio, holding opinion that was his house, and that there he kept his beastes as a sheppherd" (*The Travels and Life of Sir Thomas Hoby, Kt. . . . 1547–1564*, edited for the Royal Historical Society by Edgar Powell, 1902, in *Camden Miscellany*, x. 13). It will be noted that

morning early sailing on the Mincius, and I am told I shall there see a true idea of the little humble village

> *quo sæpe solemus*
> *Pastores ovium teneros deponere fœtus.*[5]

I am also told that I shall see the very Palace where Virgil lived; but this I look upon as the Neapolitan tradition that he kept a school, or the tradition which I myself invented that he stood a furious siege of Swans.

My Dear Freind, Mantua will remain in my mind as one of those pleasing scenes the recollection of which cheers me in my dullest hours. I ever remain your sincere freind

JAMES BOSWELL

To Johnston, Wednesday 31 July 1765

MS. Yale (L 763).

ADDRESS: No. 32. To John Johnston Esq: of Grange.

Guastalla, 31 July 1765

MY DEAR JOHNSTON: When one finds in a little Country Church a young Lady of a tollerable good air with a cap somewhat fashionable and a few pretty ribbands, is not one mightily pleased, and does not Miss appear extremely agreable? And what think you is the reason of this? In short we are glad to find what we did not expect, and therefore the object has a superiour value to us. Just

JB reached his "Birth-place" by sailing down the river. He gives a moving account of his visit in a letter to John Wilkes, 31 July 1765. The casetta di Virgilio (which probably did not antedate the Middle Ages) had disappeared before 1628, and 18th-century visitors were shown as the site of Virgil's farm the large farm-establishment La Virgiliana, formerly a splendid villa of the Gonzagas, which stands a little to the east of Pietole vecchia (Vasco Restori, *Mantova e d'intorni*, 1937, pp. 535–37; Ferrucio Carreri, "Pietole, Formigado, e il Fossato di Virgilio", in *Atti e memorie della R. Accademia Virgiliana di Mantova*, 1903–04, 1904, pp. 19–82; Bruno Nardi, *The Youth of Virgil*, trans. Belle Palmer Rand, 1930, Appendix I; E. K. Rand, *In Quest of Virgil's Birthplace*, 1930; Gilbert Highet, *Poets in a Landscape*, 1957, pp. 45–62). Since the 18th century the identification of Andes with Pietole has been challenged by various scholars, notably, in our times, by Professor R. S. Conway (*Harvard Lectures on the Vergilian Age*, 1928, pp. 14–40), but the traditional site still has powerful advocates (Carreri, Nardi, Rand, as cited).

[5] Virgil, *Eclogues* i. 20–21, *depellere* not *deponere*: "Where we shepherds often drive our tender lambs". JB seems to misapply the lines, for if the countryside of the First Eclogue is that of Virgil's birth-place, as has generally been supposed, Tityrus, who is comparing "our town" with Rome, must mean not Andes, but the market-town, Mantua.

so my freind does the Town of Guastalla[1] strike me with uncommon satisfaction. I had not the least idea of it, and supposed
that I should find one of the poor Italian Villages which I have seen
so many of with pitifull shattered houses, and narrow dirty streets.
Instead of that I find Guastalla very well built. I find a very decent
fortification, very good houses, handsom streets and even *Places*
or Squares, and what is extraordinary, I have met with no bad
building nothing little, nothing mean. I have walked about with a
Jewish Merchant. He carried me into the Synagogue where I saw
a Levite teaching some Boys to read the sacred Books. It was
curious to find mere Children bawling out Hebrew.

I began this letter with a Country Church, and if you have no
objection I will end it with a Country Church-Yard. I would
imitate a little Mr. Gray's celebrated Elegy in that passage where
he supposes that perhaps the Country Church-Yard may contain
the bones of People equal to the greatest names whom we have
preserved

> Some Village Hampden that with dauntless breast
> The little Tyrant of his fields withstood etc.

I cannot at present write a word of verse, so you must be contented
with a prose imitation. Perhaps in this humble Village may be concealed an Abraham worthy to live in the primitive Patriarchal
dignity to rule a numerous seed, and to posess vast herds and
flocks. Perhaps there is here a Pitt of superiour fire to Him whose
Eloquence bears the British Senate along as a Tide sweeps away
every thing near it. Perhaps there is here a Bute unexposed to the
rude blasts of popular caprice. Perhaps a Wilkes uncorrupted by
Party

> Some Wilkes yet guiltless of the fall of Bute.[2]

Perhaps too there is here a Johnston who is Philosopher enough
to be content with a small fortune, hoping to have it made better

[1] Guastalla, though a very small place
and the capital of an inconsiderable area,
was an ancient cathedral town, and until
1748 had been the seat of a duchy later
divided between Parma and Piacenza.

[2] JB here attributes the resignation of
Bute on 8 Apr. 1763 to the attacks on his
administration made by Wilkes in *The
North Briton*, and no doubt they had
contributed to the popular mistrust of
Bute's government. But Bute himself

indicated that he felt he would serve the
King best by retiring and thus removing
"the only unpopular part of government"
(the Earl of Bute to the Duke of Bedford,
2 Apr. 1763, in *Correspondence of John,
Fourth Duke of Bedford*, ed. Lord John
Russell, 1846, iii. 226). JB had been till
recently the intimate associate both of
Bute's son and of Bute's hated enemy:
"Fine to be well with Wilkes and Lord
M." (Mem. 14 May 1765).

but in the mean time enjoying life with a consciousness of independence. And who knows but what we might find here a Boswell solemn and gay by turns who is sometimes the favourite of the Ladies, but more often a pensive and gloomy Metaphysician. Adieu Dear Johnston

JAMES BOSWELL

To Johnston, Saturday 24 August 1765

MS. Yale (L 764).
ADDRESS: No. 33. John Johnston Esq: of Grange.

Florence, 24 August 1765

MY DEAR JOHNSTON: You have often heard it observed that Men are carefull in small matters, and negligent in matters of consequence. I have this day been very near having a strong proof of that observation. You must consider that Consequence is merely proportional and then you will understand me. Since I began to write you the suite of letters, while upon my travels, there is hardly a little town where I have not been mindfull of my engagement and now when I am in Florence the Capital of Tuscany I have omitted it till within a few hours of my setting out[1] and I can see that it has been by mere chance that I have at last recollected it. I must however own that it is easier and pleasanter to write from little towns than from large towns for in a small place you have no crowd of ideas to confuse you whereas in such a Place as this there is so much to be seen that it cannot be described in a hasty letter. Therefore my good freind I reserve an account of what has amused me at Florence till I have the happiness of meeting you in Edinburgh. I ever remain Yours with great truth

JAMES BOSWELL

To Johnston, Saturday 28 September 1765

MS. Yale (L 765).
ADDRESS: No. 34. To John Johnston Esq: of Grange.

Siena, 28 Septr. 1765

MY DEAR JOHNSTON: It is with great difficulty that I now prevail

[1] He had been in Florence since 10 Aug.

with myself to write you a few words; for I am in a situation so extraordinary, that all my ideas are wavering and extravagant. I have been living for five weeks in Siena, a Provincial town of Tuscany, where I have given myself up entirely to the delirium of love, and have experienced a cessation of serious thought which a Man of your calm good sense cannot imagine possible in a man of my parts and knowledge. But I am formed in a most singular manner and can be known only by my very intimate friends.

There is no vanity in telling you that I have been a happy lover.[1] Indeed my Friend I have experienced all the delicious enjoyment of Italian Gallantry, which I used to fancy in gay prospect while eating your Currant Jelly on a Summer afternoon. I have taken resolution, and this morning I leave my Enchantress. But I am like a Man weakened by a fever and am melted down in tender regret. Adieu My Dear Friend. My next will be more reasonable Ever Yours

JAMES BOSWELL

To Johnston, Saturday 5 October 1765

MS. Yale (L 766).
ADDRESS: No. 35. To John Johnston Esq: of Grange.

Lucca, 5 Octr. 1765

MY DEAR JOHNSTON: It is just a week this morning since I left the sweet Siena, and altho' I am not yet restored to the Stoical firmness of mind, I have been able to fortify myself so much, that I can think with calmness of the charming woman who possesses my affections and who shall ever possess my gratitude.

I was recommended to one of the first nobles of this Republic a knowing sensible polite Man, a Man truly of the world for he has the prejudices of no particular country. You and I My Dear Friend must like him for another reason. He is often as Hypo-

---

[1] Of all JB's self-conscious attempts at gallantry in Italy, the only affair which could be called successful was with Maria Girolama Piccolomini (1728–92)—Momina, or Moma, for short—who returned his affection and kept up a correspondence with him long after he had left Siena. She was of good family, was married, and had four children. Two years later JB wrote: "My Italian Angel is constant" (To W. J. Temple, 12 June 1767); and again, "I had the other day a letter from my Signora at Siena written with all the warmth of Italian affection" (To W. J. Temple, 11 Aug. 1767).

chondriac as we are. His name is Signor Romano Garzoni.[1] He has carried me into the best company here and has taken care to have me shewn the curiositys of the City. What I value still more He has given me much information with regard to the Political Administration of this State. There is an excellent Opera here which has soothed my evil spirit. The first Woman is a Prodigy.[2] There never was so extensive a voice as her's. Adieu My worthy friend. I am ever Yours

JAMES BOSWELL

To Johnston, Wednesday 9 October 1765

MS. Yale (L 767).

ADDRESS: No. 36. To John Johnston Esq: of Grange.

Leghorne, 9 Octr. 1765

MY DEAR JOHNSTON: By some strange dissipation of mind I neglected to write to you from the large and ancient City of Pisa where the hanging Tower alone would have furnished me subject enough for two Pages. You are therefore to take this letter as the joint Salutation of Pisa and Leghorne You are to look upon it as a Member of Parliament who represents two Burrows. But as a Member who represents five Burrows is not expected to have a better head than He who represents only one, You are not to expect that this letter will have any superiour excellence to the common Epistles which I write to you from every town I come to.

I have little to say of Leghorne. I have been very well pleased with myself here, for my health and Spirits are perfect. I am waiting for a fair wind to carry me upon a very singular Expedition to visit the Island of Corsica. I have a letter from M. Rousseau to

[1] Romano Garzoni (1721–86) had inherited, at the death of his father Alessandro Garzoni in 1724, the family estate near Lucca, with the Villa di Collodi and its remarkable picture-gallery. He remained a bachelor, and with him ended the main branch of a distinguished Lucchese family. When he died, the Villa di Collodi passed to his sister Maria (Vincenzo Baroni, "Notizie Genealogiche delle Famiglie Lucchese", MS. genealogies in the Biblioteca Gobernatura, Lucca, MS. 1113, p. 455).

[2] She was probably the "truly wonderful performer", Lucrezia Agujari (1743–83), otherwise known as "La Bastardina", who was brought to England to sing at the Pantheon in the season 1775–76 "at the enormous salary of £100 a night, for singing two songs only" (Charles Burney, *A General History of Music*, 1789, iv. 504; *Grove's Dictionary of Music and Musicians*, 5th ed. by Eric Blom, 1954). JB had heard her on his first day in Lucca, 29 Sept.: "At 8 Opera Bastardina delicious. Lucquese Cavaliers in raptures like Schaw Stewart—was bashfull" (Mem. 30 Sept. 1765). On the day before this letter to JJ was written he had again visited the opera, in company with Romano Garzoni, to hear her (Mem. 5 Oct. 1765).

Paoli, and hope to be received with great distinction. I am quite full of my Project. I would fain talk very pompously Cras ingens iterabimus Æquor etc.[1] But my Vain glory is now in it's decline and I shall give you no big words. Possibly when I return from my Expedition I may borrow a few of Othello's phrases about his hair-breadth 'scapes[2] for indeed Johnston I do run some little risque from the Sea and from Barbary Corsairs and from Corsican Banditti. If I do not return fare you well. I have had my Portion of existence here and remember this compleats the third dozen of these my letters to you. I ever remain My good old friend Most sincerely yours

JAMES BOSWELL

To Johnston, Thursday 14 November 1765

MS. Yale (L 768).

ADDRESS: No. 37. To John Johnston Esq: of Grange.

Island of Corsica, 14 Novr. 1765

MY DEAR JOHNSTON: I have written you many a letter when in good health; I now write you one when confined by a tertian fever. How does it affect you, old freind? Do you perceive a strong smell of Peruvian Bark?[1] Or does it act upon you like a cold Electrifyer, and make you shiver from head to foot?[2]

After travelling over Mountains and Precipices which your comfortable Indolence would never have attempted, after passing ten days with Signor De Paoli General of the Corsican Nation and

[1] Horace, *Odes* I. vii. 32: "Tomorrow we embark again on the mighty ocean."

[2] *Othello* I. iii. 136.

[1] In the 18th century quinine was administered for malarial complaints in the form of powdered bark from the Peruvian cinchona-tree. JB's "tertian fever" was malaria, which he had picked up at Sollacarò.

[2] That is, does this piece of paper induce a shivering fit in you when you touch it, as contact with an electrical machine would give you a shock? Frictional electrical machines of a primitive sort had been invented in the 17th century, and the design had been improved in the 18th, notably (1742) by Andrew Gordon, Scots Benedictine monk and Professor of Philosophy at Erfurt. JB would have seen a friction engine in his class in Natural Philosophy at the University of Edinburgh (1757–58), but not necessarily then for the first time, for Gordon's machine rapidly became available for amateur experimentation or as a plaything. Experiments in the medical use of electricity began as early as 1744. John Wesley took treatments for his lameness, and believed so strongly in the therapeutic value of electricity that he bought four machines to treat the people of London, and published a popular pamphlet on the subject, *The Desideratum, or, Electricity Made Plain and Useful*, 1759 (Sidney Licht, "History of Electrotherapy", in *Therapeutic Electricity and Ultraviolet Radiation*, ed. Sidney Licht, 1959).

making myself acquainted with one of the greatest Men in Europe, after having traversed the greatest part of this Island, and observed the free spirit of it's brave Inhabitants, I am very well satisfy'd with the singular tour which I have made,[3] and shall reflect upon it with a manly pleasure, when five and twenty more years have fixed me in a good easy chair, and a good easy Philosophy; When you and I Johnston shall lay a log upon the fire with hearty complacency, and tell old Storys over a bottle of old wine.

This tertian fever has distrest me much. I carried it about for eleven days, having no Assistance that I could confide in. I arrived at last at Bastia, where is the Commander in Chief of the french troops in the Island, M. de Marbeuf,[4] the best man I ever met with. He has insisted on my living in his house, where I am attended by a very able french Physician,[5] and have every thing I can desire. In short one would think that the ancient alliance between the french and the Scots is renewed. I am allmost quite well and sail for Genoa in a day or two. Dear Freind Adieu

JAMES BOSWELL

To Johnston, Sunday 24 November 1765

MS. Yale (L 769).
ADDRESS: No. 38. To John Johnston Esq: of Grange.

Island of Caprara, 24 Novr. 1765

MY DEAR JOHNSTON: In my passage from Corsica to Genoa I have been forced by bad weather to land on Caprara[1] a little rocky Island about six miles long, where there is not a tree to be seen, and hardly any subsistence. Allmost all their grain and other necessarys

[3] JB sailed for Corsica on 11 Oct. and having landed at Centuri, on the northern tip, travelled down the island to Sollacarò, near Ajaccio, where Paoli had gone to attend a circuit court. He made his way back over the hills, by way of Corte to Bastia, and left Corsica on 20 Nov.

[4] Louis-Charles René (1712–86), Comte de Marbeuf, to whom Paoli had given JB a letter of recommendation, was in command of a body of French troops sent to Corsica in 1764. The French were observing neutrality between the Genoese government and the Corsican insurgents led by Paoli (Colonna de Cesari-Rocca and Louis Villat, *Histoire de Corse*, n.d.).

[5] In his published *Account of Corsica*, 1768, p. 369, JB gives this physician his name: "M. de la Chapelle was the physician who attended me. He had been several years physician to the army at Minorca, and had now the same office in Corsica. I called him the physician of the isles. He was indeed an excellent one."

[1] Capraia (called by the ancients Capraria, "goat island") is a rugged volcanic island off the north coast of Corsica, which had been Genoese property since

of life must be imported. There are however about two thousand Inhabitants who are all gathered together in a Village built upon the brow of the eminence which overlooks the harbour. The Genoese to whom the Island belongs, have here a Commissary, a Castle, and a garrison of about Sixty Men. I have been four days confined on this barren Spot.[2] But am by no means so ill off as you would imagine. I am very comfortably lodged in a Franciscan Convent, and I have a Soldier who goes about and caters for me with great diligence. He brings me fowls, eggs, honey, and yesterday I was regaled with a bit of veal. The Reverend Fathers, altho' extremely poor, supply me with bread and wine. This is Sunday, and I have amused myself by comparing your situation and mine, and upon my word Johnston, I would not change with you. You have been obliged to attend the Presbyterian Kirk where you have tired sorely, and from the dregs of your dismal education have suffered many a gloomy thought. I have heard Mass the solemn ceremonys of which have affected me with a pleasing reverence. It is ten to one but you have past the evening in some company by no means to your taste, and I have past mine in writing to M. Rousseau,[3] and to my worthy old freind. In short, Johnston, I have it all to nothing: Only the apprehension of a still longer confinement saddens me a little. There is fine air here. I at first indulged the idea that it would be an excellent place for retirement from the world. But when I consider that Vessels are constantly landing in the harbour I find it would be too public. Adieu My freind

JAMES BOSWELL

To Johnston, Monday 9 December 1765

MS. Yale (L 770).

ADDRESS: No. 39. To John Johnston Esq: of Grange.

Genoa, 9 Decr. 1765

MY DEAR JOHNSTON: Ligurian Letters[1] must not be long ones. Happy is it for me that I am writing this night to my plain honest

the 16th century. If JB's estimate is correct, it supported in the 18th century a population fully three times as large as now. "Their vineyards produce wine enough for the Island. They export only honey" (Mem. 22 Nov. 1765, expanded by F. A. Pottle, BP vii. 10–11).

[2] He was obliged to remain there for four more days and was thankful to get away in a Neapolitan felucca, in which he reached Genoa on 30 Nov.

[3] This letter to Rousseau has not been recovered.

[1] Letters from that part of Cisalpine Gaul called by the Romans *Liguria*, which

old freind; for indeed I am bad. My nervous system is totally un-
strung, and I am incapable of thinking with the smallest force or
Precision. I set out with a play of alliteration which has no meaning
but carrys with it the sagacious air of a maxim. I could shew you
many Maxims not unlike this stile were I to turn over a few of
your Collections of modern Maxims[2] for indeed Johnston a man
may abuse the greatest part of what mankind have written, and
not be illnatured or envious. I have been ten days in this stately
City which I find truly what Mr. Addison made me expect. Do you
know I have had my own fears at Genoa for being just arrived from
Corsica where I was very intimate with their terrible Ennemy
Paoli. I am pretty certain that the Noble Merchants of this despicable Republic would have been very well pleased to have had a
Stiletto slipt into my back, or to have got me into Prison and very
quietly given me a little poison; But the British flag makes them
tremble, and good Captain Robinson of the Vultur[3] rides at Anchor
in their Port. Farewell Honest Freind.

JAMES BOSWELL

To Johnston, Sunday 15 December 1765

MS. Yale (L 771).
ADDRESS: No. 40. To John Johnston Esq: of Grange.

Nice, 15 Decr. 1765

MY DEAR JOHNSTON: In a City where a famous General Council
was held I ought surely to be in an orthodox humour, and whatever
difficultys I may make to receive the hard doctrines of St. Athanasius I should for this evening at least be a firm Supporter of the

included Genoa and parts of Piedmont
and Savoy.
  [2] Such as *Maxims, Characters, and
Reflections, Critical, Satyrical, and Moral,*
by Fulke and Frances (Macartney)
Greville, published in London in 1756.
Bringing out such collections was a not
uncommon practice of the age.
  [3] H.M.S. *Vulture* was a sloop of fourteen guns (David Steel, *Navy List*, 1750).
Her Captain, Mark Robinson, had been
commissioned a lieutenant in 1746, a
commander in 1758, and a captain in 1760

(*The Commissioned Sea Officers of the
Royal Navy, 1660–1815,* comp. David
Bonner Smith *et al.,* 1954). He had
served in the war which had ended in
1763, and was later to see active service off the Falkland Islands in 1767 and
off Ushant in 1778. In 1780, as Captain
of the *Shrewsbury*, he led the fleet into
action off Chesapeake Bay, where he
lost a leg from a cannon-shot wound.
He was superannuated soon afterwards
as a rear-admiral (John Charnock, *Biographia Navalis,* 1794–98, vi. 404–06).

Nicene Creed.[1] Just as I entered the City the ringing of bells and firing of guns proclaimed a grand Procession. It was that of the Madonna Annunciata which being a pleasing subject made a fine mixture of solemnity and elegant sweetness. Our Lady was borne by a number of white masks on a scaffold richly gilded. She was a handsom figure and stood upright with her hands modestly folded on her breast. "Be it unto thy Handmaid" etc.[2] She was drest in a scarlet gown and had over it a loose flowing robe of blue with gold flowers. Round her head was a garland of stars, and above hung a magnificent crown. She was preceeded by the Franciscan friars with torches and followed by a vast crowd many of whom had also torches. I own I think that Processions representing the principal facts of our Holy Religion may have a very good effect on peoples minds. I am sure I felt it on this occasion. Warmed with devotion I entered a venerable church and payed fervent Adoration to the Father of Spirits. I was much of a Catholic. I find a Man now and then comes just round to what he has been and changes again he knows not how. But I enjoy a perfect tranquillity on that head. God grant it may last. Johnston I visited this day the little state of Monaco, from whence I ought to have written you a letter, but was so hurried I realy forgot. To make up matters I here promise that I shall never stop at any town long enough to dine sup or sleep without writing to your honour. Adieu My Dear Johnston.

JAMES BOSWELL

To Johnston, Monday 16 December 1765

MS. Yale (L 772).

ADDRESS: No. 41. To John Johnston Esq: of Grange.

Antibes, 16 Decr. 1765

MY DEAR JOHNSTON: At length I am fairly arrived in france[1] and

---

[1] The oecumenical council called by Constantine in 325, at which Athanasius was present and at which the Nicene creed was formulated, was not held, as JB supposed, at the town of Nice but at Nicaea (Bithynia) in Asia Minor.

[2] "And Mary said, Behold the handmaid of the Lord; be it unto me according to thy word" (*Luke* i. 38).

---

[1] JB had on the morning of this day travelled from Nice to Antibes (Journ. 16 Dec.). As Nice was at that time in the Kingdom of Sardinia, he had only now entered France.

see what large white clear paper I have got to write upon. *Il n'y a point de Pais comme la France*, says the happy Frenchman. I shall tell you by and by if he is in the right. Antibes is however hardly to be reckoned in france and every body tells me not to begin to judge of this Kingdom, till I get a good way into it, till I find excellent Inns, noble roads and most agreable *table d'hotes*. There is nothing to be seen here but the fortifications, and these the Sentry would not permit me to look at, so I have been reduced to amuse myself by considering impartially my own character. Not to enter into detail, I have an infinite variety of agreable talents, but I cannot be called an able man for upon my honour I am a very weak one for the world as it goes, and till the world be realy turned upside down as we see it in the set of prints[2] it must be the standard to which we appeal. I have however the happiness to think that I am a perfectly honest Man. But in this I cannot glory, for I am not conscious of having parts enough to be a Villain. I remember as well as any Student fresh from the university that famous line of Pope

An honest Man's the noblest work of God.[3]

But Poets are allways extravagant in the praise of what happens to please them at the time, and never fail to give it the preference to every thing else; as indeed even the ordinary race of Men do upon occasions. Have not you heard a hundred different dishes called the best in the world by different men who happened to be exceedingly hungry when they eat them, and therefore I look upon Popes general praise of simple honesty to be similar to the Sally of a young dragoon officer in Country quarters, who has got a keen appetite and as he enjoys his dinner, calls out "Well Gentlemen a piece of good salt Beef is the very best dish that comes upon a table." My opinion of human Nature is such that an honest Man of great abilitys is truly a noble work; but alltho' able men are indeed scarce, honest Able Men are ten times more so. Let you and

[2] JB is probably referring to "The Folleys of Mankind Expos'd or the World Upside Down", a print in sixteen divisions, first printed in 1733 (British Museum *Catalogue of Prints and Drawings . . . Division I. Political and Personal Satires*, No. 1999).

[3] Pope's *Essay on Man* iv. 247–48:

A Wit's a feather, and a Chief's a rod;

An honest Man's the noblest work of God.

Burns later used the line in *The Cotter's Saturday Night*:

Princes and lords are but the breath of kings,
"An honest man's the noblest work of God."

I My old freind be allways honest and as able as our Creator intended us. But let us never sowr the present moment by anxious cares for the future. This is the old Classic System. Adieu.

JAMES BOSWELL

To Johnston, Wednesday 18 December 1765

MS. Yale (L 773).

ADDRESS: No. 42. To John Johnston Esq: of Grange.

Lucces,[1] 18 Decr. 1765

MY DEAR JOHNSTON: In my letter from Nice I promised to write to you from every place where I either should dine, sup or sleep. I dined yesterday at an Inn which I don't know the name of, and supt and lay at Frezius, where I was entertained as if I had been at the great Inn at Stamford,[2] or any other of the noble Caravansarys in old England. But from neither of my yesterday's Inns did I write to my freind;—and yet I am not a bit the worse man, nor is my promise a bit less to be depended upon than it was at Nice. In short Johnston I forgot to write, and this to a thinking Man is excuse enough. You know I am a Metaphysician in my own way, allways reflecting allways endeavouring to get a more perfect knowledge of the human mind. Every little circumstance which occurs in my life is to me an Experiment in Philosophy, and my neglect of writing to you yesterday has led me to think very curiously of the faculty of Memory. Certain it is that Memory is not in our power, for to remember is not an active faculty, and I cannot help smiling when I think how gravely we charge one another "Now remember this". To explain myself, suppose the idea of what a man has promised to remember once fairly effaced

---

[1] Le Luc in the department of Var, an ancient town with Roman and medieval remains on the road from Fréjus to Toulon.

[2] The George Inn, of great age, is still one of the principal hotels at Stamford. Its position on the Great North Road made it a busy place, and it was familiar to all travellers between London and Scotland: ". . . well-known, long-established, and excellent INN called THE GEORGE, in St. Martin's, Stamford Baron, in the county of Northampton . . . comprising 10 sitting-rooms, 38 bed-rooms, spacious kitchen, bar, laundry, larder, and most extensive Out-houses of every description, Stabling for 86 horses, and large Garden. These premises . . . possess all the advantages that can possibly belong to a large inn which has for a great number of years been resorted to by the first families in the kingdom. Seventeen pairs of horses in capital condition are daily employed in the above concern" (Advertisement in *The Lincoln, Rutland, and Stamford Mercury*, 12 May 1815).

from his mind, pray tell me by what known power can he recover that idea. You will tell me let him try well, and I'll warrant he recovers it, as I have done a name which I had forgotten, by combining letters at random till I hit upon what I wanted; but My dear freind, your forgetfullness in that case was a very imperfect one, for you remembered that it was necessary for you to recall a name; but suppose the idea of name entirely out of your mind, and give me your secret for bringing it in again. Now Johnston to make an application, I yesterday had not the most distant thought connected with that of a letter. Had I recollected that I had a letter to write to some one the Alphabet would not have been much tortured by me with a *Bons. Cons. Dons* etc. before the good old name of Johnston would have presented itself. But this idea did not enter my mind till I was a mile or two advanced this morning, when other ideas at last made a little room for it. I maintain then that no Man ought to be punished for forgetfullness; and yet in the course of ordinary Society we all agree in punishing him. There are two reasons for this in the first place because we are not sure that he realy forgot, in the next place because blows do actually so work upon our frames, that we Some how or other remember better: a strange effect this. How in the name of wonder can beating my carcase at three o'clock be the cause of a certain idea's rising in my mind at Six. In short My Dear Freind, Memory is to us a real Mystery.[3] I therefore promise to write to you from the french Inns as often as I shall remember. Adieu.

JAMES BOSWELL

To Johnston, Friday 20 December 1765

MS. Yale (L 774).

ADDRESS: No. 43. To John Johnston Esq: of Grange.

Toulon, 20 Decr. 1765

MY DEAR JOHNSTON: When you have been reading the *Edinburgh Evening Courant*, or our more favourite *Caledonian Mercury*,[1] when

---

[3] Rather more than a year before, JB had written a letter on the mystery of memory to the Abbé Jerusalem, director of the Collegium Carolinum, whom he had met at Brunswick in June 1764.

[1] *The Edinburgh Evening Courant* was a thrice-weekly paper which survived under various ownerships for the long period from 1718 to 1886. It had no connexion with Defoe's *Edinburgh Courant*, which was a short-lived publication. *The Caledonian Mercury* was also published thrice weekly and lived on through many

sitting gravely in Forrest's Coffeehouse, or lying at your ease on a bank at Grange, has not Toulon roused your soul to war? has it not made you think of the insulting Gaul, the perfidious french, Cannons and Mortars, twenty sail of the line and a terrible invasion?[2] I own to you I love to recollect such feelings of the untravelled Scottish comfortable Laird, and I have done what I could to make myself feel in the same manner now when I am at Toulon that I might have the satisfaction of changing in a moment my ideas of the Spot where I find myself. Captain Keith Stewart[3] whom I have met several times unexpectedly is here. He has shewn me the Ships of war lying in the harbour but could not possibly get me to see the Arsenal. They are exceedingly cautious here of letting Strangers see any thing which it is worth while to remark. Captain Elliot who has brought from Constantinople Mr. Grenville our late Ambassador At the Porte,[4] is also here with his Ship. It is curious to see British Ships in a french harbour and the Sailors of the two Nations talking and laughing together in all safety, when without doubt they will very soon be doing all in their power to blow out one another's brains. Human life My Dear Freind is not a whole it is an aggregate of parts which are entirely unconnected. He who calls life absurd takes a false view of it. He considers it's

vicissitudes for almost as long—from 1720 to 1867. Besides news and advertisements, it printed current odes, epitaphs, elegies, and similar literary matter (W. J. Couper, *The Edinburgh Periodical Press*, 1908, ii. 19–62; Mary E. Craig, *The Scottish Periodical Press 1750–1789*, 1931, pp. 24–25).

[2] Toulon had been made, in the reign of Louis XIV, one of the strongest fortresses of France and was the headquarters of the French navy.

[3] *Ante* 29 July 1765. "I found at the Inn here Captain Keith Stewart who had frightened me so much with regard to my Corsican Expedition. He joked me very heartily and realy did not enter into the spirit of my singular tour" (Journ. 20 Dec. 1765). It is clear that in temperament Keith Stewart and JB were incompatible. More than twenty years after these encounters in Italy, Stewart, meeting him by chance at Knaresborough, was so flippant about JB's cherished hopes of becoming M.P. for Ayrshire that, in

recording the episode, JB was moved to write: "I knew his cold selfish character well, and did not mind him" (Journ. 5 July 1788).

[4] H.M.S. *Thames*, a ship of thirty-two guns of the Mediterranean fleet, commanded by Captain John Eliot, was conveying the Hon. Henry Grenville and his wife back from Constantinople, where he had been ambassador for the past three years: "I saw here Captain Elliot who had brought Mr. Grenville the Ambassador, from Constantinople. How manly these Captains [Eliot and Stewart] look'd, while I was conscious of having no firm hold of any plan" (Journ. 20 Dec. 1765). JB found Grenville "stately but affable". Mrs. Grenville was "gay and easy as a foreign woman and said I had seen nothing, as I had not seen Turkey the true Paradise on earth" (Journ. 22 Dec. 1765). Eliot (d. 1769) was Governor of West Florida from 1766 until his death (John Charnock, *Biographia Navalis*, 1794–98, vi. 391).

parts as one whole whereas he ought never to think but of one part at a time and it will appear tollerably well. He who would make a whole of life by connecting it's parts is as unreasonable as if he should insist on finding a connection among the goods of a Toy Shop and be in a passion because he cannot see what a pair of pinchbeck buckles can do to a Lady's neclace, or a pocket knife to a Snuff box in the shape of a drum. Worthy Johnston let us divert ourselves in this same Toy shop, till death lets us in to a better. I only desire that you may never talk of the chain of life for the links of our existence are realy never joined above two or three at a time. Adieu.

JAMES BOSWELL

To Johnston, Friday 20 December 1765

MS. Yale (L 775).

ADDRESS: No. 44. To John Johnston Esq: of Grange.

Cuges, 20 Decr. 1765

MY DEAR JOHNSTON: This is the first day that I have perfectly remembered my promise of writing to you from every Inn of any consequence; so this day you have both a morning and an evening Epistle. In the morning I was in an excellent frame as you may judge from the vivacious flow of my Epistle. I cannot say much for myself, this evening, for either the fatigue of being dragged slowly along, or a very plentifull Supper has dulled my finer facultys. Shall I tell you what I had for Supper? Captain Erskine wrote once what he called a Culinary Ode,[1] and why may not I write a Culinary letter? I had then for supper a couple of well-roasted *grives*[2] exceeding savoury with a slice of bacon and bread burnt and buttered. I had some ribs of delicate lamb which I eat with a Sallad that I drest to my liking. Lastly I had a choice cold Partridge, and as is allways the custom abroad a desert of several little things. This supper with half a bottle of good Provence wine is I think no bad repast even to a Man who has not dined, which is my case today. Perhaps You may think my Supper no great matter, and think me very easily pleased. I remember my Brother David used to

---

[1] JB himself published " To Gluttony. An Ode" (a parody of one of Erskine's serious odes) in Donaldson's *Collection*, ii. 106–08. In the same volume, pp. 28–32, is a poem (not an ode) by Erskine called "The Dinner". [2] Thrushes.

laugh at me for talking so sumptously of my entertainment wherever I had been. He used to say "Well you no doubt had some elegant bread and some magnificent salt." I must make a reflection Johnston. A Man when a Boy and when grown up is much the same in reality. He only changes his manner. This morning I said to Captain Stewart, "Come pray let us go aboard your ship that I may see you command for five minutes." Could any wish be more childish and had I exprest it in a childish tone he had despised me, but alltho' I realy had the childish wish, by expressing it in a deep rough tone Stewart could not positively conclude me in earnest and it appeared singular humour. I must also give you an Anecdote. I this day on the road had a hot dispute with my Valet de Chambre[3] on the dutys of inferiors to their superiors. He maintained that He was my Superior, and I boiled with fiery indignation. And what occasioned all this think you? Nothing but my english pronunciation of a french word which made him mistake me. I pronounced *Sooperieur* which made him think of *sous* under so he thought *Sousperieur* was an inferior in french. A most ridiculous Logomachy or rather *Syllabomachy*. Cuges where I now am is a small village it was dark when I entered it and dark will it be when I leave it; so food and sleep are all I can get of it. Farewell.

JAMES BOSWELL

To Johnston, Monday 23 December 1765

MS. Yale (L 776).

ADDRESS: No. 45. To John Johnston Esq: of Grange.

Marseilles, 23 Decr. 1765

MY DEAR JOHNSTON: Tell me honestly if you are not tired of reading such a suite of singular Epistles? Such will be the question which your freind will put by the time you have read thus far, and he is realy uncertain what will be your Answer. I am on this occasion like an Advocate who does not know for which Party he may be retained, like a Political Pamph[l]eteer who does not know

---

[3] *Ante* 9 Nov. 1764, n. 2. JB had been discussing at some length with Jacob Hänni the relationship between masters and servants, and Jacob, distressed at the frankness and intimacy of JB's manners, had been trying to instruct him how to conduct himself with becoming reserve and dignity towards his inferiors (Journ. 18 Dec. 1765).

which Great Man's emissarys may bring him five guineas. I am equally ready to abuse my letters or to praise them, and it is only because praise is more pleasing than abuse that I determine myself to chuse the former. You cannot tire of my letters Johnston for you are singular as they, alltho' your plump and swarthy Countenance would denote as common an honest boild-beef family sort of a Gentleman as old Edinburgh can produce. But I who have seen you on Arthur seat, in bed of a morning, in the tavern at night, drinking tea and drinking twopenny, heartily merry, and comfortably serious, happy as you could wish and sad as the Owl on the ruined towers of Lochwood,[1] I know what you are, and therefore regard and love you. My letters Johnston abound in uncommon sallies and I would fain hope in easy humour. I know my producing them easily does not prove them to have that true ease which constitutes the excellence of such light pieces, but I realy think that they have that admirable quality. I know but of one way that you can tire of these my letters which is by reading too many of them at a time, for you know Johnston that an excess of what is good becomes most disgusting. You may prove it in honey, in Italian Music, and in love. Therefore my freind take my letters in moderation.

This is my third day at Marseilles which is one of the prettiest towns in france. Their Theatre is a very handsom one, and they are a gay free sort of people. There are here just now a great many of our Countrymen. I must tell you a curious Anecdote. I arrived here without money and without a credit. I wanted fifty Louis and could not do without them. I found here Mr. Pennant,[2] an ancient Briton whom I had the pleasure of knowing at Florence. I applyed

[1] *Ante* 19 July 1763.

[2] Edward Pennant (c. 1729–78), of whom JB wrote: "I had neither money nor credit but trusted to Pennant an ancient Welchman of very large fortune. I ask'd him to answer for me for 50 Louis which he most readily agreed to. Nothing is to be had in this world as one would have it. By making Pennant answer for my 50 louis I deprived myself of one excellent Subject of my Satyre for he is indeed a most absurd Mortal and now it would be shocking in me to pourtray him as I well could" (Journ. 21 Dec. 1765).

Pennant was the owner of Bagillt Hall, near Holywell, Flintshire, and of extensive lands in the neighbourhood. In 1766 he sold the Hall and all these estates to his distant relative, Thomas Pennant the naturalist, and made his home in France, where he died some twelve years later. He had matriculated at Christ Church, Oxford, in 1746, and had been High Sheriff of Flintshire in 1753–54, so he could not have openly professed Roman Catholicism before 1754. Possibly he embraced that faith only later and retired to France for that reason (Burke's *Commoners*, 1836, iii. 35; Henry Taylor, *Historic Notices . . . of Flint*, 1883, p. 56; Thomas Pennant, *The History of the Parishes of Whiteford and Holywell*, 1796, p. 272; *Alumni Oxonienses*).

to him, and he let me have the Money immediatly, on my drawing a bill on My Banker in London. I call this the right way of doing among Men who by the course of things have the advantage to be Gentlemen. Let Tobacco Merchants[3] try to laugh at this. We wish them a good stomach to eat the fruit of their labours; but let them keep their distance. Pennant knows nothing of me more than by having lived some weeks together. He is a Cambrian Catholic tho no great Beleiver, and in Politics I fear he holds to the precept of the civil law, Suum cuique tribuito.[4] Eat a welch rabbit in honour of this worthy Gentleman. Yours

JAMES BOSWELL

To Johnston, Tuesday 24 December 1765

MS. Yale (L 777).

ADDRESS: No. 46. To John Johnston Esq: of Grange.

Aix en Provence, 24 Decr. 1765

MY DEAR JOHNSTON: If I praised my letters yesterday I am sure I did not promise that they should be all equally good. This Morning's Epistle will help you to follow the advice which I gave you to take my letters in moderation. It will be a very poor one and when you have read it you will be like a man who when eating cherries finds an unripe one which disgusts him for a little and interrupts his luxurious Banquet. I have stroled an hour in Aix and looked at the Townhouse the Cathedral and two or three more of the principal things. The Course[1] is a walk where I could meditate long enough. In short I could pass half a summer at Aix very well. I am hurried by a rascal of a Postilion who insists on my mounting a vile hack this instant. It is hard to be so hurried to mount, when I am sure of falling so soon. Adieu My Dear Freind.

JAMES BOSWELL

---

[3] Glasgow tobacco merchants were the merchant-princes and typical parvenus of JB's day.

[4] Justinian, *Institutiones* I.i.l: "Justitia est constans et perpetua voluntas jus suum cuique tribuendi"; cf. also Cicero, *De officiis* L.v.15). JB's adaptation may be translated: "Thou shalt render to every man his due."

[1] The wide thoroughfare, planted with double rows of plane-trees, known as the Cours Mirabeau, which today divides the newer from the older part of the town. In JB's time it was on the south side of the city.

To Johnston, Friday 27 December 1765

MS. Yale (L 778).

ADDRESS: No. 47. To John Johnston Esq: of Grange.

Avignon, 27 December 1765

MY DEAR JOHNSTON: You know I am half a Catholic. I love the solemn and magnificent worship of the Church of Rome and allthough I cannot beleive some of her tenets I have a great respect for the many learned and holy men that have lived and died in a firm perswasion of that faith, and therefore I treat with reverence what to my understanding appears strange. I came to this City on Christmas eve and heard high Mass at Midnight in the Cathedral. I contrived it so as to pass the agreable festival of the nativity of our Saviour in this ancient seat of the Dominion of the Pope. I have seen one or two of the Churches with satisfaction and have been in the best frame I could wish. The Jesuits have taken sanctuary here.[1] It rejoyces me to meet in my walks the genteel fathers of that Order so much distinguished for Science and for Nobility. I have been much with My Lord Dumbar and My Lady Inverness[2] who are most excellent People true old Scots Nobility with the ease of foreign manners. They are of that sort of people which is wearing out in this interested debauched and republican age of Britain. Their attachment to The Royal Family of Stuart does them honour with liberal Minds. Their long acquaintance with the unfortunate Court has given them a turn of thinking which it is pleasing to sympathise with, and the variety of Anecdotes which they know makes them very entertaining. I have enjoyed a singular scene here. It is true I have my melancholy hours, but I

---

[1] The Society of Jesus had been expelled from France in 1765, by royal edict. Avignon, a papal dominion, was not under the sovereignty of France.

[2] James Murray (c. 1690–1770), son of David, 5th Viscount Stormont, and brother of Lord Mansfield, was given the titles of Earl of Dunbar and Viscount of Drumcairn by the Pretender, whose cause he served during the Fifteen. His sister, Lady Marjory Murray, had married another Jacobite leader, Colonel John Hay of Cromlix, the Pretender's secretary, who had also been given a title, and was known in Jacobite circles as the Duke of Inverness. He had died in 1740 (*Scots Peer.* v. 231, viii. 205). JB had an introductory letter to Murray from Andrew Lumisden, and when he called on him was invited to stay and have a meal with him and his sister. They were so pleased with his company that they urged him to stay another day in Avignon and visit them again (Journ. 25 Dec. 1765). JB's spelling "Dumbar" is not inadvertent, but follows Lumisden's (To JB, 7 Sept. 1765) and that of the old man himself (To JB, 25 Dec. 1765).

own, that I am perswaded no man has tasted a greater diversity of ideas than I have. Adieu Dear Johnston

JAMES BOSWELL

To Johnston, Saturday 28 December 1765

MS. Yale (L 779).

ADDRESS: No. 48. To John Johnston Esq: of Grange.

Nismes, 28 Decr. 1765

MY DEAR JOHNSTON: Were you with me this morning you would value me more than you could have done for these several Months. Nismes is another Rome in regard of Antiquitys. I have seen here some as magnificent remains of Roman grandeur as are in the world over which those noble Conquerors ruled.[1] The contemplation of those Antiquitys banishes from my mind every frivolous and mean idea and gives me a manly and virtuous tone which makes me happy in myself, and estimable to others. The regret which one feels on the reflection that the Romans are no more throws a cast of melancholy into my disposition which tempered by resolute Philosophy has a very good effect. At this Moment Johnston I am what I wish ever to be. I embrace you with all my heart. This is a french Expression of freindship and I think it so good a one that I venture to adopt it. Ever yours

JAMES BOSWELL

To Johnston, Monday 30 December 1765

MS. Yale (L 780).

ADDRESS: No. 49. To John Johnston Esq: of Grange.

Montpelier, 30 December 1765

MY DEAR JOHNSTON: Allthough in a hurry to get to Paris, I have come a day out of my road in order to see this Seat of Salubrity where so many of our sickly Countrymen have been restored to the ordinary state of imperfect humanity, which by comparrison appears to them a state of health.

What is the matter with me this morning I realy cannot say;

---

[1] In his journal he mentions the so-called Temple of Diana, the Maison Carrée, and the Amphitheatre.

but I find myself a formal and tedious talker, a man who gives you a long warped period for what might be very easily said in three words. I am a dull frenchman. I have past a day here, and seen what was curious, which does not require much time. I must not rob my Journal to tell you what I have seen. These my letters are intended rather to tell you what I feel, to give you the ideas which employ my mind at the time I write. If they have some connection with the place where I happen to be so much the better, if not they are allways the thoughts or reveries of your freind who never fails to remember you in all Citys and in all Countrys. I have been kindly entertained here by Mr. Alexander Ray an honest east Lothian man and a most admirable Banker and what I like as well when my Purse is not empty He is a good Classical Scholar and an Antiquarian.[1] Adieu My Dear Freind Yours ever

JAMES BOSWELL

To Johnston, Sunday 5 January 1766

MS. Yale (L 781).

ADDRESS: No. 50. To John Johnston Esq: of Grange.

Lyons, 5 Janry. 1766

MY DEAR JOHNSTON: Let me wish you many happy new years, as is the cordial custom in good Scotland, where you are now eating *Buns* and Short-bread of most excellent taste, savoury to your palate and comfortable to that honest Stomach which must allways partake of the best. I can say hardly any thing of this ancient and stately City renowned for it's roman remains, for it's printing and for it's beautifull stuffs. I am lame Johnston. I have got sore toes and in this severe frost it is necessary for me to stay quietly at

---

[1] Andrew Lumisden (MS. Yale C 1798) had recommended JB to Ray, who, because of his antiquarian tastes, was nicknamed "the Doctor". JB spent two days in his congenial company and found him "a free sensible goodhumoured man with a variety of agreable knowledge" (Journ. 29, 30 Dec. 1765).

The Scottish banking firm at Montpellier was one of the partnerships established at suitable points on the Continent by Robert Herries (*ante* 4 Aug.

1763, n. 2; *post* 9 Oct. 1767, n. 7). After being apprenticed to his own uncles, Robert and Charles Herries, merchants, of Rotterdam, the younger Robert had established himself in 1754 at Barcelona, and his ability had quickly earned him a great reputation in the business world. Much about his early career can be found in Forbes, pp. 17–18 and *passim*. This work (at p. 18) states that the Montpellier house was styled "Herries, Ray, and Burnet".

home in my warm room;[1] therefore Johnston I can only bid you good night. I might dash you down a few flashes of imagination; but I set out tomorrow morning at five in the Diligence for Paris and it is now Midnight so I must go and have a few hours repose. Adieu My Dear Freind

JAMES BOSWELL

To Johnston, Thursday 9 January 1766

MS. Yale (L 782). The letter was written in the diligence; the writing is very uneven.

ADDRESS: No. 51. To John Johnston Esq: of Grange.

Auxerres, 9 Janry. 1766

MY DEAR JOHNSTON: My last from Lyons was written in a very great hurry and this from Auxerres will be written as the Scots Blackguards[1] say in *a couple of hurries*, for I am now upon my route to Paris in the *Diligence* of which you have certainly read. Let me assure you it is the best Stage Coach in the world.[2] You pay a hundred livres for which you travel a hundred leagues and are *nourri* and *couché* the whole way. The Coachman is a Personage of

[1] JB had been suffering, since before Christmas, from ingrowing nails on both great toes, and by New Year's Day one of his feet had become badly swollen. He had thought of buying a horse and riding part of the way to Paris, but as he could not bear to wear riding-boots for long, he continued on his way by coach, reaching Lyons on 2 Jan. There he had his feet dressed by a surgeon and did little walking about during the four days of his stay (Journ. 24, 31 Dec. 1765; 2, 3, 14 Jan. 1766).

[1] The term seldom carried in the 18th century the full sense of opprobrium it has since acquired. JB was probably thinking of the Edinburgh caddies. The word was usually applied to odd-job men or servants of the lowest class with no reflection on their characters.

[2] For contrast with the comfortable Paris diligence JB had in mind the German post-wagon, of which he says: "The Post Waggon is a remain of barbarity of

manners. It is just a large cart mounted upon very high wheels which jolt prodigiously. It has no covering, and has three or four deal boards laid accross it, to serve for seats. In this manner do the Germans travel night and day" (Journ. 4 Aug. 1764). And even the English stage-coach compared unfavourably with the Diligence: "These vehicles, however cumbrous they may appear, are much more easy and agreeable for the passenger than our own stage-coaches. . . . the comfort of the inside, from having plenty of room, and the pleasure of travelling in the Cabriolet, which is their outside, where your neck is not risked, but you are shaded from the sun, and, if necessary, can be shielded from the rain, enjoying the scene around, is so agreeable, contrasted with our own mode, that not to notice it would have been unjust. We boast, that the word *comfort* is unknown in France; here, however, is a luxury we do not enjoy in England" (Henry Sass, *A Journey to Rome and Naples*, 1818, pp. 21–22).

very great Consequence, for besides his being Chief Conductor of our Coach, It is He who orders every thing at the Inns where we have most excellent entertainment I promise you and very good beds. If any of us is not content with what the Inn has furnished him, The Coachman is called in and talked to with such manly vigour as the Cook of a College at Oxford or Cambridge is chid by the eaters of Commons. But you Johnston know nothing of those Anecdotes of English Universitys. You must apply to my freind Temple of Trinity Hall Cambridge who will soon instruct you as to this as much as he has done me. Diligence Passangers like University Students are glad to improve the little opportunity they have of domineering. The Coachman I have said is respectable, but not from his figure which is not like the bluff square jolly grumbling British Coachman. No no. The Materials of which Man is made in france cannot make a true Coachman. We are eight Passengers in The Diligence. When we meet, you shall laugh at our History. At present let me tell you that I have the health of a Hercules dining and supping heartily every day and sleeping soundly every Night. I have great vigour and a pure absence of thought. I have an existence without pain which some would prefer to the anxious sensibility of taste and passion; but for my part I prefer being an unhappy man with the prospect of perfection to being a contented Brute with no prospect. We have just time to sup before we go to bed as we are called up between two and three. I write you one Diligence letter. Adieu.

JAMES BOSWELL

V

March 1766–July 1786

During this period, which stretches from his twenty-sixth to his forty-sixth year, Boswell was called to the Scottish bar on 29 July 1766 and became an advocate in Edinburgh; was married on 25 Nov. 1769 to his cousin Margaret Montgomerie; succeeded on 30 Aug. 1782 to the estate of Auchinleck; and on 13 Feb. 1786 was admitted to the English bar.

V

March 1766–July 1786

To Johnston, Monday 31 March 1766

MS. Yale (L 783). Sent 31 Mar. 1766 (Reg. Let.).
ADDRESS: To Mr. John Johnstone, Writer in Edinburgh.

Auchinleck, 31 March 1766

MY DEAR JOHNSTON: I would willingly write you a long and entertaining letter. But I am at present under such a cloud that I am incapable of executing my wish. You must therefore be contented with an assurance of the continuance of my regard and with being told that I am studying Scots Law and conforming entirely to the inclinations of my worthy Father.[1] I hope to be at Moffat[2] by the 8th or 10th of May. If you could come up at that time we might look at lodgings together. Order that matter as you see best. I expect to hear from you soon and am ever yours

JAMES BOSWELL

Since writing the above the cloud is much disperst and I could now write to you long enough but have not time. Such is life My Dear Friend. But be it as it may You and I have enjoyed many a good hour and I hope shall enjoy many more, and above all I trust we shall meet in a better life where there is "no night."[3] Adieu Continue to be the worthy man I have allways found you and beleive me most sincerely yours.

[1] JB had returned to Scotland on 5 or 6 March, after more than three years of absence, and was now applying himself seriously to the study of Scots law in preparation for the examination which would precede his call to the Scottish bar in July of this year.

[2] Moffat had a high reputation at the time as a watering place. JB knew it of old, for he had been sent there in his thirteenth year to "take the cure" at a time when a bad cold had left him with nervous indigestion and scorbutic symp-

toms. A serious depression, which occurred towards the end of his seventeenth year, sent him back again ("Ébauche de ma vie", MS. Yale L 1107; Journ. 11 Dec. 1762). He recalled with pleasure the experience of taking warm baths there, and spoke of Mr. Little, the innkeeper at Moffat, as "my old acquaintance" (French theme, c. 14–15 Oct. 1763, MS. Yale M 87; Journ. 14 Mar. 1783).

[3] *Rev.* xxii. 5: "And there shall be no night there."

From Johnston, Saturday 26 April 1766

MS. Yale (C 1624). Recd. 2 May 1766. "Mr. Johnston" (Reg. Let.).

ADDRESS: To James Boswell Esqr. Younger of Auchinleck, By Ayr.

POSTMARK: AP 29.

Edinburgh 26th. April 1766

MY DEAR SIR: I received your kind Letter of the 31st. March, and have delaid writing to you, till I could fix the time of my leaving the Town, where I have Staid much longer than I intended at parting from you, owing to Some occurencies in bussiness, which I nowise regrete, as at present I have no place at home that I could lodge in, and you know Edinr. is never dissagreeable to me, while I am under no necessity of leaving it. I hope you have lived comfortably at Auchinleck these 4 weeks. The Scene would appear new after three years absence, and recall some agreeable ideas, tho' you Complained a little of not being quite well when you wrote me. I imagine it has been owing to the Tooth ach. You did not mention it to me, but Davie informs me you was much troubled with it at that time. If it is owing to Antiquity Endeavour to Combate it Stoutly. It is to be got the better of, and to believe this firmly, I am Convinced is a great Step towards it. Your young friend Mr. Boswell[1] will be very acceptable to you, he is a fine young fellow, and well liked by his Companions, tho' I have not the pleasure of his acquaintance. He will read Scots Law with you, which will make it a more easy and agreeable study. If you can acquire as much as to make you pass in the summer session with a tolerable grace, I think it Shews no Small degree of resolution. After this you cannot have any doubt of giving that application necessary for a man of bussiness at the bar. What do you think of Mr. Dundas's Success in this way? Tho' he has not been three

---

[1] Claud Boswell (1742–1824), the son of Lord Auchinleck's uncle John Boswell of Balmuto, was preparing at Auchinleck, under Lord Auchinleck's supervision, for an examination in Scots law, and like JB was to be called to the bar that summer. In 1780 he became Sheriff-Depute for Fife and Kinross, and in 1799 was raised to the bench as Lord Balmuto (*College of Justice*, p. 544). In later years, JB thought him sensible but unimaginative, and did not care much for his company: "There is little congenial sympathy between him and me; so that though I regard him as a worthy cousin, we meet seldom" (Journ. 8 Dec. 1775). In *Original Portraits* ii. 277–78, he is depicted as a plain and slow-witted man, a judge of a different sort from the brilliant coterie which included Kames, Monboddo, and Hailes.

years at the Bar, he is to be Solicitor in place of Mr. Montgomery, who is to be Lord Advocate, and My Lord is to have a Double Gown. These promotions are in Consequence of the Lord Justice Clerks Death[2] which you'll have heard of, and are mentioned here as fixt and certain.

I am now determined to leave this on the 8 or 9th of May, which is much about the time you propose going to Moffat, So I may probably have the pleasure of finding you there; if not, I will leave you a letter giving an account of my rout, and when I can return to you. As I must be at Langholm,[3] and in that Neighbourhood for a few days, I propose a great deal of happiness with you at Moffat. We Shall Converse, read, walk etc. and live quite easie and without Constraint. I have not wrote to take Lodgings for you at Moffat, as I think it is better to delay it till you go there yourself, when you'll have a Choice of the whole, as there is no Company at present in that place. Put up your Horses at Little's[4] in Moffat, he keeps the best publick house, and you can lodge a night or two there till you take Lodgings. You'll receive this in time to write me before I leave Edr. I beg you'll do it, and write me a long or Short Letter according to the humour you are in for writing. I have Seen our friend Captain Erskine frequently of late, about two weeks ago we walked to the top of Old Arthurs Seat, upon a fine Serene day, and Basked ourselves a while in the Sun, and Enjoyed the Charming prospect. I hope My Lord Auchinleck is recovering his former State of health. The Jaunt to the Ensuing Circuit[5] will have a great Tendency to Confirm his

[2] Sir Gilbert Elliot, Bt., Lord Minto, the Lord Justice-Clerk, had died on 16 Apr. He was to be succeeded by Thomas Miller, Lord Barskimming (later Lord Glenlee), who had been Lord Advocate since 1760, and who in his new office would have the double gown of a judge in the Court of Session and in the Court of Justiciary (*College of Justice*, pp. 500, 530). The new Lord Advocate was to be James Montgomery, a special friend of Robert Dundas, who, on being made Lord President in 1760, had secured at the same time Montgomery's appointment as joint Solicitor-General (G. W. T. Omond, *The Arniston Memoirs*, 1887, p. 162). Montgomery had become sole Solicitor-General in 1764. Henry Dundas, nominated to succeed to the post of Solicitor-General, was the Lord President's half-brother, and only twenty-four years old. He had been a class-mate of JJ and JB in Edinburgh College, 1755–56. All these preferments indicated by JJ are confirmed by *Scots Mag.* (1766) xxviii. 224.

[3] On the Esk, between 8 and 9 miles east of Grange.

[4] *Ante* 31 Mar. 1766, n. 2.

[5] He was due to make the northern circuit, and in the following month travelled with Lord Coalston to Perth, Aberdeen, and Inverness, where they held courts on 8, 16, and 24 May (*Scots Mag.*, 1766, xxviii. 279).

health. Adieu My Dear Sir, and I remain most Sincerely yours while

JOHN JOHNSTON

About 3 weeks ago I had a Letter from Schaw acquainting me of the death of his Mother, the good old Lady.[6]

To Johnston, Sunday 4 May 1766

MS. Yale (L 784).

ADDRESS: To Mr. John Johnston, to be left at Forrest's Coffeehouse, Edinburgh.

Auchinleck House, 4 May 1766

MY DEAR SIR: I rejoice to find that you are well, and that your long delay of writing to me, has been occasioned by nothing worse than your usual indolence, for which your letters when they at length arrive, never fail to attone. There is no wonder that I felt myself a little dull on my first coming out to this Place where the recollection of the severe loss we have had of my Dear Mother[1] and a way of life very different from what I had long been accustomed to could not fail to sink my spirits a little. But I thank the God to whom I offered fervent adorations for his assistance I have enjoyed a continuation of health and spirits beyond what I expected. I have studied Scots Law with a good deal of care under as good a Professor as ever lived My Worthy Father. My Cousin Claudius has been several weeks with us which has been a great advantage to us both. He is a worthy sensible fellow, and I am perswaded will make a figure. He and I ought to be great Lawyers, Who have had a Lord of Session for our Professor. Johnston let me assure you that I have had more real satisfaction these two months past, than I had for years before. I have been doing my duty. I have been giving sensible comfort to a most affectionate Father, and been preparing myself to be of use in the World. I would fain hope that my idle days are now over, and that the rest of my life shall be employed as it ought to be.

You my friend who have been the confidant of all my errors

[6] Margaret (Anderson) Graham, the widow of William Graham of Shaw, and mother of George Graham, younger, of Shaw; she died 30 Mar. 1766 (*Scots Mag.*, 1766, xxviii. 223).

[1] Lady Auchinleck had died, after a three-weeks' illness, on 11 Jan. The news reached JB while he was at Paris (Journ. 27 Jan. 1766; From Lord Auchinleck, 11 Jan.).

must assist me to make up for them. You can hardly beleive what happiness I have enjoyed in walking in the venerable shades of Auchinleck after so long an absence and such variety of adventures. My Father talks to me whole evenings of my Ancestors which inspires me with worthy resolutions. One circumstance alone disturbs my peace of mind. It is a very strange one, but in character for me.[2] You shall have it all when we meet. And now My Dear Johnston let me enjoy the happy prospect before us. I leave this on the 7 and shall be at Moffat on Thursday. Pray set out so as to be there much about the same time. You will find me at Littles. We will consult together as to every thing, and We shall pass a few weeks most agreably at Moffat which I know so well and have had so many a meditative walk at.

In short We may promise ourselves much happiness. I am sorry to hear of worthy Lady Shaw's death. You and I must go down and have one cordial day with the family. Adieu Dear Sir

JAMES BOSWELL

From Johnston, Saturday 10 May 1766

MS. Yale (C 1625). Recd. 13 May. "Mr. Johnston" (Reg. Let.).
ADDRESS: To James Boswell Esqr. Younger of Auchinleck, at Moffat.

Edinburgh 10th. May 1766

MY DEAR SIR: Late on Wednesdays night, I had the pleasure of receiving Yours, informing me of your Intending to be at Moffat on Thursday last. I wish I had been there to have received you, but things have occurred to detain me that I did not forsee. The weather was So Stormy here last week, That I would fain hope you

[2] Almost certainly an allusion to his passing infatuation for the gardener's daughter. "The Gardener's Daughter who was named for my Mother, and has for sometime been in the family as Chambermaid, is so very pretty that I am entirely captivated by her. Besides my principle of never debauching an innocent girl, my regard for her Father a worthy man of uncommon abilitys restrains me from forming the least licentious thought against her. And therefore in plain words I am mad enough to indulge imaginations of marrying her. Only think of the Proud Boswell with all that you know of him, the fervent adorer of a Country Girl of Three and twenty. I rave about her. I was never so much in love as I am now" (To W. J. Temple, 28 Apr. 1766). Euphemia Bruce (1743–1827), eldest daughter of James Bruce, gardener and later overseer of Auchinleck, on 28 Sept. 1769 married Thomas Edmonson, JB's former servant (information, 1 Oct. 1957, from Mrs. Laura Douglas Pfitzner, Upway, Victoria, Australia, a descendant of James Bruce; Lt. John Boswell's journal, 1768–69: MS. Yale C 404:3).

did not Set out at the time you mentioned. It would be very uncomfortable to travell through a Wild Country in Such a Storm,
and might hurt your health. I am now determined to leave this on
Tuesday Morning, and if my Horse can make out the Journey will
be with you that night, if not, I will Dine at Littles on Wednesday
where I hope to meet you and I am yours most affectionately

JOHN JOHNSTON

From Johnston, Wednesday 21 May 1766

MS. Yale (C 1626). Recd. 24 May. "Mr. Johnston" (Reg. Let.).
ADDRESS: To James Boswell Esqr. Younger of Auchinleck, at Moffat.

Knottyholm[1] 21st May 1766

MY DEAR SIR: I Staid at Schaw till Monday Morning, having
Sent for Some people there with whom I had bussiness, thinking it
better to dispatch it at that time, than to delay it till I Should
return there in my way to Moffat. I was one night at Grange, and
found the reparation of the house nowise advanced,[2] So could not
have Staid there comfortably, though I had inclined it, and had
been quite at leisure to Stay there. I came here last night and hope
to finish my bussiness against Saturday, and I expect to have the
pleasure of being with you on Tuesday's night or Wednesday's
forenoon at farthest. You would See Mr. Graham[3] on Monday. I
could not perswade him to delay his visit till I returned, he Seemed
quite determined to go,—But whether to wait on you, or his
Mistress[4] is a mute point.

I have not Seen Mr. Ferguson.[5] You would have a visit from
him on Wednesday, in his way to Edinburgh where I understand
he is gone to Attend the General Assembly. I am just now in a
most agreeable retirement, the place is Situated upon the Side of
a fine River,[6] whose Banks are Covered with Aged Oaks, mixed

[1] The small farm, on the east side of
the Esk, south of Langholm in Dumfriesshire, just north of Canonbie, occupied
by the widow and daughter of JJ's cousin
Francis Scott of Johnston (Grange MSS.).
JJ was Mrs. Scott's man of business.

[2] In Nov. 1763 JJ's brother Thomas
had agreed to "build a House of Stone and
Lime with sufficient Timber consisting of
three Rooms and Closets, before the term
of Whitsunday 1765" (Grange MSS.,

Contract, 10 Nov. 1763). The new house
was probably built as an addition to the
older house of Grange. Thomas had failed
to carry out the terms of the contract.

[3] Probably Graham of Shaw (*ante*
26 Apr. 1763, n. 5).

[4] That is, his wife.

[5] *Ante* 26 Sept. 1759, n. 2.

[6] Knottyholm stands on a fine stretch
of the Esk above Jock's Pool.

with a variety of forrest Trees and Shrubs. I am convinced it would please you much. Were it not at too-great a distance, I Should think it well worth your while to pay it a visit; I wish you much happiness, and always am My Dear Sir Yours most Sincerely

JOHN JOHNSTON

From Andrew Erskine to Johnston, Monday 2 June 1766

MS. Yale (C 1199).
ADDRESS: To John Johnston of Grange Esq., at Moffat.
POSTMARK: JU 2.

Edinburgh June 2d. 1766

DEAR JOHNSTON, Instead of that warm love of your country, that blaze of Patriotism, that tender sensibility and strong affection for Mary King's close[1] instead of these William Wallace and Fletcher of Saltoun-like[2] qualities that I used so much to admire you for how am I astonished to get a letter from you[3] full of pert wit, and coxcomical vivacity. In reality I thought I had been address'd by a young Ensign or a French Abbé or an Edinburgh Advocate. What in the name of nonsense had I to do with Cable-ropes Bears, bathing Tubs, Lasses, wames,[4] Corpulency, Spurs and young Ladies. Why you certainly are not that thickleg'd, broad-shoulder'd Johnston of Grange that I once knew. When next we meet I suppose you'll be for one turn in Comely Garden[5]

[1] Mary King's Close, a narrow vent running north from the High Street, was a place of superstitious awe, for it was full of empty, half-ruinous houses, haunted by the ghosts of those who had died there in the plague of 1645 (*Old and New Edinburgh*, i. 227–28). Alarming stories were told of the apparitions seen there, and some of these were vouched for by the respectable authority of George Sinclair, Professor of Moral Philosophy in the University of Glasgow, who published his *Satan's Invisible World Discovered* in 1685. The upper (southern) portion of the close had been cleared in 1753 for the building of the Royal Exchange.

[2] Andrew Fletcher (1655–1716) of Saltoun was like Wallace in that he was a Scottish patriot, though he was of a different sort and of a different age. Of the Scottish statesmen who opposed the Union, he was perhaps the wisest, most influential, and most disinterested.

[3] Not recovered.   [4] Scots: bellies.

[5] Comely Gardens in the middle of the 18th century were open as an amusement park, a kind of Tivoli or Vauxhall for the lower classes in Edinburgh. An advertisement by the proprietor in *The Edinburgh Courant* (Sept. 1761) is as follows: "As the ball nights happened to be rainy these three weeks past he is to keep the gardens open every day for this season, that gentlemen and ladies may have the benefit of a walk there upon paying 2d. to the doorkeeper for keeping the walk in order, and may have tea, coffee, or fruit any night of the ball nights" (*Old and New Edinburgh*, iii. 128). The Gardens were located on the Abbey Hill, east and a little north of the ruins of the abbey

at seven o'Clock before the dew falls, and then you'll propose passing the evening together over Orgeat, or the noble syrup of
Cappalaire.[6] For shame! Let the days of Brose[7] and border incursions revive in your memory. Let me see you brandish the
rusty broad sword and bend the tough bow of your forefathers.
Have you mused in the Piazza of the Abbey? Have you walk'd by
moonlight through the Parliament Close? Have you perused
Joannis Major, and Fordun's *Scoti-Chronicon*[8] To sink at last into
effeminacy. Has that deluding Traveller Boswell instill'd the
French conciet or the Italian softness into you? I repeat it again
Johnston for shame! Let the days of Brose and border incursions
revive in your memory. I did not know till I receivd your letter
that my Company at Moffat would have given you any pleasure.
James Boswell of Auchinleck with a heart very well form'd for
friendship is notwithstanding frequently so whimsical that the
personal appearance of those he likes best on many occasions is
very apt to disgust him. I remember well when I follow'd him up
to London, instead of recieving me with that warmth with that
Cordiality which I expected he look'd upon me with a degree of
horror,[9] to make the matter clear to you Johnston, with that
aversion with which you in your present pretty and affected state
would survey a mouse or a spider. To tell the truth I would gladly
pass some days with you, but unfortunately about a week ago I
reciev'd most peremptory orders, without any delay to join my
Regiment at Gibraltar.[10] I have been enquiring for a Ship from

church of Holyrood, and on the right of
the road leading to Berwick.

[6] Orgeat and capillaire were popular
"soft drinks". Orgeat was barley-water
flavoured with orange-flower. Capillaire
was a syrup or infusion of maidenhair
fern; '*Connoisseur* No. 38, 'Whatever
orgeat or capillaire can inspire'" (OED).

[7] A dish consisting, in its simplest
form, of oatmeal mixed with boiling
water. In days of border-warfare, when
the Annandale Johnstons were active in
raids and forays, it was the staple diet of
Scottish troops, and because its ingredients were readily obtainable or easily
transported, as well as being quickly
prepared, it contributed to the mobility
which made them so hard to subdue, even
with larger and better-trained forces.

[8] The *Historia Majoris Britanniae tam
Angliae quam Scotiae* of Johannes Major
or John Mair (1469–1550), historian,
philosopher, and divine, published in
Paris in 1521 and republished in Edinburgh in 1740, was the first history of
Scotland to be written in a critical spirit.
John of Fordoun, or John Fordun (d.
c. 1384) made the compilation on which
Walter Bower or Bowmaker (d. 1449),
Abbot of Inchcolm, based the earlier
part of his *Scotichronicon*, a Latin history
of Scotland from mythical times to the
death of James I. Of this work, first
printed in the 18th century, an edition
had appeared in Edinburgh in 1759.

[9] *Ante* 6 Dec. 1762, n. 4.

[10] Erskine had been placed on half
pay in 1763 when the 71st Regt. of Foot

Lieth but can hear of none so I believe I shall be obliged to go by London, in which case if I can prevail upon my agreeable Companion to go up the west road I'll probably spend one evening with you at your scorbutick and sulphureous abode.[11] I got Boswell's letter some time ago[12] and shall certainly answer it before I leave Britain. Your droll Shopkeeper who was ask'd by the Minister whether he being in bed with a Lass would be guilty of the sin of omission or the sin of Commission should have answer'd that he certainly would be guilty of the Sin of Emission. I would tell Boswell what Pitt said of him at Bath[13] but why feed vanity? I would be the last person in the world to say to Colonel Skene[14] that he had white hands. I can say to you Johnston with safety that you have an honest good heart, because you don't pride yourself on these qualities and because you see nothing in them but what you think natural and the lot of many. The only way to get praise is to seem not to expect it. I don't know whether this is a secret to you but I'm sure its one to Boswell. Believe me Johnston yours very sincerely and affectionately

ANDW. ERSKINE

had been disbanded (*ante* 22 Mar. 1763, n. 6), but on 15 Nov. 1765 he was commissioned lieutenant in the 24th Foot. This regiment was stationed at Gibraltar from 1763 to 1769, when it was posted to Ireland, but it is clear that Erskine did not remain in Gibraltar for long. Early in 1767 he had returned to Scotland (James Bruce to JB, 23 Feb. 1767). Various letters from him to JJ, dated from Scotland during the years 1767–69, are extant (*post*). See, in particular, his letter of 9 Feb. 1769, in which he discusses his absence from his regiment. A year later, on 10 Feb. 1770, he is reported to have retired from it (*The South Wales Borderers, 24th Foot*, ed. C. T. Atkinson, 1937, p. 486).

[11] The sulphureous waters at Moffat were prescribed for scorbutic complaints. The agreeable companion is not identified.

[12] Sent 8 May 1766 (Reg. Let.).

[13] Immediately after his return from Corsica, JB had written to Pitt asking for an interview (To William Pitt, 15 Feb. 1766). Pitt had received him, and had listened sympathetically, though non-committally, to his appeal on behalf of Paoli's cause. Later JB renewed his appeals to Pitt (To Lord Chatham, 18 Sept. 1766; 3 Jan. 1767), but Pitt was unable to take any action on Paoli's behalf, though he expressed his admiration for him as a leader (From Lord Chatham, 4 Feb. 1767). Pitt's flattering remark about JB, made at Bath, which he was accustomed to visit for protracted periods in the hope of relieving his gout, does not appear to have been recorded.

[14] Probably Lt.-Col. Robert Skene (d. 1787) of Halyards, Fife, who during the next two decades held important posts in the army in "North Britain", being appointed Baggage-master-General and Inspector of Roads in 1767 and succeeding Sir James Adolphus Oughton as second in command in 1778 (*Scots Mag.*, xxix. 448, xl. 336). Promoted colonel in 1772, major-general 1777, and lt.-general 1782, he was also M.P. for Fife from 1780 until his death, and is several times mentioned in JB's journal.

From Johnston, Friday 25 July 1766

MS. Yale (C 1627). Datable by the reference to JB's illness and the fact that he is in Edinburgh, which he left on the rising of the Court in August, not to return till it sat down again in November. James Bruce, writing on 19 July 1766, expresses concern on hearing from JB that he has had a return of the ague; on 29 July Bruce has heard (probably from a letter from JB dated 24 July: Reg. Let.) that JB is "restored to some considerable state of health". JB passed his trials in Scots Law on 11 July (Faculty Records) and the public trials on his thesis on 26 July.

ADDRESS: To James Boswell Esqr.

[Edinburgh] friday 8 at night

DEAR SIR: I have been at home all this afternoon, and do not propose going abroad to night, So take this method of enquiring after your health, which you'll be So good as to inform me off by the Cadie, if you are so well and at leisure to do it; what would you think of going abroad a little to Morrow, if the day is good. I am convinced it would be of service to you, after ten days Confinement;[1]

Last night I read over again Six of the Letters[2] which afforded me much Comfort and Satisfaction, and I hope will be no less so thirty years hence if I live so long. Of the many Marks of your friendship and goodness, I must reckon this a particular one, and whilst I have the pleasure of reading them, I Shall always have a gratefull Sense of the favour.

I do not remember that I told you so, but I now write it with great Sincerity. I will wait on you to Morrow forenoon. Yours while

J. J.

To Johnston, Tuesday 27 January 1767

MS. Yale (L 785).
ADDRESS: To Mr. Johnston

[Edinburgh] Tuesday

I am to give a very curious pleading this morning.

[1] "Sometime ago I was favour'd with yours But was sorry to hear your Corsican trouble (the Ague) had pay'd you a visit" (From James Bruce, 19 July). Boswell suffered three or four returns of the ague later in this autumn, after going to the country (To Sir Alexander Dick, 23 Oct.), but the illness referred to here clearly occurred while he was in Edinburgh.

[2] Probably six of the unposted series written while JB was abroad. It happens that six and only six of the series were endorsed by JJ: letters 6 (*ante* 7 Nov. 1764), 7, 8, 9, 10, 11.

A woman whose Husband is absent in England has been de-
famed as a Whore by a Tidewaiter.[1]

I am for her in a Process of Defamation.[2] Pray come. I shall
speak a little after ten. I have sent for Erskine.

From Andrew Erskine to Johnston, no date, c. 1767

MS. Yale (C 1200). Datable only by the address and the reference to
"Ramsay's", both of which set wide limits. JJ was certainly in Roxburgh
Close by 4 Aug. 1767 (*post*, Andrew Erskine to JJ of that date) and may
have been there as early as the summer of 1763 (*ante*, From JJ, 20 June
1763). He remained there at least to June 1772 (*post*, To JJ, 3 June 1772).
Peter Ramsay operated the Red Lyon inn at the foot of St. Mary's Wynd
from at least 1760 to 1785 (J. H. Jamieson, "Some Inns of the Eighteenth
Century", *Book of the Old Edinburgh Club*, 1925, xiv. 134–36). The note is
somewhat arbitrarily placed here with other undated notes from the early
days of JB's legal career in Edinburgh.

ADDRESS: To Mr. Johnstone, at Mrs Stuarts, Roxburghs' Close.

[Edinburgh] Nine o'Clock

Your honour's presence at Ramsay's[1] is most earnestly intreated.
We are all privacy and sociality and cannot dispence with you.
We beg your attendance.

[1] A port official sent on board incom-
ing vessels to inspect their cargoes.

[2] James Storrie, formerly tide-waiter
in Saltcoats but now in Irvine, had been
charged with slander before the commissary court of Glasgow by Jean Robertson,
wife of a Saltcoats sailor named Robert
Boyd. Storrie was alleged, among other
offences, to have called her a friend of
smugglers, an adulterous whore, an
adulterous bitch who had given him the
clap. On 28 Aug. 1766 he had been
found guilty, fined, and ordered to
apologize in open court. Two months
later letters of suspension were issued at
Storrie's request, postponing the sentence pending its review in the Court of
Session. The cause came up on Tuesday,
27 Jan. 1767, JB appearing for his client,
but at Storrie's request it was adjourned
for a week. On Tuesday, 3 Feb., possibly
the date of this note, JB again appeared
and presumably gave his pleading, but
it was not until 12 June that the cause

was finally settled in his client's favour.
One of the four documents concerned
with the process is "Answers for Jean
Robertson to the Representation of
James Storrie", 14 pp. signed by JB
(Warrants for Acts and Decreets, Dal.
7 Feb. 1767). In his Consultation Book
under date of 27 Jan. JB lists this cause,
naming Matthew Dickie as agent, W.
Wallace as opponent, and Lord Kennet
as the Lord Ordinary. His fee was a
guinea.

[1] Peter Ramsay's inn was for a long
period not only a terminal point for
coaches arriving in Edinburgh, but a
centre for convivial gatherings. It was
at Ramsay's that General Paoli, visiting
Scotland at the instigation of JB, alighted
in 1771 (*Scots Mag.*, xxxiii. 481; Robert
Chambers, *Traditions of Edinburgh*, 1912,
pp. 171–73. Cf. also source reference in
head-note above).

To Johnston, no date, c. 1767

MS. Yale (L 786). The seal in black wax indicates a date in 1766 or early in 1767. Lady Auchinleck had died 11 Jan. 1766. JB's entry in the Notes, 20 Feb. 1767, "Supt Lady Betty's Grange at last introduced there" shows that he had previously—and probably recently—made attempts to bring JJ and Lady Betty together. As the "season" of the Assembly opened only during the latter half of November, this note can be dated within narrow limits.

ADDRESS: To Mr. Johnston.

[Edinburgh] Monday

I am this evening to dance at the Assembly[1] with Lady Betty. The Captain[2] is also to be there. Pray come if you would oblige me much. Pray do—Dont be indolent. Yours

J. B.

To Johnston, no date, c. 1767

MS. Yale (L 787). This letter bears no seal and is arbitrarily placed here as probably of this period.

ADDRESS: To John Johnston Esq: of Grange.

[Edinburgh] Thursday

Mr. Boswell and Lady Betty present their compliments to Mr. Johnston, and desire the honour of his company this evening to supper.

To Johnston, no date, c. 1767

MS. Yale (L 788). No evidence for dating, except red wax seal.

ADDRESS: To John Johnston Esquire of Grange.

[Edinburgh] Saturday

It is intreated by those who have a sincere regard for you that your honourable honour would not engage yourself to dinner this

[1] The Assembly Room in Bell's Wynd was that which Goldsmith described in his student days as being the centre of a social life so staid as to be almost dismal (Oliver Goldsmith to Robert Bryanton, 26 Sept. 1753, in *Letters of Goldsmith*, ed. K. C. Balderston, 1928, pp. 10–11). It was here that Miss Nicky Murray (Helen Nicolas Murray, 1707–77, sister of Lord Mansfield) acted for many years as hostess and upholder of the proprieties. Opened in 1736, the hall in Bell's Wynd remained in use, with minor extensions of its amenities in 1765, for almost fifty years, before being abandoned for new premises in George Street, in the New Town (James H. Jamieson, "Social Assemblies of the Eighteenth Century", *Book of the Old Edinburgh Club*, 1933, xix. 31–91).

[2] Andrew Erskine.

day as a Message is just going down to Lady Betty to anounce your approach. So come to the Parliament House like a Man who thinks of the days of Brose and Border Incursions.[1]

To Johnston, no date, c. 1767

MS. Yale (L 793). No evidence for dating, except red wafer seal.
ADDRESS: To Mr. Johnston of Grange.

[Edinburgh]

DEAR GRANGE: Pray be at our aunts[1] at eight o clock, or soon after it. Yours

J. B.

From Johnston, c. 1767

Missing. A note, presumably on a matter of legal business, to which in his reply JB says he has attended.

To Johnston, no date, c. 1767

MS. Yale (L 789). No evidence for dating, except fragment of red seal.
ADDRESS: To Mr. Johnston
ENDORSEMENT: And half the thought Content may gain
　　　　　　　Which Spleen employs to purchase pain[1]

[Edinburgh] Saturday

DEAR SIR: I was abroad last night when your note came. It was

[1] Apparently a favourite phrase—possibly a favourite toast—of JJ's (see *ante* 2 June 1766).

[1] Lady Betty Macfarlane's. The style of aunt had its origin in a prank of Erskine's obscurely recorded in JB's notes of early 1762: "Erskine came to Town—introduced to Aunts—in love with Lady Jenny—had Ersk at Break twice—. . . supt Aunts" (Notes, undated summary between 2 Jan. and 15 Feb. 1762). The passage cannot mean that JB was then meeting Erskine's sisters for the first time, for his letters to Erskine show that he had known all three of them familiarly from some time before Aug. 1761. Perhaps Erskine invited him to meet certain aunts who turned out to be the sisters he already knew, and he and JJ kept up the joke by adopting them as aunts of their own. The joke would have had a special aptness in Lady Betty's case. Because of her marriage to the elderly Walter Macfarlane, she might well have been facetiously assigned to an older generation and accorded aunt-like dignities.

It is possible that the meeting here referred to is the one thus described: "You supt Lady Betty's with Grange, Dr. Gregory, Arbuthnot and his Ladies. Pleasant, but you was a little drowsy" (Journ. 28 Feb. 1767).

[1] The couplet is so conventionally imitative of the style and sentiment of Matthew Green, author of *The Spleen* (1737), that if JJ did not compose it himself, he may have found it among the verses of any one of many contributors to the magazines and verse-collections of the age.

223

left upon my table as I supped out. I did not observe it till pretty far on in the forenoon. You will observe I have paid due attention to it. Sign the joint Epistle[2] and send it to the Post. Ever your friend

J. B.

From Johnston, Friday 24 April 1767

MS. Yale (C 1628).

ADDRESS: To James Boswell Esqr., Younger of Auchinleck, By Ayr.

POSTMARK: AP 27.

Edinburgh 24th. April 1767

MY DEAR SIR: I intended to have wrote to you every Post for these three weeks past,[1] but found myself unable to do it on account of an illness I had during that time, and which Still Continues. It has put me So much out of humour, that I am peevish and not in friendship with myself. A most unhappy Situation! My Good friend, I may in Confidence tell you, That it is owing to my own folly, in Indulging an irregular passion with a wretch full of disease. At first, when I found myself affected, my mind was So totally unhinged, that for some days I was quite miserable, untill Reflection and Cool Philosophy brought me back to reason more Justly, and to think of attending to my Recovery, which I am now doing with great attention, in Complying most Strictly with every prescription. The disease is of a worse kind than yours,[2] and more virulent, So must lay my account with Staying in Town all the vaccation, tho' I have bussiness in the Country that Cannot well be delaid, which will oblige me to employ another, a Circumstance that vexes me a little, besides I am much at a loss how to account for my Staying in Town, without forging some palpable falsehood. Were I to go to the Country at present, the want of assistance, Cold houses, and living improperly, might ruin my Constitution, which a man certainly ought to attend to, if he wishes to live anywise

---

[2] Possibly a communication in some legal case in which JB and JJ were associated as advocate and agent (*post* 28 May 1767).

---

[1] During these weeks JB was at Auchinleck, writing his *Account of Corsica*,

studying the Douglas case, composing *Dorando*, and carrying out, as usual, a varied programme of letter-writing, legal business, and social engagements.

[2] JB had also been under medical care since early March (To W. J. Temple, 8 Mar., 30 Mar.; Notes, 13, 17, 28 Mar., 2, 8, 13 Apr.).

Comfortably in this world; Let me ask you Seriously what is your sentiments upon reading this, do you laugh at me, or Sympathize with me. Suppose the former is the case, I can really forgive you, as I deserve no quarter from my friends. I hope you are now well. I have often wished to hear from you on that head, but you have not been so good as to inform me. Perhaps you may blame me for not inquiring after your wellfare before this time, which I had all the inclination to do, if I had not been prevented by this unlucky Illness: Your leaving the Town so suddenly without Seeing you, or hearing from you, hurt me a little. I had no doubt of your being hurried, and would have waited on you that morning, but as the day was bad, I had not the least notion of your going away untill I called about an hour after you Set off.[3]

I See David frequently, he is a prudent Boy, and has Good Sense and Discretion far beyond his Years.[4]—A fortnight ago, our friend Erskine went with his Brother Lord Kelly to visit Houston Stuart.[5] They are not yet returned. I long much to See Erskine, his honest heart will suggest some Consolation during my Confinement when all my other friends are absent. Amongst the ill Consequences that attend my present situation, I will be deprived of the pleasure of waiting on Lord Auchinleck and you at Dumfries,[6] which I intended. But I must Learn patience and rest Satisfied, a very usefull Lesson in Life.—What progress have you made in the *History of Corsica*? If I may believe the Letter in last Mondays *Chronicle* genuine, you are far advanced with it. The late acquisition of the Island of Capreo[7] will furnish you with an

---

[3] JB had set out with his father on 19 Mar. after having been detained for a day by bad weather.

[4] David Boswell was now nearing the end of his apprenticeship to John Coutts and Co. (*ante* 22 Mar. 1763, n. 11).

[5] Houston Stewart (d. 1785) was the second son of Sir Michael Stewart of Blackhall and elder brother of Archibald Stewart who had been a helpful friend to JB in Rotterdam (*ante* 23 Sept. 1763, nn. 1 and 11). In 1752, when he succeeded to the entailed estate of Carnock in Stirlingshire, he assumed the additional surname of Nicolson. He was so casual and unruly as a young man that JB used him as a cautionary example: "Be firm

and shun falling back to Houst Stewart" (Mem. 16 May 1764); and finding in himself "something of Houston Stewart", he solemnly warned himself, "Let me take care" (Journ. 8 Sept. 1764). Quite recently he had written: "Captain Erskine and Houston Stewart drank tea with you. Houston was dissipated as ever. You felt calm superiority; but not to shock him you assumed dissipation a little" (Journ. 15 Mar. 1767).

[6] Lord Auchinleck was to hold a court at Dumfries, during the circuit on which JB was to accompany him.

[7] JJ does not mean the number of *The London Chronicle* for Monday 20 Apr. (the paper appeared on Tuesdays, Thursdays, and Saturdays) but the

Anecdote[8] of that Brave warlike people. I had almost forgot to wish you Joy of your purchase.[9] Davie gave me a particular account of it. I think it a good bargain, neither is the Title amiss.[10] In Spite of my distress I will remember it. If the ground is Capable of Improvement, you ought to lay a plan of Carrying it into Execution. You have a Good Master to assist you, and it will beget in you a liking for the Country. To be Employed in that way, is the Most agreeable Relaxation from business, and alwise turns out to great advantage when Conducted with Judgment and discretion. You'll Laugh to hear me Speak in this way, when you know that I have done little or nothing Myself. But My Case is widely differrent from yours, and that of most people. I have it not in my power to Show my taste that way, unless I was to Stretch my Credit, which might be a little hazardous. Remember the young trees that you promised to give me when at Moffat. Settle with James Bruce as to the kinds and Size, which he can most easily afford. It will please me much to have a few Trees on my Domains That were reared at Auchinleck, and if it is practicable to Convey

number for 14–16 Apr., which he received on that day. It contains an "Extract of a Letter from Mr. Boswell" concerning the capture by the Corsicans of the island of Capraja, which ends as follows: "The unavoidable occupations of a laborious employment have retarded my account of Corsica. I am now however very busy with it, and you may depend on having it by the beginning of winter" (xxi. 368).

Although JJ gives no hint of it in this letter, JB's pretentiousness in thus venturing to refer in public print to the weight of his legal labours at the end of what was only his first full session of the courts had aroused disapproval in Edinburgh even among his friends. Earnest young David Boswell was particularly upset and took his brother to task in letters dated 28 Apr. and 19 May 1767. Two passages in the latter help to reveal JJ's actual opinion: "Your Friends the Laird of Grange and Captn. Andrew Erskine both agree with me"; "Grange told me, he heard you very much taken to pieces about this one day in a Coffee house". Though JJ sometimes ventured to reprove JB face to face (e.g. Journ.

13, 14 July 1769), he was extremely cautious about doing so by letter.

[8] MS. "Anecddote".

[9] With his father's consent and with his father as cautioner (security), JB in this year bought the small estate of Dalblair adjoining Auchinleck, which, with a liability attached to it of a £25 annuity, had cost at auction £2,410 (Journ. 12, 16 Apr.). Further financial details of this purchase are given in Journ. 17 Nov. 1775, at the time when JB's inability to meet his obligations on the Dalblair estate without Lord Auchinleck's assistance led to violent quarrels between father and son.

[10] "We drove over the very heath where Macbeth met the Witches according to Tradition. Mr. J repeated solemnly again 'How far is't called to Forres?' etc., parodying it to me: 'All hail Dalblair' " (Journ. 26 Aug. 1773). When JB published this passage in 1785, he explained it thus: "I had purchased some land called *Dalblair*; and, as in Scotland it is customary to distinguish landed men by the name of their estates, I had thus two titles, *Dalblair* and *Young Auchinleck*" (*Tour*, 1st ed., 1785, p. 123).

them to Annandale next Season, I would wish to have them then.
I beg you may write to me before you leave Auchinleck. It will do
me much good, and revive me in my Solitude. I read a little, and
have Several things to write, that will both divert me, and in a
great measure defray my Extraordinary Expence, a Circumstance
very worthy of my attention. Perhaps I will write again before you
go to Dumfries, and from that place I will expect to hear from you.
My Good wishes attend My Lord Auchinleck and You and I am
Yours most affectionately while

JOHN JOHNSTON

To Johnston, Monday 18 May 1767

MS. Yale (L 790).

ADDRESS: To John Johnston Esquire of Grange in Annandale, to the care of
Mr. David Boswell, Edinburgh.

Dumfries, 18 May 1767

DEAR SIR: Allthough you have desired me to write to you "rather
from Ayr" I think it would be an odd story if I who have written
to the Laird of Grange from so many towns in Europe, should
omit to write to him from his honour's own County Town.

Indeed my writing from hence, will be more to keep up the
form, than to communicate to you many of my thoughts, since the
dissipation of a Circuit[1] has still such an effect upon me, that I can
hardly write at all. I sincerely sympathise with you in your misfortune. I by no means laugh at you. But I must give you the

---

[1] By "dissipation of a Circuit" JB does
not necessarily mean that he had been
indulging in heavy drinking (although
see *post* 21 Sept. 1768), but that his time
had been frittered away on the legal and
social pursuits incidental to a circuit
(Notes, 11–19 May 1767). There were
nine Scottish circuit towns, each the
centre of a country district, and the great
social events of the year in their hum-
drum existences were the visits each
spring and autumn of the King's justices,
their arrival heralded by their trumpeters.
The judges, in addition to their salaries,
received special circuit allowances from
the Exchequer in order to enable them
to entertain on an adequate scale. Not all
of them, by any means, expended the
whole of their allowances in this way,
but Ramsay of Ochtertyre comments
thus on the hospitality maintained by
Lord Auchinleck on circuit: "It was his
rule to spend every shilling of his allowance for the circuit—a thing less to have
been expected that in everything else he
was supposed to be fond of money and
abundantly economical. He had a plentiful
table; and as most of his guests liked a
bottle of good wine, he did not balk them,
taking care to avoid every appearance of
excess. He used to tell the company that
the circuit table was not his but the king's,
whose representative he was then; and
the oftener he saw them the more agreeable to him" (*Scotland and Scotsmen*
i. 165).

advice which I take to myself to be very carefull against drinking. It is a vice to which both of us are inclined but which You are in most danger from because you want my obstinacy and cannot refuse an honest fellow who asks you. Improve the present time of painfull reflection and form good resolutions for the time to come.

I think you may pass your time tollerably. I would have you study the Douglas Cause with great care. Pray send to Lady Betty a respectfull card and beg She would allow you to take a copy of my *Errata* in that cause.[2] Tell honest Erskine that I have received his and shall write him fully from Ayr as I shall you Grange. Tell my brother David that I shall answer his last very soon and that I have received the £25 for Madame Scott.[3] I ever am Dear Sir yours sincerely

JAMES BOSWELL

To Johnston, Thursday 28 May 1767

MS. Yale (L 791).

ADDRESS: To Mr. John Johnston of Grange, Writer in Edinburgh.

Auchinleck, 28 May 1767

DEAR GRANGE: You who are a Laird must well know that one is not allways able to entertain a friend as He deserves. He may come late, or even to tell the plain truth of the matter, there may be very little in the house. In such cases instead of a regular Dinner

[2] These notes, probably a list of detailed criticisms of the recently printed volumes containing the *Memorial* (written by Sir Adam Fergusson) and *Proofs* for the Hamilton side in the Douglas Cause, no doubt formed the basis for the pamphlet called *The Essence of the Douglas Cause*, written by JB later in the year and published by Wilkie on 5 Dec.

[3] Magdalen Scott, *née* le Mercier, presumably French by birth or recent descent, was the second wife of William Scott (d. 1735), Professor of Moral Philosophy in the University of Edinburgh. She lived with the Rev. Pierre Loumeau Dupont (1695–1786), minister of the French Church in Edinburgh, and appears to have occupied much the same position in his household that Anna Williams did

in Johnson's. In a letter to JB of 7 Apr. 1767 Dupont reports her in ill health, and she died on 29 Mar. 1770 (*Scots Mag.*, xxxii. 168). Dupont left all he possessed to Madame Scott's daughter, Magdalen Scott, who was living in his household at the time the present letter was written and took care of him after her mother's death (communication from John Hamilton, C.A., Edinburgh, 5 Sept. 1938). Boswell had drunk tea with Madame Scott and Dupont two days before he left Edinburgh (Notes, 17 Mar.), but nowhere explains the business which he was transacting for Madame Scott. David Boswell had written to him on 28 Apr., "I have got the Receit from Madame Scott, which shall be sent to you by Mr. Menzies."

we set him down a cold Goose and Mustard with a Bottle of strong ale after it. Apply this if you please.

Whatever may be the reason, I cannot now give your honour a regular letter. So take a Scots Song for the Goose, and for the strong ale take the assurance of a Cause from Ayrshire in which I have a Commission to employ you.[1] I hope you are by this time allmost well. ⟨I⟩ long for a cordial meeting with you, and I ⟨ever⟩ am Your affectionate friend

JAMES BOSWELL

The Bl⟨aeph⟩lum   [*hoax, deception*]
S⟨cots song⟩.

1.

Gif ye a dainty Mailing want   [*farm, or holding*]
And idle-seat prefer to working
Ablins ye'll get it by a Plea   [*perhaps*]
That far aff owr the seas is lurking.

2.

Gang ye your ways to Paris town
Blaw in the lug o' lown and Sorner   [*rascal and sponger*]
And I'se be Caition ye'se bring hame   [*security*]
An *enlevement* frae ilka corner.   [*abduction*]

3.

French proofs! howt man gae hawd
   your tongue;
For, to sic proofs nae Judge e'er lippens;   [*trusts*]
Gowpins o' gowd your cause has cost,   [*handfuls*]
And after aw it's no worth tippence.

4.

Tho' your Memorial's braw and lang
And tho' your Sequel like a Curple   [*crupper*]
Would keep it sicker steeve and tight,   [*sure, sound and trim*]
'Twill faw before the men in purple.

[1] JB's MS. Consultation Book in the National Library of Scotland shows that he and JJ were associated in five cases during the years 1766–72: Carruthers *v.* Queensberry (1767–69); Graham of Shaw (1770); Johnstons *v.* Stothart (1771); Grieves *v.* Borland (1771–72); and McDougals *v.* Stewart (1772). Since, however, the agent employs the advocate and not *vice versa*, the "cause from Ayrshire" is not likely to have been one of these. It was probably a litigation of some Ayrshire friend of JB's who needed the services of an agent practising in the Court of Session.

5.

Your *Procureurs* ⟨may b⟩y their art
Cast glamer in the e'en o' Dunces;
But Conscience Callands the Fifteen
Are owr auld-farind for the Munsies.

[i.e. callants: *lads*]
[*too experienced for the Frenchies*]

6.

Since ye a worthy Lady's name
Wi' muckle foul abuse hae pelted,
By Jinks I'd turn up aw your tails
And hae you aw fu' soundly belted.[2]

From Andrew Erskine to Johnston, Tuesday 4 August 1767

MS. Yale (C 1202).
ADDRESS: To John Johnstone of Grange Esq:, Roxburgh's Close, Edinburgh.
POSTMARK: Dumbarton.

New Tarbet[1] Augst. 4th. 1767

DEAR JOHNSTON, It will I believe be necessary before the close of

[2] These stanzas are a comment on the Douglas Cause, which was approaching final judgement by the Court of Session (*post* 4 Aug., n. 4). The first stanza suggests that the Duke of Hamilton and his associates, in claiming the Douglas estates, had fabricated their whole case and brought it before the parliament of Paris in 1762 to avoid the more searching inquiry to which a Scottish court of law would have subjected it; the second, that the witnesses in the Paris action were all either unreliable or suborned; the third, that decisions taken in France could not be expected to carry any weight in Scotland, and that the Duke of Hamilton's outlay on his litigation had been wasted money since his case was worthless; the fourth, that no rhetoric or legal artifice would deter the Court of Session from arriving at a just decision; the fifth, that the fifteen Scottish judges, with their old-fashioned common sense, would not be misled by the kind of facile pleading which could influence a French court; and the sixth, that the whole action had been so grave a defamation of the innocent name of Lady Jane Douglas that those who brought it ought to be punished. JB had composed some verses on the same theme a few days before while out riding: "Good ride to Ayr made *Douglas Cause* a Song" (Notes, 20 May). *The Douglas Cause* was printed and circulated as a broadside (*Lit. Car.*, p. 27). It was not his first attempt at a song on the theme: "Had composed song on Hamilton Cause. Lord Hales—very witty. But put it in the fire---You'll make yourself ennemys. He had frightend you, such is still your weakness. Shewed it to Sr. Adam [Fergusson] D. Hume etc. all lik'd it—no venom—No said D.H. 'Tis not in you. Sung it in Parliament House with Circle round you. Had the *vivida vis* of Wilkes. Resolved to follow your own Plan" (Notes, 14 Feb. 1767). He sang it again at Lord Coalston's (Notes, 5 Mar. 1767). *The Hamilton Cause* was printed in *Scots Mag.* (1767) xxix. 119.

[1] New Tarbet, on the shore of Loch Long, Dunbartonshire, and also close to

this Session—black with the fate of Douglas, to fulfill my promise of writing to you which though it was made in all imaginable Drunkenness I confess I remember. Never was man so sick never had man such a headach as I had in the Glasgow Fly the day after I parted with you. As you had foreseen I met with Temple,[2] with whom before breakfast I had little or no conversation. He as is the Custom of the English before they have eat sat profoundly silent wrapt in his great coat, but when he had recruited his stomach and his spirits we did very well, sat next one another and turn'd tolerably easy. I think he has both sense and spirit with a good deal of knowledge and thinks for himself. I press'd him as much as I decently could on so slight an acquaintance to go along with me to New Tarbet and see the wonders of Loch Lomond but I could not prevail, so we parted and I proceeded on my Journey and reach'd New Tarbet that night. I regretted much he did not go with me as nothing could be more beautiful than the banks of the Loch that evening which was remarkably still and calm. The water was asleep below me, the trees were nodding above me, the mountains were in deep repose, nothing seem'd awake but the streams that were dashing all around me down the rocks, and the wheels of the Post chaise that rattled wonderfully during the silence of the night season, and "Would," says I to myself in Soliloquy, "the Laird of Grange were here. How would he venerate the awful mountains of his native country, how would his soul expand as the deeds of Sir William Wallace came rushing on his mind, and how as he revolv'd the various misfortunes of the beautiful and unhappy Mary and the memoirs of her faithful

Loch Lomond, was the family seat of the Macfarlanes of that ilk. Walter Macfarlane, husband of Lady Betty Erskine, and brother-in-law of Andrew Erskine, had died two months before (5 June, *Scots Mag.*, xxix. 334). As he was childless, his estates passed to his younger brother William (Sir Robert Douglas, *The Baronage of Scotland*, 1798, p. 97), but Lady Betty may have had dower rights and would anyhow not have had to move out quickly. On 1 Oct. 1768 (*Scots Peer.* ii. 563) she married Lord Colville, but in 1770 was widowed again (*post* 31 May 1770).

[2] Temple had been on a visit to his relatives at Berwick-on-Tweed, and JB had invited him to come farther north to Edinburgh. When he came, JB, though unable to accompany him, had arranged for him to visit Auchinleck, with a special view to getting his opinion of Catherine Blair, an Ayrshire neighbour on whose hand JB had serious designs. If Temple approved of her, JB hoped also to have some assistance from him in the tricky task of winning her, for she had so far given him no great encouragement. As the letter shows, Temple, when setting out on his journey from Edinburgh to Auchinleck, was joined by Erskine, who accompanied him part of the way.

Ambassador Mellville, would the tears trickle from[3] his patriot eyes, down his cheeks, and how as these Ideas soften'd him and the dead silence and gloom of the night brought the superstition of his Ancestors full in his mind, would the witches of Macbeth strike horror through his soul. The Prophecies of Thomas the Rhimer would seem all accomplish'd. Scotland again would be chear'd with a race of monarchs of her own, it would be treason to talk of Queen Mary but as a saint and a martyr, again the hardy Borderers would rise, and the warlike Johnstons chase the affrighted English and despoil them of their fattest oxen, and their most full-fleeced sheep." Now Johnston knit your brows at Boswell for me who promised faithfully to write me the whole proceedings in the cause of Douglas but has entirely forgot it. I was really much affected with that decision which was so unexpected. I think it really iniquitous. I suppose Boswell is still raging about it. Let me know what people think, and if it's imagined he has any chance in the house of Peers.[4]—Now Johnston farewell. Cherish Mellville's *Memoirs*, continue to beck on[5] Arthur's seat and let me

[3] MS. "from from".

[4] Public opinion in Scotland had for some years been bitterly, if fairly evenly, divided as to the merits of the opposing claims in the Douglas Cause. The question at issue was whether Archibald Douglas (b. 1748) was the son of Sir John Stewart and Lady Jane Douglas, his wife, or a French child, fraudulently obtained in Paris to impose upon Lady Jane's brother, the Duke of Douglas. The Duke had died in 1761 and on this question hinged the ownership of his great estates, for Archibald, if a legitimate son of Lady Jane, was heir of entail and provision, while otherwise the property would go to some unquestioned relative of the Duke, the Duke of Hamilton, as heir-male, being the most prominent claimant.

After protracted legal proceedings in Scotland and France (the cause had begun in 1762), the judges of the Court of Session had delivered their individual judgements during the week from 7 to 14 July 1767. The result had been very close, for seven judges had declared for each side, so that it was only the casting vote of the Lord President which enabled the Court to record its decision that Archibald Douglas was *not* the son of Lady Jane and that his service as heir to the Duke of Douglas should accordingly be reduced (i.e. cancelled). As Erskine knew and indicates in this letter, JB was a fanatical supporter of the claims of Archibald Douglas and was deeply distressed by the adverse decision of the Court of Session. An appeal to the House of Lords against this decision was the next legal step, and JB exerted all his powers as pamphleteer and paragraph-writer in *The London Chronicle* to sway opinion in favour of Archibald Douglas. His efforts undoubtedly had considerable effect on public opinion (*post* 9 Oct. 1767), but as the decisions remained from first to last in the hands of professional judges, it may be doubted whether they had any influence on the actual outcome. On 27 Feb. 1769, after a lengthy hearing, the House of Lords gave a final decision on the matter by reversing that of the Court of Session (*post* 9 Feb. 1769; see also *The Douglas Cause*, ed. A. Francis Steuart, 1909).

[5] To bow towards, or salute with some other significant gesture. It was JJ, it

hear from your honour. Again I say knit your brows at Boswell.
Yours very affectionately

ANDW. ERSKINE

To Johnston, Friday 9 October 1767

MS. Yale (L 792).
ADDRESS: To John Johnstoun Esquire of Grange in Annandale, By Langholm.
POSTMARK: OC 10.

Edinburgh, 9 Octr. 1767

MY DEAR SIR: You will wonder to find me still here. But this
unhappy distemper has been very obstinate and as I have done so
well hitherto, I have determined to finish my course of medecines
in the most compleat [manner.] I am now, I may say, perfectly
recovered.[1] Tomorrow I go to Sir Alexander Dick's,[2] where I
shall stay till Monday: And on Tuesday morning, David and I
set out for Auchinleck in a postchaise, with trusty Thomas riding
by us. We are to stay a night at Bothwel Castle. I wrote to the
Dutchess of Douglas to let me have a warm, orthodox room, and
she with great good humour sent me word that the warmest bed
in the house was her own, to which I should be wellcome.[3] How

would seem, who established Arthur's
Seat in the minds of his friends as a
national symbol and instituted among
them the sort of ceremony that JB performed so punctiliously on the day of his
setting out for London (Journ. 15 Nov.
1762).

---

[1] "I must tell you that on Tuesday
last . . . I got myself quite intoxicated,
went to a Bawdy-house and past a whole
night in the arms of a Whore" (To W. J.
Temple, 26 June 1767). "I am an unhappy Man. The consequences of my de-
bauch are now fatal; for I have got a
disease from which I suffer severely. It
has been long of appearing and is a heavy
one" (To W. J. Temple, 29 July 1767).
"You must know that my present unhappy distemper joined with a cold,
brought on a most terrible fever, and I
was for several days in a very allarming
situation. I am not yet got up, though I
am in a fair way of recovery" (To W. J.
Temple, 11 Aug. 1767).

[2] Sir Alexander Dick (1703–85), born
Cuninghame, had been trained as a
physician, but after inheriting in 1746
a baronetcy and the elegant mansion of
Prestonfield, near Edinburgh, which went
with it to him as heir of entail, he re-
linquished active practice. In addition to
his scientific and intellectual tastes,
which he then indulged, he had great
talents for serenity and friendship. JB,
although so much his junior, was for
many years happy to enjoy his company
and hospitality, and was a frequent visitor
at weekends. He had written to Sir
Alexander during the preceding winter,
"I am sorry to lose a Saturday with you:
but I comfort myself by reflecting that
I am now a sort of established Man at
Prestonfield, and can come and go as if
I had a claim to the Place" (9 Dec. 1766).

[3] Margaret Douglas (d. 1774), Duchess
of Douglas, at this time at least in her
fifties, was "very free and outspoken,
and quite a character" (Scots Peer. ix. 13).
The warmth of her invitation to JB was

far this would be orthodox, Your honour and Mr. Joseph Fergusson may judge.

Having said so much of myself, let me now treat of you my friend. A letter which I had this morning from Mr. William Hay[4] has thrown me into great concern. He tells me you have *a new attack of the old complaint*. Does he mean that some latent poison has broken out? Or that you have again been infected. Either of the two suppositions is distressing. Pray take care of yourself, and let me know by the very first post how you are. We are unhappy Mortals no doubt. But in the present state of society a great part of our unhappiness is occasioned by our own vices and follies. You know I am an austere Philosopher in principle; and even my practice has often been so. Could either you or I act in consistency with our principles, we should not be in danger of suffering from a malady the most dreadful which Nature has ever produced and which has been well said is the cause of poisoning the very sources of the human species. As far as man can be depended on, I trust that I shall henceforth maintain such a conduct as is the best for this life and for that which is to come. I have been busy with the Douglas Cause and have made out the *Essence* of it,[5] which I hope will be of considerable service. The Scheme[6] which I communicated to you will make a great noise. Wishing to hear comfortable accounts of you I ever am Dear Sir your affectionate friend

JAMES BOSWELL

due to her approval of the ardour he had shown in the cause of her husband's nephew, Archibald Stewart, who took the name of Douglas when he was served heir to the family estates in 1761 (*ante* 4 Aug. 1767, n. 4).

[4] William Hay (d. 1796), son of a Dumfries physician, was a member of JJ's intimate circle of friends. A clerk apprenticed to James Hay of Cocklaw, W.S., he was himself admitted W.S. on 20 June 1769 (*Writers to the Signet*, p. 188). [5] *Ante* 18 May 1767, n. 2.

[6] Probably the scheme was to publish the *Letters of Lady Jane Douglas*, which appeared on 28 Nov. 1767 (*Lit. Car.*, pp. 45–50). This was perhaps the most effective of JB's efforts to influence public opinion in favour of the claim of Archibald Douglas to be the son of Lady Jane

Douglas and Sir John Stewart. From the many letters printed in the "service and proof" submitted to the Court of Session by the Douglas lawyers, he selected and edited those most calculated to convey an impression of the integrity and pathos of Lady Jane Stewart's character. These selections, with a little additional matter, he published in London, where they undoubtedly did much to establish in the English public mind, which up to now had known little about the case, an image of Lady Jane which might well have aided Archibald Douglas's claim if the appeal in the House of Lords had gone to a general vote. As matters turned out, both law lords (Mansfield and Camden) spoke strongly for Douglas, and the verdict of the Court of Session was reversed without a division.

The Seal of this Letter will shew you the perfection of Berry,[7] and my present to honest David, when He is going to a far country.

From Andrew Erskine to Johnston, Monday 28 December 1767

MS. Yale (C 1204).

ADDRESS: To John Johnston Esq: at Mrs. Stuart's Roxburgh's Close, Edinburgh

Kelly Decbr. 28th. 1767

DEAR JOHNSTON, A man is always so hurried in the Country that he has no time to be tedious with his friends which is a great loss to you. All I have to say is go to Balfour's Coffee house and ask George the Waiter if he has any letters for me; and tell him if any come to send them to me at Kelly by Anstruther. Buy at Donaldson's shop for my Sister Lady Betty a volume of Fables for a present to a child,[1] most gorgeously bound and gilt. Æsop's fables wont do. Boswell and you are expected with impatience on Wednesday. Bid[2] him bring his *Essence*. I acknowlege your kind care of me in my last mortal state of Inebriation—Yours etc.

ANDW. ERSKINE

[7] The seal on the ring intended by JB as a parting present for his brother David has left on the wax a clear imprint of a wreathed figure, in loose-flowing Grecian garments, carrying a draped vessel. It was the seal used by David in signing his oath of allegiance to the House of Auchinleck (MS. Yale M 22) 18 days after the date of this letter. He was preparing to leave for Valencia to enter into partnership in the trading firm of Honorius Dalliot & Co. The senior partner was a Frenchman, but the ubiquitous Robert Herries had a financial interest in the concern and his brother Charles was also a partner (To W. J. Temple, 24 Aug. 1768). David probably owed his partnership to the association between his Edinburgh principals and Robert Herries (*ante* 4 Aug. 1763, n. 2, 30 Dec. 1765, n. 1; *post* 25 Apr. 1768, n. 2). The ring is now in the possession of Dr. Robert F. Metzdorf, who purchased it from Mrs. Elizabeth Mary (Cumberlege) Hailey, great-great-granddaughter of JB, and the granddaughter of Mrs. Elizabeth Margaret Montgomerie Williams, T. D. Boswell's grand-niece and representative.

William Berrie, or Berry (1730–83), was an Edinburgh seal-cutter with a high reputation for the delicacy and precision of his engraving. A portrait of him, engraved from a portrait painted by William Delacour in 1765, is in *The Bee*, 1793 (G. H. Bushnell, *Scottish Engravers*, 1949, p. 5).

[1] Perhaps one of the three daughters of Lady Janet Anstruther, his own and Lady Betty's sister. The eldest, Janet, was now three years and seven months old (date of birth furnished by Mrs. Marguerite Anstruther, Balcaskie).

[2] MS. "Wednesday bid". The visit by JB and JJ to Kellie is not otherwise recorded. JB appears to have kept no journal or notes during the latter half of 1767.

To Johnston, Thursday 14 January 1768

MS. Yale (Lg 13).

ENDORSEMENT: Mr. James Boswell.

[*Verso*] Mr. Boswell's compliments to Mr. Johnston, and sends him all that is necessary for the Petition[1] of which they spoke together this night.

[*Recto*] 14th January 1768.[2] Unto The Right etc. The Petition of John Caruthers of Hardriggs.

Humbly Sheweth

That in the Process of division of the Commonty of Dornock a Petition was on the 17 of Decr. 1767 presented by me to your Lordships and Answers thereto have been given in for his Grace the Duke of Queensberry and Robert Irving of Woodhall.

That in these Answers there are some new facts which make it necessary for your Petitioner to give in Replies.

May it therefore please your Lordships to allow your Petitioner to give in Replies any time between [now] and Thursday next. According to Justice etc.

To Johnston, Monday 25 April 1768

MS. Yale (L 794).

ADDRESS: To Mr. John Johnston of Grange, to be left at Forrest's Coffee-house, Edinburgh.

POSTMARK: ⟨2⟩6 AP.

London, 25 April 1768

MY DEAR JOHNSTON: Your unkindly indolence never hurt me so much as it has done since we last parted. Did not you positively

[1] This petition rose out of the long litigation over the division of the commonty (common pasture) of Dornock in Dumfriesshire, which commenced in 1750 or 1751 and did not end till 1789. Carruthers, who had lodged a claim in 1765 and had lost his cause twice before the Lord Ordinary, was reclaiming to the entire bench. On 2 Feb. 1768 JB submitted his most extensive writing in the case, a twenty-six-page document of "Replies for John Carruthers of Hardrigs to the Answers for Charles Duke of Queensberry and Robert Irving of Wood- hall". The Court found for Carruthers, and on 20 Oct. 1769 he reached an agreed settlement with the other parties. Car- ruther's cause appears for the greater part to have been in the hands of David Armstrong; the documents on the other side during this phase of the proceedings appear to be all signed by Andrew Crosbie or David Dalrymple, younger (Scottish Record Office: Court of Session, Warrants of Acts and Decreets, Mack. Office, 17 Jan. 1789; Court of Session Papers, Sig. Lib. Coll. cvii. 5; cxxxv. 28).

[2] MS. "1767".

engage to look after my young acquaintance,[1] to make a proper trial, and to write to me a full and distinct account of what passed; and yet here have I been a month without hearing from you. Tell me not that you knew not how to address as long as Messieurs Herries & Co.[2] are known to you. Indeed my friend, you are much to blame. I am really vexed at this. I must however forgive you; for what can I do? I love you, and I fear you never will be better; so I must bear with you as you are.

To punish you, I will not give you a word pro or con concerning myself, save that I am negociating the *treaty of Utrecht*,[3] and may perhaps be in Holland before June.

I must also confess to you that I have lost my Five Guineas.[4] I am exceedingly unfortunate. Last year's evil was nothing to this. Direct for me at Mr. Russell's Half-moon-street Piccadilly London. I ever am Dear Sir Your affectionate friend

JAMES BOSWELL

From Johnston, c. May 1768

Missing. Referred to in letter of 10 June.

To Johnston, Friday 10 June 1768

MS. Yale (L 795).

Grantham, 10 June 1768

MY DEAR JOHNSTON: Your kind and judicious letter made me full amends for the silence of which I complained so much. I in my

[1] A young Edinburgh girl whom JB hoped to save from a life of prostitution. In order to test her and discover if she was driven to street-walking from need or from desire, he gave her as much money, before he left Scotland, as she said she would need to keep her till he came back, making it a condition that she remain continent. He then asked two of his friends to tempt her to break the agreement (Journ. 16 Mar. 1768).

[2] *Ante* 4 Aug. 1763, n. 2.

[3] JB's *Account of Corsica* had been published in February, and in the following month, seen off by JJ, he had set out for London to collect the compliments and congratulations of his friends there. He had revived the intention, formed while he was on the Continent and then abandoned, of marrying Isabella de Zuylen, "Zélide" (*ante* 11 May 1765, n. 12). But though he proposed to her in a conditional way, his "treaty of Utrecht" was not ratified by the lady, and he did not, after all, proceed to Holland in June; for after giving him some encouragement, she finally repelled his advances with an "acid epistle", which he sent to Temple as proof that she could not make a satisfactory wife for him (To W. J. Temple, 14 May 1768).

[4] This bet was of the same nature as the one mentioned in the letter dated 25 Jan. 1763.

turn am to blame for not having answered that letter long e'er now. I delayed to do it, till I should be well, and when that was the case I had such a multiplicity of objects distracting my attention, that I could not settle a moment to put pen to paper. I cannot however come out of England without saluting you and informing you that I have been perfectly cured of the severe distemper which distressed me so much. But whether I may not have received some fresh wounds, time must try.

I am sorry to find that there is not a spark of virtue in Mary.[1] This instance will be some cure to me of my disposition to be made a dupe.

I have received a long letter from my brother David who makes cordial mention of you. You shall read it, as also my journal during this jaunt.[2] I shall be in Edinburgh on Monday night. My best compliments to our friends at Shaw, Mr. Fergusson etc. I ever remain my worthy Sir your affectionate friend

JAMES BOSWELL

From Andrew Erskine to Johnston, Monday 4 July 1768

MS. Yale (C 1205).

ADDRESS: To Mr: Johnston, Roxburgh's Close.

July 4th. 1768

DEAR JOHNSTON, I'm just this moment going to Fife, and must beg you will transact a little business for me which I can't do myself the Gentleman being out of Town. It is with Mr. Samuel Michelson Writer and Flute player. I was informd by Mr. James Steuart[1]

---

[1] *Ante* 25 Apr., n. 1.

[2] JJ had the good fortune to read more of this journal with its variegated blend of "philosophy and raking" than we can, for the latter portion (from 30 Mar. to some date in Apr.) has suffered heavily from family censorship. Only disjointed notes exist for the period 21 Apr. to 22 May. The letter from David has not been recovered. He had left Scotland early in November 1767 and had travelled by way of London, Paris, and Barcelona to Valencia, which he had reached by 19 Jan. 1768. Two extant letters written to JB shortly after his arrival in Spain show him in a despondent mood (From David

Boswell, 30 Oct., 16 Nov., 3, 13 Dec. 1767, 1, 19 Jan. 1768). David soon found that his first name, like all other typically Jewish ones, was very unpopular in Spain, and harmful to his business. Lord Marischal, who well knew Spanish conditions, eloquently explains the situation in a letter of 12 Mar. 1771 to JB. David then adopted an extra forename, and was known as Thomas David for the rest of his life.

[1] James Steuart (d. 1779), son of Charles Steuart of Ballechin, Perthshire, and Samuel Mitchelson (d. 1788), son of John Mitchelson of Middleton, Mid-

Writer to the Signet that Mr. Michelson had mention'd to him that he had a Company of Foot to dispose. Will you ask Mr. Michelson about this. Enquire what Regt. it is in and what is the lowest price,[2] write me at Kelly all the particulars fully, direct to me there by Anstruther. I'm sorry I have not seen you again. Remember me kindly to Boswell. Yours etc.

ANDW. ERSKINE

To Johnston, Tuesday 2 August 1768

MS. Yale (L 796).

ADDRESS: To Mr. Johnston.

ENDORSEMENT: 2d. August 1768.

[Edinburgh] Tuesday night

DEAR SIR: I enclose you the subject on which I wanted to talk with you.[1] I own that although I would willingly advance for the Captain in any real useful affair, I am unwilling to *throw away* so

---

lothian, were both Writers to the Signet (*Writers to the Signet*, pp. 329, 264). Samuel Mitchelson was for many years before his death a Director of the Musical Society. in Edinburgh, and Henry Mackenzie described him as an "uncommonly good performer on the German Flute" (*The Anecdotes and Egotisms of Henry Mackenzie 1745–1831*, ed. H. W. Thompson, 1927, p. 77). He is mentioned by name by Smollett in *Humphry Clinker*, the famous "Haggis scene" taking place in his house in Carrubber's Close. Here, too, near the end of his life, he entertained Robert Burns, whose friend Robert Ainslie was one of his apprentices (*Old and New Edinburgh* i. 239).

² A commission in the army was, at this time, a kind of investment. The capital sunk in its purchase could be recovered by its sale, or if the regiment was disbanded, could be considered to yield interest in the form of half-pay. The colonel was the proprietor of his regiment, the inferior officers joint-proprietors, since each had "bought" his company or commission. A board of general officers had sat in Jan. and Feb. 1766 to

fix the standard prices of commissions and had duly issued a report on the subject. According to this the purchase price in a "Marching Regiment of Foot" was £1,500 for a captaincy or £800 for a captain-lieutenancy, as against £550 for a lieutenancy. (A captain-lieutenant was a company commander with a captain's rank but a lieutenant's pay. OED) In practice, as this letter implies, prices varied according to the standing of the regiment, the circumstances of the sale, and other factors, but it is clear that Erskine would have had to find a considerable sum over and above the value of his lieutenancy in the 24th Foot in order to purchase a company. Even if the funds were available, the purchase required the approval of the colonel of the regiment concerned, which was often not easily obtained (*post* 9 Feb. 1769; J. W. Fortescue, *The British Army, 1783–1802*, 1905, pp. 9 ff.; *Scots Mag.*, 1766, xxviii. 53, 251).

---

¹ The enclosure, which has not been preserved, was presumably Erskine's letter to JB requesting a loan.

much.[2] I think he may let his *honourable* Creditor wait till he is richer and let this debt hang over his head as a warning. Have your thoughts upon the matter, and I will come and breakfast with you tomorrow precisely at nine. Yours ever

J. B.

From Johnston, Thursday 18 August 1768

MS. Yale (C 1629).

ADDRESS: To James Boswell Esqr. Younger of Auchinleck, By Ayr.

POSTMARK: AU 19.

Edinburgh, 18th. August 1768

DEAR SIR: You Slipt away on Monday Morning very quietly without the knowlege of Some of your friends that wanted much to have Seen you for an hour or two. I called on you upon Saturday and was told that you was gone to Pinkie[1] and would not return till Monday, So did not inquire for you on Sunday, tho' it Seems you returned on the Saturday evening. Indeed I had many things to talk over with you, which must be delaid till we have the Comfort of Meeting again in the Old Capital. I am really anxious about poor Mrs. Scots farm.[2] Nothing can be done at present, as The Duke of Buccleugh leaves Dalkeith on Tuesday next, and it's impossible that a Letter from you Could reach Mr. Smyth[3] before that time, but as I think a Conversation with Mr. Smyth will have

---

[2] Andrew Erskine, a younger son of an impoverished house, with little if any income other than his army pay or half-pay, was often in debt, and appealed to JB for loans on several occasions. Erskine's gambling debts finally led to his suicide in 1793.

---

[1] *Ante* second letter of 14 Dec. 1762, n. 3.

[2] Isabella Woodhouse, widow of Francis Scott of Johnston (a descendant of the Buccleuch family), held her farm of Knottyholm, in the parish of Canonbie, Dumfriesshire, in feu from the Duke of Buccleuch. She did not lose it, as at this time she feared she might. It remained in her family, and in 1796 was in the hands of her granddaughter Mrs. Russell (Grange MSS.).

[3] At JJ's instance, JB wrote from Edinburgh to Adam Smith, then living at Kirkcaldy, asking for his help on behalf of Isabella Scott (To Adam Smith, 28 Aug. 1769). Adam Smith was a close friend of the Duke of Buccleuch, whose tutor he had been. He had resigned his Glasgow chair in 1764 on being invited by Charles Townshend, the Duke's stepfather, to become travelling governor to the young Duke, and together they had made the Grand Tour between Feb. 1764 and Nov. 1766 (*Scotland and Scotsmen* i. 463–65). As tutor to the Duke he was paid £300 a year, and the same amount was paid afterwards as a life-pension, so that he was able to give full attention to the writing of *The Wealth of Nations* (William Fraser, *The Scotts of Buccleuch*, 1878, i. 489–91).

a better effect than a letter, we must rest Satisfied till winter when
you will have an opportunity of meeting with that Gentleman. I
wanted likewise to have had a Consultation with you and Mr.
Armstrong anent the writing An Answer to the Duke of Queens-
berrys Petition,[4] which you know must be put into the boxes[5]
upon the 24th. of September. Mr. Armstrong Says that before
writing the Answer he would incline to go to the Commonty and
view the tract of ground which the Cattle of our Clients tenents
are in use to pasture over, and after viewing it attentively he can
easily guess the extent to an Acre or two, or he may Cause a Man
to make a Sort of Measurement privately, and in the Answer
Mention the Extent with a degree of Certainty, without assigning
any other Cause of knowlege than the proof already Adduced;
He goes to the Country on Saturday or Monday and is to write the
Answer there and Send it into me in order to be printed. I hope
you'll approve of this plan. The Answers when boxed I Suppose
will be Sent to my Lord Auchinleck, pray read them Carefully
and give me your Opinion. I have wrote a long letter to our
friend David, let me know his Address and how to forward it. I
hope you have had an agreeable Journey. I wish you could acquire
a taste for the Beauties of the Country. Write me Soon, My Good
wishes attend Lord Auchinleck and the Lieutenent,[6] I remain My
Dear Sir Yours Most Sincerely

JOHN JOHNSTON

To Johnston, Thursday 25 August 1768

MS. Yale (L 797).

ADDRESS: To Mr. John Johnston of Grange, Writer in Edinburgh, to be left
at Forrest's Coffeehouse.

Auchinleck, 25 August 1768

MY DEAR SIR: I received your friendly letter, and am heartily
sorry that we did not meet before I left Edinburgh. However that
cannot now be helped, and I hope we shall meet at Dumfries. I
approve entirely of your resolution as to the Answers for our
Client Hardriggs.[1] I enclose you a letter for Erskine which you
may take a copy of and seal and send if you approve of it. I give

---

[4] *Ante* 14 Jan. 1768.
[5] *Ante* 16 Apr. 1763, n. 1.
[6] John Boswell.

[1] *Ante* 14 Jan. 1768.

you my word Johnston, I am under some difficulties; and I cannot think our friend can take the letter amiss.[2] When I arrived at Lainshaw, I found the charming *Mary Anne* the beautiful irish Lady just sixteen.[3] I own Grange I never was perfectly in love till now. Wait till we meet. I have hours of conversation for you. I am quite in a state of enchantment.

David's Address is: To David Boswell Esq: chez Messieurs Honorius Dalliot et Co., Negociants á Valencia, Spain. You had better send your letter to some friend at London, or speak to one of the Clerks of the Post office at Edinburgh. It will cost you the price of a bottle of wine.[4]

I am ever Dear Johnston your affectionate and faithful friend

JAMES BOSWELL

From Johnston, September 1768

Missing. Sent from Grange to Dumfries. As appears from the letter below, JJ persuaded JB not to refuse Andrew Erskine the loan he had asked for.

To Johnston, Wednesday 21 September 1768

MS. Yale (L 798).

ADDRESS: To John Johnston Esq: of Grange in Annandale, By Edinburgh and Langholm.

Auchinleck, 21 Septr. 1768

MY DEAR SIR: A friend such as you is a great treasure. Your letter which I received at Dumfries shews me that I may at all times depend upon your advice, and that I never should take any step of any consequence without first advising with you; for however a

---

[2] The letter, which has not been preserved, was apparently a refusal to grant the loan asked for by Erskine.

[3] While visiting his cousins, the Montgomeries of Lainshaw, JB had met an Irish cousin of theirs, Mary Ann Boyd, who had struck him at once, because of her looks, her sensibility, and her expectations, as an eligible wife.

[4] Something between a shilling and two shillings, depending on the quality and supply. In Scotland seven dozen bottles of port were bought for £4. 17s. 2½d. in 1775; in 1780, when there was a war-shortage, one dozen cost £1 (*James Beattie's Day-book, 1773–1798*, ed. R. S. Walker, 1948, pp. 62, 104). Letters to foreign countries were handled through the Foreign Office section of the Post Office in Lombard Street, London. "If a foreign letter came up from the country, it had to be prepaid to London, where it was the rule to prepay the letter to a given point on the Continent" (Howard Robinson, *Britain's Post Office*, 1953, pp. 35–36).

man may think himself right, a friend may see a thing in another point of view, and convince him that he is mistaken. I am entirely convinced by you in the affair under consideration. I am sensible that I was wrong, and I am resolved to feel all the uneasiness of being in immediate straitened circumstances rather than do any thing that can have the least appearance of being ungenteel or unfriendly.[1] You will therefore burn the letter which I enclosed to you, and let us trust to Providence.

I ought to have written to you sooner; but to tell you the truth we have had such a riotous circuit[2] both at Dumfries and at Ayr that I have not been able to write at all. Such are *the anecdotes of the Circuit*, which you bid me tell you. I give you my word, I must henceforth resolve to observe the strictest sobriety; for my inclination towards drinking is twice as strong as your honour's; and that is saying not a little.

The Irish Lady is Miss Mary Anne Boyd eldest daughter to Charles Boyd Esq. of Killaghy of the Kingdom of Ireland. She is one of the finest girls I ever saw. She is quite to your mind; for I know what pleases you; and she is sure of having £10,000 besides the prospect of the best share of £1000 a year, for Mr. Boyd has but two daughters, and She is the favourite. Whether this scheme is practicable I know not; but you know *Faint heart never won fair Lady*. At any rate, it affords me pleasing meditations in the mean time.

Do you know all is over between the Heiress and Sir Sawney?[3] I was at Adamtown some time ago, and walked with Catharine by the side of her wood, till it was pretty dark, and she told me the whole story, while I told her how I adored the fair Hibernian. Were it not that I am in love beyond the Salt Sea,[4] I have a notion

[1] It appears that JJ had pressed the claims of Erskine's long-standing friendship on JB in such terms that he decided after all to advance the money (*post* 9 Feb. 1769).

[2] *Ante* 18 May 1767, n. 1.

[3] JB had been occupied, during the previous year, in furthering his "safe and rational plan" to marry Catherine Blair of Adamton near Auchinleck, a relative of his own and heiress to a small fortune. But this had not been a smooth courtship: for one thing, Catherine Blair had never taken him seriously, and for another, there had been rivals to contend with—chief among them Sir Alexander Gilmour of Craigmillar ("Sir Sawney"), a wealthy young baronet and M.P., who was also an officer in the Guards; and William Fullarton of Rosemount ("the Nabob"), descended from the old Ayrshire family of Fullarton of that ilk, who had acquired a fortune while serving as a surgeon in India. Catherine Blair later married Sir William Maxwell of Monreith.

[4] Perhaps a line, or a refrain, from some forgotten song, or lost Jacobite ballad.

that my neighbour Miss Gordon of Stair[5] would be the woman. I have as good as told her so. I am truly an extraordinary man; and it will be hard if I do not make a good match after all.

I saw Mr. Armstrong at Dumfries. He told me what had passed between him and you concerning our client Hardriggs; and I approved entirely.

I hope Mr. Lochs marriage with my Cousin[6] will turn out well. I never saw her; but I have heard you speak of her; and if she is not very ill to please, I think she may live happily with him.

We expect great entertainment at Ayr, during the races, which begin on tuesday senight. I am to be there for a day or two, and am to sojourn at my friend the Nabobs.[7] His present residence is but a mile from Ayr. Pray let me hear from you again, before you go to Edinburgh; the sooner you write the better, as I shall be anxious to hear that my enclosed letter is destroyed. I ever am Dear Johnston your most affectionate and faithful friend

JAMES BOSWELL

To Johnston, Sunday 25 December 1768

MS. Yale (L 799). The limits of dating are set by David Boswell's departure from Scotland (Nov. 1767) and the opening of the New English Chapel, when the building which JB calls "Porter's meeting house" ceased to be

[5] JB records in his notes a dinner-party at Stair on 26 May 1767: "Miss Gordon and I [sat] at [the] sidetable [and were] very gay." Catharine Gordon was the only daughter of Thomas Gordon, younger of Earlston, who had died the previous year, leaving her heiress to the estates of Stair and Afton (P. H. M'Kerlie, *History of the Lands and their Owners in Galloway*, 1877, iii. 425–26). In 1770 she married Capt. (later Maj.-Gen.) Alexander Stewart, of the family of Stewart of Castle Stewart. Burns praised her "benevolence of temper and goodness of heart" (*Letters of Robert Burns*, ed. J. De L. Ferguson, 1931, i. 43).

[6] James Loch (d. 1793), a particular friend of JJ and an executor under his will, was admitted Writer to the Signet on 4 July 1769 and was later H.M. Remembrancer to the Court of Exchequer. He was the third son of William Loch of Hawkshaw, an Edinburgh solicitor (*Writers to the Signet*, p. 223). On 29

May 1768 he had married a not very distant cousin, Margaret, daughter of James Loch of Drylaw. As indicated in this letter, she was also a cousin of JB, her relationship to him being closer than that to her husband. Both her maternal grandparents had been of the noble family of Erskine, her grandmother, Margaret Erskine (1685–1730) having been an elder half-sister of JB's mother. Thus JB and she were first cousins of the half blood, once removed (A. L. Reade, *Johnsonian Gleanings* x. 186).

[7] "The Nabob", William Fullarton, had struck up a friendship with JB during their rivalry for the hand of Catherine Blair. Doubting the seriousness of her intentions towards them, they had agreed to go, one after the other, and put their standing with her to the test. She had discovered and resented this collusion, and their friendship for each other had grown warmer as they reached agreement that Miss Blair was a coquette.

used as a place of Anglican worship (9 Oct. 1774: Hugo Arnot, *The History of Edinburgh*, 1788, p. 285). In that period, Christmas fell on a Sunday only in 1768.

ADDRESS: To John Johnston Esq:

[Edinburgh] Sunday

DEAR SIR: I beg you may get yourself ready to go to Porter's meeting house with me, and dine at Thom's at one, in a comfortable and agreable manner, to keep Christmas, and drink the health of Temple and David. Much yours

J. B.

P.S. Let nothing prevent this. I will call on you soon.

From *Andrew Erskine* to *Johnston*, *Thursday 9 February 1769*

MS. Yale (C 1206).

ADDRESS: To Mr: John Johnston—Writer—at Forrest's Coffee house, Edinburgh.

POSTMARK: 9 FE.

London, Febry 9th 1769

DEAR JOHNSTON: You will not be pleased to hear that I have laboured unsuccessfully in my own affairs. Lord Granby has put a negative on my purchasing the vacant Company as there is a positive order that no such thing can be done without the Colonel of the Regiment's recommendation. Cornwallis has refused this in the most positive manner, and has even gone so far as to say there is not a Lieutenant in the whole Corps that he will give leave to purchase.[1] The only step I can now take is to have the matter laid before the King which would infallibly bring on a Court of Enquiry or a general Court Martial, and though I'm confident such a Court would acquit me of all blame for my absence from the Regiment,[2] yet after that, Cornwallis might still refuse his recom-

---

[1] John Manners, styled Marquis of Granby, was at this time commander-in-chief, though he was shortly to resign as a result of the repeated accusations of Junius that he had "degraded the office to that of a broker in commissions". The Hon. Edward Cornwallis (1713–76), uncle of that better-known military commander of this period, Charles, 2nd Earl Cornwallis, was, in addition to being Governor of Gibraltar, Colonel of Erskine's own regiment, the 24th Foot (*ante* 2 June 1766, n. 10).

[2] In absenting himself from his duties without explanation, Erskine had merely done what many others habitually did.

mendation, and I would just remain where I set out. I am now applying for leave till the Regiment comes home, which will be in a month or two hence as orders for that purpose are already issued. In the meantime I must endeavour to find a purchase somewhere else which I'm afraid I'll hardly make out, for there are numberless applications and more money is offered than I possess. In short I suspect I shall be obliged to go out on half pay for I'm determined never to join a Regiment where I have met with such exceeding bad usage. You may tell Boswell that I believe I shall now have no use for the money he was so kind as to propose lending me, and pray tell Fairholme[3] to pay in again to Philip Anstruther[4] the money that was lodged on my account, and acquaint Davie Stewart[5] that I shall have no occasion for Houstoun's money. So much for any Business. You'll now naturally expect something lively, or if your expectations don't soar so high you'll at least expect news, yet I'm apprehensive you'll be mistaken in both, for my present scituation is not so eligible as to bring on any remarkable flow of Spirits, and as for news you know as much at Edinburgh as we do here. The Douglas cause is as yet quite misterious. The friends of each party are sanguine, Douglas however engages the general affections and the Betts run in his favour but any opinion formed from that circumstance must be fallacious. The knowing ones are too often taken in to lay any stress on that account. Wedderburn[6] is reckoned to have done wonders I heard

"There were, of course, numbers of officers who knew nothing, and were content to know nothing, who shirked their duty continually, and were able to do so by the connivance, for purposes of political complaisance, of the political jobbers who reigned at the War Office. Most notably was this true of regiments quartered abroad in unpopular stations like the West Indies, Gibraltar, and Nova Scotia. No human power had ever yet succeeded in driving a large number of officers to do duty in these quarters. Some never joined their regiments; others contrived to get leave of absence; a few were always at home recruiting" (J. W. Fortescue, *The British Army, 1783–1802*, 1905, p. 32).

[3] Probably Thomas Fairholme (d. 1778), one of a Scottish banking family of this name, and the only one listed among the bankers in Williamson's *Edinburgh Directory*, 1773–74.

[4] Several members of the Anstruther family bore the Christian name Philip, but this was most likely Philip (b. 1737), fifth son of Sir Philip Anstruther of Balcaskie, and thus a younger brother of the husband of Erskine's sister, Lady Jennie.

[5] David Steuart (1744–1823) of Steuarthall, Writer to the Signet, was a second cousin of Houston Stewart (*ante* 24 Apr. 1767, n. 5).

[6] Alexander Wedderburn (1733–1805), an Edinburgh man, had practised first at the Scottish and then at the English bar. He was counsel, before the House of Lords, for the respondents in the Douglas Cause, and made a great impression by his speech, though the

him on Monday, 'twas his middle pleading for he spoke thrice. In my opinion it was as dull, and as unentertaining a narrative as ever I had the mortification of listening to. He tried to be ironical and to raise a laugh, but he failed egregiously for there was not a smile on the countenance of one of his auditors.[7] This pleased me, and made me smile though from a very different reason from what Mr. Counsellor Wedderburn in the Pride of his parts would have imagined. The Companion[8] you saw me depart with I found dull sleepy and agreeable. Dulness and sleep form the two chief and choice Ingredients for a Partner in a Post Chaise. We had little communication, as the learned Samuel Johnson would say, of sentiment and small interchange of Idea: by the faculty of speech, which distinguishes us from the animal world, we were little distinguished. I hope Dear Johnston your head is better. I have no hopes of bettering your heart. I'm anxious to know if the gloom which overspread the scotian lineaments of your Countenance at the fall of the Chapel of Holyroodhouse,[9] is beginning to be

final judgement went against his clients. A man of unbounded ambition, he was successively Solicitor-General, Attorney-General, Chief-Justice of the Court of Common Pleas, and Lord Chancellor. He was raised to the peerage as Baron Loughborough and later created Earl of Rosslyn (*Comp. Peer.* xi. 172). JB was excessively envious of his meteoric and spectacular career.

[7] As indicated in the last note, not everyone agreed with Erskine's estimate of the effect of Wedderburn's pleading. He had begun on 25 Jan., speaking for four hours, had continued for half an hour the next day, and on Monday, 6 Feb.—the day on which Erskine heard him—had spoken for another four hours. The following day he concluded his speech, to be greeted with "greater applause than was almost ever known", according to Horace Walpole (A. F. Steuart, *The Douglas Cause*, 1909, p. 21; Horace Walpole, *Memoirs of the Reign of King George III*, 1894, iii. 204).

[8] Not identified.

[9] The roof of the Abbey Church of Holyrood had become ruinous by the middle of the century, and had been restored with flagstones too heavy for the old arches, which collapsed under their weight on 2 Dec. 1768 (Sir Herbert Maxwell, *Official Guide [to] the Palace of Holyroodhouse*, 1936, p. 155; Francis Grose, *The Antiquities of Scotland*, 1797, i. 29). According to a note appended to JB's poem *An Evening-Walk in the Abbey-Church of Holyroodhouse* (*Scots Mag.*, 1758, xx. 420) it was JB's great-uncle, Major Thomas Cochrane, later Earl of Dundonald, who was instrumental in getting that disastrous roof put on. "Major Thomas Cochran, one of the Commissioners of Excise in Scotland, out of a laudable desire of preserving this piece of antiquity, which does honour to our country, made application to the Barons of Exchequer, and obtained their order to have it repaired at the public expence. The work is now going on." The abbey has remained roofless since 1768, a fact which later was a contributing cause to the permanent estrangement between JB and Archibald Douglas, whose claims he had done so much to further. Among those buried in the chapel was Douglas's mother, Lady Jane, and when in 1785 JB published his *Tour*, he rashly included some remarks, greatly resented by Douglas, on his challenged

dispell'd. I shall tomorrow breathe a sigh in your name over the chair in which our Scottish monarchs used to be crowned at Scone. I have got as a present for you a real underpetticoat of Mary Queen of Scots, as also the false Pego[10] with which David Rizio was wont to tickle certain susceptible parts of that un⟨fortun⟩ate ⟨Lad⟩y, his real Pego I'm convinced from his age must have been ⟨very⟩ unfit for the office. Remember me kindly to all our friends, particularly to the little mouse[11] who is so busy gnawing the net spread over the hapless Corsican Lion, tell him I shall not apply to him the famous line in Horace—

Parturiunt montes, nascetur ridiculus Mus.[12]

filiation and his neglect in allowing "the sacred spot where his mother lies interred, to be unroofed, and exposed to all the inclemencies of the weather" (*Tour*, 1st ed., 1785, p. 454).

[10] This word will be sought in vain in the OED, though it was of common occurrence in four-letter-word English verse from at least the 1660's to the 1780's. To the one example cited by Farmer and Henley (*The Second Volume of the Writings of the Author of "The London Spy"* [Edward Ward], 4th ed., 1709, p. 8) may be added four occurrences from three poems in *Poems on Several Occasions by the Right Honourable the Earl of R[ochester]*,1680 (pp. 35, 36, 76, 80, the first piece of uncertain authorship, the second by Sir George Etheredge, the third probably by the Earl of Dorset); twelve in the *Essay on Woman* and associated poems, 1763, by John Wilkes and Robert Potter (pp. 3, 14[bis], 16, 17, 18[bis], 25, 29bis, 33, 34 of John Camden Hotten's reprint, 1871); and one in Burns (*The Letters of Robert Burns*, ed. J. De L. Ferguson, 1931, ii. 283). The derivation from Greek πηγή (fountain) proposed by J. S. Farmer and W. E. Henley (*Slang and its Analogues*, 1890–1904) is surely fanciful. Professor Helge Kökeritz and Professor Louis T. Milic have independently suggested Italian *pigo*, now archaic, which Baretti glosses as "a lover, gallant, cicisbeo" and Battisti and Alessio (*Dizionario etimologico italiano*, 1950–57), citing it from the 16th century, as "damo, damerino, cicisbeo".

This etymology would indicate a pronunciation with "long e": pēgo.

[11] *British Essays in Favour of the Brave Corsicans: by Several Hands. Collected and Published by James Boswell, Esq.* (1769) had recently appeared. The frontispiece, engraved according to JB's instructions, shows Corsica, personified, imploring help from Britain, and also contains the figures of a lion and a mouse, thus explained in a note by JB: "In a corner is a Basso Relievo of the old fable of the Lion and the Mouse. The Lion had shewn kindness to the Mouse. Some time after, the Lion was entangled in a net, and could not help himself, when the Mouse came, and discovering his benefactor, gnawed the net, and let the Lion escape. The Fable shews, that a very inconsiderable man, or a very small state, may have an opportunity of repaying a kindness to the greatest."

[12] "The mountains are in labour: a ridiculous mouse will be born" (*Ars poetica*, 139). Horace was quoting a Greek proverb preserved by Athenaeus. Present-day texts, following the best MSS. and the early commentators, read *parturient* (future), but Erskine was not quoting carelessly. Bentley had thrown the great weight of his authority behind *parturiunt* (*Q. Horatius Flaccus, ex recensione et cum notis atque emendationibus Richardi Bentleii*, 1711). English editions of Horace in the 18th century (e.g. Philip Francis, 1746; Richard Hurd, 1749) generally gave that reading.

Farewell—believe me on all occasions, and in all Scituations your most affectionate friend

ANDW. ERSKINE

P.S. I shall see you in Scotland in a few weeks. Write me immediately.

To Johnston, Friday 31 March 1769

MS. Yale (L 800). Dated by letter mentioned in n. 5.

ADDRESS: To John Johnston Esq: of Grange

[Auchinleck]

DEAR SIR: We had an agreable journey west and a comfortable meeting with our cousins at Lainshaw, whom we found much better than we expected. We stayed six nights there. And now we are safe at Auchinleck where is also my brother John.[1]

I am endeavouring to acquire a taste for country affairs, and hope by degrees to do quite well. If you will give orders about the planting of the trees, I will fall on a method of getting them sent to Grange. But I would fain hope you may contrive matters so as to come here and stay a while, before you go home. My Cousins of Lainshaw intend going to Ireland; so I shall have good company.[2] We are to set out the last week of April or first of May.

[1] John Boswell (*ante* 13 Sept. 1762, n. 11; 8 Feb. 1763, n. 3) had some days earlier come to Auchinleck to rejoin the amily circle. Following his illness in 1762–63, he had gone back into military service as first lieutenant in the 21st Regt. of Foot (commission dated 9 Dec. 1763), but had almost at once decided that he wished instead to be a farmer, had got leave of absence, and had spent the last months of 1764 in the north of England, supposedly preparing himself for his new way of life. When, early in 1765, the 21st Foot was ordered abroad, he had negotiated to be placed on half pay (Apr. 1765) and had left active service for good. Returning to Newcastle, he had spent most of the next few years there. Although his mental condition was morbid and rendered him incapable of carrying on a profession, John had been for several years usually able to live an independent life and control his personal affairs, as his surviving diaries and papers show. He had lived with various people at or near Newcastle, among them the Rev. Edward Aitken, a dissenting minister who had once been tutor of Lord Auchinleck, and two well-known physicians, Dr. John Hall, who kept a private hospital, and Dr. Andrew Wilson (*post* 27 Aug. 1771, n. 8). From time to time he had gone on "jaunts", these excursions including a brief visit to Scotland in 1767 and a long one in 1768. Now, in Mar. 1769, he had returned to live with or near his father. (The sources for this note, which are numerous and minute, will be found in the *vita* of John Boswell in the Biographical Supplement appended to the appropriate volume of JB's journal in the present edition.)

[2] JB had asked to be allowed to visit the Boyds in order to pay court to Mary

James Bruce tells me that the trees fit for sending you at present are the Red fir of Hannover the Larix and the different sorts of pines. I can get a parcel sent to Dumfries, from whence you can have them taken to Grange. Perhaps you have these kinds of trees already.[3] If so, it is needless to send them. But if they will be an acceptable present to you, please let me know.

I have done nothing for my black friend,[4] these many weeks, which is very wrong. I therefore enclose you a draught for £10 which you may negociate, and deliver the money, together with my letter to Mr. Hamilton Surgeon in the Back Stairs.[5] If you think it needless for me to correspond with him about my black friend, you need not deliver the letter; but just at my desire inquire how all goes, and just say what I have said in the letter, and then inform me. I think it would be proper to have as little interference as possible. If you would call yourself with Mr. Hamilton and deliver the money, it would be obliging. You will judge if any receipt is necessary.

Ann, and he hoped to travel in company with the Montgomerie-Cuninghames. In the event, only his cousin Margaret Montgomerie went with him, rather unwillingly, to pay the visit which led to his engagement, not to Mary Ann Boyd, but to Margaret Montgomerie herself. They set out from Auchinleck on 25 Apr. The events of their journey and part of the happenings during their visit to Ireland are recorded in the unfinished portion of Journal headed *My Jaunt to Ireland* (Journ. 25 Apr. to 7 May 1769).

[3] In leasing the estate of Grange to his brother Thomas, JJ had reserved to himself "the little Parks or Inclosures which are planted with Firrs and other Forrest Trees, with full power and liberty to inclose such pieces of Ground on the said Lands as he shall think proper for planting" (Grange MSS., Contract, 10 Nov. 1763).

[4] This was Mrs. Dodds, black-haired and perhaps also swarthy of complexion, whose acquaintance JB had made at Moffat, and with whom he carried on a passionate love-affair during 1767 (postscript to letter of 8 Mar. 1767 printed in *Boswell in Search of a Wife*). She bore him a daughter (Sally) in Dec. 1767. JJ

strongly disapproved of the attachment, and together with Andrew Erskine tried to argue JB out of it (Journ. 3, 14, 16 Mar. 1767). "Johnston an old friend of mine a Writer in Edinburgh, but too much of an indolent Philosopher to have great business, being rather a worthy Country Gentleman, with a paternal estate of £100 a year, was much distressed with my unhappy Passion. He was at Moffat when it first began, and he marked the advance of the fever. It was he who assured me upon his honour, that my fair one had a very bad character, and gave me some instances which made my love-sick heart recoil" (To W. J. Temple, 30 Mar. 1767).

[5] A series of flights of stone steps leading down from Parliament Close to the Cowgate (*Old and New Edinburgh*, ii. 243). Alexander Hamilton (1739–1802) specialized in the practice of midwifery and was later for many years Professor of Midwifery at Edinburgh University, as well as the author of various works on the subject (*Original Portraits* i. 330). The letter to him asking him to deliver £10 "to my friend whom you know", is dated 31 Mar. 1769.

I am now as calm and quiet as if I had not been from Auchinleck for years. Do come my dear friend. Is it not very odd that one with whom I am in such intimacy should hardly ever be here. You ought never to be a year absent. I ever am with most sincere regard Your affectionate friend

JAMES BOSWELL

From John Boswell, younger of Knockroon, to Johnston, Saturday 1 April 1769

MS. Yale (C 393). This was, in fact, not a separate letter but a cover addressed by JB. Knockroon added a note on the inside before sealing the cover to enclose JB's own letter, above, and the bank draft.

ADDRESS, in JB's hand: To John Johnston Esq: of Grange, to be left at Forrest's Coffeehouse, Edinburgh.

Ayr 1 Ap⟨ril⟩ 1769

Mr. Boswells[1] Complts. to Mr. Johnstone. He has inclosed Mr. Johnstone Ten pounds Sterl. at desire of Mr. James Boswell Adt. the receipt of which Mr. Johnstone will acknowledge to Mr. J. Boswell at writting him.

[1] John Boswell (1741–1805), younger of Knockroon, was a "writer", practising at Ayr, whose father and mother were both descended from John Boswell, 3rd Laird of Auchinleck, by his first and second marriages respectively. The father, John Boswell, was a younger son of a line which had become impoverished, and he had inherited no landed estate. But he had married Margaret Fergusson, heiress (via her mother, Elizabeth Boswell, who died c. 1764) of the estate of Knockroon, which had been given (c. 1600) by the 3rd Laird of Auchinleck to his son by his second marriage. So in this year 1769 the mother was "of Knockroon"; the father had no territorial designation (although JB often refers to him as "Old Knockroon" to distinguish him from his son); the son was "younger of Knockroon" (i.e. heir to his mother's estate). "Young Knockroon" did eventually inherit the estate on the death of his mother (c. 1788), but as he had been one of the unfortunate partners (virtually shareholders not enjoying the benefits of limited liability) ruined by the failure of the Ayr Bank (Douglas, Heron & Co.) in 1772 (*post* 20 Oct. 1771, n. 9) the estate had to be sold for the benefit of the bank's creditors. The purchaser (for £2,500) was JB himself, because his pride of family made him reluctant to see this old Boswell estate pass into the hands of a stranger. His own circumstances were straitened at the time (winter 1790–91) and only £1,500 could be raised by a mortgage on the property, so in effect he laid out the whole of his hoped-for profits on his soon-to-be-published *Life of Samuel Johnson* in support of the prestige of the Boswell family (To Bruce Campbell, 16 Sept. 1790; To Edmond Malone, 29 Jan. 1791).

To Johnston, Saturday 12 August 1769

MS. Yale (L 801). Dated from Journ. 11 Aug. 1769.

ADDRESS: To Mr. Johnston of Grange.

[Edinburgh]

MY DEAR FRIEND: Erskine and I conjectured the reason of your absence, and excused you. I had drank too much at Lord Gardenston's.[1] However honest Andrew and I took a bottle apiece.[2] I am not uneasy as you are. But am really uneasy in mind, to think of my strong propensity to riot. My present situation gives me a physical excuse for indulgence. I however hope that by and by you shall see me a pattern of sobriety. I send you a letter from the Lord Lieutenant of Ireland's Secretary, which you will please communicate to worthy Baillie[3] with whom we both rejoice as far as the thing is worth. I wish to see you this forenoon, and ever am your affectionate friend

JAMES BOSWELL

[1] Francis Garden (1721–93) had been raised to the bench as Lord Gardenstone in 1764, after serving since 1760 as joint Solicitor-General with James Montgomery. He had been one of the counsel in the Douglas Cause and had appeared before the Parlement of Paris on behalf of Archibald Douglas (*College of Justice*, pp. 527–28). Notable for much of his life for his wit, and in his later years for his work as an early social reformer, he was a true eccentric, even in an age when the species was not uncommon, and something of the peculiar flavour of his character has survived (*Scotland and Scotsmen* i. 369–80; *Original Portraits* i. 22).

[2] On the previous day JB had gone out to dinner, with Lord Galloway and Sir Thomas Wentworth, at Lord Gardenstone's country house at St. Catherine's, Newington. He had returned to town, after drinking more burgundy than he thought wise, and (having apparently sent for JJ without success) had supped with Andrew Erskine at Charles Small's tavern, where, on Erskine's advice, they limited their drinking to a bottle of claret apiece (Journ. 11 Aug. 1769).

[3] The letter from Lord Townshend's secretary, John Lees, a Scot from Cumnock whose acquaintance JB had probably made during his recent visit to Ireland, is dated 4 Aug. 1769. Its purport is not altogether clear, but it appears to indicate that JB had concerned himself in arranging for the sale of the commission of a "Mr. Bayley" in "Lord Blayney's Regiment" and its purchase by some other person unnamed. George Bailie (the name is spelled Bayley in the index of the Army List) had been since 1760 ensign in the 38th Regt. of Foot, Ireland, commanded by Lt.-Gen. Lord Blayney (*Army List*, 1769, p. 92); his name disappears from the *Army List*, 1770. "Worthy Baillie" of the present letter seems likely to be, rather than the late ensign, that common friend of JB and JJ, James Baillie, the Edinburgh lawyer. JB's qualified congratulation probably means that, while he is pleased that Baillie's relative (?) has obtained his wish in selling out, he himself still has a high opinion of the Army as a career.

From Johnston to Andrew Erskine, Tuesday 5 September 1769

MS. Yale (C 1630): JJ's copy.

ENDORSEMENT by JJ: Copy Letter To A. Erskine dated 5th Septr. 1769, Sent off on the 6th To Kelly.

Edinr. 5th Septr 1769

DEAR ERSKINE: On friday I sent the Pittenweem Carrier[1] a Bundle directed to you at Kelly, Containing the Six pair of Stockings and two Reviews that you wanted. My friend Abercromby, who is much Skilled in matters of this Sort, assisted me in buying the Stockings. He Says they are of a good quality, and a great penny worth at 3 sh. the price you fixed. We were Something affraid of the Small Size of the feet, tho' the largest that could be had. If any of them does not answer, return them by the same Pittenweem Carrier. The Merch[an]t will Change them or return the money. I find upon a Sheet Cal[c]ulation that I owe you a Balance of 8d. for which you Shall have Credite in our Acco[un]t Current. My Good friend I Strongly Suspect that you have Some Slye designs Against the partriges. If you are Successful, and at any loss how to dispose of the Killed and wounded, there is a certain friend of yours, who lives at the foot of Roxburghs Closs,[2] that can assist you much, I have long known his abilitys in this way.

I regrete that I cannot comply with your Invitation. It would have enlarged my old Scots Ideas, to have passed Some days quietly with you at Kelly, but I am Doomed to Stay here a fortnight, after that I must repair to the Border.

Monday last week I Saw James Boswell with his agreeable Companion Set off in a Post Chaise for London.[3] Boswell was in good Spirits, though not in good health. The rage of Matrimony has taken such a firm hold of him, that he seems to feel nothing else.[4] He had an Eye towards Stratford upon Avon, where I

---

[1] The weekly carrier to and from Pittenweem in south-east Fife, near Kellie, the Erskines' home, arrived at Kennedy's Close, Edinburgh, on Thursdays and left again on Fridays (Peter Williamson, *Edinburgh Directory*, 1773–74, p. 91).

[2] Roxburgh's Close, where JJ lodged, opposite the Luckenbooths and St. Giles', was very convenient for the Parliament House, which was just across the High Street.

[3] "My worthy friend Grange came to me, and we had some kind, cordial conversation. Mr. Surgeon MacDonell and he breakfasted with me; and then came Mr. Farquhar Kinloch Merchant in London my companion for the journey" (Journ. 28 Aug. 1769).

[4] *Post* 16 Oct. 1769, n. 1. JB was

Suspect he is Just now.[5] A post or two will bring some acco[un]t of him. I am really uneasy anent his health. If you can find as much time in your great hurry of bussiness, pray let me hear of your Wellfare before I leave this place and believe me alwise to be Dear Erskine yours most sincerely

[JOHN JOHNSTON]

From Andrew Erskine to Johnston, Tuesday 26 September 1769

MS. Yale (C 1207).

ADDRESS: To Mr. John Johnston, Writer, at Mr. Stewart's, Roxburgh's Close, Edinburgh.

Kelly, Septr. 26th 1769

Good your honour are you still in Town. If you are let me know by the return of the Post, as I have something particular to communicate to you which I should be sorry fell into any hands but your own. You are excellent at a Commission, and I have not even yet recovered my surprise at the cheapness and Goodness of the stockings. Alas for the Partriges. It has not been in my power to kill any thing like a present worthy of being sent to the Metropolis. I have[1] had a letter from Boswell. I find him still marriage mad with an accession of Jubilee madness. If I have not an answer by return of Post I shall conclude you gone. Yours etc.

ANDW. ERSKINE

From Johnston to Andrew Erskine, Thursday 28 September 1769

MS. Yale (C 1631): JJ's copy.

ENDORSEMENT by JJ: Copy Letter To The Honble Andw. Erskine, 28th Septr. 1769.

Edinr. 28 Septr. 1769

DEAR ERSKINE: Owing to my keeping the house and to the neg-

now engaged to Margaret Montgomerie, and the marriage had been arranged for November. With the intention of "clearing his constitution" before marriage, he had gone to London at the end of August to undergo a course of treatment by Dr. Gilbert Kennedy.

[5] The Shakespeare Jubilee celebration, inspired and largely organized by Garrick, was held at Stratford on 6–8 Sept., and was attended by a fashionable crowd. JB was present, and at the masquerade made his memorable first public appearance in the costume of a Corsican chief.

[1] MS. "have have".

lect of the Coffeehouse-man, I have only received your letter Just now when the post is going out which I ought to have had yesterday, otherwise you Should have known this day that your friend is Still here. You say, "that you have Something particular to tell me." This has roused all my female Curiosity. As this will reach you to morrow let me have a letter left at Forrests on Saturday or Monday with every particular. Agreeable to my wishes, I have Sugested Something favourable in your own affairs, which you'll recollect we have Sometimes Spoke of. Good or bad let me have it;

Boswell has been very kind in writing to you, not one word have I had from him, in spite of a very Serious promise nowise extorted by me. Perhaps he may reckon what I see in the Newspapers Sufficient Intelligence,[1] but let me not blame my friend wantonly, he had no reason to think I was to stay here so long, and perhaps he has wrote to me at Grange where I intended to have been ten days ago. I have Staid here a week longer than I intended transacting Some affairs of a friend[2] of mine who is Just now in London. A letter from him which I expect to morrow or Saturday will determine the time of my going away, tho at any rate I have fixt upon Tuesday or Wednesday at furthest for my Journey. There is not a Creature here that I am acquainted with except my dear Self to render this old Metropolis agreeable. In Spite of that and very bad weather I have been pretty Comfortable. Adieu my good friend and believe me allwise to be yours most sincerly while

JJ

---

[1] JB contributed a long account of the Jubilee festival to *The Public Advertiser* (16 Sept. 1769), which was reprinted in *Lond. Mag.* (Sept. 1769) and *Scots Mag.* (Sept. 1769). He also wrote "An Account of the Armed Corsican Chief at the Stratford Jubilee", which appeared in the same issue of *Lond. Mag.* and was reprinted in *The London Chronicle* (5 Oct. 1769) and in *The Edinburgh Advertiser* (13 Oct. 1769). The "Verses in the Character of a Corsican", which he wrote to deliver at the masquerade, were printed as a broadside at Stratford by the local bookseller, James Keating, with the date 6 Sept. and at Birmingham by Baskerville with the date 7 Sept., and were reprinted in *The London Chronicle* (12 Sept. 1769), *The Edinburgh Advertiser* (15 Sept. 1769, with a variant title to the verses), *Lond. Mag.* (Sept. 1769), and *Scots Mag.* (Sept. 1769); *Lit. Car.*, pp. 84–85, 218, 222, 245, 252, 257; BP viii. 100 n.).

[2] Not identified.

From Andrew Erskine to Andrew Forrest, Monday 9 October 1769

MS. Yale (C 1208).

ADDRESS: To Mr. Forrest at his Coffee house, Edinburgh.

Kelly, Ocber. 9th 1769

SIR: About eight days ago I sent a letter directed to Mr. John Johnsson, Writer, at Forrest's Coffee house Edinburgh,[1] and below there was written: "To be sent immediately by Mr. Forrest to Mr. Johnson." I'll be obliged to you if you'll inform me if you reciev'd such a letter and if Mr. Johnson got it; and if Mr. Johnson is in Town be so good as ask him if he answer'd the letter, and tell him if he did that I never reciev'd it, and beg the favour he'll write to me again. My letter was about Business which required an immediate answer, and I'm very much surprised that no answer has arrived.

I am the Gentleman you may remember lodged once or twice in your house. It will be very obliging if you'll answer this letter by return of Post. Direct for me at Kelly house by Anstruther. I am Sir your most obedient Servant

ANDW. ERSKINE

To Johnston, Monday 16 October 1769

MS. Yale (L 802).

London, 16 October 1769

MY DEAR JOHNSTON: Instead of making an apology to you, for having been all this time without writing to you, I shall very calmly tell you that my love of justice is pleased, when I find that I have appeared negligent of a friend, who has so often appeared negligent of me. And I do believe that both appearances have been similar in this, that neither of them has been intended. The fact is that we have both been negligent in our turn, even while our friendship remained as warm as ever. So let us have a mutual indulgence.

My history since we parted has been various. In one respect

---

[1] Andrew Forrest's "coffee-house, at the cross" is listed in Peter Williamson's *Edinburgh Directory*, 1777–78, p. 32. He had been admitted a Burgess in 1756, when he was described as "master of the Caledonia Coffeehouse" (*Roll of Edinburgh Burgesses, 1701–1760*, p. 72).

only has it been uniform, that is to say in the constancy of my attachment to my valuable *Spouse*; for, so I may call her.[1] We have corresponded very frequently; and, believe me, Johnston I have had no wavering. This assurance will satisfy you, that at length *my time is come* as the proverb goes. I hope to be happy, and I hope my worthy friend shall be better with me by and by, than he has ever been. I could not resist Shakespeare's Jubilee at Stratford upon Avon. I enclose you some of its productions. The Print was done for *The London Magazine*.[2] After the Jubilee, I observed faithfully the Plan which I had laid down, living quietly in the house of my Bookseller Mr. Dilly,[3] and drinking Kennedy's Decoction. I felt a sensible recovery. But Duncan Forbes my Surgeon found it necessary to perform some chirurgical operations.[4] Upon which, I removed to lodgings nearer him. I was only one night in them. For, General Paoli[5] arrived, and then I came immediately

[1] The marriage had not yet taken place. JB probably means that because he and Margaret Montgomerie have privately joined hands and solemnly engaged themselves to marry (Journ. 7 Aug. 1769) their relationship is morally the same as though they had executed a formal contract of marriage with witnesses. In the standard form of marriage contract still used in Scotland the parties "accept of each other for lawful spouses and bind and oblige themselves to solemnise their marriage with all convenient speed", i.e. "spouse" bears the otherwise obsolete sense of its ultimate etymon, Latin *sponsa*, "betrothed". But he may mean merely that he considers himself as good as married, for when, shortly after the date of the present letter, he did draw up a marriage contract of his own devising, he seems to have given the word its usual meaning of married person (MS. Yale M 21, 31 Oct. 1769).

[2] An engraving by John Miller, from a sketch by Samuel Wale, of JB dressed as an armed Corsican chief had appeared as frontispiece to *The London Magazine* (Sept. 1769), which contained, as its leading article, a long letter by JB describing the Stratford Jubilee (C. B. Tinker and F. A. Pottle, *A New Portrait of James Boswell*, 1927, plate 6).

[3] Edward Dilly (1732–79), with his brother Charles, conducted the famous publishing-house in the Poultry. The brothers were very hospitable, and JB, telling of Dr. Johnson's meeting at Dilly's with Wilkes, says he met a greater number of literary men at their table than at any other except that of Sir Joshua Reynolds (*Life* iii. 65).

[4] JB had consulted Dr. Gregory in Edinburgh on 9 Aug. Gregory had thought he could be cured at home, but he had determined on the visit to London, where he intended to take a course of the nostrum of the elderly Dr. Gilbert Kennedy, which then enjoyed a great reputation. This he duly did, but he also, on the advice of Sir John Pringle, put himself in charge of a surgeon named Duncan Forbes, moving his lodgings to Carey Street to be near him (Journ. 9 Aug., 2, 14, 15, 20 Sept.).

[5] In May 1768, Genoa had surrendered the island to France in payment for subsidies received, most of which had been spent to support the French garrisons in the coastal towns. The French, who had previously observed neutrality towards the insurgents who held the interior, now increased their forces and Corsican resistance at last broke down. Paoli arrived in London, as a much-to-

to Old Bond Street and took elegant appartments a few doors from his. I was then obliged to alter my system. I bought some genteel clothes, got a foreign servant, and appeared to due advantage. My illness has taken various turns. At last I see a prospect of being soon perfectly well, and you may believe I am very much relieved; for I have been under sad anxiety. The Knife[6] has been absolutely necessary. And you know I am a very bad bearer of pain. However, the thoughts of being made well once for all cannot fail to cheer me.

You may believe that I have felt very great joy on being again with the illustrious Corsican Chief. He is in good health and spirits, and is actually the most agreable man that can be imagined. He is just now gone on a jaunt to Portsmouth Plymouth, Bath Bristol and other places. I could not go with him, being obliged to attend close to my health. He has promised me that he will go to Scotland. And I have hopes that he will go down the beginning of next month, and be present at my marriage. I shall go next week down to Devonshire to visit my worthy friend Temple;[7] and be back to London, about the fourth or fifth of November; and then I will try to prevail with the General to set out with me. Or perhaps, I may go down first, and let him come after. I doubt much if I shall insist on Temple's going. I shall determine, when I hear him and Mrs. Temple on the subject. The General will stay but a very few days in Scotland. I hope the chance of seeing him will bring your honour to Edinburgh by the 14 of November. How unpardonable will it be, if you miss seeing perhaps one of the greatest men that ever lived, one whom all Europe admires in his lifetime, and who will be the admiration of all ages, after he is gone from this world.[8]

be-fêted refugee, on 20 Sept. 1769. JB, Paoli's friend and self-appointed agent in Britain, put himself much in the public eye by accompanying him from place to place, showing him the sights and introducing him to notabilities.

[6] The passages in the Notes run: "yesterday break Forb. He saw that Incis was to be performed" (15 Oct.); "yesterday morning Dunc Forb came and with kindness to save dire forebodings *cut*" (16 Oct.). Dr. Harry Keil suggested to the editors of *Boswell in Search of a Wife, 1766–1769*, that the incision was made in the treatment of

some form of local infection, or (more probably) to relieve a paraphimosis (To Frank Brady, 6 May 1956).

[7] In 1766 Temple had been instituted rector of Mamhead, near Exeter, and in the following year had married his cousin, Anne Stow. He had since then given JB some help with the preparation of the Corsican Journal, and had secured him as godfather to his first-born son.

[8] In the event, through pressure of more important concerns, General Paoli did not make his visit to Scotland until the autumn of 1771.

My father's strange scheme still alarms me.[9] I have written to him in very strong terms. I have not as yet come to any resolution what I shall do. I am shocked at the idea of what you know affected me so much; and cannot think of it rationally. Pray write to me, under cover to George Dempster Esq: M.P. London. Remember me kindly at the Shaw and Tundergarth Manse, and believe me ever your sincere friend

JAMES BOSWELL

To Johnston, no date, c. 1770

MS. Yale (L 803). Of this letter, which is somewhat arbitrarily placed at the head of JB's letters to JJ after his marriage, it can confidently be asserted only that it was written after 25 Nov. 1769 and before 27 Jan. 1786, when JB left Edinburgh never to return as a householder. In style of writing it resembles the letters of 1769.

ADDRESS: To John Johnston Esq: of Grange.

[Edinburgh]

MY SAD FRIEND: Nothing can occur to excuse you from supping with us tonight. There is an unanimous Decision against you. Half an hour after nine, you must come. You shall go when you please. If possible do not dissapoint me. My *Jack*[1] creaks for you. I know where you are. So no excuse. I have a prior claim. Adieu till meeting

J. B.

P.S. My Wife says if you break your word, she will lose her opinion of you.

---

[9] Lord Auchinleck, who had been a widower for more than three years, was thinking of marrying again. The emotional shock to JB was severe: "After a wretched feverish night I awaked in a dreadful state. I have no doubt that evil spirits enemies to Mankind are permitted to tempt and torment them. Damn him. —Curse him sounded somehow involuntarily in my ears perpetually. I was absolutely mad. I sent for worthy Grange, and was so furious and black minded and uttered such horrid ideas that he could not help shedding tears, and even went so far as to say that if I talked so, he would never see me again. I looked on my father's marrying again as the most un- grateful return to me for my having submitted so much to please him. I thought it an insult on the memory of my valuable mother. I thought it would totally estrange him from his children by her" (Journ. 16 July 1769). On 25 Nov. 1769, Lord Auchinleck married his cousin Elizabeth, daughter of John Boswell of Balmuto. This marriage took place at the house of the bride's mother in Edinburgh on the same day as that of JB and Margaret Montgomerie at Lainshaw (*Scots Mag.*, 1769, xxxi. 615; Diary of Lt. John Boswell, MS. Yale C 404:3).

[1] A mechanical turnspit.

To Johnston, Thursday 31 May 1770

MS. Yale (L 804).

ADDRESS: To John Johnston Esq: of Grange in Annandale, by Langholm.

POSTMARK: JU 1.

Edinburgh, 31 May 1770

DEAR SIR: Though according to strict form, you ought first to write to me, and let me know that you got well home, I now sit down to write first to you, as I well *know the nature of the beast*.[1] I have been quite well since you left this; and my Wife has been as well as could be expected. We have had much hurry and confusion with *flitting*.[2] We got into our house in the Canongate,[3] on friday last. It is really an admirable one; but we have little use of it just now: for all the fore rooms are painting. We submit to that inconvenience, in order to have a future elegance. You will have seen in the Newspapers that Lord Colville is dead.[4] He has proved to be a strange man. My Lady has £200 a year jointure, with the liferent of his place at Drumseugh.[5] He has left the fee of all he had to two natural sons, except £1000 to his brother,[6] and some trifle to one of his Nephews. It is terrible to see a man pay no regard to his family, especially when there is a Peerage to support. He had kept his settlements a dead secret. Every body was stunned. I hear something may be done towards setting aside the deed. Our friend Erskine is violent about it. *Lady Betty* is well released. I was at his burial which was a grand one.

[1] A proverbial phrase listed by John Ray, *A Collection of English Proverbs*, 1678, p. 77.

[2] Scots: moving house.

[3] When they returned to Edinburgh after their marriage, the Boswells took lodgings for a few days in the flat above Lord Auchinleck's in Blair's Land, Parliament Close. On 5 Dec. 1769 they moved into a house in the Cowgate, near the Excise Office (Diary of Lt. John Boswell, MS. Yale C 404:3, 1 and 5 Dec. 1769; From Lt. John Boswell, 4 Apr. 1770, address). Leases in Scotland generally ran from Whitsunday (15 May), and on Friday, 25 May 1770 they moved into a house in Chessel's Buildings in the Canongate (as above, 31 May 1770; Mrs. Margaret Stuart to Mrs. Boswell,

8 Sept., 26 Oct. 1770, addresses; Journ. 29 Dec. 1781).

[4] Lady Betty Macfarlane, Andrew Erskine's sister, had been left a widow in 1767, at the age of thirty-three. In Oct. 1768, she had married Vice-Admiral Lord Colville of Culross. This second marriage lasted barely twenty months, for she was left a widow for the second time on 21 May 1770.

[5] Drumsheugh, Lord Colville's home, was less than half a mile northwest of the Castle, on the road to Queensferry.

[6] John, Lord Colville of Culross, succeeded his brother Alexander (1717–70), Lady Betty's husband. He was the fourth in a family of six sons and three daughters (*Scots Peer.* ii. 561–63).

I visited Harris[7] the evening before he was executed, and insisted to know from him as a dying man, the truth as to his Accomplices. He persisted in what I told you, and added something stronger. I shall tell you all about it, when we meet. In the mean time, I can hardly believe him. I saw him hanged yesterday. He seemed very penitent, and not at all frightened. He suffered great pain to all appearance. I was much shocked, and am still gloomy. I have pleaded a cause before the General Assembly.[8] Old Sir Hugh

[7] William Harris, a merchant in Ayr, had been arrested on 25 Aug. 1768 on suspicion of forging and uttering many 20-shilling bank-notes counterfeiting those of the Thistle Bank of Glasgow. Letters from him (27 Aug.) and his agent, James Neill (30 Aug.) ask that JB undertake his defence. JB consented, but the authorities showed no hurry in bringing Harris to trial and he had lain in jail for almost fifteen months when he succeeded in escaping from the Edinburgh Tolbooth on the night of 7 Nov. 1769, after cutting the bars of his window. A substantial reward was offered for his apprehension, and he was taken on 15 Nov. at Shields, where he had hoped to secure a passage for foreign parts. He was returned to the Tolbooth and put in irons. A statement by the jailer concerning this phase of his imprisonment records that JB visited him and gave him a guinea. On 6 Feb. 1770 he made an unsuccessful attempt to strangle himself, shortly before his extended trial before the Court of Session on the forgery charge. The prosecution was made in the name of the Lord Advocate, James Montgomery, with Henry Dundas and Andrew Crosbie actively assisting him, while the defence counsel were Alexander Lockhart, James Ferguson, and JB. The Boswell papers at Yale contain a great mass (nearly 200 folio and quarto pages) of manuscript and printed documents dealing with the case: MS. Yale Lg 16, 17, 18, 19. The prosecution's printed Proof runs to 88 quarto pages.

On 10 Mar. Harris was found guilty by interlocutor and was remitted to the High Court of Justiciary to face criminal trial. When this began on 24 Apr., he feigned insanity, but the jury, after hearing witnesses give evidence as to the state of his mind, pronounced him sane. Another jury was then chosen for the actual trial, and this next day delivered a unanimous verdict of guilty, whereupon Harris, still playing the madman, was sentenced to be hanged in the Grassmarket on 30 May. He dropped his pose of insanity at his execution. In an account of his life, said to have been written by himself, which was published after his death, he severely attacked many persons for having wronged or mistreated him, but said nothing definite about the crime for which he suffered, and nothing at all about his accomplices. (Sources for this note, in addition to the papers at Yale mentioned above and a copy of *An Account of the Life of Mr. William Harries, Late Merchant in Air*, Edinburgh, 1770, in the National Library of Scotland, are *Scots Mag.*, 1769, xxxi. 669 and 1770, xxxii. 337.)

[8] The General Assembly of the Church of Scotland sat each May in an apartment appropriated to its use in St. Giles's church. It was customary for advocates to be employed to argue causes at the bar of the Assembly and this was JB's first appearance in the role of church lawyer. His letter implies some reluctance on his part to accept General Assembly business, possibly because so many of the causes offered to him would have required him to argue for patronage, and patronage did not seem quite consistent with the libertarian principles he had advanced in *An Account of Corsica*. Whatever the reason for his initial aversion, there is no doubt that he increasingly disliked practising before the Assembly

Paterson[9] prevailed with me to undertake it. Our friend Mr. Fergusson lodges in your room.[10] He is much with me. I have been joking with him on the risk his spoons run. Compliments to you and all friends from my Wife and me. I am Dear Sir your affectionate friend

JAMES BOSWELL

as the years passed: "There is *de facto* something low and coarse in such employment, though *upon paper*, it is a *Supreme Judicature*. But guineas must be had" (To W. J. Temple, 3 June 1775); "Found *that vulgar and rascally* court too much for me" (Notes, 26 May 1777).

This particular cause, recorded in JB's Consultation Book as "Patron etc. of St. Ninians v. People", and debated on 29 May, was a very important one in the history of the Church of Scotland and was now before the Assembly for the fourth successive year. First heard in 1767, it was not finally disposed of by the Assembly until 1773, and there were repercussions even in 1774. *Scots Mag.* in its accounts of the proceedings of the General Assembly, and elsewhere, records in its volumes from 1767 to 1774, inclusive, much detail of the nature of the dispute and its slow progress towards solution. The facts can be briefly summarized as follows. The minister of the parish of St. Ninians, in the presbytery of Stirling, had been translated in 1765 to an Edinburgh church. In 1766 the patron of the living, Sir John Stewart of Allanbank, presented to it the Rev. David Thomson, at that time minister of Gargunnock. The people of Thomson's new parish objected to him, ostensibly on account of his delicate constitution, and the presbytery of Stirling and the synod of Perth and Stirling supported them and refused to induct him. Important aspects of church policy were involved, such as the popular party's disapproval of the translation of ministers and of presentation by patrons, an aggravating circumstance in this case being the fact that the presenters were mainly Episcopalians, and even adherents of non-juring congregations. The popular party was in a minority in the General Assembly at this period, and in 1767,

when the cause was first heard, and in each succeeding year, the Assembly ordered that Thomson's presentation be sustained. The synod and presbytery, under various pretexts, succeeded for several years in avoiding settling Thomson in St. Ninians. At last, in 1773, the Assembly gave a definitive sentence, with a threat of disciplinary action against the presbytery of Stirling, that Thomson must be settled by a fixed date. This was effective, and he was duly admitted on 29 June 1773, but his induction was made in such an unusual and grudging manner that the 1774 Assembly appointed a commission to investigate the conduct of the minister responsible. This appears to have ended the matter and Thomson held the parish until his death in 1787. JB was one of the advocates for the patron in this cause for the four years 1770 to 1773, and he wrote a long account of the debate on it in the 1771 Assembly which he published in *Lond. Mag.*, 1772, xli. 181–87, 237–42.

[9] Sir Hugh Paterson (1686–1777) of Bannockburn was one of the principal heritors of the parish of St. Ninians. He had held various public offices before associating himself with the Jacobite cause in 1715, but by his attainder he had forfeited, with his baronetcy, his prospects in public life. In spite of his losses, he had remained faithful to the Pretender, and during the rebellion of the Forty-five had put his house at Bannockburn at Prince Charles's disposal (*Comp. Bar.* iv. 342).

[10] Joseph Fergusson was no doubt a commissioner to the General Assembly, and was occupying JJ's lodgings during JJ's absence at Grange. Fergusson was a bachelor, and had presumably left his manse empty: hence the joke about the spoons.

From Andrew Erskine to Johnston, Saturday 18 August 1770

MS. Yale (C 1210).

ADDRESS: To Mr. John Johnston Writer, at Mrs. Stewarts, Roxburgh's Close, Edinburgh.

Balcaskie[1] Augst. 18th 1770

DEAR JOHNSTON, To give you any Commissions in this hot Weather would be very unconscionable, therefore if thou canst find out Johnston the Cadie and deliver him the following orders you will oblige me much. Tell him to get from Boswell the Reviews which should have been sent last week, and bid him go to the Pittenweem Carrier's Quarters and recieve from him the Doe skin Breeches which Macansh[2] made for me, which said Breeches he must give to Macansh with orders to make another pair as these will not go on, which other pair must be at least four inches wider in the Waistband, and an Inch wider at the knees and they must likewise be a little longer in the knees and must come well up in the seat and I shall expect them next week, and the Reviews I must have this week. And so I conclude the subject of Reviews and Breeches, heartily wishing thee a merry harvest Vacation and that thou wilst excuse this trouble. I remain thine in all friendship

ANDR. ERSKINE

A Post, A Place, a Pension, a sinecure.

To Johnston, Wednesday 29 August 1770

MS. Yale (L 805). For date see To W. J. Temple, 1 Sept.

ADDRESS: To Mr. Johnston.

[Edinburgh,] Wednesday Forenoon

MY DEAR FRIEND: It was not kind in you to leave me alone yesterday. I had a terrible day. My Wife after much trouble and danger

[1] The home, in Fife, of Sir Robert Anstruther of Balcaskie (1733–1818), 3rd Bt., who had married in 1763 Erskine's sister, Lady Janet. She died in Oct. 1770. The Balcaskie family is a cadet branch of the Anstruthers of Anstruther (*ante* 9 Feb. 1769, n. 4).

[2] Alexander M'Ansh was a breeches-maker in the Horse Wynd (Williamson's *Edinburgh Directory* 1774–75, p. 59).

was at last delivered of a son.[1] But the poor child lived but a very short while. Pray come to me directly. Yours

J. B.

From Johnston, October 1770

Missing. Recd. 24 Oct. 1770. "Grange" (Reg. Let.).

To Johnston, Wednesday 22 May 1771

MS. Yale (L 806).

ADDRESS: To John Johnston Esq: of Grange in Annandale, By Langholm.
POSTMARK: MY 22.

Edinburgh, 22 May 1771

MY DEAR SIR: You will perhaps have blamed me for not having written to you, before now. But I declare to you, that I was so hurried from the time I left this our old capital till my return to it, that nothing but absolute necessity could make me settle to put pen to paper. My wife and I had a very good journey west. I left her at Treesbank with her sister;[1] and went by myself to Auchinleck where I was four nights. I then accompanied my father on the Western Circuit.[2] I past six days at Inveraray, without seeing a shower; and being in perfect good health I fully saw the whole of that place, which is truly a magnificent seat.[3] It has all the highland wild grandeur, and a vast addition from art. I have written a pretty good description of it, which you shall see.[4] I then came on the Circuit to Glasgow; where I past two days; and then returned to

---

[1] This was the first child born to JB and his wife. Of the three daughters and three sons subsequently born to them, all survived childhood except David, born 15 Nov. 1776, who lived for only four months.

---

[1] Mary Montgomerie, of the Lainshaw family, JB's wife's elder sister, had married James Campbell of Treesbank in 1768. Mrs. Boswell remained at Treesbank, owing, presumably, to the coolness which had developed between her and Lord Auchinleck and his new wife. She appears to have accompanied JB to Auchinleck in the autumn of 1770 on his

first visit there after his marriage, and to have taken offence at the treatment she then received (To W. J. Temple, 6 Oct. 1770; From W. J. Temple, 27 Dec. 1771). She never visited Auchinleck again until she went there in 1782 to take possession.

[2] Lord Auchinleck went on circuit with Lord Pitfour and held courts at Inveraray on 2 May, and Glasgow on 9 May (*Scots Mag.* 1771, xxxiii. 323).

[3] Archibald Campbell, 3rd Duke of Argyll, had wholly rebuilt the Castle at Inveraray. JB was later to be entertained there with SJ (*Tour*, 25 Oct. 1773).

[4] JB's description of Inveraray has not been recovered.

Treesbank where I remained two nights comfortably and quietly; and then my wife and I with a little daughter of Treesbank[5] came in to Edinburgh.

I am now in my house in James's Court,[6] which we find large enough for us, very convenient, and exceedingly healthful and pleasant. My wife is very fond of it. Her jaunt to the country has done her great good, made her fatter, and given her a much stronger look, than when we parted.

We were out this day dining at our noble friend Lady Colville's, Nobody there but ourselves the old Countess Lady Anne and Captain Andrew.[7] Every thing was perfectly genteel, and we were all happy: And guess you what was the first toast after dinner—proposed by *her handsom Ladyship*—upon honour?—It was—GRANGE. And what was Captain Andrew's toast?—"Miss Johnston of Lockerbie."[8] So you see the good humour we were in. Her Ladyship said she really thought your honour had forgotten her; as you had been so long of seeing her. But we convinced her of the contrary. So when you come to town, remember you must acquit yourself accordingly. She looks vastly well, has resumed her usual spirits, and is in short quite *Lady Betty*. Dash[9] said "She is just ripe for Grange." That you know is ripe for sociality and ancient *stark love and kindness*.[10]

[5] James Campbell of Treesbank, a first cousin of Lord Auchinleck, had married Helen Macredie in 1763 (From Lord Auchinleck, c. 3 Sept. 1763) and this was a daughter, Jean, of that marriage. After the death of his first wife, Treesbank had married in 1768 Mary Montgomerie of Lainshaw, elder sister of JB's wife. Jeanie was an especial favourite of Sir John Pringle, as various references to her in JB's journal and correspondence show. In 1787 she married Robert Reid of Adamton; she died in 1789.

[6] At the May term the Boswells moved from the Canongate into a flat in James's Court belonging to David Hume. After two years this flat proved too small, and in May 1773 they moved downstairs to a larger flat in the same building (From W. J. Temple, 18 Jan. 1771; W. J. Temple to Mrs. Boswell, 19 Apr. 1771; Notes 15 May 1773, MS. Yale J 29;

17 May 1773, MS. Yale J 31; E. C. Mossner, "Dr. Johnson *In Partibus Infidelium*", *Modern Lang. Notes*, 1948, lxiii. 516–19).

[7] Referred to here are Lady Betty, now a widow for the second time; her mother, the widowed Lady Kellie; her unmarried sister, Lady Anne Erskine; and her brother, Andrew Erskine. It was probably from the mother, Janet, Lady Kellie, that the children inherited their brains, for she was a daughter of Dr. Archibald Pitcairne, the celebrated Jacobite physician and Latin poet.

[8] The lady with whom JJ was thus significantly linked by his intimate friends was Grace, eldest daughter and co-heiress (with her sisters Susan and Catherine) of William Johnstone of Lockerbie (*post* 27 Mar. 1772, n. 3).

[9] Andrew Erskine's nickname.

[10] A proverbial expression which was still current in Scotland in Sir Walter

I am immersed in General Assembly Business, having no less than five causes, before that Venerable Court, and being in expectation of a Sixth.[11] I am engaged on different sides both for

Scott's time (*Provincial Antiquities*, 1826, i. 177–78). The popular belief was that Robert Gibb, Master of Horse to James V, when asked by the King why he served him, replied: "For stark love and kindness" (A. M. Bisset, *Episodes in West Lothian History*, 1927). The name "Rob Gibb" came to signify disinterested loyalty and was used in that sense as a Jacobite toast: "Rob Gibb's *Contract, stark Love and Kindness.* An Expression often used when we drink to our Friends" (James Kelly, *A Complete Collection of Scotish Proverbs*, 1721, p. 283). When Prince Charles was leaving her house in Skye, "Mrs. MacDonald [of Kingsburgh] made up to him and offered him a snuff out of a little silver-mill with two hands clasped together upon the lid of it, and the common motto, ROB GIBB" (Robert Forbes, *The Lyon in Mourning*, 1747, ed. Henry Paton, 1895, i. 81). A stone dated 1779 on a building near Strichen in Aberdeenshire is inscribed: "In This Hunters Lodge Rob Gibb Commands."

[11] One of the causes was the famous Patron etc. of St. Ninians *v.* People already mentioned (*ante* 31 May 1770, n. 8); the other five, in the order in which JB entered them in his Consultation Book (italic indicating his client) were: Patron etc. of Kinglassie *v. People*; *Patron etc. of Kirkhill v.* People etc.; *People etc. of Lintrathen v.* Pr[esumptive] Patron; Elders etc. of Portpatrick *v. McMaster*; *Patron etc. of Alness v.* Monro. Bannatyne MacLeod was opposing counsel in the first three new causes, Henry Erskine in the other two, as also in the St. Ninians cause. Boswell's fees in the six causes, 15 May–6 June, amounted to 27 guineas; he in effect won three of them and lost three. The St. Ninians cause was debated on 28 May (*Scots Mag.* 1771, xxxiii. 274–75) and the McMaster cause on the 30th. McMaster was the anonymous probationer "opposed in his application to be inducted,

because it was alledged that he had been guilty of fornication five years before" whom JB discussed with Dr. Johnson on 5 Apr. 1772, eliciting the memorable remark, "A man who is good enough to go to heaven is good enough to be a clergyman" (*Life* ii. 171–72). The Assembly in 1771 reversed the sentences of the synod and presbytery in this cause on the ground of a defect in the libel, but a new libel was lodged with the presbytery, McMaster was found guilty, and the Assembly of 1772 dismissed the cause, ruling that no regular appeal had been taken (*Scots Mag.* xxxiii. 277, xxxiv. 275; MS. Register of Proceedings of the General Assembly, 1771, pp. 541–46, 1772, pp. 161–64; MS. Assembly Papers, 1771, 1772; the MS. records are in the Register House, Edinburgh, deposited by the Church of Scotland in 1958, on indefinite loan). The remaining four causes all concerned patronage. In the Lintrathen cause JB's clients attempted to show that Walter Ogilvy of Clove, who had exercised the right of presentation, was not the patron; at Kinglassie, Kirkhill, and Alness the question was whether a particular presentee should be settled in spite of opposition. At Kirkhill (a parish near Inverness) the people objected to the settlement of Mr. George Mark, probationer, on the ground that he was deficient in Gaelic (*Scots Mag.*, 1771, xxxiii. 328–30). The Alness cause (which was remitted to the presbytery "to use their best endeavours to reconcile the people of the parish to the presentee") seems to have been heard of no more in the Assembly, but the other three causes came up again in 1772, and the Lintrathen cause continued to 1773 (*Scots Mag.*, 1772, xxxiv. 269–70, 273, 396; xxxv. 273; *Fasti Scot.* v. 98; vi. 473–74. MS. records of the General Assembly refer to these causes in Register of Commission, 1771, pp. 162–69, 171–75, 176–81, 183–89; Register of Assembly, 1772, pp. 71–83, 94–99, 111–15;

and against Patronage. But you know I am to have no opinion.
I am only to speak in the person of others. So that the Judgments
of the assembly do not affect me.

> But let them say or let them do
> It's aw ane to me
> If I but get into my pouch
> A braw swinging fee etc.[12]

My wife sends you her best compliments; and I ever am My Dear
Sir your affectionate f⟨riend⟩

JAMES BOSWELL

Pray let me hear from you soon.

To Johnston, Tuesday 27 August 1771

MS. Yale (L 807).

ADDRESS: To John Johnston Esquire of Grange in Annandale, Writer in
Edinburgh, to be left at Forrest's Coffeehouse, Edinr.

ENDORSEMENT: Alnwick 27th August 1771. I received this Letter from Mr.
Boswell's hand when he returned on Wednesday the 28th. having changed
his mind in returning by Melrose as he mentions within.

Alnwick 27 August 1771

MY DEAR GRANGE: Without any preamble, I shall give you a
short account of our jaunt since we parted from you.[1] We called for
a few minutes at worthy Sir Alexander Dick's and were put in
good spirits by him. We dined at Norton and got to Cornhill at
night, so that we slept the very first night in old England. On
Thursday we set out about seven, dined at Morpeth, and got to
Newcastle at night.[2] During these two days, the most remarkable
places were Dalkeith, Newbottle,[3] Lauder Castle or Lauder Hall
an ancient seat of the Earl of Lauderdale, Redbreas the seat of
the Earl of Marchmont, Hume Castle, Hirsel the seat of the Earl
of Hume, the bridge at Coldstream the ancient Castle on the

1773, pp. 277–78. JB's signature appears
among the miscellaneous MS. Assembly
Papers of both 1771 and 1772.).

[12] Lines of a type common in the 18th
century, when Edinburgh lawyers formed
a convivial fraternity and had their own
repertoire of professional drinking songs.
Examples are to be found in *The Court of*

Session Garland, ed. James Maidment,
1839.

[1] His companion on this tour was Mrs.
Boswell (To Dr. Percy, 26 Aug. 1771).

[2] These were regular posting stages
on the main road to England by way of
Coldstream.

[3] Newbattle Abbey.

english side, Mr. Pringle's Place,[4] Ford Castle,[5] Flowdon Field, Milford Plain the finest sheep ground and hunting ground that can be imagined and several seats whose names the Post boys could not tell. We had fine weather and my travelling companion was delighted with the quick lively motion of driving post. When we got to Newcastle we found that my brother John was set out for London.[6] Sandie Maxwell the Wine Merchant[7] happened to be at Parker's the house where we put up. He supt with us, and was very good company. Sandie is really a very agreable man. He is very knowing with regard to all the places and persons in the north of England, where he sells a great deal of Claret, and he has the most cheerful disposition and communicative way that can be and is at the same time quite a well bred man. On friday morning we sent for Dr. Wilson the Physician[8] who came and breakfasted with us, and was very angry with us for not having come first to his house. Poor Sir Francis Blake Delaval's Corpse[9] had lain in

---

[4] George Pringle (1700–80), of Torwoodlee, near Galashiels, which had been a property of the Pringles since 1509 (Thomas Craig-Brown, *The History of Selkirkshire*, Edinburgh, 1886, i. 459–67).

[5] Ford Castle, Northumberland, seat of the late Sir Francis Blake Delaval (see n. 9, below).

[6] *Ante* 13 Sept. 1762, n. 11; 8 Feb. 1763, n. 3; 31 Mar. 1769, n. 1. John had remained either in Edinburgh or at Auchinleck from Mar. 1769 until the month in which the present letter was written. After a disagreement with his stepmother, he had returned to Newcastle (To W. J. Temple, 21–24 Sept. 1772) and then almost at once had left on the jaunt JB mentions.

[7] Alexander Maxwell (d. 1781) was an Edinburgh wine-merchant, a son of Sir William Maxwell, 4th Bt. of Calderwood.

[8] Andrew Wilson (1718–91), physician in Newcastle, was a Scot, M.D. of Edinburgh and Fellow of the Royal College of Physicians there. John Boswell lived with him at various times until 1775, when he moved to London to become physician to the Medical Asylum (DNB; Journ. 18 Mar. 1768,

10 Feb. 1775; To W. J. Temple, 21 Sept. 1772).

[9] Sir Francis Blake Delaval (1727–71), K.B., had been M.P. for Hindon, Wiltshire, from 1751–54, and for Andover, 1754–68 (G. F. Barker and A. H. Stenning, *Record of Old Westminsters*, 1928, i. 258). The Delavals were large landowners in Northumberland and knew how to cultivate popularity. Sir Francis is said to have canvassed for the votes of prospective constituents at Andover by discharging a gun loaded with gold coins into the midst of them. "The manner of his death was as extraordinary as the general plan of his life. He dined with some intimate friends, and eat very heartily, particularly of a haunch of venison. After dinner he found a pain in his stomach, which he attributed to indigestion, and desired some usquebagh, of which he drank pretty plentifully, and it afforded him a temporary relief. Finding it however insufficient to remove his complaints, he was supposed to make an effort to call his servant, but unfortunately fell down, struck out one of his teeth, contused one side of his head, and immediately expired" (*Town and Country Magazine*, 1771, iii. 422–23). JB was surprised at the meagre attendance at his

state here the night before, and this day it was carried through the town in solemn procession in its way to the family vault. Dr. Wilson carried us to the house of Mr. Davidson an Attorney and presently under-Sherrif,[10] where we saw the procession. Sir Francis was the head of the Patriots here; so it might have been expected that his funeral would have had a great following. But it seems a dead Patriot is not minded in England; for there were only a few people of fashion, some mourners, and his tenants and we could perceive no grief in any of their faces. We this day took an early dinner at the Inn and then took a drive to Tinmouth Castle about nine miles down the Tyne. Here we saw the ruins of a very fine old Abbacy and fortifications; but the stone is much mouldered away by the sea air. The Driver told us that in his remembrance there were statues of the twelve Apostles there; but no vestiges of them are now to be seen. This ancient fabrick is demolished by people who carry away the stone for building. We had here a fine view of the mouth of the Tyne. We then saw the Barracks hard by this. They were built during the last war and seem to be very comfortable quarters. There is a fort just below them. We then drove to the town of North-Shiels which is one of the strangest places I ever saw. It is just one narrow street along the river quite crowded and mostly filled up with butchers stalls as they kill the beef here for victualling the ships. We observed here a most extraordinary Advertisement posted up in the form of a Play Bill telling that there was to be seen *A lively Representation of our Saviour's Passion*. This was a strange Shew in a Protestant Country. I remember Mr. Whitefield gives an account of his seeing such a Representation on the stage at Lisbon.[11] But this was only a set of Basso Relievos in Marble which had been taken in the Spanish Ship the Hermione[12] and were exhibited over England.

funeral because he had been a supporter of Wilkes's popular policies and had impoverished himself by his extravagant generosity.

[10] Thomas Davidson, attorney and Clerk of the Peace for Northumberland, had offices in the Bigg Market, Newcastle. He married Eleanor, daughter of William Lowes of Ridley Hall, and they had five sons and two daughters. He died at Long Benton on 27 Nov. 1781, aged 59, and was buried in All Saints Church, Newcastle (*Gent. Mag.*, 1781, li. 594;

information from the City Librarian, Reference Library, Central Library, Newcastle, 17 May 1963).

[11] Letter IV in George Whitefield's *Brief Account of Some Lent and Other Extraordinary Processions and Ecclesiastical Entertainments Seen Last Year at Lisbon. In Four Letters to an English Friend*, 1755.

[12] The *Hermione*, a Spanish register ship on its return from Lima to Cadiz, had been captured on 21 May 1762 off Cape St. Vincent by three English frigates

They were gone by this time; so we could not see them. We saw the Keels going down the river with Coals. The Keels are small open boats which carry the coals down to the mouth of the river where they are thrown with shovels into the Vessels that carry them to the different harbours and are called Colliers. It is astonishing how extensive the coal trade here is But the Coallieries near the sea are beginning to fail. They drive them now twelve miles at some places. They have waggon ways made from all their Coalpits and a Gentleman will get £500 a year merely for allowing such a way to pass through his estate. And sometimes one who has a great Coalliery will hire the exclusive privilege of a waggon way through an estate merely to prevent a neighbouring proprietor of coal from getting it conveyed to the shore. We supt at Dr. Wilsons, where was Mr. Stothart a Surgeon a droll talkative fellow.[13] Dr. Wilson is truly a Philosopher.[14] He is constantly meditating and prying into the reasons of things and has hit upon many ingenious thoughts. He is a good Physician and is coming into great business. On Saturday we breakfasted at Dr. Wilson's, and then he shewed us the town. An old friend of mine Mr. Bigge[15] the present High Sherrif of Northumberland came to town and walked a while with us. We dined at Dr. Wilson's, and

and carried into Gibraltar. Its treasure, after deduction of all charges, was valued at £519,705. 10s., the 110 common seamen involved in its capture each receiving £484. 2s. 5d. in prize money. The "Basso Relievos in Marble" (no doubt a set of stations of the cross) are not itemized in the condensed "Account of the Value of the *Hermione* Prize", but may be included in the general article "By sundry trinkets, etc. etc. sold to sundries" for £424. 7s. 7d. (*Gent. Mag.*, 1762, xxxii. 339, 549; 1763, xxxiii. 385). George A. Kubler, Professor of the History of Art at Yale, suggests that they may have been polychrome carvings in a kind of alabaster found in the Central Andes of Peru, called Huamanga stone. Examples, showing both secular and religious subjects, are spread throughout Latin America and occur in Spain. Some of these are described in an illustrated article by Mercedes Gallagher de Parks, "La Escultura costumbrista y popular en

piedra de Huamanga", *Actas y trabajos científicos del XXVII Congreso Internacional de Americanistas*, Lima, 1939, ii (1942). 3–15.

[13] Not identified.

[14] Andrew Wilson's publications included not only medical but also philosophical works, e.g. *Short Observations on the Principles and Moving Powers assumed by the Present System of Philosophy*, 1764. On one occasion he showed JB "a little essay he had written on the Douglas Cause" (Journ. 18 Mar. 1768).

[15] JB had formed his friendship with Thomas Charles Bigge (1739–94) in Rome in the spring of 1765 and had renewed the acquaintance in London in the spring of 1768 (Burke's *Commoners*, 1834, i. 632; Mem. 13 Apr.–13 June 1765 *passim*, 8, 9 Aug. 1765; Notes, 22, 27 Apr. 1768). Bigge's seat, Benton House, was three miles beyond Newcastle on the road to Tynemouth (John Cary, *New Itinerary*, 3rd ed., 1806, p. 438).

then drove to Durham. Here Mr. Maxwell joined us again. On Sunday we went to the grand Cathedral which is truly a noble Gothick structure and heard solemn service. We then saw the Prebends walk which is romantick and most agreable. I then called on Miss Dick sister to Sir John.[16] We then dined, and drove back again to Newcastle. We put up at Dr. Wilson's and spent the evening very comfortably. Yesterday we set out, dined at Morpeth and got here at night. I sent for the Rev. Mr. Percy who published the *Reliques of Ancient English Poetry*[17] and he came and sat an hour with us; but was obliged to return to the Castle where the Duke of Cumberland[18] was. This morning all the Northumberland family are gone to Berwick with the Duke of Cumberland. The Corporation gives a dinner and the Duke of Northumberland a Ball. We are invited to the latter; but I doubt much if we shall get forward; for all the horses have been engaged and we are afraid the Duke and his retinue may carry them on to Berwick.[19] We have however

[16] John Dick (1720–1804), British Consul at Leghorn since 1754, whom JB had met at Florence in the summer of 1765, had been very helpful in collecting materials for the *Account of Corsica*. He believed himself to be heir to the dormant baronetcy of Sir William Dick of Braid (c. 1580–1655), Lord Provost of Edinburgh, from whom Sir Alexander Dick of Prestonfield was also maternally descended, but he had not claimed the title because he had no child to inherit it and did not wish to incur the expense involved. JB brought him to the attention of Sir Alexander, who searched the family papers in his possession for proofs of the claim. As a result of their activities, John Dick was in 1768 served heir to Sir William Dick by a jury in Edinburgh, and assumed the baronetcy. The *Complete Baronetage* (ii. 448–49) is sceptical, maintaining that Sir William Dick was probably not a baronet, and that in any case John Dick's claim to be his heir male was a doubtful one (Notes, 13–24 Aug. 1765 *passim*; From John Dick, 6 Oct. 1766, 6 Mar., 11 May, 17 June, 29 July, 29 Oct. 1767, 30 June 1768; To Sir Alexander Dick, 16 Apr., 2 Sept. 1767, 18 April 1768; *Edinburgh Advertiser*, 18–22 Mar. 1768, ix. 189). John Dick is reported to have had two sisters, Isabella and Mary (Sir Robert Douglas, *Baronage of Scotland*, 1798, p. 274) but it is uncertain which of these JB now called on.

[17] Percy's *Reliques of Ancient English Poetry* had appeared in 1765. A second edition had been published in 1767, and a third was to be called for in 1775. At this time he was vicar of Easton Maudit and rector of Wilby, both in Northamptonshire, and also chaplain to the Duke of Northumberland, to whom he claimed to be distantly related. He had edited the *Household Book of the Earls of Northumberland in 1512*, and was frequently in attendance on the Duke when he was in residence at Alnwick Castle or Northumberland House, London.

[18] Prince Henry Frederick (1745–90), 4th son of Frederick, Prince of Wales, was "probably the most foolish of Frederick's sons" (*Comp. Peer.* v. 744). It was his marriage, in Oct. 1771, to Mrs. Anne Horton of Catton Hall, Derbyshire, against the wishes of George III, that led to the passing of the Royal Marriage Act in 1772.

[19] That is, JB cannot follow the Duke and his party until some of the Alnwick horses are sent back from the next post stage, Belford, and he is afraid that the

been making the most of it. Monsieur Dutens[20] formerly Resident at Turin and now an English Clergyman, who has been making the tour of Europe with Lord Algernon Percy is left in the Castle. He shewed us the inside of it—and an old Porter shewed us the outside. We have also seen the Garden. When we meet, you shall hear more particularly about it. This is but an unpleasant Situation to be as we say in Scotland *poinded*[21] at an Inn. However the weather is fine, and we are in good spirits.

Some horses are just come back; and we find the horses at the next stage will be taken up, and there will be such a crowd and confusion at Berwick which we could not reach till ten or eleven o clock at night, that we have resolved to shun it, and cross into the road we came and turning off a little visit the Abbacy of Melrose. So my dear Grange adieu and believe me ever your most affectionate friend.

JAMES BOSWELL

My wife sends you her best compliments.

To Johnston, Sunday 20 October 1771

MS. The Misses Carlyle of Waterbeck, Dumfriesshire. Sent 21 Oct. 1771 (Reg. Let.).

ADDRESS: To John Johnston Esq: of Grange in Annandale. By Langholm.

POSTMARK: DUMFRIES

ENDORSEMENT: Auchinleck 20th October 1771, received at Langholm the 31st Octr.

Auchinleck, 20 October 1771

DEAR GRANGE: Since we parted at the foot of the Bow, I believe

shortage of horses there may be such that the Alnwick ones will not be returned. As he indicates later in this letter, some horses did come back, but not in time to give the Boswells a chance of reaching Berwick at a reasonable hour. So JB decided to cross to the Coldstream route and from Coldstream follow the Tweed up to Melrose.

[20] JB had met Louis Dutens (1730–1812) at Turin in 1765 (Journ. 9, 11 Jan.). A French Huguenot, Dutens was already at that time in Anglican orders, though JB seems not to have known it.

He had gone out as chaplain to the British Ambassador at Turin, Stuart Mackenzie, Lord Bute's brother, and had twice served the Crown as *chargé d'affaires* there. Having been appointed to a living in the north of England, he spent much time at Alnwick, where he was a favourite of the Duke and Duchess. Lord Algernon Percy, their second son, was put in his charge while making the tour of Europe which is described in Dutens's *Memoirs of a Traveller now in Retirement*, 1806.

[21] Scots: impounded.

I may say at the foot of the gallows,[1] I have been as well as you could wish me. The complaint[2] which I had is quite removed by sober regular living, country air and exercise. I have been serving an apprenticeship with my father in the art of pruning, and I hope in time, to be a skillful and diligent Guardian of the trees here. My father has been as good as his word, in giving me a college[3] upon the Election-Law of Scotland, mixed with it's Antiquities, which illustrate it in an entertaining manner, and without which, one cannot have a full and clear knowledge of it. My father just dictated to me a System, which I took down in writing, and which will be a valuable collection.[4] I can say with truth that I have been employing my time to good purpose.

At the same time, I must tell you that I have suffered much more than any body would imagine, on account of so long a separation from my wife.[5] You know my worthy friend with what uncommon affection and true happiness she and I live together. To be deprived of that inestimable blessing for day after day and week after week (for so I have counted the time though it is not four weeks yet since I left her) has seriously distressed me. I have been seised with fits of impatience and my heart has fluttered like a bird confined in a cage, and I have had the most anxious apprehensions about her, while my strong imagination has in the silence and solitude of night presented to me such dreary thoughts as are the more afflicting that we can have no certainty but they may be realised. Thank God she is in much better health than when I left her; and although I find that she has been suffering in the same manner with myself, I please myself with the cheerful prospect that when we meet all our uneasiness will at once fly away and it's remembrance only serve to increase our happiness. This, my good friend, is not a very polite letter, as it is all taken up in

---

[1] The gallows in Edinburgh were erected for public executions in the Grassmarket at a point opposite the foot of the West Bow. William Pickworth, a 24-year-old soldier in the 22nd Regiment of Foot, convicted of a robbery, had been hanged there on 25 Sept. 1771 (*Scots Mag.*, 1771, xxxiii. 497–98). It sounds from this letter as though JB and JJ had attended the execution together, immediately before JB left Edinburgh for Auchinleck.

[2] This complaint is not otherwise recorded.

[3] *Ante* 23 Sept. 1763, n. 11.

[4] JB's MS. of Lord Auchinleck's *Observations on the Election Law of Scotland* has been deposited in the National Library of Scotland by its owner, Lady Talbot de Malahide. The text was privately printed in 1825.

[5] Mrs. Boswell had probably remained in Edinburgh.

writing about my wife; but I know how much you rejoice at my happiness; and I am sure I wish you to be as happy as I am.

I am to attend a ⟨::::::::::⟩ poor cause[6] on Thursday; and on friday I set out from Treesbank, and hope to be in town on Saturday. My sister in law Mrs. Campbell is to go in with me and stay a forthnight with us.[7] ⟨She⟩ is a worthy good woman, and you would like her much. I wish you would come in a day or two before the Session sits down, that you may see her. I fear we shall not be able to keep her above a forthnight from her family. Lady Mary Scott's Elopement[8] would surprise and vex you. Poor young Creature, to reduce herself at once from such grand prospects to absolute misery and disgrace, in the very bloom of life. I sincerely pity her relations. Sir John Douglas and Mr. Grierson of the Ayr Bank[9] are here tonight. I send this by them to Dumfries. Pray why do you not exert yourself? why not boldly jump at the hass[10] of her? *Verbum sat Sapienti.* I hope you have enjoyed health and

[6] This may refer to a meeting of the Kirk Session and Heritors to draw up lists of poor persons in need of relief, and to fix the contribution to be paid by the proprietors and tenants of the parish, or (less probably) to a meeting of the Justices of the Peace to appoint an overseer of the poor. It is not likely that JB is referring to any appearance by himself as counsel.

[7] *Ante* 22 May 1771, n. 1.

[8] Lady Mary Hay (b. 1754), eldest daughter of the 15th Earl of Erroll, had married, less than twelve months before, General John Scott of Balcomie, M.P. for Fife, a fortunate gambler who had acquired many estates and was considered the wealthiest commoner in Scotland (*Scots Peer.* iii. 581; ix. 87). In 1771 she eloped with James Sutherland of Duffus, a captain in the 26th Regt. of Foot (see *Town and Country Mag.*, 1771, iii. 516–18, for a highly coloured account of this affair). General Scott divorced her on 18 Dec. 1771 (*Consistorial Processes and Decreets, 1658–1800*, No. 583), and in 1773 married as his second wife Margaret, third daughter of the Lord President, Robert Dundas of Arniston.

[9] The ill-fated Ayr bank was also known as Douglas, Heron & Co. from the names of its chief promoters, Archibald Douglas of Douglas and Patrick Heron of Heron. Founded in Nov. 1769, it suspended payments in June 1772 and closed all transactions in Aug. 1773, ruining many Ayrshire families (James Paterson, *History of the Counties of Ayr and Wigton*, 1863, i. 38–39). JB was moved by its failure to write his pamphlet *Reflections on the Late Alarming Bankruptcies in Scotland* (*Lit. Car.*, pp. 89–92) which appeared in Nov. 1772. Sir John Douglas of Kelhead (c. 1708–78), 3rd Bt., was the son of a half-sister of JB's mother, Euphemia Erskine. He had been imprisoned after the Forty-five on suspicion of treason, but had never been brought to trial and had finally been released for want of clear evidence against him (*Comp. Bar.* iv. 266–67). JB visited Kelhead during his Harvest Jaunt of 1762, and wrote an account of it and of the family (Journ. 6 Oct. 1762). Mr. Grierson was presumably Charles Grierson, sub-cashier at the Edinburgh branch of the bank (*Scots Mag.*, 1769, xxxi. 669).

[10] That is, "halse", meaning either "neck" or "embrace". William Johnstone of Lockerbie, father of Grace Johnstone, lived at The Hass, Lockerbie (*ante* 22 May 1771, n. 8; *post* 27 Mar. 1772, n. 3).

tranquillity this autumn. But you are really too indolent. Mr. Dun[11] complains that he never hears from you. I tell him that I would not hear either, were it not that I am allways attacking your indolence, so that every letter which I write to you, is serving you with a libel. It is giving you a Charge which you must answer in so many days. Make my kind compliments to Shaw Mr. Christopher Caruthers, Mr. Joseph Fergusson and all friends, and pray let me hear from you before the Session. I am ever your most sincere friend

JAMES BOSWELL

From Johnston, Saturday 2 November 1771

MS. Yale (C 1632).

ADDRESS: To James Boswell Esqr. Younger of Auchinleck, Edinburgh.

POSTMARK: LANGHOLM.

Knottyholm, 2d. Novr. 1771

DEAR SIR: I have been here two days. Just now when I was Setting out for Grange I received your letter[1] from Langholm. I ought to have had it on Thursday Se'ennight at Dumfries, where I met with Sir John Douglas at a Meeting of the Gentlemen of this County. He very politely informed me that he had been at Auchinleck, and of the wellfare of you and the family, but certainly had forgotten that he had a letter for me, and afterwards upon recollecting it, had put it into the post office;

I have been variously employed Since we parted, though neither in a way very agreeable or profitable, but I am determined to be alwise as well pleased as I can, and make the most of life. Upon the road from Edr. I was Seized with a violent pain in my back, Something like a Rheumatism. It confined me three days at Crook a publick house twelve miles from Moffat. I felt great pain, and was a little dreary, by being ill in So remote a place where I had none of my friends nor proper assistance. I found out that Mr. Hunter of Polmood was at home Lady Caroline Drakes husband[2]

---

[11] *Ante* 19 July 1763, n. 1.

[1] *Ante* 20 Oct. 1771.
[2] Walter Hunter (d. 1796) of Polmood and Crailing had married Caroline, a daughter of George Mackenzie, 3rd Earl of Cromartie, who was the widow of a Captain Drake (*Scots Peer*. iii. 81). The ownership of the estate of Polmood, in Peeblesshire, situated about 15 miles north of Moffat, was the subject of litigation in the Scots courts for some half-century after the death of Thomas Hunter in March 1765. Some weeks earlier he

who lives in that neighbourhood. As I was a little acquainted with him and knew he was bred a Surgeon, I Sent to him to come to me, which he very frankly did, and after blooding me plentifully I was much relieved, and after Staying two days, found myself able to travell. I thank kind heaven that I am almost quite well. I have been obliged to travell a good deal, in very bad weather, that prevented my being well Sooner. I find it is usefull to be ill Sometimes, it makes one think Seriously, and gives a double relish to good health.

You know I proposed taking a proof in Johnstons Reduction this vaccation. After finding out proper witnesses, being at much trouble on that hand, fixing a day for the proof and Mr. Crosbie[3] to attend it, our Client who had come from England to See how the proof turned out, very foolishly agreed with his brother on most disadvantageous terms, without, nay Contrary to my advice, as I had good reason to believe that we could have proven the incapacity of the Father very Clearly. I have a notion that he was affraid of the proof of Character that induced him to make it up.[4]

had executed a disposition of the estate in favour of Alexander Hunter, banker in Edinburgh, to whom he was not related, and it was this deed which persons claiming to be the rightful heirs of the old family of Hunter of Polmood endeavoured unsuccessfully to have reduced by the courts. Walter Hunter, who assisted JJ, although described by him as "of Polmood" was not at this date the legal owner but nephew and heir of Alexander Hunter, who did not die until 1786 (*Scots Mag.* xlviii. 51). Doubtless his uncle had placed the estate in his care soon after he acquired it. He was eventually served heir to it in 1787, when he was described as a "surgeon in the artillery at Guadeloupe" (*A History of Peeblesshire*, ed. J. W. Buchan and Henry Paton, 1925–27, iii. 456–61; *Original Portraits* i. 44–45).

[3] Andrew Crosbie (1736–85) of Holm was one of the most distinguished advocates then at the Edinburgh bar, and JB had a profound respect for his knowledge and abilities. Ramsay of Ochtertyre gives an account of him (*Scotland and Scotsmen* i. 449), and he is said to have been the prototype of Scott's Councillor Pleydell in *Guy Mannering*. He built up a fortune by his practice and lost most of it in the failure of the Ayr Bank of Douglas, Heron, & Co. When he died he left so little to support his widow that she was obliged to apply for a pension of £50 a year from the Faculty of Advocates (Frank Miller, *Andrew Crosbie: a reported Original of Paulus Pleydell in "Guy Mannering"*, 1925; James Maidment, *The Court of Session Garland*, 1871, p. 93).

[4] Presumably in this case one of the sons of a man named Johnston sought to have the provisions of his father's will "reduced", i.e. annulled, on the ground that his father had been induced in some illegal way to leave an undue proportion of his property to another son. JJ, believing his claim to be sound, had spent much time assembling evidence of the father's incapacity and the second brother's complicity, and had planned to get Andrew Crosbie to present the case as advocate for his client. He had been obliged to abandon it because his client had come to some arrangement with his brother, on terms disadvantageous to himself, in order to avoid a too searching inquiry into his own record.

I was a little vext at his yeilding up his right So tamely, when it appeared to me So plainly that this Deed was obtained by unfair means, but I believe both brothers are very worthless, that we are well quit of them. I fancy I shall find Some difficulty in being repaid my outgivings, with very little if any thing for my trouble.

My best wishes to Mrs. Boswell. I am happy to hear that you are both recovered So well. Your meeting in good health and Spirits would make a return for the uneasieness occasioned by your absence; I return you my hearty thanks for your kind letter, and your good wishes and friendship that I have So long enjoyed without any interruption; I hope to See you about the end of the week after next. Farewell my dear Sir and believe [me] Yours most Sincerely while

JOHN JOHNSTON

P.S. I saw Captain Huggan[5] at Dumfries and had much Conversation with him. I think him a Worthy Young Man. He made the most kind inquirys about your Lady and You. He speaks of being in Edinburgh a few days this Winter, before he goes abroad to join his Regiment. You'll hear if Lord Auchinleck advises Borelands process[6] before I come to Town.

---

[5] James Hoggan, a captain in the 51st Regt. of Foot, had been in Ireland when JB visited Belfast in 1769. He had been a classfellow of JB and JJ at Edinburgh University (Robert Hunter's matriculation list, 10 Mar. 1756) and was well known to them both, as well as to Joseph Fergusson, who, writing to JB in 1780, after Hoggan's death, recalled him as a "sprightly youth" (20 Mar. 1780). He was presumably the eldest son of Captain James Hoggan of the 3rd Dragoons, who was factor to the Earl of Mansfield and lived at Comlongan Castle. It was there, in Jan. 1746, that the elder James Hoggan managed by his pleading to save from the retreating Highlanders the horses of the Marchioness of Annandale, who rented Comlongan at that time from Lord Stormont (C. L. Johnstone, *History of the Johnstones*, 1909). He had married Sophia, daughter of Sir James Johnstone of Westerhall, and had four sons—James, who died in Bath; Charles, an officer in the navy; John, in the merchant service; and George, a nabob, who bought the estate of Watersyde for £4,300 in 1782 (*Local Parish Histories and New Statistical Account. 16th parish. Keir. Presbytery of Penpont and Synod of Dumfries. No. V*, a typescript supplied by Mrs. Molly Johnston, née Hoggan, Portland Square, Carlisle).

[6] Grieves, &c. *v.* Borland, with JJ as agent and JB as advocate, is listed four times in JB's Consultation Book during 1771 and 1772. The first mention after the date of this letter occurs on 25 Jan. 1772. Apparently the case did not come up for some time after the sitting of the Winter Session.

To Johnston, Friday 27 March 1772

MS. The Misses Carlyle of Waterbeck, Dumfriesshire. Sent 24 Mar. 1772 (Reg. Let.).[1]

London, 27 March 1772

MY DEAR FRIEND: You will not as yet I hope have allowed yourself to imagine that there has been any neglect on my part towards you. I know indeed that in the present state of your mind, you cannot help being much readier to feel in a strong manner the slightest and most innocent appearances, than you would be at another time to feel greater ones. You know how much I sympathise with you under every uneasiness, and I am sure you cannot doubt my sincere wishes to be able to comfort you and make you happy. I hope your little jaunt northwards did you some good. Loch wrote me in a jocular way that amidst the frost and snow Grange had set out on a jaunt of *pleasure*. It was however really so, in a certain sense, for I can figure such scenes suiting your imagination better, than all the gayety of summer. Honest Hoggan is here.[2] He has found me excellent lodgings and is most kind and obliging in every respect. We often talk of you with much regard. I suppose he knows nothing of a certain affair. He however says that a certain Lady will repent her marriage, all her life.[3] Her husband has never called upon me: Pretty curious.

I find myself somewhat hurried and dissipated amidst this hurry and noise and variety; but not much so. The Schoolmaster's cause is fixed for Monday the 14 of April.[4] I am not afraid of his cause; nor under any uneasiness at the thoughts of appearing at the bar of the house of Lords; for I see that a man has the fairest and most mild and candid hearing.

[1] Probably an error in recording this letter.

[2] JB, who had arrived in London on 19 Mar., tells in his journal (20 Mar. 1772) of driving with Captain Hoggan in a hackney coach to look at lodgings in the house of a glover named King, in Conduit Street.

[3] Grace Johnstone (*ante* 22 May 1771, n. 8; 20 Oct. 1771, n. 10) had married in Edinburgh on 21 Mar. JB's cousin William Douglas, who was to succeed in 1778 to the baronetcy of Kelhead. Her eldest son Charles became 5th Marquis of Queensberry, and the family of Johnstone-Douglas is descended from her (*Scots Peer*. vii. 151).

[4] JB was to plead before the House of Lords on behalf of John Hastie, the Campbeltown schoolmaster who had been dismissed for being too severe in his punishment of the children in his charge. In an appeal to the Court of Session Hastie had won his cause and had been restored, but his accusers had carried the matter to the higher court. For an argument dictated by Dr. Johnson for JB's use in this case, see *Life* ii. 183-85.

Adieu my worthy friend, for this time. Keep up your spirits, and let me hear from you from time to time. I ever am most cordially and steadily Semper Idem.

JAMES BOSWELL

From Johnston, Saturday 18 April 1772

MS. Yale (C 1633). Received 24 Apr. 1772 (Reg. Let.). Forwarded from Auchinleck to London.

ADDRESS: To James Boswell Esqr Younger of Auchinleck.

Edinburgh, 18th. April 1772

MY DEAR SIR: I return you my most hearty thanks for the obliging Letter[1] you Sent me. It gave me real comfort and relieved me much. To have the Sympathy of an honest worthy friend gives Strength and Courage to the Mind that is depressed. This I have felt very Sensibly from the kind concern you have Shown for me in a late affair; Your last Letter has done me much good, I often read it when I find myself uneasie. I will Carry it with me to the Country to peruse when I am Solitary and thoughtfull. There you know I have no person that I can Communicate my mind to, but I propose taking much exercise, which with a little time will put me right: My late Jaunt was of great Service to me. You guessed right with respect to the Weather, the Sharpness of the Air and bleakness of the Country Suited me better than Softer Scenes. I went round by Stirling to Dunkeld and returned by Perth, Falkland, St Andrews, and then alongst the Coast of Fife to Kinghorn. I was out Seven days, and during that time was in good health and Spirits, and very happy with my Companion G. Kirkpatrick,[2] but in a few days after I returned, I found myself relapse to my former State, and Still am very uneasie, and incapable of fixing my attention on any particular Subject. I could not even think of writing you, being oppressed with a foolish timidity that makes me affraid of putting my thoughts upon any Subject in Writing.

I have Seen Mrs. Boswell frequently. She is pretty well, and by the time you return, I hope you'll find her perfectly recovered.[3]

[1] *Ante* 27 Mar. 1772.
[2] George Kirkpatrick (d. 1796), Depute Clerk of Session, one of the friends whom JJ appointed trustees under his will.

[3] Mrs. Boswell had suffered a miscarriage. See Notes 28 Feb., 3 Mar. 1772; From W. J. Temple 26 Mar., 3 Apr. 1772.

I was blaming her for being So much alone, indeed She has not many people here at present that She can be quite easy with, and these you know are the only company that are agreeable to a person recovering from any illness. I Saw her last night. She was anxious anent your appearance in the house of Lords. I hope it is now over to your liking.[4] Let me know how your Cause is determined, and how you felt on that occasion. I am Just now Setting out for Annandale, which I do with Some reluctance, but I find it necessary to go there. To morrows night I will be with honest Schaw. Remember me kindly to Captain Hoggan. I Suppose the Letter I wrote him did not come to his hand before he left the Country, but there is no loss to him in that. When you are at leisure be So good as write to me at Grange by Carlisle and Langholm. Accept of my best wishes and believe me alwise Yours Most Sincerely while

JOHN JOHNSTON

To Johnston, Saturday 9 May, Monday 11 May 1772

MS. The Misses Carlyle of Waterbeck, Dumfriesshire.

ADDRESS (in Dempster's hand): John Johnstone Esqr. Grange, Carlisle and Langholm.
FRANK: Free G. Dempster
POSTMARK: 11 MA

London, 9 May 1772

MY DEAR JOHNSTON, Your kind letter written just before you left Edinburgh, gave me sincere pleasure, because it shewed me that amidst your own uneasiness you still retained a warm friendship for me. I hope that before this time, the air and exercise of the country, seeing your trees grow and necessary occupations will have dissipated any clouds, and that you are as cheerful and happy as I wish you. For my part I have passed a most agreable spring here. I only regret that my valuable spouse and I have been separated, which has given considerable anxiety and uneasiness to both of us, and which therefore I am resolved shall never again happen for so long a time while we are in this world. Excepting this circumstance I have had almost compleat felicity since ever

---

[4] The judgement of the Court of Session was reversed and JB's client lost his case (Journ. 14 Apr. 1772).

I came to London, admirable health fine spirits, the conversation of the first geniuses. I am now sitting in Mr. Samuel Johnson's study. Dempster and I are to dine tête á tête at the St. Alban's Tavern, at six I go and see Mr. Garrick act in *The Wonder*,[1] and after the Play I sup at his house. There is a Specimen of a day. My Journal will shew you all the rest.[2]

I pleaded my Client the Schoolmaster of Campbelltown's cause in the House of Lords; and though Lord Mansfield spoke for reversing the Decree whi⟨ch I was defending⟩ he spoke won-de⟨rfully well. As for me,⟩ although my C⟨lient lost, I myself⟩ gained credit⟨. Lord Mansfield said⟩ that I really spoke very ⟨well.⟩

On monday morning, the ⟨day⟩ after tomorrow, I set out.[3] Our friend Hoggan is to be my companion. We are to go the west road by Carlisle and Langholm, and he engages to give me a convoy as far as Hawick. I hope my wife will meet me there. You must be kind enough to be at Langholm on friday forenoon, and meet us there, and go with us to Hawick. It will be an admirable friendly meeting, and you will return with Hoggan. Now pray come. God bless you My Dear Johnston. I am ever your most affectionate friend,

JAMES BOSWELL

Monday 11 May

DEAR GRANGE: Mr. Johnson dined with Mr. Dempster and me on Saturday. I set out only tomorrow. If this reaches you in time we shall meet on friday.

[1] *The Wonder! a Woman Keeps a Secret*, by Mrs. Susannah Centlivre (largely borrowed from *The Wrangling Lovers*, 1676, by Edward Ravenscroft) was first performed at Drury Lane, 27 Apr. 1714. The character of Don Felix was a favourite part of Garrick's. It was as Don Felix in *The Wonder* that he was to make his farewell appearance in June 1776 before retiring from the stage (John Genest, *Some Account of the English Stage, 1660–1830*, 1832, ii. 526; v. 497–98).

[2] The journal for the period, which exists only in rough jottings (MS. Yale J 25), seems to indicate a change of plans. SJ having offered to join JB and Dempster at dinner, JB appears to have given up the play, so as to have more time for conversation. When SJ and Dempster left him, he went to the Bedford Coffee-house and wrote letters till it was time to go to Garrick's. It was on this occasion that Garrick displayed "his exquisite talent for mimickry" by taking off SJ and his wife Tetty "so as to excite the heartiest bursts of laughter" (Notes 9 May 1772; *Life* i. 99, ii. 195).

[3] JB's condensed journal for Monday 11 May indicates that he spent the day in leave-taking calls. He left early on the following day, after only two hours' sleep, stayed overnight at Loughborough, Manchester, Shap, and Hawick, and was home on the 16th (Notes 11–16 May).

To Johnston, Wednesday 3 June 1772

MS. Yale (L 808).

ADDRESS: To John Johnston Esq: of Grange in Annandale, By Langholm.

ENDORSEMENT: Edinr. 3d. June 1772, received on the 24th. from the Country, James Boswell.

POSTMARK: JU 3.

Edinburgh, 3 June 1772

MY DEAR JOHNSTON: If the letter[1] which I wrote to you a little before setting out from London has reached you, I dare say you will regret that we did not meet at Langholm, as I flattered myself we might do. I went to the Post-house there; but could get no intelligence about you; nor did they remember a letter having lately come for you. However I trust that before this, you have received it, and probably have also seen our worthy friend Hoggan. He has his uneasy circumstances as well as others. But by this time I hope your uneasiness is over, and you have seen that your own generosity deceived you, by making you expect that valuable quality in a mercenary being. I will not let you excuse her; for if ever there was a faithless, Lammas-fair conduct[2] hers was so. Were you an ordinary kind of man, you have met with a loss; but as you are a man of real honour and delicacy, you are well rid of her.[3]

I have just got free from the Church Court,[4] by which I cleared

---

[1] *Ante* 9 May 1772.

[2] Lammas, the 1st of August, a quarter-day and general holiday in Scotland and the occasion for holding fairs in many localities, provided plenty of opportunity for short-lived flirtations.

[3] *Ante* 22 May 1771, n. 8; 20 Oct. 1771, n. 10; 27 Mar. 1772, n. 3.

[4] The Consultation Book records fees of thirty-five guineas in ten causes. Five of these (St. Ninians, Kinglassie, Kirkhill, Lintrathen, and Portpatrick) had been debated in 1771 and are annotated above, 22 May 1771, n. 11. The five new causes were *People of Marykirk v.* Patron, *People of Neilston v.* Patron, *People of Rathen v.* Patron, *Haddoway, etc. of Leith v.* Robertson, etc., and *Wallace v. Steven.* The last named, according to JB's own note, "did not come on", but some particulars of the others are avail-able. The Neilston and Rathen causes, which were heard by the Commission on 2 June 1772, consisted of the usual objections of parishes to presentees not of the people's choice (*Scots Mag.*, 1772, xxiv. 396). Haddoway *v.* Robertson, heard by the Commission on 1 June, concerned efforts by the parties to control the election to the second charge of the South Church at Leith by packing the representation from the kirk session (*Scots Mag.*, 1772, xxiv. 395–96). By far the most interesting of the new causes was that of Marykirk, pleaded before the General Assembly on 27 May 1772. In 1766 King's College, Aberdeen, had sold at auction the patronage of sixteen churches in its gift. John Brymer of Marnock-kirk, styled by the respondents a merchant and by the appellants an inn-keeper, had purchased

my house-rent, and five guineas in to the bargain. My wife is really very well; and I believe we shall go out for a few days to Sir Alexr. Dick's.

This has been a melancholy season in one respect. Within these few days we have heard of the death of Mr. Boyd at Donaghadee[5] a very worthy Gentleman husband to my wifes cousin german—of Mr. Wellwood's second son[6] and of Mr. Chalmers brother to Miss Chalmers in company with Miss Cochran,[7] and of poor Sandie Preston[8] who died yesterday morning at Valleyfield of a few days illness. We must endeavour to make the best improvement of such *mementoes*, and hold life loosely, though with a due care.

I suppose you know of the death of poor Mr. Stewart your Landlord.[9]

I beg you may be so good as pay Captain Hoggan eight pounds

the patronage of Marykirk, and when the parish became vacant in 1771, had presented his own son to the charge. The settlement had been appealed on the ground of simony. After full hearing, the Assembly affirmed the sentences of the synod and presbytery without a vote (*Scots Mag.*, 1772, xxiv. 271). Nearly a year later *The London Magazine* printed a series of articles by JB on "Debates in the General Assembly of the Church of Scotland" in which this cause was prominently featured, with reports of various speeches, including JB's own and that of the opposing counsel (*Lond. Mag.*, xlii., April–July 1773, *passim*. The MS. records of the General Assembly refer to these causes in Register of Assembly, 1772, pp. 102–05, 170; Register of Commission, 1772, pp. 218–26, 236–41).

[5] Hugh Boyd of Donaghadee, an Irish Collector of Excise, was the uncle of Mary Ann Boyd whom JB had visited in Ireland on the occasion when Margaret Montgomerie had been his reluctant companion. Margaret Montgomerie's grandfather had been rector of Donaghadee, and "Aunt Boyd" was the Collector's wife.

[6] George, second son of Robert Wellwood of Garvock and of Mary Preston of the Valleyfield family, who was first cousin of JB's mother, is said by Burke's *Landed Gentry* (1846) to have died in Batavia. He cannot have been more than 26.

[7] The Misses Chalmers and Cochrane were milliners and mantua-makers in Miln's Square (Williamson's *Edinburgh Directory*, 1773–74, p. 19). The identity of Mr. Chalmers remains uncertain; he was probably from out of town or JB would not have identified him for JJ by reference to his sister. A plausible suggestion is that Miss Chalmers the milliner, who appears as such in Williamson's *Directory* of 1777–78, but not in that of 1778–79, was the Cochrane Chalmers, daughter of James Chalmers of Fingland, who in July 1778 married her cousin, Sir Hector Mackenzie of Gairloch. She was descended via her mother from the Cochrane family and her father was tenant of Braehead, one of the farms of the Auchinleck estate. If this identification is correct "Mr. Chalmers", like the others in this small group of persons, would have been related to the Boswells, even if distantly.

[8] Alexander Preston was the second son of Sir George Preston of Valleyfield and an uncle of the Wellwood boy mentioned above. His mother, Anne Cochrane, was JB's great-aunt.

[9] JJ's landlord in Roxburgh's Close. Some time between this date and Oct. 1775, JJ moved into the flat in James's Court which had earlier belonged to hi relative Francis Scott of Johnston.

for me, if you are in cash, as I am unwilling to trust money to the Post. I want to borrow £250 on my personal bond. I will tell you the reason when we meet. In the meantime I wish you would be on the look out for the money.[10] Let me hear from you, and pray come as soon as you can. I ever am most sincerely yours.

JAMES BOSWELL

Tell Hoggan I have received his letter[11] and will write to him soon. My wife joins me in compliments to you and him.

From Johnston, November 1772

Missing. Recd. 7 Nov. 1772. "Grange" (Reg. Let.).

To Johnston, Monday 24 May 1773

Missing. Sent 24 May 1773. "Grange" (Reg. Let.).

From Johnston, June 1773

Missing. Recd. 12 June. "Mr. Johnston" (Reg. Let.).

To Johnston, Wednesday 20 October 1773

MS. Yale (L 809).
ADDRESS: To John Johnston Esq: of Grange.

Cathedral of Icolmkilm,[1] 20 October 1773

MY WORTHY FRIEND: I promised to write to you from this vener-

[10] JB's particular reason for requiring this loan has not been ascertained, but he had probably been living above his income since his marriage and wished to pay off accumulated smaller debts. It was an unfortunate time for anyone to attempt to borrow money, for only a few days later news of the failure in London of the banking firm in which Alexander Fordyce was a partner reached Edinburgh and started a run on the Scottish private banks which was to cause many of them to fail too (Forbes, pp. 39–44). But JB may have obtained his money from the (public) Bank of Scotland, for it is on record that he was at one time allowed by it "credit for £350 on current cash account, his Cautioners being Alexander Donaldson, bookseller, and Matthew Dickie, writer" (*The Bank of Scotland, 1695–1745*, C. A. Malcolm, n.d., p. 275, in which the date of the credit is misprinted 1722 [?1772]).

[11] Received 25 May (Reg. Let.). It has not survived.

[1] JB wrote this letter in pencil and later traced it with ink. It is impossible now to decide whether he really intended a final *m* or produced a character that looked like one by not putting the ink precisely on top of the pencil strokes.

able spot.[2] You know I never fail either in my promises or good offices to you. But at present I would less fail than at any other time; for the sanctity of the place and the sight of the ruined monuments of religion and learning now arround me have thrown me into so excellent a frame that our long friendship has the most lively impressions upon my soul. I am all superstition and warmth of heart. I fervently pray GOD to bless us and make us eternally happy in heaven. It is grand to see the Rambler stalking about[3] as I write   I am ever your most affectionate friend

JAMES BOSWELL

To Johnston, Saturday 21 May 1774

Missing. Sent 21 May 1774. "Grange" (Reg. Let.). Written from Edinburgh, probably to inform JJ of the birth of JB's second daughter, Euphemia, the previous day.

From Johnston, June 1774

Missing. Recd. 13 June. "Grange" (Reg. Let.).

To Johnston, Friday 12 August 1774

MS. Yale (L 810).
ADDRESS: To Mr. Johnston.

[Edinburgh] Friday 12 August 17⟨74⟩

MY DEAR SIR: Mr. Nichols,[1] an english Clergyman an old

[2] Perhaps he wrote Icolmkiln on the analogy of kiln (pronounced "kill"), but he always appears to have used the spelling Icolmkill in his contemporary Hebridean journal.

[2] Touring the Hebrides, JB and SJ had reached Iona on 19 Oct. The letter was written inside the cathedral ruins, after JB had prayed to God and to St. Columba, and had read aloud the 5th chapter of St. James and a sermon of Dr. Ogden's. "I had promised to write to my worthy old friend Grange from Icolmkill. I therefore wrote a short solemn letter to him here. While I was writing it, Mr. J entered, that he might attentively view and even measure the ruins" (Journ. 20 Oct. 1773). JB was no doubt led to write

from this spot by the strong association existing in his mind between JJ and ancient Catholic Scotland.

[3] "As I knew that many persons had already examined them, and as I saw Dr. Johnson inspecting and measuring several of the ruins of which he has since given so full an account, my mind was quiescent; and I resolved to stroll among them at my ease, to take no trouble to investigate minutely, and only receive the general impression of solemn antiquity, and the particular ideas of such objects as should of themselves strike my attention" (Tour, 1785, 20 Oct. 1773).

[1] JB had met Norton Nicholls (c. 1742–1809) in the spring of 1763. Like

acquaintance of mine and a great friend of worthy Temple's sups with me tonight. I insist then that you shall be with us, though you should have to get off from an engagement. Sincerely yours

JAMES BOSWELL

From Johnston, Friday 15 March 1776

MS. Yale (C 1634). Received 29 March 1776. "Grange in friendly concern about me" (Reg. Let.).

ADDRESS: To James Boswell Esqr.

Edinburgh, 15th. March 1776

MY DEAR SIR: I dined to day with Mrs. Boswell, Miss Cunningham[1] and the Children,[2] all in good health. Before we rose from the Table Mr. Lawrie[3] brought from the Post office your Letter to Mrs. Boswell, dated on Tuesday from Newcastle. Mrs. Boswell afterwards told me that you Complained of your Spirits that morning you left this,[4] but that You became better from Some Occurrences in the Coach, nothing so good as exercise and variety of Objects. I hope by this time you have felt the good Effects of your Journey. Take as much exercise as your present Situation will admit of, avoid every thing that leads to dissipation, and even business that requires any Extraordinary Exertion of the mind untill it recovers it's former firmness.

I am not a little Sorry to find you So much hurt by the talk of

his friend Temple, Nicholls had been at Trinity Hall, Cambridge. They had literary tastes and ambitions in common, and had both abandoned thoughts of a legal career to take orders in the Church of England. Nicholls was rector of Lound and Bradwell, near Lowestoft, and was a bachelor. The *Correspondence between Thomas Gray and the Rev. Norton Nicholls* was published in 1843. JJ came to supper, "but there was little intercourse between his honour and Nichols, who was full of spirits quite the fine Gentleman, and talked of nothing but of his travels in Italy" (Journ. 12 Aug. 1774).

---

[1] Annie Cuninghame, daughter of Captain Alexander Montgomerie-Cuninghame, and sister of Sir Walter

Montgomerie-Cuninghame of Corsehill, 4th Bt., was Margaret Boswell's niece— a daughter of her elder sister Elizabeth. She had come in January to pay a protracted visit to the Boswells. In the following year her health failed, and there is occasional mention in the journal of the progress of her illness. She died of consumption in Aug. 1779.

[2] In Mar. 1776 the family consisted of Veronica, on whose third birthday this was written, Euphemia, aged twenty-two months, and Alexander, aged five months.

[3] John Lawrie was JB's clerk.

[4] JB had left for London in a state of great gloom, having seen a vision of a death's-head during the night, and with the parting wish to his wife: "GOD grant we may meet in a better World!" (Journ. 10, 11 Mar. 1776).

a certain Set of people anent the late Decision in the Fife Politicks.[5]
I Really think it is rather a laughable Subject than to be treated
Seriously. Every person who knows your father or his character
will pay no regard to the Clamours of a disappointed party, who
Seldom regard truth, and often propogate Malicious and ground-

[5] The cause was a complicated one, arising from the parliamentary by-election held at Cupar on 24 Jan. 1776 to elect a successor to the deceased General Scott of Balcomie as M.P. for the county of Fife. The rival candidates were James Oswald of Dunnikier and John Henderson, eldest son of Sir Robert Henderson of Fordell, and Oswald had been returned member by a majority of a single vote. The result hinged entirely on the (property) qualification to vote of a certain Captain Dalrymple, who had been admitted to the roll of freeholders on the very day of the election. Henderson accordingly petitioned the Court of Session to find that the admission had been wrongfully made and should be expunged, which decision would have necessitated a new election. In the petition, two different objections to Dalrymple's qualification were specified, and when the cause came before the Court of Session on 7 March it became evident from the opinions of the judges who spoke (two of the eleven present remained silent) that about half of them would sustain the first objection and repel the second and the other half *vice versa*. Thus, if the single question was put: "Is Captain Dalrymple qualified?", the vote in the negative would be carried by a large majority, even though the reasons for the decision would differ as between individual judges. Dalrymple's counsel thereupon moved that each objection should be voted on separately, to which the Court agreed. The first objection was then repelled by six votes to four, but the second one found five judges voting on each side. Lord Auchinleck, in the absence of the Lord President, happened to be in the chair, and he gave his casting vote against the objection, with the effect that Oswald's election as M.P. remained valid (*Scots Mag.*, 1776, xxxviii. 160–

61). There was wide dissatisfaction with the decision, and caustic criticism of Lord Auchinleck, not only because he, as acting chairman, had been responsible for the mode of putting the questions to the vote, but because many felt that the tenor of his own speech had been at variance with his decisive casting vote. The Dundas political faction, whose interest had been exerted in favour of Henderson, was particularly annoyed at the unexpected outcome of the petition, and Henry Dundas, the Lord Advocate, said to JB: "I would rather lose all the elections in Scotland than have to represent his conduct at the bar of the house of Commons as I must do. Speak one way, and vote another" (Journ. 6 Mar. 1776, an incorrectly dated entry, as the case was heard on the 7th). Though Lord Auchinleck declared it a misunderstanding, and JJ advised JB "not to make a stir about the matter; but laugh it off with indifference" (Journ. 9 Mar. 1776), the incident got on JB's nerves and he even contemplated challenging Dundas to a duel. Ramsay of Ochtertyre believed that Lord Auchinleck was at fault, having become unreliable in his old age and inclined to become involved in political inconsistencies: "When verging fast to dotage, he gave an inconsistent vote in a political cause, which gave great offence to one of his political friends" (*Scotland and Scotsmen* i. 177 n.).

Henderson had also petitioned the House of Commons against Dalrymple's right to vote in the election. Oswald had duly taken his seat on 14 Feb., as was normal in cases of contested elections. The committee appointed by the House to try the objection sat on 21 March and next day reported that it found Capt. Dalrymple's vote a good one, and that the sitting member had been duly elected (*Scots Mag.*, 1776, xxxviii. 161).

less Storys of their opponents, and which in the end never meet with Credit from the Worthy and unprejudiced part of Mankind. Pray treat this affair in the way you once proposed, that is, to take no Nottice of it, nor appear to know any thing of the Matter, and even avoid conversing on the Subject. I cannot Suppose any person So rude as to introduce it in your presence. Avoid Likewise being with Lord Advocate at present, as he is warm and keen in this affair, and were you to meet, it might happen that this disagreeable Subject may be Spoke of, nay I beg you'll not think of being present when it is determined, but Endeavour to be cool and collected in every thing relating to this affair, and be assured that in the end your Father will Stand Justified in the opinion of those you think well of. I would fain hope the Committee will affirm every thing done in relation to that Election, and then You'll soon See the partizans of the other Side, like good and true politicians Smooth their countenances and become as Supple and as civil as formerly. I take the opportunity of Mrs. Boswells Frank to enquire after your Wellfare, and let me beg you'll favour me with a few lines when you have leisure to write. If you See Temple acquaint him of my best wishes—I alwise am My dear sir Yours Sincerely

JOHN JOHNSTON

Remember Doctr. Johnson's Copys of his *Tour to the Hebrides* that he presented you with, and Send them down with your baggage.

To Johnston, Monday 22 September 1777

MS. Yale (L 811).
ADDRESS: To John Johnston Esq: of Grange.

Ashbourne,[1] 22 Septr. 1777

MY WORTHY FRIEND: Upon getting to Carlisle the second day, whom did I meet at Lupton's but Captain Scott and the Revd. Mr. Dow.[2] We dined together and talked cordially of *the Laird* which upon honour was said by Scott and well understood by the rest.

[1] SJ had written on 30 Aug. to say he was at Ashbourne, in Derbyshire, staying with his friend Dr. Taylor, and that JB was invited to join them (*Letters SJ* ii. 198). They had been there together before, in Mar. 1776 (*Life* ii. 473–75).

[2] On his way south JB had reached Carlisle in the afternoon, and had dined at Lupton's inn with John Dowe, minister of Canonby in Cumberland, and a friend of JJ's named Scott (Journ. 11 Sept. 1777). In his journal record of the encounter JB describes Scott as "Captain Scott near Langholm, whom I had seen at Grange's", and thus connects him with "A Captain Scott from the East Indies"

No companion in a postchaise could be had, and no Stage went till the afternoon of next day. So I took posthorses, and rode and chaised on as I found it agreable, and got hither on Sunday evening. The two Doctours[3] were at the door ready to wellcome me, before I got out of the chaise. The Rambler has been upon the whole very well and has convinced me that I did right to make out my scheme of meeting him. You shall hear me read excellent Wisdom and Wit from my Journal. I shall set out the day after tomorrow, and hope to be home on saturday or monday next. I have had the comfort to hear good accounts of my Wife and Children.[4] I ever am with most sincere regard Your affectionate friend

JAMES BOSWELL

From Johnston, October 1777

Missing. Recd. 27 Oct. 1777. "Grange—that my Wife has been very ill, and is anxious to have me home—Very friendly" (Reg. Let.).[1]

To Johnston, Thursday 6 November 1777

Missing. Sent 6 Nov. 1777. "Mr. Johnston of Grange that my Wife is somewhat better—That I fear our Client Smith's predecessor has encroached on the Water of Irvine" (Reg. Let.).[2] Written from Edinburgh.

To Johnston, Sunday 6 June 1779

Missing. Sent 6 June 1779. "Grange a kindly letter. N.B. He never received it" (Reg. Let.). Written from Edinburgh.

with whom he had dined at Grange's lodgings the previous year (Journ. 27 July 1776). He may have been a member of the family of Scott of Johnston and a relative of JJ.

[3] SJ and his host, John Taylor (1711–88), prebendary of Westminster, a schoolfellow of SJ's. Taylor was a wealthy man who kept establishments both in London and at Ashbourne. Though SJ often stayed with him in Derbyshire, he found life there tedious, for there was little intellectual society and Taylor had his own affairs to attend to. Consequently he welcomed for a change the stimulating company of JB. He was even contemplating another tour with him, this time to the Baltic. JB was lukewarm about this

project, and suggested Wales, or Ireland, instead. In the event, they stayed at Ashbourne, which JB had reached on 14 Sept. and which he left on 24 Sept. (*Life* iii. 135–208).

[4] 18 Sept. 1777; received at Ashbourne: "Mr. Lawrie that my Wife and Children are all well." 22 Sept. 1777; received: "My Wife." (Reg. Let.). Neither letter has been recovered.

[1] JB was at Auchinleck, but because of this letter left the next day for Edinburgh.

[2] JJ had gone to Annandale on 31 Oct. (Journ.).

To Johnston, Thursday 28 October 1779

Missing. Sent 28 Oct. 1779. "Grange of my Chester felicity"[3] (Reg. Let.).

From Margaret Boswell to Johnston, ? 15 February 1780

MS. Yale (C 435).

ADDRESS: To John Johnston Esqr. of Grange.

[Edinburgh] Tuesday[1]

DEAR SIR: If it is not inconvenient for you, Mr. Boswell and I beg you will favor us with your Company to supper to night as there is nobody to be with us and your friend wishes to have a *sober* Chat with you. I hope it will be in your power to Come which will give sincere pleasure to your oblig'd and obedient servant

M. BOSWELL

To Johnston, Wednesday 22, Thursday 23 March 1780

MS. The Misses Carlyle of Waterbeck, Dumfriesshire. Sent 24 March 1780 (Reg. Let.).

ADDRESS: To John Johnston Esq. of Grange in Annandale, By Langholm.

POSTMARK: MR 24.

ENDORSEMENT: 27th Mar. paid 2 d. [?] W.S.[1]

[Edinburgh, 22 March 1780]

⟨DEAR⟩ FREIND, It is after supper, and my letter will not go till tomorrow evening. But, I will not delay writing to you, while I am

[3] In writing to SJ on 7 Nov. 1779, JB similarly described his Chester journal as "truly a log-book of felicity" (*Life* iii. 415). He had arrived at Chester on 19 October with Colonel James Stuart, and they spent some two weeks in the town, where the regiment raised by Stuart for service in the American war (the 92nd Foot) was then stationed. Unfortunately, this particular journal has not been recovered and little more is known of JB's happy stay in Chester than the brief account given in his letter of ‹Jan. 1780 to W. J. Temple.

[1] No date can be assigned with cer-

tainty to this note. JJ supped alone with the Boswells on several Tuesdays between 1770 and 1785, e.g. 15 Feb. 1780, 11 Dec. 1781, 8 Jan. 1782. On Tuesday 15 Feb. 1780, JB was unwell, which might account for a note of invitation being sent by Mrs. Boswell instead of the more usual invitation from JB by word of mouth. "But was persuaded to sit up, and have Grange to eat a bit of supper and drink some negus with us, which releived me a little" (Journ.).

[1] The endorsement is in the hand of the payer, whose initials both here and in letter of 9 May 1782 are unclear.

in clear cheerful spirits. I dined at worthy Sir Alexander Dick's today, accompanied by Sandie[2]—no company there. The excellent Knight exceedingly well; but three makes a better company than two. We would have been the better of you. Howev⟨er⟩ he proposed your health, and I drank ⟨::::::::.⟩

I hope you got safe to Grange, and executed the dreary duty, and weathered other dissagreable circumstances better than you imagined beforehand.[3] It is certain that one often finds an immediate supply of resolution in the very occasions themselves which require it.

Your absence I can assure you has been felt by me very sensibly. To be ⟨without the com⟩fort of your s⟨ociet⟩y ⟨and⟩ sympathy ⟨is no sm⟩all loss, though it may be argued that the mind may be the better of being hardened as it is when no such tender medicinal aid is administered.

How are you likely to get your country affairs settled? I have had most discouraging accounts of mine[4] from Hallglenmuir[5] and

[2] JB's eldest son Alexander, now four years old.

[3] "Grange had received an express that his Mother was just dying, and the man who came had heard she was dead; so he was to go south next day. She was very old, and had not been a kind mother to him; so he was not grieved" (Journ. 13 Mar. 1780). JJ's mother, Agnes Laggart, lived at Grange with his brother Thomas, to whom he paid £6 a year towards her maintenance (Grange MSS., Contract, 10 Nov. 1763).

[4] JB is referring to the letting of his property of Dalblair, a small estate in the valley of Glenmuir, adjoining Auchinleck (*ante* 24 Apr. 1767, n. 9). His existing tenants, Andrew Howatson of Craigdarroch (a nearby property) and Robert Chisholm, a tacksman of one or more farms of the Auchinleck estate, had not always been prompt in paying their rents, and JB also seems to have felt that the total rental was too low (Reg. Let. 1778–80, *passim*). A year before this letter he had agreed that they should remain in occupation on the same terms as before until Whitsunday 1780 (Reg. Let. 19 Feb. 1779), but he had determined to "roup", or offer by public

auction, the renting of the estate after that date. There was much correspondence about this with his Ayrshire friends and connexions, and JB sent down advertisements to be circulated regarding the auction, to be held at Cumnock on 15 March 1780 (Reg. Let. Mar. 1779–Mar. 1780, *passim*). As the present letter reports, nobody would bid at the roup. Consequently, JB retained his former tenants, but apparently added a third: "My three tenants of Dalblair each a letter offering them their possessions for four years Howatson £17—Lockie £19 and 3d. of Cess and publick burthens—Chisholm £48 and two 3ds Cess and publick burthens. Hoping Craigdarroch will assist me in getting a good set and he may [have] the whole himself at £84 clear—Chisholm to make a sufficient low house at the sight of Mr. Jas. Bruce" (Reg. Let. 7 Apr. 1780). Surviving records (Reg. Let. and estate papers) indicate that the three accepted the terms offered, but that Chisholm subsequently became bankrupt (see *post* 9 May 1782, n. 5) and had to be replaced by another tenant.

[5] Alexander Mitchell of Hallglenmuir, an Auchinleck neighbour, was in financial

291

James Bruce. At th⟨e roup⟩ of Dalblair (I am now writing on thursday the 23 after dinner) there were many farmers present, but not one offered, though the lands were set up £10 under the present rent. £80 was offered to Hallglenmuir after the roup. But I have written to him that rather than let the lands under the present rent, I will take them into my own hands. I am really uneasy about this ⟨matte⟩r. Hallglen⟨muir comes to town⟩ next week, and after talking ⟨bills with me⟩, ⟨he⟩ may probably go west some time next month. But such uneasiness as this is nothing compared with what you and I know. I met honest Dash[6] today on the bridge and walked with him as far as the West Kirk. He is at present in high spirits, goes tomorrow for *Sir John's*,[7] and talks of walk⟨in⟩g all the way. I asked him if he drove the ⟨wor⟩ld before him.[8] He said he did. I observed that it was quite unaccountable. But the world sometimes appears to one ⟨like a⟩ Lion grinning in the way, and then of a su⟨dden⟩ turns a hare, scours off, and we pursue it briskly. I yesterday paid Mr. Walter Scott[9] £200 on his acknowledgement. Jamie Baillie informed me today that he had my £150 ready

difficulties. The Ayr Bank of Douglas, Heron & Co., to which he owed money, was about to foreclose a mortgage and sell the estate. He was a distant relative of the Boswells; his mother was a sister of the elder John Boswell of Knockroon. JB wanted his father to advance him the money, but Lord Auchinleck refused. Hallglenmuir was obliged to leave the country two months later in order to escape his creditors (Journ. 18, 21 Apr., 28 May 1780). JB had sent a letter to him on 18 March: "Sorry that Dalblair is so discouraging. Will rather take it into my own hand than lower the rent. Will talk bills with him when he comes to town" (Reg. Let.). The two met on 5, 6, and 8 April. "Hallglenmuir had been at Dumfermline getting some money due to him, and was to go west next day" (Journ. 8 Apr.).

[6] Andrew Erskine.

[7] Sir John Whitefoord (d. 1803), 3rd Bt. He was a particular friend of Andrew Erskine with whom he was caricatured by John Kay (*Original Portraits*, ii, facing p. 56; and pp. 59–60). Erskine's walk would have been a long one, for Sir

John's country estate was that of Ballochmyle, near Auchinleck in Ayrshire, which he had inherited from his uncle, Allan Whitefoord (*ante* 21 July 1763, n. 7). It remained in his possession until at least 1785, but then had to be sold for the benefit of the creditors of Douglas, Heron & Co. in whose failure Sir John was involved.

[8] JB is quoting Johnson. He had recorded the phrase in his as yet unpublished journal of the Hebridean tour, 23 Aug. 1773: "He said when he read Warb[urton] first, and observed his force, and contempt, he thought he had driven the world before him." It may well have been an habitual, as well as a characteristic, expression, for in a letter to Mrs. Thrale in the last year of his life, 13 May 1784, Johnson wrote: "I do not now drive the World about, the World drives or draws me. I am very weak."

[9] Walter Scott, W.S. (1729–99), father of Sir Walter, was an acquaintance of JB's, with whom, as the Journal shows, he came occasionally in contact both socially and professionally.

and will pay it whenever you return.[10] I do not like to touch on it, as it is a distinct sum of interest. So would rather lend it again on good prompt security. We shall settle this when you come. Let me know when that will be. I go to Bothwel Castle tomorrow for a few days. The Solicitor and I go together and return.[11] We are all ⟨we⟩ll; only my Wifes cold still troubles her. Come soon and beleive me to be ever most affectionately yours

JAMES BOSWELL

To Johnston, Monday 21 August 1780

Missing. Sent 21 Aug. 1780. "Grange to read seal and send Mr. Fergusson's letter.[1] Wishing to hear from him" (Reg. Let.). Written from Auchinleck.

To Johnston, May 1781

Missing. May 1781. "Grange" (Reg. Let.). Written from London.

To Johnston, Thursday 9 May 1782

MS. The Misses Carlyle of Waterbeck, Dumfriesshire.

ADDRESS: To John Johnston Esq. of Grange, By Langholm.

POSTMARK: MY 9.

ENDORSEMENT by JJ: Edr. 9 May 1782, Mr. Boswell.

ENDORSEMENT by payer (*ante* 22 Mar. 1780, n. 1): 10th May paid post at 2d. W.S.

Edinburgh, 9 May 1782

MY DEAR SIR, The newspapers will probably have informed you

---

[10] Some particulars of this financial transaction are given by JB in a later letter (*post* 17 Dec. 1787).

[11] JB went on 24 Mar. with Alexander Murray (who had succeeded Henry Dundas in 1775 as Solicitor-General) to Bothwell Castle to visit Archibald Douglas of Douglas, in support of whose claims JB had expended so much energy at the time of the Douglas Cause. Douglas's wife, Lady Lucy Graham, daughter of the Duke of Montrose, whom he had married in 1771, had just died at the age of twenty-eight. The visit was in-

tended as one of condolence (Journ. 24–27 Mar. 1780).

---

[1] The letter which was enclosed was to inform Joseph Fergusson that JB's brother David had returned from Valencia, and was looking forward to meeting him. "[Sent 21 Aug. 1780] Rev. Mr. Joseph Fergusson that my brother David would be happy to see him, that he is to be at Auchinleck till the 10 or 12 of Sept and at Edr. till about the 20. Suggesting to him to try if he could get my brother John to board with him" (Reg. Let.).

of my being dissappointed of the office of Judge Advocate,[1] which I understand was obtained by the Duke of Buccleugh and Lord Advocate for Mr. Mark Pringle. But I have not been dissappointed of Mr. Burke's friendship; for, I received from him a most freindly letter, enclosing a letter from him to General Conway soliciting the office for me, in such terms, as make me very much indebted to him, as also General Conway's answer.[2] You shall see them all when you return. I am also happy to inform you that my alarm of bad health was a false alarm. I am quite well.[3]

You desired me to write to you to comfort you, while in the country. You may be assured of the full comfort of my steady freindship; as also that I by no means view your affairs in the way that you are sometimes unhappy enough to do. Our freind Abercrombie has informed me of what Lord Elliock has said about your engagement for Mr. Armstrong to the Royal Bank, and that their agent Mr. Anderson is to do nothing without letting Mr. Abercrombie know.[4] I am going west tomorrow, my principal

[1] "Was told in street by Dr. Gillespie that Mark Pringle had got Judge Advocates office. Was a little disappointed, but soon recovered" (Journ. 4 May 1782). JB's disappointment was allayed by his conviction that he had Burke's interest and that Burke would soon get him some office as good as the Judge Advocateship (Notes, 29 Apr. 1782).

[2] Burke's letters to JB and to Conway (a copy), and Conway's reply to Burke, all dated 23 Apr. 1782, have been preserved (MSS. Yale C 685, C 686, C 820). The appointment was virtually in the gift of General Conway, Commander-in-Chief of the army, because its main duties consisted in acting as legal adviser to the army commanders and advising the Crown on matters relating to military law, particularly in connexion with courts martial.

[3] During the month of February JB had been carrying on a gross affair with a landlady in Liberton's Wynd. Mrs. Boswell, having learned of it from reading the journal, had announced that all connexion between them was at an end (Journ. 2, 3, 9, 16, 18, 27, 28 Feb. 1782); she relented on 10 Mar. On the 28th JB reported "Folly" and on 6 Apr. "Lib.

Wynd"; on 10 Apr. he became appropriately "miserable" both because he was "affraid of virus" and because Mrs. Boswell had heard of his being back in Liberton's Wynd. He continued in an agony of apprehension through the rest of the month, trying to persuade himself that his disquieting symptoms were due to "hard drinking of punch on tuesday the 9th" (Notes, 12–18 Apr. 1782). By the 27th the symptoms had disappeared, and he decided they had been illusory.

[4] David Armstrong was the advocate with whom JB had been associated in the case of Carruthers v. Queensberry (ante 14 Jan. 1768). JJ and "Mr. Bell" (perhaps Adam Bell, another "writer" with whom JB had legal associations) were cautioners (sureties) for Armstrong in respect of some sum owing by him to the Royal Bank of Scotland. Armstrong, like so many others, had been one of the partners in Douglas, Heron & Co. and was now, presumably, in such financial difficulties that his cautioners were likely to be called upon to fulfil their obligations. JJ's share was apparently £150, but attempts were being made to persuade the Royal Bank to abstain from pressing

tenant in Dalblair[5] having become Bankrupt, so that I must exert myself. I shall apply to Mr. Dun to be your Cautioner. Or rather, if he will lend you £100, I shall let you have £50 of mine which I have lying at £4 per cent; so that I shall be a gainer by your borrowing it. I really think it will be better to pay up the £150 if you can borrow the money. Mr. Abercrombie tells me your Coobligant Mr. Bell is to do so.

I shall be about ten or twelve days in Ayrshire, and should be happy to hear from you while there, and at any rate by the time I get back to Edinburgh for the General Assembly.

Adieu my dear Sir. Read the *Rambler* and (which I should have said first) read the Gospel and pray to GOD, and I hope you will be easy and enjoy hope. My kind compliments to Mr. Fergusson. I am ever your very sincere freind,

JAMES BOSWELL

From Johnston, Friday 25 October 1782

MS. Yale (C 1635).

ADDRESS: Mr. Boswell.

ENDORSEMENT: Grange coming to Auchinleck, 25 Octr. 1782.

Edinburgh, 25th. Octr. 1782

DEAR SIR: Before this time I would have thanked you for your present of partridges, had I not intended to have done it in person

for immediate payment. Lord Elliock (James Veitch, 1712–93), a judge of the Court of Session, was also a Director of the Royal Bank, while "their agent Mr. Anderson" was probably the most distinguished of the five Writers to the Signet of that surname, David Anderson (1707–86). Abercrombie would be JJ's friend, Alexander Abercrombie, W.S. (*ante* 25 Jan. 1763, n. 5). As this letter shows, JB was doing his best to assist his friend in the matter. Three months later he paid a visit to Lord Elliock "partly on Grange's account, that My Lord, as a Director of the Royal Bank, might get things made easy to him as one of Mr. David Armstrong's Cautioners, which his Lordship, who expressed a regard for Grange, obligingly engaged to do. I had

spoke of it to him before" (Journ. 12 Aug. 1782).

[5] This was Robert Chisholm (*ante* 22, 23 Mar. 1780, n. 4). His increasing financial difficulties in the previous two years, since his lease of a farm in Dalblair had been renewed, are reflected in the summaries of letters in the Register of Letters for this period. From these, JB appears to have given Chisholm every chance, until it became clear that he was insolvent. At last a letter was sent "By Fly—Knockroon with Mandate for Sequestration against Chisholm" (Reg. Let. 7 May 1782). JB himself went to Ayrshire and, assisted by another Dalblair tenant, Alexander Howatson of Craigdarroch, let the vacant farm to James Weir (Journ. 10, 11, 15 May 1782).

above ten days ago. I have been twice disappointed, when I was ready to take out a Ticket in the Fly, but as I have laid aside all thoughts of going to Annandale this Season, I cannot resist your kind invitation, and the Strong desire I have of Seeing you at the head of your family Comfortably Set down at the Seat of your ancestors,[1] which I hope you and your posterity Shall inherit for ages to come. I propose Setting out, if it please God, on Tuesday Morning, and to be with you in the Evening. By no means Send a horse to Ochiltree. It will be much more agreeable to Stretch my Limbs, after Sitting So long in the Carriage, by walking to the house. I can easily have a boy at the inn to carry a Small trunk with a few Shirts to Serve me till friday when I must return. Mr. Du-pont[2] was highly pleased with your present, and more So by your kindly remembering him at a time of life, he Said, when most people are forgotten or neglected by their former acquaintance. He desires you to accept of his hearty thanks.

I dined at Prestonfield on Tuesday. I found the good family well. I Sat with Sir Alexander an hour before dinner. He is in good Spirits. We had much Conversation about you and Mrs Boswell. I told him of my intended visit to Auchinleck. He and the Ladys[3] have Loaded me with Compliments and good wishes, particularly for Mrs Boswells perfect recovery. Thank God for the favourable account you gave me of her health in your last Letter. From what I saw in your Letter to Mr. Lawrie, I find She continues to recover; Mr Lawries Wife has brought him a 3d Son the other day. Poor

[1] Lord Auchinleck had died on 30 Aug. For some weeks JB's wife had been ill, with ominous symptoms of the consumption from which she had undoubtedly suffered, intermittently, since at least 1777, but she had been well enough to travel on 17 Sept., when the Boswells went to Ayrshire to enter into possession of Auchinleck. After that she had had some ups and downs which had caused great anxiety.

[2] Pierre Loumeau Dupont, minister to the French Protestant congregation in Edinburgh, though more than forty years older than JB, seems to have taken great pleasure in his company. He was now in needy circumstances, for he was old and frail and most of his congregation had fallen away from him. JB lent him a small sum, asked Alexander Kincaid, the Lord Provost, to use his influence in the town council to get him an augmentation of salary, and helped him to draw up a formal petition for relief to the Edinburgh magistrates (Journ. 1, 14, 15 Jan. 1777). Before anything could be done, Kincaid's sudden death brought John Dalrymple back into office as his successor, and in the following month Dupont wrote asking Dalrymple's brother, Lord Hailes, to support his appeal (Dupont to Lord Hailes, 21 Feb. 1777, MS. Yale C 1165, a copy in JB's hand).

[3] Lady Dick, her two stepdaughters, Janet (now aged 33), and Anne (23), and her own three daughters, Elizabeth (18), Mary (16), and Margaret (11).

fellow, it may for a while Increase his difficultys, but who knows the advantages he may receive from them at an after period. My good wishes attend you all. Farewell and believe me to be most affectionately and Sincerely yours

JOHN JOHNSTON

To Johnston, Tuesday 22 April, Monday 28 April 1783

MS. Yale (L 812). Sent before 1 May (Reg. Let.).
ADDRESS: To John Johnston Esqr. of Grange, Langholm, Dumfries, N.B.
FRANKED: Free Edm Burke.
POSTMARK: T.O. [i.e. *Treasury Office*] 29 AP.

Butler's Court, 22 April 1783

MY DEAR FREIND: I now write to you from the delightful Country Seat of my highly admired and very kind freind the Right Honourable Edmund Burke Paymaster General of his Majesty's Forces.[1] Long may he enjoy that good office. This place is in Buckinghamshire just one and twenty miles from London. I came to it yesterday forenoon by special invitation, and am to stay till tomorrow. The Country here is as beautiful as you can imagine; a dry gravelly soil which bears a fine verdure, the ground varied with swells and hollows as if it had been cast in a mould by an Artist of exquisite taste, and abundance of Wood. There is in particular a vast number of cherry trees some of them very large, which are now all in blossom and give a most gay appearance to the scene. As we walked Yesterday between dinner and tea, in the same humour as you and I have been in in our pleasantest days at Prestonfield, He was admiring a cherrytree among a cluster of pines and other coarser trees. I said it was like a Tory among Whigs. Though he is a Member of the present coalition at the head of which is the Duke of Portland, and great Whig Champions in the first ranks of it, yet I trust he is a mild Tory at his heart;

---

[1] Burke had first been appointed to this office in 1782, when the Whigs in power had excluded him from the Cabinet, but had resigned it on the death of Lord Rockingham (1 July 1782). Two weeks before this letter was written he had been reappointed to it on the formation of a new Whig–Tory coalition under the Duke of Portland. "I have served the publick for seventeen years with great fidelity and Labour, and just at the decline of my Life there comes to me a temporary Office of some emollument, considerable expence, and no power" (From Edmund Burke, 23 Apr. 1782).

and to tell the truth Government at present is indeed a mixed government Tories and Whigs being blended in it. Nay the Prime Minister himself though a Dutchman and consequently a Revolutionist by the Father's side, is descended by the Mother's side of the great Lord Treasurer Oxford so that I call him a *Harleian Miscellany.*[3]

There is at this place perfect hospitality and the best conversation whether instructive or pleasant. Let me add too that we live well, which both you and I think of some consequence.

London has been more agreable to me this time than ever. The consciousness of being Laird of Auchinleck, and being independent of any controul gives me a steadiness which I had not before. I have experienced variety of kindness, and I have relished exceedingly my existence.

I found Dr. Johnson not at all well on my first coming; but his mind was as vigourous and lively as ever. He is now a good deal better; and I would hope may live some years.[4] I have collected a great many more of his excellent sayings, which I shall communicate to you when we meet. I regret much that you are not along with me to enjoy a portion of what I enjoy. Some time or other I flatter myself I shall go over the classical scenes of London with you and revive the finest ideas of our younger years which the *Spectator* gave us. ⟨I am⟩ very desireous to be enabled to pass the winter months in London. But as yet I do not see a *rational* probability of it, and I am disposing my mind to acquiesce in not having my desire gratified. I would upon no account be deprived of the comfort and I may say dignified happiness of passing part of the year at Auchinleck, which you know well.

I have had a full conversation with Lord Advocate concerning

---

[3] The family name of the Dukes of Portland is Dutch in origin. Hans-William Bentinck, confidential adviser to William of Orange, accompanied the King to England and was raised to the peerage as the 1st Earl of Portland. His descendant, the 3rd Duke, who had just become Prime Minister, was a great-grandson, through his mother, Margaret Cavendish Harley, of the 1st Earl of Oxford, who began collecting the great library of books and MSS. to which his son, the 2nd Earl, made many additions before parting with it (*Comp. Peer.* x.

267). A selection was published in eight volumes, entitled *The Harleian Miscellany,* 1744–46.

[4] When JB visited SJ on 21 Mar. (the day after his arrival in London), the first words SJ said were: "I am glad you are come. I am very ill" (Journ.). But JB's presence stimulated SJ to animated talk, and his frequent visits may have contributed to the improvement which took place in SJ's health during the spring. SJ was now nearly seventy-four: he had little more than twenty months to live.

you.[5] But at present he has nothing to say; and I can suppose if he had, would have many many demands upon his influence. I asked him if Mr. Burke could get me a small pension for you. He said he could. I have talked of it warmly with Mr. Burke; and he tells me that when once the Duke of Portland is well settled, he will see what can be done. I really indulge a fond expectation of it. Be assured that my earnest endeavours shall not be wanting.

London, 28 April 1783

I had written so far, when amidst my felicity, there was *the handwriting upon the wall*. An express came, informing me that Lieutenant David Cunninghame had killed his Antagonist Mr. Riddell of the horseguards in a duel,[6] and that he himself was shot through the body and lay dangerously ill; so, I hastened to town, and you may imagine was in sad agitation. Fortunately the Corroner's Inquest brought in their verdict Manslaughter so he will not I beleive be brought to a trial. His resolution was very remarkable, after being severely wounded, and in such pain and so faint that they were going to carry him off, he declared he would not quit the field, but would have his shot, which unfortunately proved mortal. He told me what passed in his mind at the moment. He thought can it be possible that Providence will permit a Man who has been so much in the wrong to prevail? And then he fired. He is recovering wonderfully well. He must behave with much propriety after this. Poor Sir James Riddell is much to be pitied.

After some hesitation Temple has resolved to come to London, and to accompany me north. I expect him in a few days. He will be a comfort to me here. But I wish his feeble spirits and con-

[5] JJ, who was getting into difficulties, largely because of the defection of his brother Thomas, and whose legal practice does not seem to have been prosperous, was anxious to obtain some public office with a fixed income attached to it, or a pension on the civil list. Under Shelburne's administration of 1782, Henry Dundas, the Lord Advocate, had been appointed patron of all government posts in Scotland (G. W. T. Omond, *The Lord Advocates of Scotland*, 1883, ii. 109).

[6] Full accounts of this duel and its causes are given in *Scots Mag.* (1783, xlv. 272–74) and *Gent. Mag.* (1783, liii. 362).

It appears that the dispute arose at cards and that Riddell challenged Cuninghame, who declined the challenge: but later, since aspersions were being made on his honour, Cuninghame challenged Riddell, who in turn, declined. Cuninghame, on next meeting Riddell, spat in his face, and thereupon the duel was arranged. George Riddell of the Horse Grenadiers was a son of Sir James Riddell of Ardnamurchan and Sunart, Bt. David Cuninghame was the second son of Alexander Montgomerie-Cuninghame of Lainshaw, and was a nephew of JB's wife and JB's first cousin, once removed.

tracted sphere of acquaintance may not produce some suspicion of my neglecting him,[7] while I am hurried round a large circle of company and amusement. I must frankly caution him.

I hope you are well in the country. Read the Rambler much, and think how I am enjoying his wonderful conversation. And be persuaded that there is a future state revealed to us by our Lord Jesus Christ, in which I trust you and I shall meet and be happy for ever. I am Your faithful and affectionate freind

JAMES BOSWELL

Be sure to write to me under cover of George Dempster Esq. M.P. London.

From Johnston, Tuesday 17 June 1783

MS. Yale (C 1636) Received 20 June 1783 (Reg. Let.).

ADDRESS: To James Boswell Esqr. of Auchinleck Advocate, Edinburgh.

POSTMARK: LANGHOLM.

ENDORSEMENT: 2d[1] Received 20 June 1783, Grange, a cordial Letter from Annandale.

Grange, 17th. June 1783

I ought my Dear Sir to have acknowledged the receipt of your kind and affectionate Letter while you was in London, but found myself Some how or other incapable of doing it. Every post I proposed Writing, and as often it was delayed. Indeed I was at a loss to express what I felt, to Shew the Sense I have of your goodness, in interesting yourself So warmly in what relates to my

---

[7] Temple came to London on 2 May, and remained there, in some impatience, till 30 May, when JB was ready to start with him for the north. JB was making for Scotland, and Temple for Berwick-on-Tweed, where he was going to settle accounts with his sister and let his farm of Allerdean (From W. J. Temple, 22 Feb. 1783). Temple was inclined at this time to be easily tired, peevish, and uncomfortable in society, and there was reason for JB's suspicion that he might be envious, for he wrote: "B[oswel]l irregular in his conduct and manners, selfish, indelicate, thoughtless, no sensi-

bility for others who have not his coarse and rustick strength and spirits. Sorry I came to town to meet him. Detaining me here to no purpose. Seems often absurd and almost mad I think. No composure or rational view of things. Years do not improve him. Why should I mortify myself to stay for him?" (*Diaries of William Johnston Temple*, ed. Lewis Bettany, 1929, 25 May 1783, p. 41).

---

[1] Presumably the postage JB paid for the letter. Cf. endorsements on his letters of 22, 23 Mar. 1780 and 9 May 1782.

Wellfare in every respect,[2] and what heightens the favour, to do it at a time when I have been desponding so much from the adverse occurrences that have depressed me of late; I hope you know me so well, as not to interpret my Silence as proceeding from the want of a Just Sense of your kind endeavours to alleviate and remove whatever gives me uneasieness; Nay though your Efforts to Serve me Should prove unsuccessful (which I hope will not be the Case) what an invaluable relief does it bring me in the mean time to have an assured and tried friend, Such as I have experienced in you for So long a time. I long much to See you again, and renew those free and agreeable Conversations that have So often afforded me pleasure. By this time you'll be with your family, who I hope you found well, and that your late expedition has turned out quite to your liking; betake yourself now to business, and the Management of your Estate, with that keenness, which both affords pleasure, and renders every pursuit in life effectual; you have[3] very flattering prospects, an agreeable family, an independent fortune, and all at a period of life far Removed from old age. These are blessings of a very Singular nature and fall but to the Share of a very few. May kind providence give you a long and uninterrupted enjoyment of them. From what you Said about Temple, I hope to find him with you when I return, it will be very pleasant to meet after an absence of near ten years. I shall Say nothing more about myself till I See you, only that I have been ever Since I came to the Country threatened with a kind of Rheumatism, attended with a Strange Sort of Antiquity, and an indifferrence about every thing, which I never felt before. I have taken a good deal of excercise which has done me much Service. I would fain hope that I Shall get free of all my Complaints by the time I return, which if it please god I intend about the Middle of next week, perhaps Sooner, if I can recover Some money I wait for; My best wishes attend you and your family. I remain My Dear Sir most affectionately and Sincerely yours while

JOHN JOHNSTON

I have procured four Hams for Mrs. Boswell. I hope they will be as good as the former, being made by the Same man. They will be Sent in next week.

[2] *Ante* 22 Apr. 1783, n. 5.   [3] MS. "have have".

To Johnston, Saturday 23 August 1783

MS. Yale (L 813).
ADDRESS: To John Johnston Esq: of Grange, James's Court, Edinburgh.
POSTMARK: ⟨C⟩UMNOC⟨K⟩.
ENDORSEMENT: Auchinleck 23. Aug. 1783.

Auchinleck, 23 August 1783

MY DEAR SIR: I am not *so well* here this year as I was the last.[1] You understand me; and therefore I need say no more. I hope you will find it convenient to come to me; and I beg you may go out and dine with worthy Sir Alexander Dick, give him my kindest compliments, let me know particularly how he is, and tell him it will make us very happy, if he will make out his intended visit.[2]

You will receive this on tuesday morning; and immediately on receipt of it, please take the trouble to go to Mr. George (alias Major) Jollie my Taylor,[3] and bid him make for me directly a *Corbeau*[4] or dark coloured frock with the fashionable white buttons, and a folding-down cape, but without lapels, as also a pair of stout black silk breeches, and let both be sent packed up in some coarse

---

[1] Within a year of succeeding to his estate, JB had tired of the life of a country laird. He was much preoccupied with his project to move to England: "But upon the whole I led a life of wretched insignificance in my own estimation, though indeed it was perhaps no worse than that of many Gentlemen of fortune. My valuable Wife and agreable children were constant objects of satisfaction. But my mental eye was often too dim or confused to relish them sufficiently. I began to despair of acquiring any knowledge in country affairs, and apprehended that my affairs would go into confusion" (Journ. summary, Autumn 1783).

[2] "On friday the 12 [Sept.] my amiable old freind Sir Alex. Dick in his eightieth year paid us a visit most cordially accompanied by his son Robert and his brother in law Captain Butler" (*ibid.*).

[3] On 12 Oct. 1792 JB wrote to his son Alexander: "I hope you will employ Jollie as your taylor, three generations of his family having worked for three of

ours." George Jollie's place of business was at the Canongate head (Williamson's *Edinburgh Directory*, various dates, including 1784–85, p. 46). There were other tailors of the same surname in Edinburgh, probably all related, but the Edinburgh Burgess Roll reveals that George (admitted Burgess in 1778) was a son of Walter Jollie (1744), and a grandson of James Jollie (1713). The family's place in the social scale seems to have been rising, for George's brother, James, was admitted W.S. in December of this same year, 1783, while the "alias Major" of this letter presumably means that George held that rank in the recently formed Edinburgh Defensive Band. He died on 9 Jan. 1793, only three months after JB had recommended him to his son (*Scots Mag.*, 1793, lv. 50).

[4] Cloth of a green so dark that it appeared almost black. This occurrence of the word is a full half-century earlier than the first example in the OED (Lamb's *Essays of Elia*).

cover, to my house on Wednesday night, to come west with the Cumnock Carrier on Thursday morning early. I am at all times and in all states of mind most cordially yours

JAMES BOSWELL

To Johnston, Sunday 31 August 1783

Missing. Sent 31 Aug. 1783. "Grange with Mr. C. Dilly" (Reg. Let.). Charles Dilly had arrived at Auchinleck on 24 Aug. 1783 and stayed there until 1 Sept., when he presumably carried with him to Edinburgh this missing letter to JJ (Journ. summary, Autumn 1783).

To Johnston, Tuesday 27 April 1784

Missing. Sent 27 April 1784. "Grange—that the Office of Clerk to the Justices of Peace for Ayrshire is obtained for Knockroon, etc." (Reg. Let.). Written from Douglas Mill (To James Bruce, 27 Apr.). It was through the great influence of Henry Dundas that JB had obtained the grant of this office for John Boswell ("Knockroon": see *ante* 1 Apr. 1769, n. 1), the intention being, as the summary of the next letter to JJ shows, that JJ was to enjoy half of the emoluments. But, to his mortification, JB soon found that he had been mistakenly informed by John Boswell that the office was vacant, whereas it had in fact already been granted for life to James Dalrymple of Orangefield, son of the former holder. Thus the commission made out in favour of John Boswell was invalid (JB to John Boswell, Reg. Let. 22 May 1784; to Henry Dundas, 14 June 1794).

To Johnston, Saturday 22 May 1784

Missing. Sent 22 May 1784. "Grange regretting that the Clerkship to the Ayrshire Justices of which he was to have one half is not vacant; but to be of good cheer, for I will get him something. In the mean time he has *credit* for a visit to London, as Sir John Dick has of his own accord settled what we talked of—that I am now *resolved* to try my fortune at the english bar, to which I am well encouraged. Mr. Dundas approves, and says it will not prevent my afterwards getting a Judge's place in Scotland, if I should chuse it" (Reg. Let.).

To Johnston, c. Wednesday 9, Thursday 17 June 1784

Missing. Entered in Reg. Let. 19 June 1784. "Grange (a day or two earlier) partly from Oxford, partly from London, consoling him on my trying the english bar and assuring him We shall meet every year and that I shall exert myself to obtain something for him etc. etc." (Reg. Let.). After accompanying SJ to Oxford on 3 June, JB had returned to London to fulfil certain engagements, in particular to attend the performance of Handel's *Messiah* in Westminster Abbey on 5 June, but he rejoined SJ on the 9th (*Life* iv. 283–86). They both returned to London on Wednesday, 16 June (wrongly printed as 19 June in *Life* iv. 311). This letter was presumably then finished and posted to JJ.

From Johnston, September 1784

Missing. A letter which appears from JB's reply below to have complained of low spirits and the involvement of JJ's affairs.

To Johnston, Sunday 12 September 1784

MS. Yale (L 814).

Auchinleck, Sunday Morning, 12 Septr. 1784

MY DEAR SIR: Last night I was favoured with yours in answer to mine by the Ayr Fly. You ask as long [a] letter of consolation. But you know the old saying *Qui nihil habet nihil dabit.*[1] My own mind is in such a state that I am ill qualified to help another. The cheerfulness which I had on my first coming to the country this autumn was a transient gleam; and I have since suffered in the most dismal manner. But I will try to make out a letter to you, which may perhaps afford you some amusement; as your communications allways do to me.

I had a letter from my noble Relation in Holland Mynheer van Sommelsdyck acquainting me of the death of his only son which puts an end to that illustrious house.[2] It has affected me deeply.

I have had two letters from Dr. Johnson from Dr. Taylor's at Ashborne. He is rather better; but he abuses me too harshly for complaining to him of melancholy and discontent. Strange that He who has felt all the torment of *Antiquity* should have so little

[1] Latin equivalent of "He who hath nothing, nothing can he pay", an English maxim quoted in *Poor Robin's Almanack*, 1675. JB may have been altering for his purpose the late-Latin proverb, *Nil dat quod non habet*: "Nothing gives what it does not possess" (C. A. M. Fennell, *Stanford Dictionary of Anglicised Words and Phrases*, 1892, p. 571).

[2] JB had made the acquaintance of Francis Cornelius van Aerssen, Heer van Sommelsdyck, Lord Auchinleck's second cousin, at The Hague in 1763 (*ante* 20 Jan. 1764, n. 4), and had arranged to carry on a correspondence with him (Journ. 6 June 1764). Francis Johan, Sommelsdyck's son, who was only twenty at the time of his death, was born some two months after JB left Holland. In 1769 JB had sent him a pony (To F. C. van Aerssen van Sommelsdyck, 13 Aug., 10 Sept. 1764; 18 Aug. 1769).

indulgence for another.[3] He seemed at a loss what to think of the state of my negociation for his getting to Italy, as Sir Joshua had never received an answer from the Chancellor. But last night I had a letter from Sir Joshua telling me that the Chancellor had called on him and told him that his application to a certain Person in favour of Dr. Johnson had not been received so warmly as he expected; but he would apply again.[4] The Chancellor spoke strongly; and said the journey should not be delayed, and desired that in the mean time Dr. Johnson should draw on him for five or six hundred pounds, and should mortgage his pension to him, which his Lordship explained to Sir Joshua was meant only that Dr. Johnson might not seem under an obligation in any greater degree than could possibly be. So I hope this matter will be adjusted pretty well.

I have been living very privately, and did not go to the Ayr races. The state of my affairs really distresses me, and the disappointment at least for a time of my scheme of active ambition vexes me.[5] I *must* have you here this autumn; and I enclose a letter

[3] "Having written to him, in bad spirits, a letter filled with dejection and fretfulness, and at the same time expressing anxious apprehensions concerning him, on account of a dream which had disturbed me; his answer was chiefly in terms of reproach, for a supposed charge of 'affecting discontent, and indulging the vanity of complaint'" (*Life* iv. 379).

[4] The MS. originally ran at this point: "This coldness vexes me. The Royal House of Stuart would have been more generous." JB was anxious to arrange for SJ to spend the winter in Italy, so that the asthma might be alleviated, which in addition to dropsy, was hastening his end. He had canvassed various friends of SJ for their views, and after consulting Sir Joshua Reynolds, had written to Lord Thurlow, the Lord Chancellor, suggesting that some special grant or augmentation of pension might be obtained for the purpose (To Lord Thurlow, 24 June 1784). Lord Thurlow had replied that he would do all he could for SJ (From Lord Thurlow, 28 June 1784, *Life* iv. 336). After telling SJ what he had done, JB, who was obliged to return to Scotland, left the negotiations

in Sir Joshua's hands. The matter dragged on for two months after JB left London on 2 July, until at last Sir Joshua was able to write to JB the letter he here summarizes for JJ (From Sir Joshua Reynolds, 2 Sept. 1784). This offer Sir Joshua at once conveyed to SJ who had gone to Ashbourne; SJ replied on 9 Sept. enclosing a letter to Lord Thurlow in which he thanked him warmly for his offer but declined it because his health appeared to have improved so much that a visit to Italy seemed unnecessary (*Life* iv. 326–28, 336–37, 348–50).

[5] JB is here referring to his scheme for transferring from the Scottish to the English bar. He had been in high spirits during his visit to London in 1784, had convinced himself that his scheme was feasible, and had taken the decisive step of absenting himself not only from the General Assembly but from the first four weeks of the Summer Session in Edinburgh in order to further his qualification for being called to the bar. On his way north, he wrote a radiantly happy letter to W. J. Temple (6–8 July 1784) informing him of his decision and expectation of success. After reaching Scotland a few

to Mr. Fergusson[6] which you will seal and deliver, and I cannot doubt he will come with you. Do you know I have an inclination to ride over to Grange and Tundergarth, and bring you and him with me. I have a farther design to ride as far as Counsellor Lee's[7] about 60 miles from Carlisle and take you with me, that there may be a conversation in your presence about my plan of life. Will you be good enough to go with me? And will you be ready upon a letter from me? Write as to this. I am going to write earnestly to Mr. Dundas about you, as well as myself.[8]

I send you two packets from Temple to peruse. As to his *Articles* or Lease Richardson did not fulfil his agreement, did not enter.[9] If you think he should prosecute him you or I can write to Mr. Willoby attorney at law Berwick.

days later, he investigated his financial affairs and was dismayed to find that the interest on his debts was so heavy a charge against his income that his plan of moving to London was hardly practicable. This discovery, aggravated by the discouragement of many of his friends, caused his spirits to slump heavily. The Register of Letters thus summarizes his state of mind: "Wrote to Dempster that I was in miserable low spirits from finding that from the situation of my affairs I could not realise my agreable prospect of going to the english bar" (July 1784; see also JB to W. J. Temple, 20 July; Journ. 12 Dec.).

[6] This letter has not been recovered.

[7] John Lee (1733–93), K.C., Attorney-General for a brief period in 1783 and known as "honest Jack Lee", had been present at the Carlisle assizes in 1778, and JB had heard him deliver a speech there. He had a reputation for stating his opinions frankly, even at times crudely, and JB, feeling he could rely on his advice, consulted him on his prospects of success at the English bar. Whatever his private doubts, Lee initially encouraged him (JB to John Lee, 24 June 1784). The visit here suggested to Lee's country home at Staindrop clearly did not take place, but at the end of Sept. 1785 JB, on his way to Scotland, called there, bearing with him an advance copy of his *Tour*. On this occasion he asked Lee to write him a letter giving his opinion on the propriety of the proposed transfer to the English bar. Lee did so, referring to the indiscretions in the *Tour* and warning him that "there is hardly any Quality more essential to Success in our Profession, than that sort of Prudence, which knows, what is fit to be said, and what ought to [be] concealed"—with more in the same vein (From John Lee, 3 Oct. 1785).

[8] Shortly after he had become laird of Auchinleck, JB had written to Dundas soliciting some small appointment for JJ (*ante* 22 Apr. 1783). JB's copy of this letter, dated 16 Sept. 1782, is extant (MS. Yale L 449). In Dec. 1784 JB arranged to consult Dundas about his own affairs and hopes of settling in London. They had a "confidential conversation", when Dundas, among other things, mentioned that "he had a note of mine concerning my freind Johnston, and if an opportunity offered would do for him" (Journ. 12 Dec. 1784).

[9] See *ante* 22–28 Apr. 1783, n. 5. During his visit to the north in June 1783, Temple had paid his sister, Sarah Forster, "£600 being the remainder of her fortune secured upon Allerdeen" (*Diaries of William Johnston Temple*, ed. Lewis Bettany, 1929, 17 June 1783, p. 43), and had busied himself about letting Allerdean from Whitsuntide 1784. Copy for an advertisement which he sent to JB to insert in an Edinburgh newspaper

You may keep all the vouchers of my money till we meet. I send three partridges two for M. Dupont with my kind compliments. One to taste your own mouth. All are well here. Sandie is earnest for you to come. Be of good cheer. I trust things will yet clear up. I am most cordially yours

JAMES BOSWELL

To Johnston, Saturday 8 January 1785

Missing. Sent 8 Jan. 1785. "Grange that I am wonderfully recovered" (Reg. Let.). Written from Auchinleck.

To Johnston, Monday 4 April 1785

Missing. Sent 4 April 1785. "Grange of my journey to London—kind wishes for him—but rallying him for being angry that my Wife talked of his love of social drinking" (Reg. Let.). JB had left Auchinleck on 21 March, and had come to London by way of Lancaster, Preston, Manchester, Lichfield, and Birmingham, arriving in London on 30 March (Journ.).

From Johnston, Thursday 21 April 1785

MS. Yale (C 1638).
ADDRESS: Mr. Boswell.

Edinburgh, 21st. April 1785

I thank you most Cordially, My Worthy and Steady friend, for your kind Letter, written So early after your arrival in the great City, when you behooved to be in a hurried State. I have often determined and even Attempted to write you Since your departure, but alwise failed in doing it. Is not this odd and unaccountable? to

describes the farm as containing six hundred acres, and as being situated three miles south-west of Berwick (From W. J. Temple, 23 June 1783). Various prospective tenants were conducted over the land, and on 5 July 1783 an agreement was signed (Diaries, pp. 43–44; From W. J. Temple, 20, 23, 27, 28–30 June 1783). But when Whitsuntide came round, Temple learned from his lawyer, Edward Willoby, that the tenant, one Richardson, had other views and could not easily be prosecuted for breach of agreement because he lived in Scotland

(From W. J. Temple, 6 May 1784). Temple solicited JB's help, continued to refer to the matter in letters written during the summer of 1784 (From W. J. Temple, 3, 17 June, 8 July 1784), and on 3 Aug. 1784 announced that he was sending under separate cover the documents to which JB here refers. The outcome is uncertain, owing to gaps in the extant JB–Temple correspondence, but on 18 April 1785 Temple reported that he had let Allerdean on terms highly satisfactory to himself.

feel Such a difficulty in writing to one, to whom I have alwise Communicated with ease and freedom my most Secret thoughts of Men and things, for Such a number of years, but Such is the nature of this vile malady, that it benumbs and freezes the powers of the Mind. Such a long and unremitting Continuation of it, alarms me, least it may bring on diseases fatal to life. Do not treat me Just now, as your learned and Eminent friend used to treat you when in the like State.—I alwise thought it unkind, nay unpardonable in him, who had Sufferred So much himself in that way.[1] This day I feel Something like a gleam towards a recovery. The weather is fine, and the cheerfull progress of Spring refreshes and Strengthens the Mind. Were it Convenient I am perswaded that a Jaunt of two or three hundred Miles upon horseback through the delightfull Country of England would restore me to perfect health, but as that Cannot happen, I do not despair of being much relieved by passing a month in my Native County; I am very Sensible of your goodness in So kindly regretting my not being with you, but I Saw So many inconveniencys attending this Journey, that I Still think I was right in not Complying with your request; I am glad to hear you are going on with the Hebridian Tour,[2] but the bustling Scene of London, You'll find not favourable to Elegant Composition. Remember you have reputation to Support, and I hope much to acquire; think not my good friend of floating any longer in uncertainty, but of Casting Anchor on a good bottom. A Seat on the bench here, the Education of your Children, the Managing of your Estate, are objects within your reach, and will afford you Sufficient Employment, and for your amusement, an Annual visit to London, where you are alwise So respectably received. Do your best at this time with the Treasurer[3] to Secure

[1] *Ante* 12 Sept. 1784, n. 3.

[2] Immediately after SJ's death, on 13 Dec. 1784, Dilly had asked JB if he could have a four-hundred page biography ready by February. But JB, not intending to produce a brief and hurried *Life*, had decided instead to prepare for early publication the journal of the tour to the Hebrides which he had made with SJ in 1773, and to proceed later to write the biography deliberately (Journ. 18 Dec. 1784; 21 Feb. 1785). He had intended to settle down, when in London, and "get the work executed easily" (Journ. 21 Feb. 1785), but though he had been there since 30 Mar. the Journal shows that he was not making much headway, for the very reason suggested by JJ.

[3] That is, Henry Dundas. In Shelburne's administration (1782–83) he had briefly held the office of Treasurer of the Navy conjointly with that of Lord Advocate. The fall of the ministry lost him the former, while he was soon after dismissed from the Lord Advocateship. But the change in political fortunes when Pitt became Prime Minister at the end of 1783 saw him restored to the lucrative

Something or a promise of Something Certain to Carry with you to the bench. As for myself, I have no doubt of your kind offices, but I have little to expect, though little would make me Comfortable.

I Saw your Lady last night, She has been ill for ten days with a Tooth ach and Rheum in her head. She had a tooth drawn which did not abate the pain for Some days, the whole Seems to be the Effects of a Severe Cold, and has distressed her exceedingly. She is in pretty good Spirits, a few days I hope will restore her to her wonted health: I have Seen her frequently since She returned from the Country. I dined with her and the Children that day She received your short Letter dated from Lancaster. I was Sorry to find Mr. Lee Still mentioning the affair of the English bar, is not the opinion of your friend the Treasurer to determine you in this important Change?[4] I beg you'll come down quite determined. Suspense is a dreadfull Situation.

You mentioned the night I last Supped with you here. My mind was so galled and fretted, that I could bear nothing. After I came down Stairs,[5] and reflected on the impropriety of losing my temper, and on what had passed,[6] I could not Sleep, and continued for many days in a very perplexed Condition. It is the only instance wherein I ever uttered a word, or even entertained a thought anywise inconsistent with the long and Sincere regard I have for you and yours. Let this night be forgotten and forgive what happened with a Willingness equal to my anxiety of having it obliterate. The two Letters inclosed, I had from Mrs. Boswell to transmit to you. They ought to have been Sent the beginning of last week, but I was really unable to write. I hope no loss can arise from the

Treasurership, and content that his supporter Ilay Campbell should become Lord Advocate.

[4] Since 1783 JJ had been doing all he could to dissuade JB from going to England: "Worthy Grange endeavoured . . . to persuade me that I should reconcile my mind to living in Scotland" (Journ. 7 Aug. 1783). Finally he prevailed on Sir William Forbes to write to SJ and enlist his help to convince JB that it would be wiser to remain in Scotland. SJ's letter, and the one to which it was the reply, "never seen", says Forbes, "by any body but honest Grange, in Con-

junction with whom it was written", do not appear to have been preserved, though they were both sent to JB, at his own request, when he was collecting material which might be useful for the *Life* (From Sir William Forbes, 19 Oct. 1787; Reg. Let. Sent Sir W. Forbes, 11 Oct., 7 Nov.; Received Sir William Forbes, 22 Oct.).

[5] To his own flat, below that of the Boswells.

[6] *Ante* 4 Apr. 1785. JB's journal does not record this incident, which must have occurred before he and Mrs. Boswell left for Auchinleck on about 16 March.

delay. I beg the favour of a Letter Soon. Let me know what progress you have made in the Hebridian Tour, and how every thing goes on in your own Expectations. Have you met with Mr. Loch, he has transacted with Mr. Stuart about the office he held,[7] and now Waits for his Commission. I told him where you Lodged. I wish he may See you before he Sets out for this Country. Have you kept well Since you left this, no man ought to Complain of the Cross occurrences in life, if he enjoys good health. May God bless and prosper you in all your Endeavours to act a proper part in life—I am My Dear Sir most affectionately and sincerely yours while

JOHN JOHNSTON

To Johnston, Saturday 30 April 1785

Missing. Sent 30 April 1785. "Grange a kind letter to cheer him" (Reg. Let.). Written from London.

To Johnston, Monday 19 September 1785

MS. Yale (L 815).

London, 19 Septr. 1785

MY DEAR SIR: I must not call you *indolent*. But what can you say to me for being so very long without writing me a single line. I fear you have been *antiquated*, and that is too good an excuse. Yet both you and I know that in such a situation the correspondence with a real friend is a great relief.[1] I now write to you a few lines just to *hail* you, and to beg that you may write to me under cover of John Lee Esq. M.P.[2] Staindrop by Darlington and put on the back of your letter to me *to lie till he comes*. Let me know if you can meet me at Carlisle on one of the early days of next month—about the 4th 5th or 6th? And if you can go with me to Auchinleck.

I have enjoyed such an abundance of happiness in this Place,

[7] In 1785 James Loch succeeded Andrew Stuart as one of the King's Remembrancers in Exchequer (*The Royal Kalendar*, 1785 and 1786, p. 247).

[1] JB was practising what he preached, for his journal-entry for this day complains bitterly of hypochondria and *ennui*.

[2] *Ante* 12 Sept. 1784, n. 7. It is unlikely that JJ went to Carlisle to meet JB, who reached Auchinleck on 3 Oct. after paying his brief visit to Lee at Staindrop.

since I saw you, that I declare I cannot help assimilating myself
to one who has ascended into a superiour state of existence the
hopes of which are the best support of our dejected minds, while
in this World. I trust you shall experience what London is. Be
assured that the *Premier* shall not be allowed to have peace until
he grants me something *for you*,[3] which is all I ask of him. I am
confident that I shall take care of *myself* in Westminster Hall.

I am still detained here by the printing of my *Tour to the
Hebrides*,[4] which is done with great care, and I hope will be finished
tomorrow. A copy of it and of my *Court of Session Letter*[5] will
come to you by and by. Believe me to be ever My Dear Grange
your most sincere friend

JAMES BOSWELL

Write as long a letter as you can.

To Johnston, Monday 13 February 1786

MS. Yale (L 816).

London, 13 Febry. 1786

DEAR SIR: I had an excellent journey to *town*, and am I thank God
in sound health and spirits, owing I am persuaded to making my
blood circulate by activity, and keeping my mind ever fixed on

[3] Though JJ had opposed JB's move to
England, he had long since agreed that if
JB went to London he would accompany
him: "He readily agreed to go to London
if I went, supposing a decent place could
be procured for him" (Journ. 17 Jan.
1777). JB appears to have made more
than one appeal on JJ's behalf to Pitt
(*post* 7 June 1786).

[4] *Ante* 21 Apr. 1785, n. 2. On 30 Apr.
1785 (Journ.) JB had arranged with
Henry Baldwin and Charles Dilly for the
printing and publishing of the *Tour*, but
made little progress in preparing the
copy till a month later he secured the
energetic assistance of Edmond Malone.
The pair had worked together revising
copy and proofs all summer, and on the
date of this letter had just concluded their
labours. JB's journal shows that four
advance copies of the book were ready
on 21 Sept. It was published on 1 Oct.
(Journ. 29 Apr.–23 Sept. 1785, *passim*;

Preface, *Boswell's Journal of a Tour to
the Hebrides*, ed. F. A. Pottle and C. H.
Bennett, 1962 [1963]; *Lit. Car.*, pp.
121–22).

[5] *A Letter to the People of Scotland, on
the Alarming Attempt to Infringe the
Articles of the Union, and Introduce a Most
Pernicious Innovation, by Diminishing the
Number of the Lords of Session*, published
26 May 1785 (Journ.). On 27 April
(*Journ. House of Commons* xl. 905) Ilay
Campbell, Lord Advocate, had introduced
a bill, actually the work of Henry Dundas,
which proposed to reduce the number of
the Lords of Session from fifteen to ten.
JB dropped work on the *Tour* and devoted
three weeks to the production of this
frothy pamphlet, which he feared might
bring him a challenge from Dundas. The
proposal was found unpopular, and was
dropped (Journ. 2–26 May 1785 *passim*;
Lit. Car., pp. 111–12).

some object. I am now called to the rank of Barrister at law.[1] I this morning took the oaths in the Court of King's Bench where I have attended the proceedings for some hours, and I am not affraid to take the field. I am by Mr. Lee's advice, to go the very first northern circuit which begins about a month hence. I shall be at York the two last weeks of March and at Lancaster the first week of April. But the news papers will by and by shew you the very days. If you could rouse yourself, and meet me at either of these places, I will answer for your being quite a new man. In the mean time I intreat of you to get up and take a walk every morning before breakfast, and go as much among your friends as you possibly can. Be assured that they regard you; and do not suffer the foul fiend to delude you into any gloomy apprehension of the contrary. He has at times made me entertain such a groundless fear even as to Courtney and Malone.[2] I need say no more to you.

Today I give a dinner in *our* Hall (Inner Temple) to some friends—Sir Joshua Reynolds Malone Courtenay, the Honble. Daines Barrington[3] etc.   My two bretheren[4] called at the same

---

[1] After long hesitation and much advice-seeking, JB had decided to leave Scotland, where no brilliant future was opening up, and make a fresh attempt at spectacular professional success. Those who knew him best were most averse to the move, but knew also how little they could influence him against the pull of his inclination. His recent visit to Scotland had been one of barely six weeks and he had left Edinburgh on 12 Nov. (Journ.), determined to make arrangements for settling his family in London as soon as possible. On 13 Feb. he took the oaths in the Court of King's Bench and assumed his seat at the bar. "I . . . felt myself a Member of the ancient Court of King's Bench, and did not despair of yet being a Judge in it. My mind was firm and serene, and my imagination bright" (Journ. 13 Feb. 1786).

[2] John Courtenay (1741–1816), the politician and verse-writer, and Edmond Malone (1741–1812), the critic and man-of-letters, were JB's chief stand-bys at this time. It was their interest and practical help which enabled him to complete the *Life*.

[3] Daines Barrington (1727–1800), K.C., judge, antiquary, and naturalist, was invited not as a close friend of JB's (they appear to have seen very little of each other before this), but as a well-known representative of the Inner Temple, of which he was a bencher.

[4] JB took the oaths along with the Hon. John Eliot, younger son and successor of JB's friend, Baron Eliot of St. Germans, and William Dowdeswell, nephew of the former Chancellor of the Exchequer. The company invited to dinner with him that evening were "The Hon. Daines Barrington—Sir Joshua Reynolds—Mr. Wilkes—Mr. Malone, Mr. Courtenay, Young Mr. Strange—Dr. Brocklesby—Mr. Dilly my Bookseller—Mr. Baldwin my Printer—and my brother T. D. Mr. Eliot's guest was the Hon. Counsellor Percival. Mr. Dowdeswell's guests were Mr. Hay nephew of Lord Kinnoul—and Mr. James Martin, M.P. . . . I sat at the head of the table, and Mr. Dowdeswell at the foot, and a more jovial pleasant day never was passed" (Journ. 13 Feb. 1786). "Coun-

time with me to the bar, have joined in the jovial treat and bring two friends apiece. We shall have an admirable day of it. How much would your honour enjoy it! and how welcome should you be!

I insist on your sending me every saturday a Logbook or Journal how you have lived the preceeding week. It will be some occupation to you, and it will oblige you to more exertion when you know you are to *give an Account*. Try this, and be assured that I ever am your sincere friend.

JAMES BOSWELL

Your nephew[5] found me at Dilly's the day after my arrival— Direct under cover of Sir Charles Preston Bart. M.P.[6]

To Johnston, Wednesday 7 June 1786

Missing. Sent 7 June 1786. "Grange,—glad to hear that Shaw took him south, but uneasy at not hearing from him, and the more so that I dreamt last night he was very ill. I have again applied to Mr. Pitt for him. How long I shall remain at the english bar must depend upon circumstances" (Reg. Let.). Written from London. JB's journal does not record or refer to this dream.

To George Graham, July 1786

Missing. Sent July 1786. "Laird of Shaw begging he may tell Grange how often I have written to him without an answer—and may inform me particularly how he is—that I have a sincere regard for Shaw's family" (Reg. Let.).

sellor Percival" was Spencer Perceval, Prime Minister 1809, assassinated 1812.

[5] John Johnston (1770–94), eldest son of JJ's brother Thomas, was a student of medicine (*post* 1 Apr. 1795).

[6] Sir Charles Preston (1733–1800) of Valleyfield, had in 1779 succeeded his father Sir George, JB's great-uncle by marriage, as the 5th Bt. He was M.P. for the Kirkcaldy group of burghs.

VI

1786–1795

Letters concerning the death of Johnston and the winding up of his affairs.

From John Lawrie, July 1786

Missing. Recd. 3 Aug. 1786. "Mr. John Lawrie informing me of Grange's death" (Reg. Let.). After JB had moved to London, Lawrie, who had been his clerk, worked for Grange (*ante* p. xli; To John Lawrie, 19 June 1784; *post* 5 Aug., 20 Nov. 1786).

From Joseph Fergusson, Monday 24 July 1786

MS. Yale (C 1246).
ADDRESS: James Boswel of Auchinleck Esqr. London.
POSTMARK: 7 AU.

Tundergarth Manse 24 july 1786

DER SIR: I was honoured with your kind and friendly letter[1] about a year ago, at a time when I was confined to bed, in a most dangerous trouble, and ever Since, have been in a poor State of health, and seldom able to preach, which made me neglect to corrispond with my best friends, amongest whom I reckoned you the first; I am now a little better, and going about visiting the Sick, and have been attending our good friend Grange who is now no more, and to be interred in my Church-yard to morrow, whose funeral I propose to attend and to help to drop him into the grave. He frequently spoke of you in time of his trouble, and showed no little respect to me, which made me go oftener to him than my health could well permit, the distence being four miles.

What shall we say   the tender ties of nature and friendship must be disolved, and the best of friends must be seperated by death.

I am Sorrie to hear that you intend to leave Auchinkleck, and to reside at London. How can you think of leaving Such a fine place which your honoured father my Lord had such pleasure in and ornamented so much? Does not every fine walk and flourishing

---

[1] Not recovered.

plant Say "Stay at home"? How ever I shall always rejoyce to hear of the prosperity of you and your family wherever you go.

I have a Nephew in Virginia which you ordered me to put to School when you was at Moffat to make a Schollar. He has been pretty fortunate, bought a plantation and built some houses in Petersburg, married and has an only son whom he calls James Boswel for you. The boy is about six years of age, and he says if he be not blinded by paternal affection, he has some of the spirit of his namefather in him. He proposes to send him to Scotland to be educated I have nothing more of importance to write you. My most respectful compliments to your Lady, young family, and your brother Mr. David I am Dear Sir with the highest Esteem Your Humble Servant

Jos. Fergusson

From John Gordon, August 1786

Missing. Recd. 4 Aug. 1786. "John Gordon Esq. Clerk to the Signet with Grange's nomination of Trustees—hoping I will accept as one" (Reg. Let.).

To Alexander Abercrombie, Friday 4 August 1786

Missing. Sent 4 Aug. 1786. "Alexr. Abercrombie Esq: Clerk to the Signet in great concern for the loss of Grange. Begging that he may get secured for me a series of confidential letters from me to Grange, in case he has neglected to leave them to me as he promised" (Reg. Let.). The executors named in JJ's will were, besides JB, Alexander Abercrombie, W.S.; John Gordon, W.S.; James Baillie, writer in Edinburgh; James Loch, King's Remembrancer in Exchequer; Alexander Gordon of Campbelton; George Graham of Shaw; John Paxton of New Orchard; and George Kirkpatrick, Depute Clerk of Session (Grange MSS.).

To John Gordon, Saturday 5 August 1786

Missing. Sent 5 Aug. 1786. "John Gordon Esq: Clerk to the Signet, in answer to his concerning Grange—regretting him much—that we his friends should be cordially united—that I shall probably be little in Scotland for some time, the trust business may be completed in my absence, but as I wish to pay all respect to his memory, I most readily accept, and shall be glad if my advice can be of any service. Begging he may get my letters secured. I am happy to think they are in the hands of gentlemen. Mr. Abercrombie will show him my letter recommending Mr. Lawrie" (Reg. Let.).

To John Lawrie, Saturday 5 August 1786

Missing. Sent 5 Aug. 1786. "Mr. John Lawrie—of Grange's death—that I have recommended him to Mr. Gordon" (Reg. Let.).

From Thomas Johnston, Tuesday 3 October 1786

MS. Yale (C 1639).

ADDRESS: James Boswell Esqr of Awchenleck at Auchenleck.

POSTMARK: OC 7 LOCHMABEN.

Grainge Octor 3d 1786

DEAR SIR: I Beg Leive to wse this freedom tho wnaquanted. But by my Late Brother's Sentiments I have often here him mention of you My Caise is hard in Regaird to his Settlement of his affairs and By the advantage Taken by an wnworth Sister who staid with him in Edinr. Till he came owt[1] No doubt the particulars you will be well acquanted with By this Time how unfavourable they are for me and a Small fammlie.[2] But Irationality of the dead[3] will planly Show his State of uncapassity Besides many Circumstances of proof which owld Be Teidous [to] mention only this I Shall notice his Left more than his funds will ans[we]r And not one Shilling for me or my fammlie I mean to Reduce[4] the Settlement Imeadiatly to proceed after of Seeing you Which I hope your goodness will geive me your advice and your aid I mean to Be in Edinr. this month Oh Be so good to write me if I Can feind you there If this Settlement is Set aside I Can by the assistance of my freind mr. Paxton[5] Keep the hole Estate excepting the hous in Edinr. and Johnston[6] And if the dead[3] Stands not one Shilling for me I am Dear Sir your most obde. Servtt.

THOS. JOHNSTON

N.B. Directe to me pr. Lochmaben

[1] On account of Thomas's insolvency, JJ had left him, instead of a fixed legacy, an annuity to be paid after all other claims had been met. To his eldest sister Janet, widow of George Brown of Cleughside, who had looked after him latterly in Edinburgh before his removal to Grange, he left a fixed annuity of £20 and all his moveable property at Grange and in Edinburgh; and to her two sons, John and Thomas, he left legacies of 50 guineas and 100 guineas respectively (Grange MSS.).

[2] Actually a *large* family of nine; but Thomas means a *young* family, for seven of them were under fifteen years old.

[3] That is, "deed".

[4] To render void (Scots Law).

[5] His father-in-law, James Paxton of New Orchard, who was one of the trustees.

[6] The flat in James's Court and the farm of Johnston.

From John Lawrie, November 1786

Missing. Recd. Nov. 1786. ". . . Mr. John Lawrie to know what shall be done with my letters to Grange" (Reg. Let.).

To John Lawrie, Monday 20 November 1786

Missing. Sent 20 Nov. 1786. "Mr. John Lawrie to send the box with my letters to Grange by the first sure private hand" (Reg. Let.).

To James Loch, Monday 20 November 1786

Missing. Sent 20 Nov. 1786. "Ja. Loch Esq. recommending Mr. Lawrie—lamenting Grange" (Reg. Let.).

From John Lawrie, January 1787

Missing. Recd. 11 Jan. 1787. "Mr. John Lawrie to know how a box of my letters to Grange shall be sent" (Reg. Let.).

To Robert Boswell, Saturday 24 March 1787

MS. Yale (L 212). "Mr. Ro. Boswell[1] to apply to Mr. Lawrie about papers of mine in a box in his possession which I desired might be sent to London by the waggon. If not sent off, let them go to Auchinleck by the Carrier, with a note upon the Box *not to be opened*" (Reg. Let.).

ENDORSEMENT: London 24 March 1787. Jas. Boswell. About mo[ney] matters etc. Recd. 27 and Ansd. 30 D.

. . . Some time ago I wrote to Mr. Lawrie my late Clerk to send me by the Waggon a box of papers of mine which were delivered to him, and I desired he would inform me when he sent them off. I have as yet had no intelligence. Be so good as speak to him; and in case they are not sent off, let them go to Auchinleck by the Carrier, and let the Box be *sealed*. . . .

From Robert Boswell, Friday 30 March 1787

Missing. Recd. 4 April 1787. "Mr. Ro. Boswell that my Box of papers in Mr. Lawrie's possession is to be sent to Auchinleck" (Reg. Let.). For date see Robert Boswell's endorsement of the preceding letter.

---

[1] Robert Boswell (1746–1804), Lyon Depute and Clerk to the Signet, a son of JB's uncle Dr. John Boswell, was JB's solicitor.

To Robert Boswell, c. Wednesday 26 September 1787

Missing. "During this month [Sept. 1787] which I passed till the 24th at Auchinleck, I . . . received . . . two letters from Ro. Preston Esq: for payment of my note for £500 . . . I wrote to Ro. Boswell from Penrith to try if he could procure me a loan of £500 to pay Preston, and to try at least to get me payment of two bills due to me by Grange" (Reg. Let.). Dated from JB's journal, which shows that he spent the night of 26–27 Sept. 1787 at Penrith. The urgent need expressed by JB, in this and letters following, for the repayment of the money due to him by JJ's estate arose, as he here indicates, from his obligation to Captain Robert Preston, youngest son of Sir George. Preston had a few years before lent him £500 against his note, apparently for an indefinite period. On 9 June 1786 JB had been "stunned" to receive a demand for repayment (Journ.). Although he had succeeded in obtaining a postponement, Preston was now insisting on an early settlement. In the event, JB was able to borrow £300 from Charles Dilly and £200 from Henry Baldwin, and he repaid Preston's £500 on 26 Oct. 1787 (Journ.), the day before again writing to Robert Boswell (*post*) regarding Grange's bills. The £200 he there refers to is Baldwin's loan, which was on a short-term basis. Temple had also been applied to for financial help, but had shown some reluctance to grant it. However, when payment from JJ's executors was not forthcoming, it was Temple who, in Feb. 1788, advanced the £200 required to repay Baldwin (JB–W. J. Temple correspondence, 8 Oct. 1787 to 25 Feb. 1788, *passim*). In Nov. 1788 (date not recorded) JB wrote to Temple "that by delay of repayment of poor Johnston's debt to me, I cannot yet pay the £200 I owe him but that it is very safe, and he has better interest than in the funds" (Reg. Let.). When JB died, JJ's debt to him was unpaid and so, it appears, was his own to Temple ("View of my Affairs", 1 Jan. 1795, MS. Yale A 52).

To Robert Boswell, Saturday 6 October 1787

Missing. Sent 6 Oct. 1787. "Mr. Ro. Boswell that my Credit must be very bad. I have been more fortunate here. A friend *offered* me £300 and if I cannot raise the other £200 will let me have that sum also for six months. Let him endeavour to get what is owing by Grange which will be about £180. . . ." (Reg. Let.). The friend was Charles Dilly (*ante* c. 26 Sept. headnote).

From Robert Boswell, October 1787

Missing. Recd. 13 Oct. 1787. "Mr. Ro. Boswell, that the debt due by Grange may perhaps be paid at Martinmas. Discouraging view of my credit" (Reg. Let.).

To Robert Boswell, Saturday 27 October 1787

MS. Yale (*L 218). *A small fragment identifiable from the summary in* Reg. Let: Sent 27 Oct. 1787. "Mr. Ro. Boswell enclosing Grange's Bills of which I hope payment may be got at Martinmas and the money remitted to me that I may pay as soon as I can £200 lent me by a friend to assist me to settle with Mr. Preston." The friend was Henry Baldwin (*ante* c. 26 Sept. headnote).

From Robert Boswell, December 1787

Missing. Recd. 5 Dec. 1787. "Mr. Ro. Boswell enclosing a card to him from Grange's Trustees with a Copy of an Account between him and me which they wish to have explained" (Reg. Let.).

To Robert Boswell, Monday 17 December 1787

MS. Yale (*L 219). Sent 17 Dec. 1787. "Mr. Ro. Boswell with a full explanation of any doubt as to the Bill due to me by Grange" (Reg. Let.). ENDORSEMENT: London 17 Dec. 1787. Jas. Boswell. Abt Grange's debt. Ans'd.

London, 17. Decr. 1787

DEAR SIR: Not having sent to Mr. Ward's for some days, I did not receive yours of the 4th. so soon as I might have done. I return the enclosures. Hunter's Account is just; so pray pay it for me.

My money transactions with my late worthy friend Johnston were many and various. I had no recollection of the stated Account of which his Trustees have sent you a copy. I see that it relates to one sum only of mine which was put into his hands, viz. £150 on 4th July 1780, to clear off which certain Articles are placed to his Credit. I think that sum of £150 was some money particularly appropriated and was lent either before he got it, in my name, or after he got it, in *his* name to Sir Robert Maxwell[1] and others. I think Mr. James Baillie was their agent, and will be able to tell. But it will be observed that this Account respects solely that sum of £150. At the bottom of it you see it is mentioned that the *vouchers* were delivered up. But no other voucher on my part

[1] Sir Robert Maxwell (d. 1786) of Orchardton (*Comp. Bar.* iii. 340 note g; BP i. 72–73, 85) suffered serious loss in the failure in Aug. 1773 of the Ayr Bank of Douglas, Heron, & Co. For an earlier reference to this transaction see *ante* 22, 23 Mar. 1780.

except the £150 Bill is stated, or could be considered at that time, as no more is stated upon his side of the Account but what was just a ballance to that Bill. Several of our money transactions were mutual operations upon our Cash Accounts by loans and repayments, of which the vouchers were given up without stating regular clearances and of these there were a number between 1780 and 1783 as to which Mr. Gordon's note very properly inquires. I have not my Accounts here, nor am I sure how many of them I have preserved; but I find in a little Memorandum Book which contains other things, that I paid and advanced to Mr. Johnston from my Cash Account with the Bank of Scotland—1781 Augt. 14 £120—1782 Decr. 27 £50—1783 March 5 £40. All these you see were between the date of the £150 Bill 4 July 1780 and the Partial Account relative to it 12 March 1784 and I know that there were several more payments and advances within that period from my Cash Account with Sir William Forbes and Co. Mr. Johnston certainly kept some Cash Books or Accounts in which his Money transactions must be stated; or even his Bank Book must ascertain some if not all of the payments and advances of which I have given the dates. I am anxious to do all that I possibly can to explain to the Trustees what Mr. Johns[t]on could have at once cleared up had he been alive. I see that between the most intimate friends care should be taken in money transactions not to leave the smallest *appearance* of inaccuracy. I have only to add that as the partial account respects only the £150 Bill I cannot perceive any objection arrising from it to the £70 Bill, which I know was a permanent loan, and which in every state of my affairs at the beginning of each year has been stated in the list of debts due to me. At the time when Mr. Johnston made a settlement of his affairs before his death, I should suppose he would enumerate his debts, and if he did, I cannot doubt that his two Bills due to me would be mentioned.[2] I am Dear Sir yours sincerely

JAMES BOSWELL

When the money is paid I wish to have it remitted by a Bill at par.

[2] The exact amount due by JJ to JB, apparently in the form of two bills of exchange, is uncertain, partly for reasons mentioned in this letter. In his "View of my Affairs", 1 Jan. 1787, JB entered the debt as £170, but in that of 19 Jan. 1788 it is reduced to £160, probably because of JB's recent investigation of his financial transactions with JJ, as reported in this letter. Subsequent

To Robert Boswell, Tuesday 22 January 1788

Missing. Sent 22 Jan. 1788. "Mr. Ro. Boswell . . . that I certainly will not take payment of one of Grange's Bills till it is settled whether I am to have both paid. That I *know* both to be due, and shall wonder if neither in word or writing he mentioned this . . ." (Reg. Let.).

From Robert Boswell, c. 8 February 1788

Missing. See next letter.

To Robert Boswell, Tuesday 12 February 1788

MS. Yale (*L 220). "Mr. Ro. Boswell that the demur of Grange's trustees as to one of the Bills is disagreable—to send me a copy of it" (Reg. Let.).
ENDORSEMENT: London 12 Febr. 1788. Jas. Boswell. Abt Grange's debt—Cunninghame's affairs etc. Recd. 15th Ansd. 18th D.

. . . Yesterday I received yours, enclosing the Minute of Grange's Trustees, which I feel to be disagreable, but I agree with you that they could not well do otherwise. I send a letter to Mr. Gordon who I trust will give me a pointed and candid answer. Pray send me a Copy of the first Bill. I cannot at this distance of time say whether it's not being upon a stamp[1] was owing to forgetfulness, or to some erroneous notion as to the Act, or to its being granted on a sudden, merely as a Memorandum, which from my great confidence in him was not afterwards transferred to a stamp. If I lose the contents of that Bill it will be very hard. . . .

From Robert Boswell, 18 February 1788

Missing. "Mr. Ro. Boswell that Dav[id] Cuninghame is not to be talked to of paying debts[2]—enclosing Minute of Grange's Trustees concerning his bills to me" (Reg. Let.). For date see endorsement of previous letter.

"Views" (all Yale MS. A 52) show:

	£
3 Jan. 1789	. . 165
1 Jan. 1790	. . 174
21 Feb. 1791	. . 180
— Jan. 1792	. . 180
1 Jan. 1793	. . 180
1 Jan. 1795	. . 195

The slight increases probably represent interest. In Jan. 1795 a large sum was repaid, but the final payment of £40. 3s. 5d.

was not made until after JB's death (Grange MSS.: Receipt and Discharge, 5 Dec. 1798).

[1] That is, JJs executors were contesting the validity of the one bill, on the grounds that it had not been written on stamped paper, as required by law. However, they were later satisfied that the claim was just (*post* c. 18 Feb. 1788).

[2] *Ante* 22–28 Apr. 1783, n. 6. David Cuninghame, now an officer in the 3rd

From John Gordon, c. 18 February 1788

Missing. Recd. Feb. 1788. "Mr. John Gordon that he is satisfied Grange's bills to me are justly due; but as his brother is a very troublesome man,[3] the trustees have raised a multiplepoinding[4] that they may pay mine and other debts with safety" (Reg. Let.).

To Robert Boswell, c. 21 February 1788

Missing. "Mr. Ro. Boswell that upon looking at the Stamp Acts I perfectly recollect that Notes *payable on demand* although *with interest from the date* did not require a stamp before *1 Augt. 1783* and Grange's first Bill is in *March 1783.* Hoping therefore the Trustees will have no difficulty to pay it" (Reg. Let.).

To Robert Boswell, Tuesday 13 January 1789

Missing. Sent 13 Jan. 1789. "Mr. Ro. Boswell . . . What is doing with my claims on Grange's trustees" (Reg. Let.).

To Robert Boswell, Thursday 29 December 1789

MS. Yale (*L 229). Sent 29 Dec. 1789. "Mr. Ro. Boswell . . . Wishing to hear of money from Lord Lyle's funds and Grange's trustees" (Reg. Let.).

ADDRESS: To Ro. Boswell Esqr. C. S., Edinburgh.

FRANK: J. B. Garforth.

POSTMARKS: DEC 29, JA 1.

ENDORSEMENT: London 29 Dcr. 89. James Boswell. Red. 1 Jany. '90.

. . . No word yet of my dividend from Lord Lyle's funds,[1] or my

---

Foot Guards, had recently been apprehended at the instance of his creditors and lodged in the Canongate Gaol, Edinburgh. Among his debts was a bond to his cousin, George Campbell of Treesbank, JB's Register of Letters summarizes several letters on the subject, mostly to or from Robert Boswell and Bruce Campbell, who were endeavouring to obtain repayment from the impecunious, if imperious, Cuninghame (Reg. Let. 1787 and 1788, *passim*).

[3] *Ante* 3 Oct. 1786.

[4] An action raised by the holder of a property to which there are several claimants who are thereby required to come together and settle their claims in court (OED).

---

[1] Sir Walter Montgomerie-Cuninghame, Bt. (d. 1814), nephew of JB's wife, claimed the title of Lord Lyle, but his

money from Grange's Trustees.[2] Be so good as to quicken those tardy measures. . . .

From John Johnston, Junior, February 1790

Missing. "Mr. John Johnston,[3] Surgeon (nephew of Grange) to get him into some appointment" (Reg. Let.).

From Joseph Fergusson, Thursday 18 February 1790

MS. Yale. (C 1247). Written in the hand of an amanuensis.

ADDRESS: Mr. Jas. Boswel, Counselor at Law, London.

ENDORSEMENT: Rev. Mr. Jos Fergusson feb 18—1790. Answerd that I can do nothing for his niece's husband. Let him apply to Glasgow Merchants. I hope yet to pay him a visit.

Tundergarth Mance, Febry. 18th 1790

DEAR SIR: I was extreemly Sory to hear of the Death of your Worthy Lady and Did Condole Much with You on that Occasion.[1] I Would be Very Glad to hear how You and Your Young family Are And What length Sandy is Come in his Education. I hope that hereafter he Will Represent the family in an "Honourable Way." I fancy you have Recd. A letter from A Nephew of Grange for Whom You Was Chosen for one of his Trustees He hath been Studing Physick for three or four Winters And Wishes Much to Get on to Some Vesial in the line of his Buisness And Expects if Any thing Casts up in that way at london you will try to get him an appointment of being A Surgeon or Surgeons Mate to the East Indeas or Any other place in the Way of his Buisness He is A Very hopefull young Man And[2] I hope Will Do Well.

Likewise a young man[3] that is Married to one of my Neices He is a perfict good Writter And Well Acquinted With Counting

right to it was not officially recognized. JB had made many loans and advances to Sir Walter and his brothers. Over £1,000 is shown as due by them in the "View of my Affairs" dated 1 Jan. 1790 (MS. Yale A 52).

[2] *Ante* 17 Dec. 1787 n. 2.

[3] *Ante* 13 Feb. 1786, n. 5; *post* 1 Apr. 1795.

[1] Margaret Boswell had died on 4 June 1789.

[2] MS. "And And".

[3] This letter is not in Fergusson's handwriting and was apparently dictated from his sickbed. The passage from "Likewise" to "Waite on you" is in such inferior language that it seems possible that it was inserted by the writer (? the niece) without the knowledge of Fergusson.

And Merchants Accounts And is at present out of Buisness. And is one that is Worthy of My Recommendation It Would be A great Obligation to Me As he Inclines to follow that line of life if You Could procure him A place And I Expect A Answer that he May [be] ready to Waite on you.

I Shall be Very Glad to hear of the Welfair of your brother David I am With My best respects to him And you your most Houmble Servant

Jos. Fergusson

As to Myself I am in a Very low feeble State of Health having been Confined to my bed for the Space of two years And Do Not Expect to live long in the World[4] Adew.

From Thomas Johnston, Wednesday 1 April 1795

MS. Yale (C 1640). Written in the hand of an amanuensis.

ADDRESS: James Boswell Esqr., Counsellor at Law, London, Post Paid.

POSTMARK: Paid Ap [*digit illegible*] 1795. 7d added.

ENDORSEMENT: Tho. Johnston, Grange 1795.

Grainge 1st. April 1795

SIR: My son John went out to the West Indies with the expedition under the command of Sir Charles Gray,[1] have had no accounts of him for twelve months past. As he had the honor of being introduced to you when in London,[2] from the many civilities which you

[4] Joseph Fergusson died on 18 Jan. 1791, in his 73rd year (*Fasti Scot.* ii 223).

[1] In 1793 Sir Charles Grey (1729–1807), afterwards 1st Earl Grey, commanded (with Sir John Jervis, afterwards 1st Earl St. Vincent) a joint expedition against the French West Indies. The islands of Martinique, St. Lucia, the Saints, and Guadaloupe were reduced, though the last was recaptured by the French. John Johnston, who had been appointed to the government hospital in Jamaica, obtained a passage in one of the transports. Before reaching his destination he saw active service as a surgeon's mate during part of the fighting (Grange MSS.).

[2] JB had befriended John Johnston in London and had tried to get him a regimental surgeoncy. References to him in the notes and journal are as follows: "Granges Nephew tea" (27 June 1787); "Wrote to . . . Granges Nephew" (21 Apr. 1790); "Two days ago I had a visit from Mr. John Johnstone nephew and heir of my old friend Grange. I was pleased to find him a very sensible genteel young man, a Surgeon's mate in the Army. He dined with me to-day, and I entertained him as well as my bad spirits would allow" (30 Sept. 1793); "Mr. Johnston of Grange and my brother David dined with me" (11 Oct. 1793); "Johnston of Grange and my brother David dined with me" (16 Nov. 1793). All these entries were made in London.

was pleased to shew him and your kind attention to his interest I think it is probable he may have done himself the honor of writing you from the West Indies. Should you have heard from him, or can put me on any plan of getting information of him, I will take it kind if you will take the trouble of writing me as soon as convenient.[3]

When you consider the feelings of a parent, I make no doubt but you will excuse the freedom I have takin. I have the honor to be, Sir, your Most. Obedient. Servant.

THOS. JOHNSTON

PS. Please to direct to me by Ecclefechan.

---

[3] Shortly after reaching Jamaica in Mar. 1794, John Johnston had died of tropical fever (Grange MSS.).

APPENDIX 1

The Johnstons of Grange

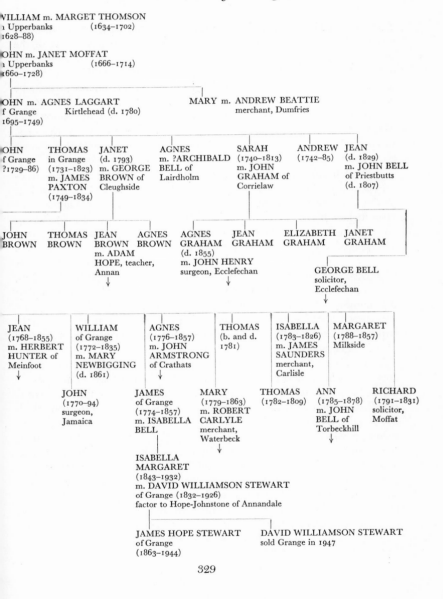

WILLIAM m. MARGET THOMSON
1 Upperbanks   (1634–1702)
1628–88)

JOHN m. JANET MOFFAT
1 Upperbanks   (1666–1714)
1660–1728)

JOHN m. AGNES LAGGART   MARY m. ANDREW BEATTIE
f Grange   Kirtlehead (d. 1780)   merchant, Dumfries
1695–1749)

JOHN   THOMAS   JANET   AGNES   SARAH   ANDREW   JEAN
f Grange   in Grange (d. 1793) m. ?ARCHIBALD (1740–1813) (1742–85) (d. 1829)
?1729–86) (1731–1823) m. GEORGE BELL of   m. JOHN   m. JOHN BELL
          m. JAMES   BROWN of   Lairdholm   GRAHAM of   of Priestbutts
          PAXTON   Cleughside   Corrielaw   (d. 1807)
          (1749–1834)

JOHN   THOMAS   JEAN   AGNES   AGNES   JEAN   ELIZABETH JANET
BROWN   BROWN   BROWN   BROWN   GRAHAM   GRAHAM   GRAHAM   GRAHAM
                   m. ADAM   (d. 1855)
                   HOPE, teacher,   m. JOHN HENRY   GEORGE BELL
                   Annan   surgeon, Ecclefechan   solicitor,
                   ↓   ↓   Ecclefechan
                                                                       ↓

JEAN   WILLIAM   AGNES   THOMAS   ISABELLA   MARGARET
(1768–1855)   of Grange   (1776–1857)   (b. and d. (1783–1826) (1788–1857)
m. HERBERT   (1772–1835)   m. JOHN   1781)   m. JAMES   Milkside
HUNTER of   m. MARY   ARMSTRONG   SAUNDERS
Meinfoot   NEWBIGGING   of Crathats   merchant,
↓   (d. 1861)   ↓   Carlisle

              JOHN   JAMES   MARY   THOMAS   ANN   RICHARD
              (1770–94)   of Grange   (1779–1863) (1782–1809) (1785–1878) (1791–1831)
              surgeon,   (1774–1857)   m. ROBERT   m. JOHN   solicitor,
              Jamaica   m. ISABELLA   CARLYLE   BELL of   Moffat
                            BELL   merchant,   Torbeckhill
                                          Waterbeck   ↓
                                          ↓

                            ISABELLA
                            MARGARET
                            (1843–1932)
                            m. DAVID WILLIAMSON STEWART
                            of Grange (1832–1926)
                            factor to Hope-Johnstone of Annandale

                            JAMES HOPE STEWART   DAVID WILLIAMSON STEWART
                            of Grange   sold Grange in 1947
                            (1863–1944)

329

APPENDIX 2

A Note on John Johnston's Age

THE date of JJ's birth is given as 1729 on a genealogical table of fairly recent compilation among the Grange papers in the possession of the Misses Carlyle of Waterbeck. This was copied, it is believed, from notes drawn up by their great-uncle, the late Thomas Johnston Carlyle, whose interest in the history of his family is apparent from the many jottings he has left among the other material in the collection. No official document confirming that date appears to have been preserved. Great quantities of Mr. Carlyle's family papers were destroyed during the two world wars, when waste-paper was in especial demand, and it is possible that among these the original source of Mr. Carlyle's information disappeared.

If the date cannot be fixed from contemporary evidence, it is nevertheless clear that JJ was born not later than the early part of 1731. According to the tombstone in Tundergarth churchyard, his brother Thomas was born in December of that year, and this date is roughly consistent with an entry in the family Bible which asserts that Thomas died on 8 January 1823, aged 92. Both these records derive from Thomas Johnston's grandson Robert Carlyle, but they are supported so far as the year is concerned by two contemporary official records made by Richard Paxton, cousin to Thomas's wife and minister of Tundergarth. In a "list containing the number of souls in the parish" which he made 31 October–17 November 1791, he entered Thomas's age as 60, and in his register of baptisms, marriages, and deaths he recorded his interment on 8 January 1823, "aged pene 92".[1]

That JJ was Thomas's *elder* brother is proved by the record of JJ's special service as heir to Grange, in which he is described as his father's eldest born son, *sui filii natu maximi*; and that they were full brothers is certified in the contract signed between them (10 Nov. 1763) in which the regular phrase "brother german" is used. Moreover, in legal documents in which both are mentioned (e.g. the Testament of their aunt, Mrs. Mary Beattie) JJ is always named first in order, before Thomas and other members of the family, and his letters to Thomas are written in the tone of mingled authority and affection which is precisely suited to such a relationship. The name of John was customarily given in that family to the eldest son: it had been the name of the father and grandfather,

[1] The Grange family Bible is in the possession of Thomas's descendants, the Misses Carlyle of Waterbeck. Paxton's records are preserved in the Tundergarth parish church.

and was given to their eldest sons both by Thomas and his sister Janet. If no other evidence were forthcoming that JJ was older than Thomas, it could be found in his apparently undisputed inheritance of all his father's landed property.

Although JJ was not served heir to the property until 1759, ten years after his father's death, this is no indication that his succession was in doubt; on the contrary, it strongly suggests that it was undisputed and entirely regular. Service was frequently, indeed usually, delayed until some legal transaction, some sale of property, or lawsuit, rendered it necessary, and had his title to inherit been challenged at the time of his father's death, service would have had to be applied for long before 1759 in order to substantiate his claim. His reason for being served in that year may have been connected with the candidature of his friend Joseph Fergusson for appointment to the charge of Tundergarth parish. The service legalized his status as one of the principal heritors of the parish. As such his word in the choice of a minister must have carried considerable weight. At any rate we find among the witnesses at his service "Joseph Fergusson, student", who in 1761 was ordained minister of Tundergarth.

The evidence that JJ was at least nine years older than JB seems conclusive, and since there is nothing in the known records that is in formal contradiction with the birth-date 1729 given in the Grange family tree, it appears reasonable to accept that date and conclude that the difference between their ages was about eleven years. It is true that they both attended Robert Hunter's Greek class at Edinburgh University in 1755, but the ages of students in the Arts classes ranged widely. Middle-aged men, often school-teachers preparing to qualify themselves for the ministry of the church, were frequently members of these classes, and professional men might attend them with a view to promotion or to self-improvement at almost any stage in their careers. JJ was older than the younger group of his classfellows to which JB belonged, probably because he had been obliged to postpone leaving home until Thomas should be old enough to assume responsibility for Grange. He may well have been a law-apprentice when he attended Hunter's class, and the direction of JB's letter of 11 Jan. 1760 to the house of a Clerk to the Signet in Wardrop's Close suggests that he was still, at that time, serving his apprenticeship.

APPENDIX 3

(See *ante*, p. 61, n. 10)

Lines possibly contributed by Boswell and Erskine to The North Briton, No. 41

No. 41 of *The North Briton* (12 Mar. 1763), which purports to be a letter from an anonymous correspondent, is epitomized by George Nobbe as follows: "[It] tells of the visit to London of a Scottish office holder and his loutish son, a 'raw chield' of eighteen. In Westminster Abbey the son gives way to a moment of prophetic inspiration when he sees there the coronation chair of the kings of Scotland and predicts that here the Scots shall reign" (*The North Briton*, 1939, p. 187). The authorship of this number has not been established (*ibid.*, p. 266). The author concludes the paper with the following riddling couplets, which are not reported as part of the happenings in the Abbey, but are presented gratuitously as "another [prophecy] which is clear and express".

> When *Andrew* shall unite with *James*,[1]
> And *Tweed* adulterate[2] with *Thames*,
> When *Cod* shall make the *Salmon* rue,[3]
> *Blue* turn to *yellow*,[4] green to *blue*;[5]
> When *John* leaves *Marg'ret* in the lurch,[6]
> And Presbyterians head the church;[7]
> When cold *Jamaica* sends for peat
> From *Florida* to roast her meat;[8]
> When *reformation*[9] turns a shrew,
> And acts as riot us'd to do;[10]
> When *England*'s lost and *Britain* wins,[11]
> When *Union*'s firm and strife begins,[12]
> When *Stuart*'s claims are all o'erthrown,
> And *Stuart* reigns without a crown;[13]
> Then triumph *Scotland*, thou hast won,
> *England* look to't—the charm's begun.

The immediate model for these lines was the "prophecy" of the Fool, *King Lear*, III. ii. 81–95:

> When Priests are more in word, then matter;
> When Brewers marre their Malt with water;

332

When Nobles are their Taylors Tutors
No Heretiques burn'd, but wenches Sutors;
   [six lines omitted]
Then shal the Realme of *Albion*, come to great confusion;
Then comes the time, who liues to see't,
That going shalbe vs'd with feet.
This prophecie *Merlin* shall make, for I live before his time.

Shakespeare (or the Fool) was satirizing the whole voluminous tradition of legendary prophecy, which, under the names of Merlin, Bede, and especially Thomas the Rhymer (see *ante* p. 232), was widely believed to have been fulfilled in the succession of James VI to the English throne. Swift's *Windsor Prophecy* and Johnson's *Marmor Norfolciense* show the mode still current in the 18th century as a satiric device. But the prophecies continued also to be taken seriously. The dark sayings attributed to Thomas (a Lowland Scot of the 13th century) were especially popular in Scotland, where they still enjoyed wide circulation through chapbooks, and had received much attention during the rising of 1745, when it was expected by many that various unfulfilled portions of the predictions would be accomplished. See J. A. H. Murray, ed., *The Romance and Prophecies of Thomas of Erceldoune*, 1875 (EETS vol. 61).

JB's statement in his letter of 22 Mar. 1763 that he and Erskine "added" certain lines, which JJ "will see", to an unidentified number of *The North Briton* does not furnish proof that he and Erskine wrote the verses printed in *North Briton* No. 41: on the contrary, as suggested above in the note on the passage, when taken with what follows, "and were to have sent it to the Gentlewoman who is very narrow, without a frank", that statement seems rather to point to a copy especially prepared by manuscript additions to tease somebody or other. JB certainly could not have meant that he and Erskine had sufficient personal acquaintance with Wilkes and Churchill to have been allowed to collaborate with them while the essay was printing, for he records that he met both men for the first time on 24 May (Journ.). The only real piece of evidence that he and Erskine wrote the verses is the conjunction of the names Andrew and James in the first verse, but that conjunction is surely very striking. It seems likely that some private allusion is involved, for one would expect "George" rather than "James" to represent England. And there is evidence that JB did try to get at least one composition of his own printed in *The North Briton*. On 14 Feb. 1763 he wrote in his daily memorandum, "By no means show any body *Hopromp* but try North *Brit*.". His holograph manuscript of this rather feeble political allegory ("Hopromp" is asserted to be a Scots rural game) has turned up among the Wilkes papers in the British Museum. It does not bear his name, but is in the form of a letter signed "Risor", and is prefaced by a brief note signed "your constant

Reader and Admirer". Furthermore, George Dempster, who was in a position to know the facts, believed that JB and Erskine had written something for *The North Briton*, or comparable to *The North Briton*, which had fortunately failed to get into print. On 19 Nov. 1763, JB being then in Holland, he told him of the Government's prosecution of Wilkes and added: "How lucky your jeu d'esprit and Erskines never was published It is you find a serious affair to Laugh at a Bishop."

By pure speculation one could reconcile all the bits of evidence something as follows: JB and Erskine collaborated in a paper which they submitted anonymously to *The North Briton*, a paper containing an extended metrical "prophecy" of the sort traditionally attributed to Thomas the Rhymer. Wilkes (or Churchill) took a hint from this and wrote No. 41. Either through design or because the copy came out short, Wilkes (Churchill) concluded with an extract from the contribution by JB and Erskine. JB and Erskine, with pen and ink, added some more lines (perhaps from their original) in a copy of *The North Briton*, planning to send this expanded copy to some one in Scotland whom they wished to tease, but relented and sent it instead to JJ. JB admitted authorship of the manuscript, but not the printed, lines (to claim any part of a printed *North Briton* would have been rash), though he hoped Johnston would make the right inference from the line naming Andrew and James.

Though full of political allusion entirely in the vein of *The North Briton*, these verses, if by JB and Erskine, were more an exercise in popular political satire than an expression of belief. They admired the subversive daring of Wilkes's wit, but as Scotsmen with Tory and Jacobite leanings they were not actually in sympathy with his politics. JB, however, cared little for Bute (see Journ. 18 July 1763), and at all times showed a willingness to write anonymously against his convictions if it enabled him to get into print. Besides, the "derne" style of the prophecies enabled one to seem to say much while actually writing nonsense. The verses may be explained point by point, as follows:

1. Perhaps Andrew Erskine and JB. This secret sense could be understood by few besides the authors, but to the uninitiated (see the next line) the names were intended to suggest Scotland and England, through the association of St. Andrew with Scotland and of St. James with the palace and court in London.

2. The reader of 1763 would inevitably have read this in the light of Wilkes's repeated insinuations (*North Briton* No. 5, Dedication to *The Fall of Mortimer*) that a criminal intimacy existed between Bute and the Princess Dowager of Wales. "Adulterate" in the sense "commit adultery" was current usage in Shakespeare's time and is cited by the OED from Vanbrugh (1698) and once even in the 19th century.

3. This line, which faintly echoes Shakespeare's *Othello*, II. i. 156, "To change the Cods-head for the Salmons taile", is probably nonsense, but

would have been taken as continuing Wilkes's reiterated attacks on Bute (*North Briton* Nos. 9, 14, 18, 24, 28, 30) for having, in the Peace, allowed the French the fishing rights on the Newfoundland Banks which Pitt had struggled to make an exclusively British possession. One could also see in the line a suggestion that a state of topsyturveydom had been produced by giving authority to men of inferior quality (Bute and his party) in place of wiser and better men like Newcastle and Pitt.

4. An allusion to the confused political scene. Various splinter groups had been formed from the old political parties and numbers of politicians (notably Fox) had recently changed sides. "In the absence of distinct, definable programmes, it was becoming increasingly difficult to say who, from the angle of practical politics, should be considered a Tory and who a Whig" (L. B. Namier, *England in the Age of American Revolution*, 1930, pp. 206–7). According to Horace Walpole, "Tories were Whigs when they got places" (Letter to Mann, 20 Dec. 1762).

There were no firmly established party colours at the time, but blue seems to have been most often associated with the Tories ("true-blues"), green and yellow with the Whigs. In the notorious Oxfordshire election of 1754, blue was the colour of the Tories: "The parties were distinguished by the names of the blues and the yellows; the blues being in the old interest, and the yellows in the new" (*Gent. Mag.* xxv. 339, Aug. 1755). R. J. Robson in *The Oxfordshire Election of 1754* (1949), p. 27, quotes a couplet which indicates that, at the same election, green was also recognized as a Whig colour:

> At present 'tis doubtful but soon will be seen
> Who deals more in falsehood, the Blue or the Green.

According to Lord Dundonald, "yellow waistcoat and breeches" denoted a staunch Whig (W. C. Sydney, *England and the English in the 18th Century*, ii. 157) and Charles Churchill in his poem *Independence* (1764), p. 16, writing of the turncoat politician, sets the yellow of the Whig against the blue of the Tory:

> A Creature of the right Camelion hue,
> He wears my colours, yellow or true Blue,
> Just as I wear them. . . .

Mention of the use of green as a party colour, presumably by the Whigs, occurs in a footnote in Wilkes's collected edition of *The North Briton* (1762, p. 93), where a reference to blue and green in the text is explained as "alluding to the different coloured ribbons wore by the two parties as badges of their affection to the cause they espoused".

5. Besides completing the picture of political confusion, the second half of the line may have been intended as a dig at Bute, who had resigned from the Scottish Order of the Thistle, with its green ribbon, on his elevation to the Order of the Garter, with its blue one. The allusion is not so abstruse as it may appear, for readers of *The North Briton* might be expected to remember the angry protest with which in No. 16 (18 Sept. 1762) that paper had greeted Bute's change of ribbon.

6. John Bull and Sister Margaret (cognomens for England and Scotland

popularized by Arbuthnot) had recently reappeared in Adam Ferguson's *History of the Proceedings in the Case of Margaret, Commonly Called Peg, only Lawful Sister to John Bull, Esq.*, 1761; in Charles Churchill's rhymed satire in *The North Briton*, No. 26 (27 Nov. 1762); and in his *Prophecy of Famine*, 1763. In Ferguson's *History* (chaps. x, xi) John is accused of leaving Margaret in the lurch because, the Militia Act having been applied only to England, Scotland had been left at that time comparatively defenceless in face of a threatened French invasion. But the topical allusion here is no doubt to Bute (John Stuart). In his misguided ambition for power, he had, according to *The North Briton*, abandoned his native land to become the unwanted ruler of the neighbouring kingdom. That he and other such place-seeking Scots should stay at home is a constantly reiterated plea of *The North Briton*.

7. In *The North Briton*, No. 10 (7 Aug. 1762) Churchill had pretended to reveal the secret plans of Scotland for the subjugation of the Church of England by a process of infiltration by Scots Presbyterians, who, under an administration headed by a Scotsman and biased in favour of Scotsmen, "will be sure of all the best preferments". The same theme recurs in Churchill's poem *The Ghost* (book iii), Sept. 1762.

8. A reference to the brilliant hoax by means of which Wilkes discomfited his antagonist Arthur Murphy, editor of the government organ *The Auditor*, and in doing so seriously discredited the administration. Wilkes sent to Murphy a complimentary anonymous letter purporting to come from a traveller familiar with Florida and the West Indies, in which he praised the government for acquiring Florida under the recent peace treaty in preference to other territories commonly considered more desirable. Its bogs were rich, he said, in a combustible turf which would prove a valuable export as it would meet a crying need of residents in the West Indies for fuel. Both the Florida turf and the West Indian demand for fuel were entirely imaginary, but as Murphy was desperately trying to make the unpalatable treaty acceptable to the public, he immediately printed the letter (which was signed "Viator") in *The Auditor* (No. 31, 18 Dec. 1762). Wilkes had the satisfaction of seeing *The Auditor* ridiculed for its credulity in *Lloyd's Evening Post* (No. 848, 20 Dec. 1762, p. 585) and in *The St. James's Chronicle* (No. 281, 24 Dec. 1762) before crowning his triumph by admitting authorship of the letter in *The North Briton* (No. 30, 25 Dec. 1762). Even after Murphy's dismissal he continued to gloat: "I would therefore, humbly submit, whether the *pension* now granted to the AUDITOR should not be withdrawn, and instead of it an *exclusive charter* be granted to him for this new branch of commerce, the *Florida Peet*" (*North Briton*, No. 35, 29 Jan. 1763).

9. The two main planks of Bute's administrative programme were "reformation" and "economy". *The North Briton* launched a number of withering attacks on the policy of economy, which the government put forward as a plea for ending the war as rapidly as possible, and on Bute's claim that he had successfully brought about a salutary reformation of the political scene: "What a shallow pretence to the least *reformation of abuses*, or to any degree of *œconomy*, the *first lord of the Treasury* has, is apparent" (No. 40, 5 Mar. 1763).

10. *The North Briton* had derided *The Auditor's* claim that a reformation of

political abuses had been achieved by Bute's ministry. "I believe Statesmen of such opposite, incoherent, and heterogeneous principles were never before huddled together. The confusion which has followed this unnatural mixture we have all seen" (No. 20, 16 Oct. 1762). Later, in the notorious No. 45 (23 Apr. 1763) the government's claim to have established a new spirit of concord was to be even more indignantly denied: "They have sent the *spirit of discord* through the land, and I will prophecy, that it will never be extinguished, but by the extinction of their power."

11. The submergence of England in a Britain dominated by ambitious Scots was a favourite theme of *The North Briton*. This line recalls the satirical verses contributed by Churchill to No. 26 (27 Nov. 1762) in which Scotland is thus addressed:

> When ENGLAND'S GENIUS droops his wing,
> So shall thy soil new wealth disclose,
> So thy own THISTLE choak the ROSE.

12. In its primary sense the line, no doubt, refers to the Union between England and Scotland, but in a secondary sense it may also intend the union between Britain and her allies which *The North Briton* accused Bute's government of wantonly breaking up: "By the *superior genius* of *one man* [Pitt], the war . . . has been successful . . . and the most entire confidence has prevailed . . . among . . . our allies abroad. By the *evil genius* of another man [Bute], . . . distrust and dissentions have arose, and the firmest bonds of union have split, and been dissolved" (No. 28, 11 Dec. 1762).

13. John Stuart, 3rd Earl of Bute (*ante* 22 Feb. 1763, n. 7).

Index

This is an index of persons and places mentioned in letters and footnotes and in the Introduction and appendixes. Under James Boswell and John Johnston of Grange the subjects mentioned in the letters are summarized. Noblemen, Lords of Session, and their wives are indexed under their titles; usually the forms chosen are those appropriate to the time of the letters. The following abbreviations are used: D. (Duke), E. (Earl), M. (Marquess), V. (Viscount), JB (James Boswell), SJ (Samuel Johnson), JJ (John Johnston of Grange).

INDEX

Baldwin, Henry, printer, c. 1734–1813, 311 *n.* 4, 312 *n.* 4, 321, 322.

Ballochmyle, 292 *n.* 7.

Bandrigg (Banriggs), farm, xii.

Bannockburn, 262 *n.* 9.

Barber, The, song, 86 *n.* 2.

Barrington, Daines, 1727–1800, 312 *n.* 3.

Barskimming, Lord. *See* Miller, Thomas.

Bartoli, Giuseppe, 1717–88, 165 *n.* 8.

Basle, 144, 145.

Bastia, 191.

Bath, 219, 258.

Bayley, C. C., xlv.

Beat, David, theatrical manager, 8 *n.* 5, *n.* 6.

Beattie, Mary (Johnston), wife of Andrew Beattie, 329, 330.

Bel, Karl Andreas, 1717–82, 137 *n.* 2.

Belfast, 277 *n.* 5.

Bell, Adam, "writer", d. 1790, 294 *n.* 4, 295.

Bell, Agnes (Johnston), wife of Archibald Bell, 329.

Bell, Ann (Johnston), wife of John Bell, 1785–1878, 329.

Bell, David, of Newhall, xii.

Bell, George, son of John Bell of Priestbutts, 329.

Bell, Jean (Johnston), sister of JJ, wife of John Bell of Priestbutts, d. 1829, xxxiii, xxxix, 329.

Bell family, xi.

Bellamy, Mrs. George Anne, actress, ?1731–88, 170 *n.* 1.

Bennet, Robert, Dean of Faculty of Advocates, 1644–1722, 97*n.*

Bentinck, Hans-William. *See* Portland, 1st E. of.

Berlin, JB in, 92 *n.* 2, 132; mentioned, xxiii, xxiv, 86, 113, 126.

Berrie (Berry), William, engraver, 1730–83, 235 *n.* 7.

Berthe, wife of Rudolph II, D. of Burgundy, d. 966, 146 *n.* 1.

Bertram, Helen, xxxv.

Berwick, 13, 23, 271, 272, 300 *n.* 7.

Bible, *Acts;* 161 *n.* 3; *James,* 285 *n.* 2; *John,* 33 *n.* 4; *Luke,* 194 *n.* 2; *Revelation,* 211 *n.* 3.

Bigge, Thomas Charles, 1739–94, 270 *n.* 15.

Bird, Mrs., pastry cook in Edinburgh, xiv, xv, xxiv, 92, 105 *n.* 1.

Blacklock, Thomas, poet, 1721–91, 4 *n.* 3.

Blair, Anne (Kennedy), d. 1782, 16 *n.* 8.

Blair, Catherine, of Adamtown, *later* wife of Sir William Maxwell of Monreith, ?1749–98, 231 *n.* 2, 243 *n.* 3, 244 *n.* 7.

Blair, Capt. John of Dunskey, d. 1772, 16, 56–57, 58.

Bologna, 156, 163, 166.

Bond, Richmond P., 72 *n.* 2.

Bonshaw, 39 *n.* 1, 41.

Borgaretto, Vittoria Enrichetta Bistorti, Countess of, 152*n.*

Boston, Thomas, 1677–1732, *Human Nature in Its Fourfold Estate,* 69 *n.* 5.

Boswall, Alexander, of Blackadder, 1728–1812, brother of Thomas Boswall, 175 *n.* 6.

Boswall, Thomas, accountant in Edinburgh, ? 1724–76, 175 *n.* 6.

Boswell, Alexander, son of JB, 1775–1822, letters from JB, x *n.* 3, xxxvii, 4 *n.* 1, 51 *n.* 5, 181 *n.* 1, 302 *n.* 3; mentioned, 286 *n.* 2, 291, 326.

Boswell, Charles (Doig), illegitimate son of JB, 1762–64, birth and christening, 25, 29 *n.* 2, 31–32; JB on maintenance of, 82, 103, 106, 120; Peggy Doig gives fine account of, 98–99; JJ visits, JB imagines scene, 102–3; JB's hopes for his future, 103; death, 103 *n.* 1, 121–22, 123; mentioned, xxii–xxiii, xxix, 27, 34, 36, 40, 44, 62, 64, 78, 80, 115.

Boswell, Claud Irvine, *later* Lord Balmuto, 1742–1824, 212 *n.* 1, 214.

Boswell, David, *later* Thomas David, brother of JB, 1748–1826, letters to JB, 226*n.*, 228 *n.* 3, 238 *n.* 2; friendship with JJ, 25, 29, 36, 44, 71, 225; goes to Valencia, 46 *n.* 7, 235 *n.* 7, 242; tells of father's anger, 51 *n.* 5, 52; apprenticed to banking firm, 58, 62 *n.* 12, 106 *n.* 2, 225 *n.* 4; JB praises, 120–21, 167, 175; JB writes to, 163; laughs at JB's talk of entertainment, 199–200; seal given to, 235 *n.* 7; changes name to Thomas David, 238 *n.* 2; returns from Valencia 293 *n.* 1; mentioned, xxiii, 24 *n.* 2, 32, 34, 47, 64, 78, 95 *n.*9, 116, 131, 134, 162, 212, 228, 233, 312 *n.* 4, 327 *n.* 2.

Boswell, Euphemia, dau. of JB, 1774–1837, 285, 286 *n.* 2.

341

INDEX

INDEX

Malone, Edmond, 1741–1812, letter from JB, 251 *n.* 1; helps JB with *Tour*, 311 *n.* 4; with *Life*, 312 *n.* 2; mentioned, xl, 312 *n.* 4; *Life of Dryden*, 37 *n.* 1.

Mamhead, 258 *n.* 7.

Mannheim, 133, 141–42.

Mansfield, William Murray, 1st E. of, 1705–93, in Douglas Cause, 234 *n.* 6; in cause of John Hastie, 281; mentioned, 203 *n.* 2, 222 *n.* 1, 277 *n.* 5.

M'Ansh, Alexander, breeches-maker, 263 *n.* 2.

Mantua, 181, 182 *n.* 6, 183–85.

Marbeuf, Louis-Charles René, Comte de, 1712–86, 191.

Marburg, 140 *n.* 1.

Maria Luisa, Infanta of Spain, wife of Archduke Leopold, 1745–92, 184 *n.* 2.

Marischal, George Keith, 10th E., 1694–1778; editorial account of, 126 *n.* 1; JB tours Germany with, 126, 132; writes to Lord Auchinleck, 133; as Governor of Neuchâtel, 148 *n.* 1; on change of David Boswell's name, 238 *n.* 2.

Mark, George, probationer, 266 *n.* 11.

Marseilles, 200–02.

Martin, James, M.P., 1738–1810, 312 *n.* 4.

Martinique, xlii.

Mary, Edinburgh girl, 237 *n.* 1, 238.

Mary, Queen of Scots, 1542–87, painting of, by Gavin Hamilton, 161–62 *n.* 4; mentioned, xxv, 15, 41, 49, 100 *n.* 6, 231, 232, 248.

Marykirk, parish, cause of, 282–83 *n.* 4.

Masserati, Countess, 182–83.

Mauchline, parish, 31 *n.* 2.

Maupertuis, Pierre Louis Moreau de, 1698–1759, 145 *n.* 3.

Maxwell, Alexander, son of Sir William Maxwell of Calderwood, 4th Bt., d. 1781, 268, 271.

Maxwell, Catherine (Blair). *See* Blair, Catherine.

Maxwell, Catherine (Douglas), c. 1707–61, 88 *n.* 4.

Maxwell, Margaret (Stewart), wife of Sir William Maxwell of Springkell, c. 1742–1816, JB considers marrying her, xxii, 96*n.*; JB asks JJ's advice on courtships, 115, 116–17; JB describes

in letter to Temple, 115 *n.* 14; marriage, 166 *n.* 11.

Maxwell, Sir Robert, of Orchardton, d. 1786, 322 *n.* 1.

Maxwell, Sir William, of Monreith, 4th Bt., d. 1812, 243 *n.* 3.

Maxwell, Sir William, of Springkell, 3rd Bt., 1739–1804, 88, 166 *n.* 11.

Maxwell family, xii.

Mecklenberg-Strelitz, Charles Lewis, D. of, 1708–52, 118–19 *n.* 5.

Mecklenberg-Strelitz, George Augustus, Prince of, 1748–85, 118–19.

Medmenham Abbey, 163 *n.* 3.

Meissen, 137 *n.* 1.

Melanchthon (Philipp Schwarzert), 1497–1560, 161 *n.* 1.

Melrose Abbey, 272.

Melville, Sir James, 1535–1617, *Memoirs*, 44 *n.* 4, 232.

Metzdorf, Robert F., xlv, 235 *n.* 7.

Milan, 153–54, 163.

Milford Plain, 268.

Milk, Water of, river, xi, xii, 92 *n.* 5.

Milkside, Grange, xxxviii.

Miller, John (i.e. Müller, Johann Sebastian), engraver, ?1715–90, 257 *n.* 2.

Miller, Thomas (Lord Barskimming, Lord Glenlee), Lord Justice-Clerk, *later* Lord President and Bt., 1717–89, JB writes to, 99; becomes Lord Justice-Clerk, 213 *n.* 2; mentioned, xxxii, 81 *n.* 1.

Miller, William, son of preceding, xxxii.

Mincio, river, 184–85 *n.* 4.

Minnigaff, 16.

Minto (Sir Gilbert Elliot, of Minto, 2nd Bt.), Lord, c. 1693–1766, 213 *n.* 2.

Mitchell, Alexander, of Hallglenmuir, 291–92 *n.* 5.

Mitchell, Andrew, British Envoy in Berlin, 1708–71, 132, 133.

Mitchelson, John, of Middleton, Midlothian, d. 1728, 238–39 *n.* 1.

Mitchelson, Samuel, W.S., d. 1788, 238–39 *n.* 1.

Moffat, xxiv, 77*n.*, 211*n.*, 213, 215, 218, 219 *n.* 11, 250 *n.* 4, 275, 318.

Monaco, 194.

Monigo, 172.

Mont Cenis, 151 *n.* 2.

Montagu, Anthony Browne, 6th V., 1686–1767, 42 *n.* 7.

INDEX

INDEX

Orr, Alexander, of Waterside, W.S., d. 1774, 57 *n.* 3, 134.

Oswald, James, of Dunnikier, 1715–69, 4–5 *n.* 4.

Oswald, James Townsend, of Dunnikier, c. 1748–1813, 287 *n.* 5.

Otway, Thomas, 1652–85, *Venice Preserv'd*, 115 *n.* 14, 170 *n.* 1, 171 *n.* 2.

Oughton, Sir James Adolphus, 1720–80, 219 *n.* 14.

Oxford, 71–72, 303.

Oxford, Edward Harley, 2nd E. of, 1689–1741, 298 *n.* 3.

Oxford, Robert Harley, 1st E. of, 1661–1724, 298 *n.* 3.

Padua, 169–70.

Paoli, Gen. Pasquale de, 1725–1807, gives JB a dog, 143 *n.* 2; Rousseau gives JB letter to, 189–90; JB meets in Corsica, 190–91, 193; visits Scotland, 221 *n.* 1, 258; in London, 257–58; travels in England, 258; mentioned, xxxii.

Paris, 113, 118, 133, 160, 206.

Parma, 155, 156, 163, 166, 175.

Paterson, Sir Hugh, of Bannockburn, 2nd Bt., 1686–1777, 262 *n.* 9.

Pavia, 179–81.

Paxton, John, of New Orchard, d. 1787, xxxiii, xxxv, xxxviii, 318, 319.

Paxton, Richard, minister of Tundergarth, d. 1832, 330.

Pennant, Edward, of Holywell, c. 1729–98, 201–02 *and n.* 2.

Pennant, Thomas, naturalist, 1726–98, 201 *n.* 2.

Pennsylvania, University of, 113 *n.* 5.

Penrith, 321.

Perceval, Spencer, 1761–1812, 312 *n.* 4.

Percy, Lord Algernon, *later* B. Loraine of Alnwick and E. of Beverley, 1750–1830, 272.

Percy, Rev. Thomas, 1729–1811, letter from JB, 267 *n.* 1; editorial account of, 271 *n.* 17; *Northern Antiquities*, 171 *n.* 3; *Reliques of Ancient English Poetry*, 271.

Persbiehall, farm, xii.

Perth, 262*n.*, 279.

Perth, James Drummond, 4th E. and 1st titular D. of, 1648–1716, 15 *n.* 7.

Petersburg, 318.

Pfitzner, Laura Douglas, 215 *n.* 2.

Philadelphia, 113 *n.* 5.

Piacenza, 154–55, 163.

Piccolomini, Maria Girolama (Momina, Moma), 1728–92, 188.

Pickworth, William, d. 1771, 273 *n.* 1.

Pietole, 184–85 *n.* 4.

Pinkie, 31–32 *n.* 3, 240.

Pisa, 189.

Pitcairne, Dr. Archibald, 1652–1713, 265 *n.* 7.

Pitfour (James Ferguson), Lord, Dean of Faculty of Advocates, 1700–77, 99, 124, 134 *n.* 8, 261 *n.* 7, 264 *n.* 2.

Pitt, Thomas, 1737–93, 155 *n.* 1.

Pitt, William, the elder. *See* Chatham, William Pitt, 1st E. of.

Pitt, William, the younger, 1759–1806, JB asks help in obtaining office for JJ, xxxvi, 311 *n.* 3; 313; mentioned, 308 *n.* 3.

Pittenweem, 253, 263.

Pliny the Elder, A.D. 23–79, 176 *n.*1.

Pliny the Younger, A.D. 62–113, 176 *n.* 1.

Plymouth, 44 *n.* 3, 258.

Polmood, 275 *n.* 2.

Pope, Alexander, 1688–1744, *Essay on Man*, 114 *n.* 13, 195 *n.* 3.

Portland, Hans-William Bentinck, 1st E. of, 1649–1709, 298 *n.* 3.

Portland, Margaret Cavendish (Harley), Duchess of, 1715–85, 298 *n.* 3.

Portland, William Henry Cavendish Bentinck, 3rd D. of, 1738–1809, 297, 298 *n.* 3, 299.

Portpatrick, parish, cause of, 266 *n.* 11, 282 *n.* 4.

Portsmouth, 258.

Potsdam, 132.

Pottle, Marion S., xlv.

Preston, Alexander, 1732–72, 283.

Preston (Anne Cochrane), Lady, wife of Sir George Preston, d. 1779, 283 *n.* 8.

Preston, Sir Charles, 5th Bt., 1733–1800, 313 *n.* 6.

Preston, Lt.-Gen. George, Governor of Edinburgh Castle, ?1659–1748, 87 *n.* 1.

Preston, Sir George, of Valleyfield, 4th Bt., 1702–79, 87 *n.* 1, 283 *n.* 8, 313 *n.* 6.

Preston, Robert, son of Sir George Preston, d. 1834, 321, 322.

Prestonfield, 233 *n.* 2, 296, 297.

INDEX

Sanvitale, Constanza (Scotti), Countess, c. 1736–94, 155.

Saunders, Isabella (Johnston), wife of James Saunders, 1783–1826, 329.

Saxe, Maurice, Comte de, Marshal of France, 1696–1750, 150 *n*. 5.

Saxe-Gotha, 139.

Saxony, 137, 138*n*.

Scarnafigi, Maria Anna Theresa Ponte, Countess of, 1733–1808, 152*n*.

Scaurus, Marcus Æmilius, 168–69 *n*. 4.

Schaw, Capt. Frederick Bridges, 96*n*.

Schaw, Isabella (Thomson), wife of preceding, 96*n*.

Scotland: Christmas not celebrated, 34 *n*. 2; weights and measures, 67–68 *n*. 5; unification in 844, 88 *n*. 2; Militia, 158 *n*. 1; marriage contracts in, 257 *n*. 1; proverbial toast, "stark love and kindness", 265–66 *n*. 10; Royal Bank of Scotland, 284 *n*. 10, 294– 95 *n*. 4.
    Scottish courts and legal system, 89 *n*. 1, 96–97 *n*. 12, 165 *n*. 6, 227*n*.; legal terms, 29 *n*. 5, 35 *n*. 5, 69 *n*. 2, 155 *n*. 4, 160 *n*. 5, 319 *n*. 4, 325 *n*. 3.
    Scotticisms: in JB's song "The Blaephlum", 230–31; blackguard, 206 *n*. 1; body, 71 *n*. 4; brose, 218 *n*. 7; caddie, 24 *n*. 3, 46 *n*. 6; diet loaf, 88 *n*. 5; flitting, 260 *n*. 2; halse, 274 *n*. 10; joe, 65 *n*. 4; milk-bakes, 39 *n*. 5; poinded, 272 *n*. 21; ramp, 65 *n*. 6; roup, 291 *n*. 4; trance, 38 *n*. 4; throng, 29 *n*. 6; wame, 217 *n*. 4.

Scots Magazine, contributions by JB, 230 *n*. 2, 247 *n*. 9, 255 *n*. 1.

Scott, Capt., 288–89 *n*. 2.

Scott, David, of Scotstarvet, d. 1766, 4 *n*. 4.

Scott, Francis, of Johnston, d. 1761, xxxiv, 68 *n*. 8, 121 *n*. 14, 216 *n*. 1, 240 *n*. 2, 283 *n*. 9.

Scott, Isabella, dau. of Francis Scott, d. 1773, xxxiv.

Scott, Isabella (Woodhouse), widow of Francis Scott, 240.

Scott, Gen. John, of Balcomie, c. 1725– 75, 274 *n*. 8, 287 *n*. 5.

Scott, Magdalen (le Mercier), wife of William Scott, d. 1770, 228 *n*. 3.

Scott, Magdalen, dau. of preceding, 228 *n*. 3.

Scott, Margaret (Dundas), 2nd wife of Gen. John Scott, d. 1797, 274 *n*. 8.

Scott, Lady Mary (Hay), 1st wife of Gen. John Scott, b. 1754, 274.

Scott, Patrick, son of Francis Scott, 68 *n*. 8, 121 *n*. 14.

Scott, Walter, W.S., 1729–99, 292 *n*. 9.

Scott, Sir Walter, 1771–1832, 265–66 *n*. 10, 292 *n*. 9; *Guy Mannering*, 276 *n*. 3.

Scott, Prof. William, d. 1735, 228 *n*. 3.

Scott family, xi.

Scotti, Constanza. *See* Sanvitale, Constanza.

Session, Court of, 12 *n*. 2, 96 *n*. 12, 232 *n*. 4, 278 *n*. 4, 280 *n*. 4, 287 *n*. 5, 305 *n*. 5, 311 *n*. 5.

Shakespeare, William, 1564–1616, Stratford Jubilee, 253, 254 *n*. 5, 257; *Hamlet*, 140; 2 *Henry IV*, 63 *n*. 4; *King Lear*, 61 *n*. 10, 332–33; *Macbeth*, 226 *n*. 10, 232; *Othello*, 190 *n*. 2, 334; *Romeo and Juliet*, 176; *Two Gentlemen of Verona*, 63*n*., 176.

Shaw (person). *See* Graham, George; Graham, William.

Shaw (estate), 72–73 *n*. 2, 76, 79, 259.

Shaw family, 134.

Shelburne, William Petty, 2nd E. of, 1737–1805, 299 *n*. 5, 308 *n*. 3.

Sheridan, Thomas, actor, 1719–88, 37 *n*. 3.

"Sherrifmuir" (song), 150.

Shields, 261 *n*. 7.

Shrewsbury, H.M.S., 193 *n*. 3.

Siena, 187–88.

Sinclair, Prof. George, d. 1696, *Satan's Invisible World Discovered*, 217 *n*. 1.

Skene, Lt.-Col. Robert, d. 1787, 219 *n*. 14.

Skinner, B. C., xlv.

Smith, client of JB, 289.

Smith, Adam, 1723–90, JB praises, 7; JB asks his help for Isabella Scott, 240– 41; editorial account of, 240 *n*. 3; *The Wealth of Nations*, 7 *n*. 3, 240 *n*. 3.

Smollett, Tobias George, 1721–71, *The Expedition of Humphry Clinker*, 239*n*.

Soaping Club, 12 *n*. 3, 16 *n*. 12.

Soleure, 146.

Sollacarò, 190 *n*. 1, 191 *n*. 3.

PRINTED IN GREAT BRITAIN
AT THE UNIVERSITY PRESS, OXFORD
BY VIVIAN RIDLER
PRINTER TO THE UNIVERSITY